342-38

SELF-CONTROL:
POWER TO THE PERSON

SELF-CONTROL:
POWER TO THE PERSON

MICHAEL J. MAHONEY
Pennsylvania State University

CARL E. THORESEN
Stanford University

BROOKS/COLE PUBLISHING COMPANY
MONTEREY, CALIFORNIA

A DIVISION OF WADSWORTH PUBLISHING COMPANY, INC.

ISBN: 0-8185-0121-9
L. C. Catalog Card No.: 73-89411
Printed in the United States of America
    5 6 7 8 9 10

Manuscript Editor: Barbara Greiling
Production Editor: Lyle York
Interior & Cover Design: Bernard Dix
Illustrations: Creative Repro, Monterey, California
Typesetting: Production Type, Inc., Dallas, Texas
Printing & Binding: Colonial Press, Inc., Clinton, Massachusetts

PREFACE

Although interest in self-control dates back many centuries, controlled scientific research on the principles and techniques of self-regulation is a relatively recent phenomenon. Five years ago, a text dealing with self-control procedures would have been very difficult to produce—there just wasn't enough evidence. During the last half decade, however, interest and inquiries into human self-regulation have mushroomed.

Our interest in writing this book stemmed from the need for a readable introduction to self-control. We have oriented our writing to students and professionals desiring a basic overview of self-control theory and research. The first part of the text discusses the basic principles and processes in self-regulation. Chapter 1 provides a brief overview of social-learning theory—operant-learning principles, modeling, and cognitive-symbolic processes. The second chapter challenges traditional views of willpower and proposes a functional behavioral model. Self-regulation is approached as a learnable skill rather than as an inborn talent. Three basic elements in human self-control are suggested: (1) awareness of controlling influences, (2) environmental changes that encourage the desired outcome, and (3) self-presented consequences. Chapter 3 discusses the crucial importance of personal-data collection in successful self-control. Methods of "becoming aware" are then discussed. Awareness by itself, however, does not result in lasting behavior change. Techniques for altering influential factors are required. In Chapters 4 and 5, the most popular and effective self-control strategies are described and evaluated. Chapter 6 concludes this first section by discussing the relevance of behavioral self-control for humanistic goals and personal freedom.

The second part of the book contains an up-to-date and relevant set of resource articles for the student or researcher interested in self-regulation. Many of our selected articles represent reviews that pull together a sizable amount of research and provide the reader with references and ideas for subsequent inquiry. Despite the rapid pace at which self-control studies are now appearing in professional journals, we feel that our collection of readings is contemporary and well-rounded. The selected articles represent both theoretical and applied approaches. They deal with topics ranging from the theoretical features of self-reinforcement and behavioral humanism to the use of pocket timers as cues to reduce smoking. Most of the articles·involve a somewhat higher degree of sophistication and complexity than do our introductory chapters. Thus, they offer an opportunity for individual pursuit of topics and issues beyond those touched on in the introduction. The articles have been chosen not only to educate but also to stimulate.

In this book, we have presented a brief introduction to what may well be the most promising frontier in modern behavioral science. We believe that self-control skills—developed and refined through careful empirical methods—offer excitingly effective means for the attainment of personally meaningful goals. In this sense, behavioral self-control represents an "applied humanism"—a humane and long-awaited technology for giving power to the person.

Many individuals have influenced and encouraged our work on this text. Our students, at both Stanford University and The Pennsylvania State University, have contributed immeasurably to our efforts, as have our many clients. Ann Van Der Meulen and Barbara Greiling of Brooks/Cole have been a constant source of support and enthusiasm. Donna M. Gelfand of the University of Utah, Marvin R. Goldfried of the State University of New York at Stony Brook, Frederick H. Kanfer of the University of Illinois, Gerald R. Smith of Indiana University, Barbara Vance of Brigham Young University, and Edward L. Walker of the University of Michigan reviewed the manuscript and offered many helpful suggestions. Ann Gladstone, Sharon Washington, and Sandy Ranio provided much-appreciated help in typing and retyping the manuscript, and Lee Appleton and Kay Thoresen assisted with the references.

People from many environments—colleagues, families, clients, and students—have helped us in countless ways, and we are deeply appreciative of their efforts.

Michael J. Mahoney
Carl E. Thoresen

CONTENTS

SELF-CONTROL:
POWER TO THE PERSON

SELF-CONTROL

AN INTRODUCTION TO
SOCIAL-LEARNING PRINCIPLES

It has been said that the purposes of behavioral science are the *prediction, control,* and *explanation* of behavior. Needless to say, these goals are quite ambitious in an area of such complexity and diversity. Over the past few decades, however, great strides have been made in identifying some of the many factors that influence our actions. One of the assumptions made by the behavioral scientist is that behavior is determined—that is, that it obeys lawful relationships. Without such an assumption, the psychologist—or, indeed, any scientist—would be helpless, since the prediction and control of a phenomenon require that it follow some consistent pattern.

Fortunately, psychological research has overwhelmingly supported behavioral determinism. It is now reasonably safe to say that *behavior is a function of the environment.* That is, we can accurately predict and control behavior by making systematic changes in the environment. This relationship was illustrated by Goldiamond (1965a) in the equation

$$B = f(x),$$

where *B* represents behavior and *x* represents specific environmental factors. There are, of course, many behavior-environment relationships that remain to be identified and explored. However, during the last few years, we have made dramatic advances in our understanding of complex human behaviors.

A. ABC'S: ANTECEDENTS, BEHAVIORS, CONSEQUENCES

Conceptually, we may think of a behavior as being "sandwiched" between two sets of environmental influences: those that precede it (its *antecedents*) and those that follow it (its *consequences*). If the scientist has knowledge of and control over both of these sets of factors, he can often demonstrate remarkable accuracy in predicting the form or frequency of a behavior.

Antecedent events are usually cues that inform the individual of which behaviors are appropriate in a particular situation. They predict the consequences of various responses in which the person might engage. For example, your driving behavior is often very powerfully controlled by such cues as road signs, traffic signals, and a parked patrol car—cues that inform you of the probable consequences of certain behaviors such as stopping, turning, and speeding. We frequently respond to environmental cues without being aware of our actions. In such instances, we may call the pattern a "habit." A somewhat humorous but informative example of a response to environmental cues is provided by the case of a four-year-old who—despite the fact that she was toilet trained—always forgot to flush the toilet. Her parents had to continually order her back to the bathroom to perform that task.

> This problem, it turned out, had persisted for at least a couple of years until finally Uncle Jim intervened. Instead of ordering the child back to flush the toilet, he instructed her to make believe that she was just finishing going to the toilet; she was to make believe to the extent that she was to take down her pants, climb up on the toilet, imagine she was just finishing, get off the toilet, pull up her pants, then flush the toilet and rejoin the adults. This exercise worked; the child gives every sign that she will grow up to be a happily married lady who flushes the toilet a lot (Homme, C'de Baca, Cottingham, & Homme, 1968, p. 429).

Prior to Uncle Jim's rather astute intervention, the child's toilet-flushing behavior had been under the control of an inappropriate stimulus—namely, her parents' commands. When an appropriate antecedent cue was associated with the desired behavior, the problem was easily remedied.

Other illustrations of the influence of antecedent cues (often referred to as *stimulus control*) can be found in eating and smoking patterns. Research has shown that these two responses often occur in the presence of specified cues. A bountiful bowl of cashews, an ice-cream commercial, and the local pizza parlor may all come to elicit eating responses even in the absence of physiological hunger. Similarly, the completion of a meal or the sight of an ashtray may cue or prompt smoking behavior. As we will see in later chapters, patterns as complex as eating and smoking can be controlled through systematic alterations in important antecedent cues.

The consequences of a behavior are those events that immediately follow it. They fall into three general categories: positive, negative, and neutral. Classification of a particular consequence varies with the individual. While one student may consider a "B" to be a positive grade, another may perceive it as negative. A clear means of establishing the value that a consequence has for a particular individual is to find out if he will work to produce it or to avoid it. If he will work to produce or prolong a certain consequence, then we are justified in calling it positive. On the other hand, if he will work to avoid or terminate it, then it is negative. Consequences that he neither seeks nor avoids may be considered neutral. In the technical lingo of the psychologist, positive consequences are usually referred to as *rewards* or *reinforcers.* Negative consequences are labeled *punishers* or *aversive stimuli,* while neutral consequences are given no special label.

Behaviors are influenced by their consequences as well as by antecedent cues. Generally speaking, we may say that reinforcing consequences strengthen a behavior—that is, they increase the likelihood that the behavior will recur. Conversely, punishing consequences weaken the behavior—that is, they reduce the likelihood of its recurrence. For example, a young child might display tantrum behavior in the presence of certain environmental cues (such as the sight of his mother bringing him his pajamas at bedtime). The probability of bedtime tantrums in the future is determined by the consequences of that behavior. If his parents provide a positive reinforcement for the response (such as giving him special attention or delaying his bedtime), then the tantrums probably will recur more frequently. However, if a negative consequence (such as a spanking) is presented, the behavior may become less likely. Notice that the latter prediction is a bit more cautious. Research has suggested that punishment may be a much less effective technique for behavior change than reinforcement is (Bandura, 1969). Many conditions must be met before negative consequences (punishment) will systematically reduce a behavior (Azrin & Holz, 1966; Johnston, 1972). For example, the consequence must be presented every time the behavior occurs. The punishing consequence must also be as strong (aversive) as possible. In addition, any inadvertent reinforcement must also be avoided. Obviously, it is difficult to use aversive consequences effectively. Too often a consequence that seems aversive is used inconsistently and actually causes the problem behavior to increase. Despite the evidence questioning the usefulness of punishment in changing behavior, many parents and teachers rely too heavily on this strategy.

Neutral consequences may influence a behavior in several different ways, depending on the nature of earlier consequences. For example, if a child has been accustomed to receiving positive attention from his parents for his bedtime tantrums, a more neutral reaction (for example, ignoring the tantrums) may reduce the likelihood of the behavior. On the other hand, if punishing consequences are changed to neutral ones, an increase in the behavior might occur. Changing from a pattern of positive or negative consequences to a pattern of neutral ones is known as *extinction*. Procedurally, this means that the reinforcing or punishing consequences that previously followed a behavior are removed. When a reinforcer is removed, the frequency of the behavior often declines. The removal of a punisher, however, often increases the frequency of the behavior. Thus, an elementary school teacher may more effectively reduce fighting between two students by *not* providing them with a lot of attention (a positive consequence) for fighting rather than by punishing them with a restriction (an aversive consequence), such as no recess.

From this discussion it may be seen that reinforcing consequences offer the most practical and promising means for behavior change. There now exists a substantial body of evidence indicating that human behaviors—from the simplest to the most complex—may be predicted and controlled through the systematic presentation and removal of reinforcing consequences.

However, if the desired behavior does not occur initially, it cannot be reinforced. A procedure for remedying this situation is called *shaping*, or the reinforcement of successive approximations. This means that we initially reinforce behaviors that are remotely related to the ultimate goal response. The behaviors that receive reinforcement are *gradually* required to be slightly closer to the desired behavior. For example, in teaching a young child to speak, we would begin by rewarding any vocal sounds whatsoever. When these sounds had increased in frequency, we could then raise the requirements for reward by waiting for sounds that were similar to consonant and vowel sounds.

Once a behavior has been shaped and reinforced, its continued occurrence still depends on environmental influences. If sufficient consequences are not forthcoming, the behavior will decrease. A very intriguing principle related to behavior maintenance is that of intermittency. The *principle of intermittency* states that, once a behavior has been established, its maintenance will be greater if the behavior is reinforced only occasionally instead of after every occurrence. For example, once a child has learned to say a few words, it is better to praise him only occasionally (for example, after every fifth word) instead of after every response. Because the intermittency principle deals with the scheduling or timing of reinforcers, it is often spoken of in terms of *schedules of reinforcement.* There are a variety of schedules, many of which produce different degrees of behavior maintenance.

This very brief description indicates that behaviors are influenced both by antecedent cues and by consequences. More detailed and comprehensive sources on the principles and techniques discussed in this section are listed at the end of the chapter.

Given that behaviors do follow consistent patterns in relation to environmental influences, we are able both to predict and to control their occurrence to some extent. In the next section, we shall explore the application of basic behavior principles through systematic environmental engineering or designing.

B. BEHAVIORAL DESIGNING

The discovery and clarification of scientific principles are frequently followed by the development of an applied technology—that is, by the development of a set of procedures that make use of the principles. Behavioral designing involves a systematic application of the research findings in behavioral science. It involves arranging an environment that will produce and maintain specified behaviors in particular situations. Returning to Goldiamond's (1965a) equation $(B = f(x))$ illustrating the functional relationship between a behavior and its environment, we find that, once the equation has been solved—that is, once the relevant environmental factors (x) have been discovered—the occurrence of the behavior can be controlled by making the necessary changes in the environment. Usually, the behavioral designer is faced with one of three technological tasks: (1) establishing a behavior, (2) increasing or maintaining a behavior, or (3) reducing or eliminating a behavior. We shall now take a brief look at his technology.

1. Establishing a Behavior.   When the behavioral designer is asked to plan an environment that will produce certain behaviors, he must determine whether those behaviors now occur to any extent. If they do occur but only at low frequencies, then the techniques to be discussed under "increasing a behavior" are relevant. If they do not occur, then the behaviors must be established.

One of the most popular response-establishing techniques is *shaping*. As was mentioned earlier, this technique involves the reinforcement of responses that are successively closer to the desired behavior. Thus, even though the young child who is learning to feed himself may initially deposit more oatmeal in his hair than in his mouth, by praising him for gradually better aim, we can shape his self-feeding responses to eventually resemble the socially approved ones.

A second procedure for establishing a response is *instruction*. That is, the desired behavior can be described to the individual either verbally or in writing. While this technique is very useful with many behaviors, there are instances in which simple instruction is not a sufficiently effective technique. Although certain responses may be acquired through verbal instruction, it is doubtful that such skills as gymnastics or shoe-tying can be taught solely by this means. Moreover, when communication problems exist (for example, with preverbal children), alternative training procedures must be used.

A third technique is called *modeling*, or observational learning. Basically, this technique involves demonstrating the desired behavior in some way. Research in a variety of areas has shown that modeling is one of the most powerful and efficient procedures for transmitting information about behavior.

Another useful procedure is *guided participation*, a technique in which the individual is first shown the behavior (modeling) and then is assisted in performing the behavior. The guidance is subsequently phased out when the individual has learned the response. For example, a shy teenager may learn how to start conversations with strangers by seeing another person model that behavior. However, the combination of observing the behavior (modeling) and then practicing it with help is usually much more effective. Of course, guided participation, modeling, instruction, and shaping can be used in various combinations to increase instructional input.

2. Increasing or Maintaining a Behavior. The fact that an individual knows how to perform a response does not, of course, ensure that he or she will do so. This is repeatedly illustrated on first dates.

The frequency of an acquired behavior is usually increased by means of systematic reinforcement. An alternative to reinforcement, of course, is punishment for the non-occurrence of the behavior. In either instance, an "if-then" relationship is established between the behavior and a specified consequence. This "if-then" relationship is called a *contingency*. For example, the parent who wishes to increase his son's lawn-mowing behavior might set up a contingency such that the desired behavior is followed by a reinforcer (such as money or privileges). On the other hand, the parent might approach the same problem by establishing a punishment contingency such that not mowing the lawn results in negative consequences (such as the termination of car privileges). As was mentioned earlier, preliminary research suggests that reinforcement contingencies are more effective than punishment contingencies in terms of long-term behavior change.

Another way to increase or maintain the performance of a behavior is to systematically alter the schedule of the consequences. We referred briefly to the principle of intermittency in the last section. Here we shall see that the behavioral designer relies very heavily on that principle in planning environments to maintain behavior. Once a response has been learned, it can be increased by making reinforcements contingent upon its occurrence. The number of responses required for each reinforcement can be gradually raised (for example, from 1 to 3 to 5 and so on) until the desired performance rate is attained. In using intermittent schedules of reinforcement, we must be careful (1) that the contingency is changed very gradually rather than abruptly, and (2) that the ultimate performance rate is both attainable and equitable in terms of the individual's efforts and abilities.

An important subtask that is often requested of the behavioral designer has to do with the development of *stimulus control.* This means that the frequency of certain behaviors is increased in the presence of one set of antecedent stimuli but decreased in the presence of others. For example, you may know someone whose jokes are well received by one group of friends but frowned upon by another. Moreover, it is very likely that your own actions vary depending on the prevailing environmental cues (for example, the presence of your parents rather than of your college friends). As was mentioned earlier, antecedent stimuli predict the consequences of various behaviors. In this manner, these stimuli gain control over the performance of responses. Basically, stimulus control may be established through certain *discrimination-training* experiences. That is, the individual can be taught that a particular behavior pattern (for example, making liberal statements about marijuana) will be reinforced in the presence of some environmental stimuli (for example, campus friends) but punished in the presence of others (for example, parents and narcotics agents). Because environmental cues can gain control over a behavior, these cues may be used to assist in increasing or maintaining a performance. For example, research has shown that study behaviors can be increased by arranging for them to occur in the presence of certain environmental cues. These cues will subsequently come to elicit, or "set the occasion for," study behaviors (Goldiamond, 1965a). For example, a college freshman could arrange his desk so that only the work to be done that day was on top. He would put other books and papers elsewhere. In addition, he would only sit at the desk to study, not to listen to records or to talk to his roommate. Thus, sitting at the desk would cue, or "set the occasion for," studying.

3. *Eliminating a Behavior.*   A behavior can be reduced or eliminated in several different ways. One of the most popular and effective techniques is *extinction.* In this procedure, the behavioral designer determines what reinforcers are currently encouraging the behavior. He then suggests the removal of those reinforcers and predicts that the behavior will subsequently decrease. Although extinction procedures are often applied successfully, their use occasionally involves some practical problems. For one thing, such procedures often take time and require patience on the part of both the behavioral designer and anyone else involved. Additionally, extinction procedures sometimes produce temporary "emotional" behaviors and a short-lived increase in the behavior to be eliminated. That is, things often get temporarily worse before they get better. For example, a frustrated young mother who tries to ignore her son's temper tantrums may find herself becoming very upset when he shouts even louder during the first few days of "extinction." Finally, the identification and control of relevant reinforcements are often a difficult task.

A second procedure for eliminating or reducing a behavior capitalizes on the principle of stimulus control. If it is apparent that a behavior is being influenced by cues that have previously been present when the behavior occurred, the cues may be altered to produce a reduction in the behavior. For example, investigations of overeating have shown that a variety of food-relevant cues powerfully influence the occurrence of eating behavior. Thus, a refrigerator that is abundantly stocked with soda and pastries may elicit (and reinforce) frequent eating. The seemingly innocuous presence of a candy machine in a frequently traveled corridor may likewise come to control (and accelerate) the purchases of candy. Research on obesity has suggested that inappropriate eating may be reduced by eliminating its eliciting cue (for example, by avoiding the tempting corridor) or by changing its availability (for example, by stocking a refrigerator with more appropriate low-calorie reinforcers).

A third technique for the reduction or elimination of a response is punishment. As was mentioned earlier, our current knowledge on the effects of punishment suggests that this technique involves some complexities that often make its successful use difficult. Too often, the person administering punishment becomes generally aversive to the person being punished. Sometimes, the "punishment" becomes a reinforcer, since it increases the problem behavior. However, punishment should not be totally ignored by the behavioral designer. There have been many reports of situations in which punishment procedures have contributed significantly to the reduction of inappropriate behaviors. "Time out" from positive consequences has proved to be an effective type of punishment. In this procedure, a person is punished by the removal of something positive rather than by the direct administration of an aversive consequence. For example, a teen-age boy who constantly interrupts the conversations of other family members during meals must leave the table for ten minutes as punishment. (This presumes that he finds being with the rest of the family reinforcing.) Similarly, an overly boisterous third grader must leave the playground and return to his classroom during recess. Indeed, a person can sometimes punish himself by denying himself some pleasant object or event if he engages in a problem behavior.

A fourth strategy that has been used to reduce undesired behavior involves the reinforcement of incompatible responses. For example, in order to reduce smoking or eating behaviors, the behavioral designer can arrange reinforcement contingencies that strengthen responses that are incompatible with these behaviors. A bit of ingenuity is required in selecting effective incompatible responses. The anxious overeater might use physical relaxation responses when he feels anxious and is tempted to eat. The chronic smoker might work small puzzles to keep his hands busy and to make smoking difficult. Of course, taking a shower is incompatible with smoking, as are swimming and relaxed deep breathing. Similarly, reinforcing oneself for acting more assertively—that is, for speaking more loudly and for maintaining more eye contact with others—is incompatible with being shy. Sometimes, a combined strategy is used. The target behaviors—that is, the behaviors to be reduced—are punished, and responses that are incompatible with them are rewarded. Research on this combined approach has shown it to be a very practical and promising one in the modification of a variety of behaviors.

The foregoing techniques and examples deal with the reduction and elimination of behaviors that probably have been maintained by occasional positive reinforcement. Another set of procedures is often used to reduce other inappropriate response patterns, such as phobic avoidance responses and sexual deviations. In these patterns of behavior, the learning history is often assumed to be somewhat different from what we have outlined, and a variety of other behavior principles are drawn upon. Briefly, these procedures involve *classical* or *respondent conditioning,* whereas our discussions have centered on *operant* or *instrumental conditioning.* (The term *conditioning,* as used here, is synonymous with *learning.*)

Recent research has questioned the distinction between these two types of conditioning, and ongoing investigations are demonstrating some very complex relationships between them (Miller, 1969). Without delving into these complexities, we may say that operant (instrumental) conditioning involves a response that is sandwiched between antecedents and consequences. The antecedent cues do not automatically produce the behavior; they influence its likelihood by informing the person of the probable consequences of his actions. Once a person acts, his response is either strengthened or weakened by reinforcement, punishment, or the absence of consequences (extinction). This type of conditioning differs from classical (respondent) conditioning, in which the performance is relatively involuntary or reflexive. For example, a very sudden loud noise will elicit fear responses (such as crying, rapid breathing, and so forth) in an infant. If a formerly neutral stimulus, such as a bathtub, is accidentally paired with the loud noise, it may become a conditioned stimulus, and, in future situations, the bathtub alone may elicit the fear response. Diagrams of these learning sequences follow.

Operant (Instrumental) Conditioning

NS ⟶ R

NS ⟶ R ⟶ C ⟨ NS / R

1. Initial State of Affairs. A neutral stimulus (NS) precedes a response (R), but no consequences occur.

2. Learning Conditions. The antecedent cue occurs, the R is emitted, and a positive (rewarding) or negative (punishing) consequence (C) is experienced.

3. Result. The R is either strengthened or weakened, and the antecedent cue becomes informative in predicting the consequences of the R. Further, the C can then precede other responses and neutral stimuli.

Classical (Respondent) Conditioning

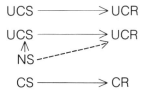

1. Initial State of Affairs. An unconditioned stimulus (UCS), such as a loud noise, will elicit a reflexive fear response, or unconditioned response (UCR).

2. Learning Conditions. A formerly neutral stimulus (NS)—that is, a stimulus that produced neither intensely positive nor intensely negative reactions—is paired with the UCS.

3. Result. The NS has now become a *conditioned stimulus* (CS) and can, by itself, elicit a reflexive fear response. Because this fearful behavior was not connected to this stimulus prior to conditioning, it is now referred to as a *conditioned response* (CR).

Table 1-1 illustrates the differences between operant and classical conditioning. More extensive discussions of these forms of learning are presented in Bandura (1969).

It should be noted that a particular behavior may be acquired and maintained as a result of both classical- and operant-conditioning principles. A child's fear of bathtubs may have been classically conditioned (for example, through pairing with a loud noise or a painful fall) and may also have been reinforced (for example, through parental attention).

Fears and sexual responses are generally believed to involve at least some classical conditioning. Some forms of addiction may also involve respondent processes. Respondent conditioning is thought to be heavily influenced by antecedent cues and by certain autonomic processes. For this reason, the reduction and elimination of classically conditioned response patterns (for example, the avoidance of elevators) usually involve procedures designed to change the cueing value of antecedent stimuli. That is, instead of altering the consequences of avoiding elevators, the behavioral designer would try to alter the fear-inducing properties of elevators through several experimentally derived procedures.

One of these therapeutic procedures involves modeling and guided participation. It is similar in some ways to the procedures that

---

TABLE 1-1.   *Operant and Classical Conditioning.*

Operant (Instrumental) Conditioning

Antecedent Cue	Response	Consequence
(1) philosophy instructor	criticizing	(1) praise (reward)
(2) church minister	religious	(2) admonishment (punishment)
(3) no one	philosophy	(3) nothing (neutral)

Classical (Respondent) Conditioning

Stimulus	Response	Comments
(X) loud noise	fear	(X) elicits this response almost automatically ("reflexively"); because (X) possesses this power without previous conditioning, it is called an "unconditioned" stimulus.
(Y) quiet commercial airliner	no response	(Y) is initially neutral.
(X+Y) noisy commercial airliner	fear	Noise-elicited fear responses become associated with the airliner.
(Y') quiet airliner	fear	The airliner has now become a "conditioned" stimulus that, by itself, elicits the fear response.

Although there are several technical similarities between operant and classical conditioning, they may be differentiated on several points:

Operant	Classical
1. major emphasis on *response*	1. major emphasis on *stimulus*
2. stimulus "sets the occasion for" a response (predicts consequences of a response)	2. stimulus produces response
3. connotation of "active, instrumental, voluntary" response	3. connotation of "passive, reflexive, involuntary" response to stimulation

are used to establish a behavior. Very gradually, the fearful individual can be shown that the experiences involved in approaching an elevator (for example, the sight of an elevator) need not be fear-arousing. The individual is then systematically guided toward engaging in the desired behavior—that is, toward approaching and entering an elevator. External support is gradually reduced as the individual acquires competence—that is, as he begins to ride elevators on his own. This fear-elimination technique, as well as the following ones, can be effectively supplemented with procedures such as systematic reinforcement and the extinction of inappropriate responses, which are derived from operant-conditioning principles.

A second procedure for reducing fears and other maladaptive response patterns is called *desensitization* or *counterconditioning*. The former term is derived from the fact that the individual has somehow become "sensitized" to a stimulus (for example, to flying), and the therapeutic goal is to remove that excessive sensitization. The term *counterconditioning* is based on the assumption that responses such as fears are conditioned (classically) through the association of arousing or painful stimuli with situations that are realistically harmless. Presumably this conditioning may be "countered" by systematically associating the harmless but feared situation with pleasant stimuli. For example, a person's fear of dentists may have been caused by the previous association of a dentist with severe pain. This kind of learning can be countered by now associating dentists with pleasant feelings (for example, with deep physical relaxation). The actual processes at work in desensitization and counterconditioning are not entirely clear. Current research is exploring this area in hopes of clarifying the behavior principles involved. However, there can be little doubt that dramatic reductions in fears and anxieties (avoidance behaviors) can be effected through the systematic use of these procedures.

The foregoing techniques have been used for the reduction of fears, anxieties, and phobias. Another technique is employed in the elimination of inappropriate approach responses, such as sexual deviance, alcoholism, and drug addiction. In this strategy, a sensitization or *aversion* is developed to the target stimulus—that is, to the stimulus that inappropriately evokes the response—by associating it with painful stimuli. At the same time, another procedure is used that associates appropriate stimuli with either pleasant stimulation or the absence of pain. For example, in the treatment of child molesters, looking at pictures of nude children may be associated with painful shock, while attending to pictures of nude women is reinforced through shock termination. Despite the rather ghoulish misrepresentation of aversion techniques in the mass media, these procedures have shown some promising success in the treatment of addictive and sexual disorders.

C.   COGNITIVE-SYMBOLIC PROCESSES

The foregoing description of behavior principles and technology has been necessarily brief. The complexities involved in both the understanding and the application of even a single principle (such as intermittent reinforcement) would require more time and space than our present purposes will allow. It is strongly recommended that the reader consult the suggested readings list at the end of this chapter for further resources detailing social-learning principles.

The principles we have discussed have been derived from decades of research in both laboratory and field settings. This research was initially carried out with laboratory animals—rats, pigeons, dogs, and monkeys. Principles developed from animal research were later applied in controlled experiments with children. Finally, during the last two decades, there has been an expansion both of learning research and of its application to the complex behavior problems of adult humans. An early criticism of the application of findings from animal research to humans was that one could not generalize from pigeons to people. Humans are, of course, extremely complex. However, the wealth of data on human performance suggests that a broad parallel does exist between the principles governing infrahuman behavior and those governing human behavior. In both cases, stimulus cues and behavioral consequences play very significant roles. Anyone who has observed a rat pressing a lever for intermittent reinforcement and subsequently has visited Las Vegas will attest to the striking parallels.

To some extent, however, many behavioral scientists have been at fault in their conceptual and practical leaps from animal to human behavior. Human behavior is remarkably more complicated than animal behavior and usually is influenced by a myriad of interrelated environmental factors. The behavioral designer who approaches an intelligent adult as if he were simply an overgrown rat will soon find that both his technology and his conceptual system need revising. This is not to say that different principles are at work in human behavior—only that more complicated factors (antecedents, behaviors, and consequences) are involved. For example, the behavioral designer may not be aware of the many stimuli that the human is capable of presenting to himself. These stimuli may take the form of thoughts, self-instructions, or images. Moreover, the human is capable of an extensive repertoire of behavior, which includes countercontrolling responses. That is, just as the behavioral designer may attempt to control the individual's responses, the individual, in turn, may control the performance of the designer. While rats and pigeons may also exert an influence over the designer to some degree, their propensity for control is far below that exhibited by humans. This high degree of control is demonstrated each day in classrooms in which teachers' efforts at encouraging certain student behaviors are countered by student actions that alter the teachers' behaviors. Parents and their children share the same experience.

The preceding statements are not intended to discourage generalizations from animal research to human behavior but are meant to discourage simplistic generalizations. As Bandura (Article Two) points out, most individuals perform very complex responses over long periods of time without immediate environmental consequences (such as reinforcement or punishment). The average college professor does not present pellets to his students each time they attend class or exhibit study behavior. Yet these responses are maintained and often accelerated. Does this mean that human performance does not obey the previously described principles of learning? On the contrary. Research has shown, for example, that when no contingencies are placed on behaviors such as attending class and studying, they follow a predictable extinction pattern. But how can we account for the development and maintenance of effortful response patterns such as writing books and hermitism when the consequences for such behaviors are either tremendously delayed or not apparent? From our present knowledge, it would appear that such patterns are mediated and maintained through complex cognitive-symbolic processes—that is, through thoughts about anticipated consequences, self-praise, self-criticism, and so forth. As a matter of fact, evidence in the area of human learning suggests that an individual's behavior patterns are largely influenced by cognitive mediation. That is, while the rat may respond in a very predictable fashion to the presence of an antecedent cue and to subsequent consequences, the human's performance is affected by his *perception* of the cue and his anticipation of the consequences. Because of his socially learned repertoire of language and thought, any behavior exhibited by the human adult is met with two types of consequences—those provided by the external environment and those supplied by his own "internal environment" (self-reactions). Thus, while even the most ambitious rat is unlikely to worry about the adequacy of a day's performance, a person is likely to exhibit such a concern, and these self-reactions are significant in the understanding of human behavior.

D. BEHAVIOR-CHANGE AGENT:
THERAPIST OR SELF?

The rapidly expanding research of the past two decades has resulted in a collection of principles aimed at predicting, understanding, and controlling human behavior. As the principles were tested and applied, a sophisticated technology was developed for reliably changing human behavior (Bandura, 1969). Given that such a technology exists, we naturally ask "who should apply it to whom?" Early arguments were concerned with the ethical issues involved—that is, why should one individual be able to engineer and control the performances of another? As our previous discussion has pointed out, however, the control process is a reciprocal one—that is, both the individual and the designer act as controlled and controlling persons. It soon became clear that behavior is always under the control of the existing environmental influences. Unfortunately, however, the existing control is usually haphazard, and it frequently results in the development and maintenance of inappropriate behavior patterns. Thus, the important question was not whether it is ethical to control behavior but whether that control should be deliberate and constructive or random and often harmful.

With the debate still continuing, it occurred to several researchers that a possible solution to the problem lay in providing the individual with a behavior technology that he could apply toward his own chosen behavior change. Returning to Goldiamond's (1965a) equation ($B = f(x)$) again, we can see that no constraints are placed on *who* alters the environment to produce the desired behavior change. Given the necessary knowledge, the individual can himself perform that task as well as (if not better than) an external behavioral designer. He certainly has more access to the responses to be changed (particularly if they involve such factors as thoughts), and he may be more capable of applying behavior-change procedures over a long period of time. This self-regulated engineering highlights the reciprocal relationship between individual and environmental influences (Bandura, 1969). Modifying Goldiamond's equation, we can say that $X = f(b)$, where X again represents environmental factors and b represents the individual's self-managed behaviors. The equation states that a person's environment (which, as we know, controls his behavior) is itself a function of his behavior patterns. While the earlier description of behavior principles may have implied a passive manipulation of the individual by environmental forces, this conceptualization highlights the fact that the individual can take an active role in arranging and regulating those forces.

We have thus come full circle. Behavior is a function of its environment, which, in turn, may be rearranged and altered. It should be noted that the act of engaging in self-regulated behavioral designing is itself a complex response worthy of investigation. Skinner (1953) describes the distinction between *controlled* responses (such as smoking) and *controlling* responses (such as refusing to buy cigarettes). If these "self-controlling" responses are not themselves reinforced (for example, by health improvements or social praise), they will decline. We are thus faced with an infinite and complex chain of interdependent behavior-environment influences that make up the phenomenon of self-control. In the next chapter, we shall talk about the concept of self-control and preview the basic strategies that can be used to produce self-change.

SUPPLEMENTARY SOURCES

Bandura, A. *Social learning theory.* New York: General Learning Press, 1971.

Ferster, C. B., & Perrott, M. C. *Behavior principles.* New York: Meredith, 1968.

Kanfer, F. H. *Behavior modification: An overview.* In C. E. Thoresen (Ed.), *Behavior modification in education, Second yearbook of the National Society for the Study of Education.* Part I. Chicago: University of Chicago Press, 1973.

Mikulas, W. L. *Behavior modification: An overview.* New York: Harper & Row, 1972.

Reese, E. P. *An analysis of human operant behavior.* Dubuque, Iowa: Brown, 1966.

BEHAVIORAL SELF-CONTROL

History is filled with descriptions of man's attempts to develop self-control. Indeed, the notion of self-control is often associated with the ideals of freedom and self-improvement. A person who is really free is one who guides and directs his own actions. Such a person is the master both of himself and of his immediate environment. Moreover, self-control is valued because of its role in sociocultural survival. A major characteristic of "civilized" societies is the degree to which their members can direct, maintain, and coordinate individual activities without external coercion. Looking ahead, we can predict that, if more individuals could become effective in their self-management skills, the need for professional helpers to deal with passive "you-help-me" patients might be sharply diminished.

A. SELF-CONTROL: WILLPOWER OR LEARNED BEHAVIOR?

The term *self-control* has meant many different things to different people. Its most popular synonym, by far, has been "willpower"—a vaguely defined inner force. Unable to fully understand how and why some individuals are able to demonstrate self-control in the face of very trying circumstances, we have attributed such behavior to willpower, to some supernatural entity, or to an underlying personality trait. These ways of thinking about the problem have unfortunately retarded understanding and discouraged research. A vicious tautology or circularity has been created. The person who succeeds in demonstrating self-control by resisting a major temptation—for example, the heavy smoker who quits cold turkey—is often described as having willpower. How do we know that he has willpower? Well, he quit smoking, didn't he? This circular route of observing a self-regulative behavior, inferring will-power, and then using the latter to "explain" the former is an all too frequent journey in self-control discussions. We have not gotten beyond the behavior to be explained. Moreover, this tautology discourages further inquiries into the factors affecting self-control. If John's unsuccessful attempt to lose weight can be attributed to his lack of willpower, then we need look no further for causes of failure (or for solutions to his problem) (Thoresen, in press). We cannot deny that some individuals have demonstrated remarkable self-management under trying circumstances. They seemingly have exhibited a great deal of "willpower." However, the issue that concerns us here is whether willpower conceptions of self-control have shown themselves to be useful in understanding self-regulatory processes. To date, the consensus among self-control researchers has been virtually unanimous: volitional approaches to self-control (such as willpower and personality-trait explanations) have seriously impeded the collection and interpretation of meaningful knowledge about self-management.

What are the alternatives to the willpower interpretation? One of the oldest examples of effective self-control was reported by Homer in the travels of Odysseus (Kanfer & Phillips, 1970). To manage the bewitching effects of the Sirens, Odysseus had his oarsmen fill their ears with beeswax. To manage himself, he commanded his men to tie him to the mast and warned them not to release him under any circumstances. Instead of beseeching the gods to give him the power to ward off the Sirens or admonishing himself to exercise his willpower, Odysseus altered some important environmental factors. Had we listened to Homer many centuries ago, our efforts toward understanding self-control might not have gone so far astray.

The key to Odysseus' success was in his recognition that self-control is integrally bound up with "here-and-now" environmental considerations. There is a rapidly expanding body of evidence indicating that effective self-regulation can be durably established if attention is given to significant person-environment relationships. Preliminary efforts have pointed toward the possibility of creating a "technology" of behavioral self-control—that is, a set of procedures that the individual can learn to use in directing and managing his own internal and external actions (Thoresen & Mahoney, 1974).

An individual's ability to regulate his own behavior is dependent on his knowledge of and control over current environmental factors. Self-control skills are significantly enhanced by the person's ability to identify the factors that influence his behaviors—namely, cues and consequences. In this sense, the Greek maxim "Know thyself" can be translated to "Know thy controlling variables."

Self-control requires that the individual know what factors influence his behavior and how those factors can be modified to produce the desired behavior change. In effect, the individual must become a sort of personal scientist. He must make careful self-observations, collecting and analyzing personal "data." Techniques for self-change may then be tested, with the individual continuing his scrutiny of self-recorded data. Thus, accurate and ongoing personal-data collection plays a critical role in successful self-management.

People are simply not used to being very systematic about observing their own actions. Yet a person must know "where he's at" if a successful self-change plan is to work. Attending to the everyday life situations in which the problem behavior occurs is crucial. What happens, for example, just before Carol, the incessant smoker, reaches for another cigarette? The "antecedents," or activities that precede smoking, include internal cues, such as Carol's thoughts and feelings, and external cues such as Carol's physical and social settings—for example, two friends, a cup of coffee, and an ashtray on the table. The immediate consequences of having that cigarette also demand careful observation, in terms of both internal self-reactions and the actions of others. Examination of the ABCs—the antecedents, the behavior, and the consequences—helps tell what may be controlling the behavior to be changed.

Thus, successful self-control generally involves three important processes: the specification of a behavior, the identification of its antecedent cues and environmental consequences, and the implementation of an action plan that alters some of these antecedents and/or consequences. But how does the person do it? Preliminary research has identified three basic elements in behavioral self-control—namely, self-observation, environmental planning, and behavioral programming. At least one of these elements has been present in every successful self-control attempt reported thus far.

B.   AWARENESS: KNOW THY CONTROLLING VARIABLES

The first self-control strategy, *self-observation,* requires that the person not only attend to his own actions but also record their occurrence for purposes of feedback and evaluation. As mentioned earlier,

few individuals are in the habit of carefully monitoring their own behaviors. Golf counters, behavioral diaries, and wall charts can increase
the accuracy of self-observation. The individual who records his own
behavior becomes more aware of himself and, in addition, receives
both immediate and cumulative feedback on what he is (or is not)
doing. Thus, a weight chart in the bathroom might reflect trends in
weight gain or weight loss (for example, increases around weekends
and holidays). It could also provide feedback on gradual changes that
might otherwise go unnoticed. Self-recorded data may also supply significant information on the rate of a behavior, its eliciting cues, and
its subsequent consequences. Moreover, recording devices can provide an objective basis for self-evaluation—that is, if my personal data
indicate that I am changing in a desired direction, then I have good
reason to feel positively about myself.

The research evidence on self-observation suggests that desired
behaviors can often be increased simply by being recorded. The
effects of self-observation on undesired behaviors, however, are not yet
clear-cut. In a recent study, an adolescent girl who was concerned with
doing better schoolwork in a history class was asked to observe and
record her studying in class (Broden, Hall, & Mitts, Article Four). In
one week, this self-observation procedure increased her study behavior
from about 30 percent of classtime to about 80 percent, an increase
that continued after the self-observation procedure had been gradually
phased out. Self-observation in this study and others can be viewed
as a kind of applied awareness or sensitivity training. The act of systematically recording a particular action—in this case, studying or not
studying—sensitizes the person to himself. Other studies have shown
that self-observation can be employed to alter a variety of behaviors.
Further research is needed to determine the most effective types of self-
observation for various behaviors. However, it is reasonably safe to
conclude at this point that the systematic recording of one's own
behavior can have a dramatic effect on that behavior.

C. ALTERING THE ENVIRONMENT

Environmental planning, the second strategy, involves changing
the environment so that either the cues that precede a behavior or the
consequences that follow it are changed. Our ancient-mariner friend
Odysseus programmed his environment by altering the antecedent
cues for his men and by arranging for his own behavior to be strongly
controlled when temptation arose.

Environmental planning often involves the elimination or avoidance of situations in which a choice is necessary. Avoiding cigarette machines, buying only low-calorie snacks, and carrying only minimal amounts of money are effective ways of controlling smoking, overeating, and overspending. Other environmental strategies require that the person rearrange environmental cues. For example, obesity is often affected by a variety of social and physical cues that prompt overeating in the absence of physiological hunger. Thus, many people eat to avoid waste (particularly in restaurants) or because a clock (instead of their stomach) tells them to eat. Likewise, environmental cues such as a television set, a cookie jar, or even an entire room (for example, the kitchen) can elicit eating behavior. Research on behavioral self-control of overeating has shown that individuals trained to detect and alter maladaptive eating cues can significantly reduce their weight (Stuart & Davis, 1972).

This finding has since been shown to be highly consistent and applicable to behaviors other than overeating. Upper and Meredith (1970), for example, have reported an interesting application to smoking reduction. They trained smokers to break long-standing (cue-elicited) smoking patterns by altering the physical cues to smoke. Smokers were asked to record their initial daily smoking rate. Their average time between cigarettes (about 15 minutes) was then computed, and smokers were asked to wear a small portable timer. Initially, the timer was set to buzz whenever the individual's average inter-cigarette time had elapsed. The smokers were instructed to smoke only after the timer's buzz. This new environmental cue to smoke displaced previous cueing situations—such as the completion of a meal, a conversation with a friend, or a stress experience. Gradually, the interval between cigarettes was increased until smoking was greatly reduced. A similar strategy was used by Shapiro and his colleagues (Article Thirteen).

These and other studies have shown that altering the environment can help a person modify chronic and resistant behavior problems.

D. ALTERING THE CONSEQUENCES
OF BEHAVIOR

The third self-control strategy, *behavioral programming,* involves altering the consequences of a behavior instead of changing its eliciting cues. Self-reward, self-punishment, and other self-administered therapeutic techniques are common examples of this strategy. Both internal and external consequences can be used in individual programming. For example, self-praise, self-criticism, and pleasant or unpleasant mental images might be used as self-administered internal consequences. External consequences could include special privileges (such as allowing oneself to watch a favorite television program) or tangible objects (such as clothing or a hobby item). Private contracts ("If I do this, then I get that") are common in behavioral programming.

An illustration of this approach is provided by a case history of a young man who was diagnosed as schizophrenic. His problem behavior involved frequent obsessive thoughts about being physically unattractive, stupid, and brain damaged (Mahoney, 1971). After he had determined the initial frequency of these maladaptive thoughts through self-observation, the man was instructed to punish himself by snapping a heavy-gauge rubber band against his wrist whenever he engaged in obsessional thoughts. When the negative thoughts had been drastically reduced, positive self-thoughts were established and gradually increased through use of a cueing procedure that was paired with self-reward. That is, the individual was asked to write down three positive things about himself on small cards that were then attached to his cigarette package. He was instructed to read a positive self-statement whenever he wanted to smoke and then to reward himself with a cigarette. A "wild card" was alternated with the other three, and it required the young man to think of an original positive self-statement. Soon he began to generate complimentary self-thoughts without prior cueing and in the absence of smoking stimuli. The treatment techniques were gradually decreased, and the young man was able to resume a normal and adaptive life without lengthy hospitalization or extended therapy. Several other studies have indicated that individual programming strategies can be very effective in the modification of a variety of both private and observable behavior patterns.

An expanding body of literature is currently adding to our knowledge of self-control phenomena. New trends in self-control techniques include the use of imaginal consequences (such as imaginary rewards and punishments) and self-instructions. In addition, as the preceding case history showed, self-control procedures are being applied to thoughts and feelings. These trends point up an intriguing aspect of self-control research and application—namely, that it may well provide the "missing link" between behavioristic and humanistic approaches to psychology (Thoresen, Article Fourteen). Research in the behavioral analyses of self-esteem, for example, seems to incorporate both an empirical rationale and an intrapersonal relevance. Indeed, many self-control endeavors seem to be characterized by behavioral humanism. Continuing research will increase our understanding of how behavior principles can be applied to self-control. To this end, self-control researchers might appropriately adopt the banner of "Power to the Person!"

The remaining chapters of this book will be devoted to expanding our discussion of the use of self-monitoring, environmental self-control strategies, and behavioral programming to effect self-change. In addition, the behavioral humanism of self-control enterprises will be explored further. Articles discussing each of these topics follow Chapter Six.

SUPPLEMENTARY SOURCES

Thoresen, C. E. Behavioral humanism. In C. E. Thoresen (Ed.), *Behavior modification in education, Second yearbook of the National Society for the Study of Education.* Part I. Chicago: University of Chicago Press, 1973.

Thoresen, C. E., & Mahoney, M. J. *Behavioral self-control.* New York: Holt, Rinehart & Winston, 1974.

SUGGESTED READING

Kanfer & Karoly (Article Eight)
Thoresen (Article Fourteen)

ASSESSMENT IN SELF-CONTROL

Having presented the view that self-control can be conceptualized as a systematic application of learning principles, we now turn our attention to the effectiveness of self-control as a behavior-change strategy. Assessment plays an invaluable role in the objective evaluation of any scientific application. Assessment procedures allow us to test whether the principle being applied is in fact a valid one, and they also allow us to perform "exploratory" applied research. For example, in many instances, a therapist does not have a predetermined cut-and-dried solution for a client's problem (that is, he has not found the value of x in Goldiamond's equation). Therefore, he evaluates the severity of the problem prior to initiating any treatment procedures. He continues his evaluation as he introduces a treatment technique. If the ongoing data do not show an improvement after technique A is introduced, then the therapist may initiate technique B. By continually collecting information on the ongoing state of the behavior, the therapist is provided with valuable feedback that can tell him when he is on the right therapeutic "track." For this reason, even when "scientific research" is not the primary concern, objective assessment procedures should be employed—if only for immediate feedback on the appropriateness and effectiveness of the treatment technique.

A.   THE DATA TELL THE STORY

Scientific assessment has several important characteristics. One of these is an emphasis on *objective descriptions* or, as Bachrach

(1965) puts it, "data language." Suppose a friend were to tell you that he had overcome a "personality crisis" through "self-therapy." Your interest might lead you to ask him exactly what he meant by those two terms. Perhaps he used the term "personality crisis" to refer to a series of thoughts and self-statements regarding personal inadequacies and an unpleasant living situation. (For example, "I'll never make it through college—I'm just too dumb. And, besides, there aren't any jobs left anyway.") His "self-therapy," on the other hand, may have involved self-instructions (such as "Stop saying such negative things to yourself") and an increased frequency of self-praise for academic performance (such as "I'm really doing well in keeping up with my assignments"). Cast in the role of a personal scientist, your friend was describing a functional relationship in his own behavior—namely, that his feelings of personal inadequacy were systematically related to what he was saying to himself.

The importance of straightforward and objective descriptions in any application of scientific principles cannot be overemphasized (see Jeffrey, Article Seven). When behavioral scientists couch their therapeutic procedures and target behaviors in vague and abstract terms (for example, by saying that "transcendental awareness produces heightened self-actualization"), they impede pure as well as applied research. If a subsequent researcher were to report that he found no relationship between "transcendental-awareness" techniques and "heightened self-actualization," the first investigator could easily hide behind the ambiguities in these two terms and claim that the proper techniques had not been applied or that the second researcher had not evaluated self-actualization correctly. This need for straightforward communication among behavioral researchers and clinicians applies to descriptions of both the *procedures* they are using and the *outcomes* (that is, behavior changes) that they observe. If an investigator were to report that he had found a cure for cancer, his claim would have little relevance (and questionable validity) if he were unable to describe the necessary procedures for the cure.

Objective descriptions are valuable not only in communicating therapeutic procedures and outcomes but also in assessing them. Once we know what behavior a term specifies (for example, that "personality crisis" refers to negative self-statements), we have the opportunity to measure the frequency of that behavior. Once we can measure its rate, we can evaluate the influence of various procedures on its occurrence. And herein lies the crux of scientific assessment: the data tell the story.

After we have defined our procedure and the behavior that we would like to change, the next major step in scientific assessment —namely, *comparison*—arises. Stating that a self-control technique produced a change in smoking behavior presumes that we have measured the rate of smoking behavior in the *presence* and in the *absence* of that procedure and have found a difference in its occurrence. This may be done in one of two ways. We can take a single individual and measure the frequency of a behavior prior to the introduction of the self-control strategy and again after the strategy has been applied. The experimental phase prior to treatment is usually called *baseline*, and the treatment phase itself is referred to as *intervention*. In order to reassure ourselves of the functional relationship between the target behavior and the treatment strategy, we can present and withdraw the strategy in a series of baseline-intervention phases to see whether the target response co-varies with the presence of the treatment procedure. In general, studies that investigate the effects of a technique on one individual at a time are called intensive, *single-subject designs* or *empirical case studies*. Their rationale and advantages are presented by Thoresen (in press). In contrast to the single-subject design, the empirical group study may be used to evaluate the effects of a self-control strategy. Again, the underlying assessment process involves the measurement of the rate of a target behavior in the presence and in the absence of a treatment strategy. However, instead of arranging for the strategy to be alternately present and absent for a single subject, the therapist uses the strategy with one group of subjects (the *experimental* group) but does not use it with another group (the *control* group). Assuming that (1) the two groups are generally equal on pretreatment measures of the target behavior and (2) there are no uncontrolled influences (such as differential health problems) affecting one group more than the other, we can conclude that any post-treatment differences in the rate of the target behavior have been caused by the presence or absence of the treatment strategy. Campbell and Stanley (1966) offer an excellent discussion of complex variations of group designs. In his analysis of methodological problems in self-control research, Jeffrey (Article Seven) presents a discussion of some of the experimental considerations involved in single-subject (or "within-subject") and group (or "between-subject") designs.

There are, of course, many other steps in scientific assessment that improve its usefulness in both research and therapy. The suggested readings listed at the end of this chapter provide further sources of information.

B. SELF-MONITORING: ASSESSMENT TOOL OR TREATMENT STRATEGY?

Since applications of learning principles are most effective when ongoing-behavior data provide information on their appropriateness, it should come as no surprise that self-collected data play an important role in successful self-control. The first step in this personal data collection is defining the target behavior. To say that a person would like to improve his "study habits" is not sufficient—many of us have very different ideas about what study habits are. Therefore, the goal behavior must be defined in a way that will allow it to be readily measured. For example, we could define study habits as the amount of time spent actually reading assignments. This provides an easily measured behavior that other people would have no trouble understanding. Once a measurable behavior has been defined, personal data collection can be initiated, and the "awareness" process described in the previous chapter is underway.

1. Self-Monitoring Devices. A wide variety of self-monitoring devices can be used to measure the frequency of a behavior. One of the simplest is the *behavioral diary,* which allows the individual to record the occurrence of a behavior along with comments about relevant antecedent cues and consequences. Standard 3 x 5 cards can be ruled off into days of the week or hours of the day to provide a useful form. Another very popular self-monitoring device is the *miniature counter.* These are hand-held, pocket, or wrist devices that can be used whenever a behavior occurs. Although frequently designed for other uses (for example, as golf counters, mileage meters, or knitting aids), they are extremely helpful as data-collection devices. Most sporting-goods stores carry several varieties of inexpensive golf counters that can be employed in measuring the rate of a behavior.

A third device that has been found useful in self-control applications is the *portable timer.* Pocket-size or key-chain timers can be used as indicators of the termination of a measurement interval or as prearranged cues for specific responses (for example, a person may be instructed to think of a positive self-statement when the timer buzzes). As we shall see in the next section, these timers can be very useful in altering habits that contain strong stimulus-control elements. Varieties of these miniature timers have been sold as "parking-meter reminders" and may occasionally be found in novelty stores. Another time device, which is less portable but still very useful in self-control applications, is a modified electric alarm clock. Installing an inexpensive switch in the cord of the clock makes it a very handy device for timing the duration of various activities. Thus, a student may set it at 12 o'clock at the beginning of the week and place it on his desk. He is told to switch it on whenever he is studying at his desk and to switch it off if he leaves the desk area. At the end of the week, the total amount of studying time can be written on a separate form or entered on a chart.

An additional type of self-monitoring device is the *behavior graph* or chart. These are often made on standard graph paper and employ basic charting procedures. Typically, the horizontal axis represents the dimension of time (such as days or weeks) and the vertical axis represents the rate of the behavior to be changed (such as the number of cigarettes smoked) or the results of a behavior-change program (such as change in body weight).

2. Types of Self-Monitoring. In addition to a variety of self-monitoring devices, there are several different methods of personal data collection. To begin with, we can choose between *actuarial-frequency* measurements and *all-or-none* measurements. For example, if a person were interested in measuring the frequency of his smoking behavior, he could count the actual number of cigarettes he smoked each day. An alternative method would be to divide the day into equal parts (for example, into 12 two-hour periods) and then record in "all-or-none" fashion whether at least one cigarette was smoked during each of those time periods. Thus, if he were keeping a behavioral diary, the individual would mark a "yes" for those two-hour periods during which he smoked at least one cigarette. No entries would be made for those time periods during which no smoking occurred. As you can see, all-or-none methods discard much of the data—for example, you may have had six cigarettes during one time period, but your diary would indicate only that you smoked at least one cigarette.

The advantages of all-or-none recording are more apparent in instances in which the behavior is of extremely high frequency or in which it is not discrete. For example, if a person wanted to measure the frequency of his self-critical thoughts, making an actual count (for example, by pressing a miniature counter after each thought) might be difficult. How would he know when *one* self-critical thought stopped and the next began? If he criticized himself every 30 seconds for ten minutes, would that be one large self-criticism or 20 small ones? Moreover, if his self-critical thoughts occurred very frequently, he might become annoyed at the ongoing task of registering each occurrence. Those of you who have tried to count calories know how tiresome it can become to write down every single instance of a high-frequency

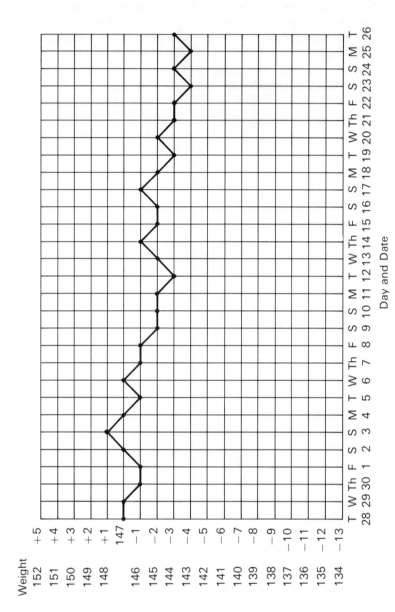

FIGURE 3-1. Daily Weight Chart. Charts such as this one may be used as self-monitoring aids to provide graphically illustrated feedback on performance.

behavior. In situations such as this, the all-or-none assessment method is very desirable. It eliminates the problem of determining the duration of one response and also lightens the self-monitoring burden. Although it may not provide data on the actual frequency of a response, over a period of time, the all-or-none technique offers a useful estimate of how often the behavior occurs. In the sample all-or-none recording system presented in Table 3.1, notice how the monitoring procedures were set up to provide information on the frequency, the nature, and the timing of the behavior.

3. The Accuracy of Self-Monitoring.   The usefulness of a measurement in any scientific application is largely influenced by its accuracy. We cannot profit from erroneous information. In general, the accuracy of measurements is determined by their reliability and their validity. Reliability usually refers to the consistency of the measurement—that is, whether the same value will be observed with repeated measurements or with measurements using more than one observer or device. Validity, on the other hand, refers to the "true" value of the phenomenon being assessed. Thus, you may weigh yourself on a bathroom scale and observe a reading of 136 pounds. If you step off the scale and back on again several times and the same reading appears, then we may say that your scale is reliable (that is, consistent). However, it may turn out that a more accurate device (such as your physician's scale) shows your real weight as 138. This would indicate that your home scale was reliable but invalid. These same terms apply in almost all forms of scientific measurement.

Jeffrey (Article Seven) and Kazdin (Article Nine) discuss some of the possible problems in obtaining accurate self-monitored data. Without going into detail here, it can be said that people are not naturally accurate observers—either of their own behavior or of others' behavior. This raises several problems in the assessment of self-control strategies. If you outline a self-managed therapy procedure for a friend who would like to quit smoking, your analysis of his success must rely on his self-monitored data (unless you plan to follow him around and observe for yourself). However, you now know that it is very likely that he will not be totally accurate in his reports to you. Moreover, as Jeffrey points out, there is always the chance that someone will falsely report a self-monitored behavior change—if only to please the therapist. Problems such as these pose a serious challenge, and self-control researchers are now developing methods for training and evaluating the accuracy of self-monitoring (see Thoresen & Mahoney, 1974). At the present time, however, several measures may be taken to increase

TABLE 3-1. Self-Recording of Eating Habits.

Record your daily eating habits on a chart like the one shown here. You will record behaviors in three different areas: (1) *quality control*, (2) *quantity control*, and (3) *situation control*. In general, quality control refers to *what* you eat, quantity control refers to *how much* you eat, and situation control refers to *where and when* you eat. Your habits may be good (+) or poor (-) in each of these areas. Specific examples follow. Be sure to read these over so that you understand what is meant by each category.

Name _____ SAMPLE _____   Week _____

		Sun	Mon	Tues	Wed	Thur	Fri	Sat
Quality	Morn	- +					+	
Control	Aft	-	+	+	+		-	- +
	Eve	-		-	-		-	
Quantity	Morn			+ -				-
Control	Aft	+	+ -					+
	Eve				+		+	
Situation	Morn		-				-	
Control	Aft	+	-		-	+		-
	Eve	-	-		-	-	-	- +

The chart represents a week, and the days of the week have been divided into morning (midnight to noon), afternoon (noon to 6 PM), and evening (6 PM to midnight). For each part of the day, record whether you showed good (+) or poor (-) eating habits in each of the categories (quality, quantity, and situation). For example, the uppermost left square is for quality control on Sunday morning. If you showed *at least one* good quality habit on Sunday morning, you would place a plus mark in that box. If you showed at least one poor quality habit, you would place a minus sign in that box. It may happen that you did both. For example, you may have had saccharin with your morning coffee (+quality) but had a doughnut for breakfast (−quality). If so, you would mark both a plus and a minus in the Sunday morning quality square. Remember, all it takes is one instance of a good or poor habit to earn a plus or minus in that category.

Use the same procedure in recording the quantity-control and situation-control categories. Again, one instance earns a plus or a minus for that entire part of the day. If a behavior fits two categories, mark it in both. For example, between-meal snacking on carrots (instead of candy) earns a plus under quality but a minus under situation control.

It is very important that you record your habits as soon as possible after they occur. That is, the first time you show a good or poor habit in one of the three categories, mark it down immediately under the appropriate part of the day. This means that you should keep the chart handy at all times; carry it with you and do not wait until the end of the day to record.

Be accurate and honest in your self-recording. It will help you to determine exactly what your eating habits are and how they may best be altered.

Quality Control

Good (+) habits	Poor (-) habits
1. *low-calorie foods* such as yogurt, boiled eggs, lean meat, cottage cheese, and so on (include *any* foods that are low in carbohydrates or fats).	1. *fattening foods* such as potatoes, bread, fatty meat, fried foods, salad dressing, spaghetti, lasagna (noodle dishes), and so on (include *any* foods that are high in carbohydrates or fats).
2. *low-calorie substitutions* such as ice water instead of beer, saccharin instead of sugar, skim milk instead of whole milk, diet soda instead of regular soda, popcorn instead of chips, carrots instead of nuts, and so on (*anytime* you eat or drink something less fattening than usual; include low-calorie snacking).	2. *fattening snacks and beverages* such as candy, nuts, pastry, chips, ice cream, nondiet soda, beer, wine, any alcohol, coffee or tea with sugar, and so on (include *all* fattening between-meal snacking).

Quantity Control

Good (+) habits	Poor (-) habits
1. *reduced portions* (*anytime* you eat or drink less than your usual amount—for example, one piece of toast instead of two, a half-glass of beer instead of a full one).	1. *extra portions* such as seconds at a meal, large servings, and so on (*anytime* you eat more than usual).
2. *ending a meal while still a bit hungry*.	2. *eating until full or bloated.*
3. *eating slowly, taking small bites, or interrupting meal by five minutes or more.*	3. *taking large bites and eating rapidly.*
4. *leaving food on your plate* after a meal at home, turning down offers of food, throwing away leftovers rather than eating them.	4. *eating to avoid waste* (for example, by eating leftovers to prevent their being thrown out or to keep them from spoiling, or by finishing a child's meal for him).

Situation Control

Good (+) habits	Poor (-) habits
1. *separating eating from other activities*—for example, by going to a special room to eat or by making an effort not to eat while reading or watching TV.	1. *eating when not really hungry*—for example, at a party, due to "nervous energy," because others are eating (such as at meals), or due to time of day ("lunch") (*anytime* you eat due to habit or just to be sociable).
2. *not eating between meals.*	2. *eating between meals.* (Note: if the item you eat is fattening, mark a minus for quality; if it is low-calorie, mark a plus.)
3. *not eating because of time of day or because you have seen others eating* (include ANYTIME you do not eat when you normally would have).	3. *eating every item at a restaurant* just because you paid for it.

the likelihood of accurate personal data. One procedure is to initially arrange for an independent observer to collect the data and then to gradually have the subject assume this task for himself. By repeated comparison of his personal data with that collected by the observer, the individual will be shaped (see Chapter One) into more accurate self-recording. However, this method requires considerable effort on the part of an independent observer, and it is often unfeasible if the target behavior is not visible (for example, as in the case of suicidal thoughts). A second method for increasing the accuracy of self-monitoring is to provide a simple and painless recording system and have the individual practice it several times before he begins his actual field work. Concise behavior descriptions and relatively effortless self-monitoring devices increase the likelihood of accurate personal data. Occasional checks on this accuracy can be made through related measurements—for example, if the individual self-reports improvements in eating habits, subsequent changes in body weight should be observed, and if improvements in study habits are reported, increases in grade-point average should follow.

4. *Reactivity of Self-Monitoring.* Up until now, we have been talking about self-monitoring as a means of collecting important information for successful self-control. However, recent research has shown that self-monitoring is often more than just an assessment tool; sometimes it is also a treatment strategy. That is, studies have shown that simply keeping track of a behavior (such as smoking) may result in changes in that behavior. In a sense, the target behavior seems to "react" to the measurement device. Because of this, self-monitoring is said to be *reactive*. The articles by Jeffrey (Article Seven) and Mahoney (Article Ten) discuss this phenomenon, which also is well illustrated in the study by Broden, Hall, and Mitts (Article Four). In addition, Kazdin's paper (Article Nine) offers an excellent review of self-monitoring research and provides some intriguing conceptualizations of the processes involved.

To date, the reactive effects of self-monitoring have been demonstrated in a variety of studies involving different target behaviors and a wide range of self-monitoring procedures. In general, however, it appears that the effects of self-monitoring as a treatment device are both variable and short-lived. That is, although keeping track of study habits, eating patterns, or cigarettes smoked may have an initial effect on the behavior involved, that effect will eventually fade, and the behavior will return to its premonitoring level. This, of course, does not mean that self-monitoring holds no promise as a significant component in self-control efforts. As we pointed out earlier, the ongoing feedback provided by self-monitored data plays such a crucial role in effective self-control that it would be hard to think of an instance in which systematic self-recording would not be recommended as a part of the treatment procedure. However, research suggests that we should not be fooled into thinking that self-recording alone will permanently change a behavior. At the present time, it appears that additional self-control techniques (to be discussed in the next two chapters) can be used as supplements to self-monitoring. For example, in addition to recording and charting his progress in weight control, a person can tell others of his efforts. Thus, other environmental influences, such as family praise for weight loss, will be enlisted.

The nature of the self-monitored response may play an important role in both the effectiveness and the accuracy of the personal data. For example, Kanfer (1971) has suggested that self-monitoring will result in increases in socially approved behaviors (such as studying and dieting) but decreases in socially censured behaviors (such as smoking and nail biting). The evidence on this point is as yet inconclusive. However, it does highlight the fact that we always have two sides of a behavior to consider for self-monitoring—the positive and the negative sides. There do seem to be instances in which one side has more relevance for self-control than the other does. For example, in a weight study reported by Mahoney (in press), the self-monitoring of inappropriate eating habits turned out to be significantly related to successful weight loss, whereas self-recording of appropriate eating habits was not. Until further research illuminates some of the relationships involved in self-monitoring, we are well advised to openly explore various possibilities and applications.

The reactivity of self-monitoring is an important consideration in making comparisons. Recall that the evaluation of a technique's effects on a particular behavior requires that we have measurements of the rate of the behavior in the presence and in the absence of that technique. Thus, to say that a particular diet has dramatically changed a person's body weight, we need a record of that body weight before and after the adoption of the diet. Otherwise, since people's body weights vary considerably from week to week, one could argue that the observed change was simply a common fluctuation and had nothing to do with the newly adopted diet. If it is true that initiating a self-record of, say, body weight, may temporarily affect one's eating habits and therefore cause a decline in weight, this should be taken into account in assessing the effects of the self-control technique. For example, if a person has self-monitored his weight for two weeks and each week it has gone down, introducing a self-control procedure (such as self-punishment) should be delayed. If the procedure were introduced and the person's weight continued to decrease, we would not know whether this continuing reduction was caused by self-monitoring or by the introduction of self-punishment. A solution to this dilemma is to *continue "baseline" self-monitoring until the behavior has stabilized.* This gives us a more accurate estimate of the pretreatment state of the behavior, and we can more confidently attribute any subsequent change to the introduction of the self-control strategy.

Although the role of many "uncontrolled variables" (such as expectancies and experimental demand characteristics) has not been discussed here in our analysis of assessment in self-control, their significance should not be taken lightly (Thoresen & Mahoney, 1974). The articles by Jeffrey (Article Seven), Kazdin (Article Nine), and Mahoney (Article Ten) discuss these influences.

SUPPLEMENTARY SOURCES

Bachrach, A. J. *Psychological research: An introduction.* (2nd ed.) New York: Random House, 1965.

Campbell, D. T., & Stanley, J. C. *Experimental and quasi-experimental designs for research.* Chicago: Rand McNally, 1966.

Thoresen, C. E. The intensive design: An intimate approach to counseling research. *The Counseling Psychologist,* in press.

SUGGESTED READING

Broden, Hall, & Mitts (Article Four)
Jeffrey (Article Seven)
Kazdin (Article Nine)
Mahoney (Article Ten)

SELF-CONTROL APPLICATIONS: ENVIRONMENTAL STRATEGIES

Many people fail to realize that they frequently employ environmental self-control strategies in their everyday lives. For example, setting an alarm clock before going to bed is a means of prearranging an important environmental cue. Similarly, leaving a to-be-mailed letter in a prominent place is a means of cueing yourself to display a behavior. Unfortunately, because of popular misconceptions about self-control, many people overlook these rather mundane instances of self-managed behavior change. They tend to equate self-control with awesome instances of "resistance" in the face of temptation. This conceptualization is not surprising in view of the early influence of religious organizations on thinking about self-control. However, as we pointed out earlier, many patterns that fall under the title of "self-control" involve increasing the frequency of a behavior (such as jogging or practicing tennis) instead of decreasing its frequency.

The popular misconceptions about self-control are particularly relevant in our discussion of environmental strategies. Environmental self-control strategies generally rely upon the prearrangement of cues that bear some relationship to the occurrence of a target behavior (that is, cues that increase or decrease the likelihood of a behavior. Environmental strategies may also call for the prearrangement of response consequences.

Interestingly, some people think that environmental strategies involve less self-regulation than other strategies do. Perhaps this is because environmental strategies employ prearranged influences that facilitate the performance of the desired behavior. For example, the devout weight watcher may avoid purchasing high-calorie foods and thus reduce the likelihood that he will eat them at home. This strategy alters the nature of a formerly troublesome choice point (that is, it reduces the temptation to snack by eliminating the snacking cues). Research subjects sometimes believe that more self-control is necessary when the tempting stimulus is available and must be resisted. The misconception that "staring temptation in the face" is a desirable self-control skill has probably spelled the downfall of all too many efforts at self-regulation. Research to date has shown that strategies that interrupt the response "chain" (that is, the sequence of behaviors) very early may be significantly more successful than those that occur later in the chain.

A.   PREARRANGEMENT OF CUES: STIMULUS CONTROL

By far the most heavily researched subtype of environmental self-control is that referred to by many investigators as "stimulus control." This strategy involves the rearrangement of cues that have come to elicit undesired responses and/or the establishment of cues that will elicit desired responses. This approach, one of the first to be employed in self-regulation research, was borrowed directly from the laboratory findings with animals. As our discussion in Chapter One indicated, the likelihood that many response patterns will occur is very different under varying situational circumstances. Instances of this stimulus cueing are particularly evident in eating and smoking behaviors. Extensive research has revealed that eating is tremendously influenced by a variety of cues—for example, by an enticing food display, a clock indicating "mealtime," the observation of someone else eating, and so on. Similarly, smoking behavior is often preceded by the sight of an ashtray, the smell of another person's cigarette, or the completion of a meal. Because of the strong stimulus components in these two behavior patterns, they have been frequent targets of environmental self-control research.

One of the earliest and most impressive investigations using environmental strategies was that reported by Stuart (1967). He outlined stimulus-control assignments for eight obese women and reported unprecedented degrees of success. After 12 months of treatment, his *least* successful subject had lost 26 pounds and the most successful subject had shed 47 pounds. The subjects' long-term maintenance of weight loss was particularly noteworthy. Stuart's research stimulated other workers to explore environmental self-control strategies in the treatment of obesity. To date, over a dozen well-controlled studies have been performed, all of them supporting Stuart's earlier findings. An exemplary study by Penick, Filion, Fox, and Stunkard is presented in Article Twelve. The techniques used in Stuart's study have, of course, been revised and extended. Some of these strategies are discussed in the paper by Penick et al. (Article Twelve). A general summary follows.

Stimulus-Control Techniques for Obesity

1. *Limit the cues you associate with eating.* Eat in one specific room and preferably at one place in that room. This means that eating should become a "pure experience"—that is, it must be separated from other activities that might gain stimulus control over it and/or reinforce it. When you eat, eat—but avoid other simultaneous activities (such as television viewing, phone conversations, pleasure reading, and studying). This means that an ongoing activity (for example, watching a football game) must be interrupted while you eat.
2. *Do not eat to avoid waste.* Childhood training and the desire not to waste money have resulted in countless extra calories for people who can't stand seeing food thrown out. A woman who consumes her children's unfinished meals is one example. Another is the individual who stuffs himself at a restaurant in order to consume everything that has been included in an entree. Get in the habit of leaving small portions of food on your plate so that the cue for meal termination will not be an empty bowl or a clean plate.
3. *Restrict your food intake ahead of time.* Bountiful bowls of food on the table are powerful cues for eating (and *over*eating). Prepare your plate ahead of time, put the foods away (or leave them in another room), and then sit down to your meal. Arrange food portions so that they look larger by spreading them out over a plate or by using small or shallow dishes. When you are eating at a restaurant, restrict tempting cues ahead of time. For example, request that the potato or bread be omitted from your plate.
4. *Make fattening foods less available and nonfattening foods more available.* You are much more likely to eat fattening snacks if they are stored in your own kitchen instead of at the local store. Don't buy high-calorie snacks. It's easier to avoid them if you *always shop for groceries after a full meal* (*never* on an empty stomach). If you must keep sweets in the house (for example, for children's lunches), buy brands that you dislike, store them in an inconspicuous place (the back of a cabinet rather than the cookie jar), and instruct your children to get them for themselves. Keep a large supply of safe snacks on hand at all times (for example, popcorn, raw vegetables, diet soda).
5. *Alter the eating process.* Eating slowly reduces the quantity of food consumed. Swallow one bite of food before putting the next bite on

your fork. (This may entail actually putting the fork down between bites.) Toward the end of a meal, get in the habit of interrupting your eating for two to five minutes to gain control over the behavior (and to dissociate it with such stimuli as a clean plate or an empty bowl).

6. *Modify the physiological cues for eating.* Many people eat in response to internal sensations of "emptiness" or "hunger pangs." Eat high-bulk, low-calorie foods (such as celery, carrot sticks, and popcorn) or drink a large amount of liquid before or during the meal to produce a sensation of "fullness." Moreover, to maintain an appropriate blood-sugar level and to avoid cravings for sweets, eat high-protein foods (particularly early in the day) and use sugar substitutes extensively (not only in coffee but also in baking and meal preparation). Reduce intake of nutrients that produce large blood-sugar swings (for example, caffeine, processed sugar, white bread, and noodle products).

7. *Arrange social cues that encourage appropriate eating.* Many people find the presence of certain other people a cue for more moderate and adaptive eating patterns. If this is the case, arrange to eat only in the presence of those people. On the other hand, if some persons model inappropriate eating habits, arrange to eat separately from them.

8. *Develop nonfattening responses to emotional upset.* Many people report very strong eating temptations when they are anxious, frustrated, or depressed. The association between these emotions and eating has two possible bases: (1) many children grow up learning that foods (particularly sweets) are used to soothe them and to lift their spirits, and (2) emotional upsets actually represent mild physiological arousal that under certain conditions may lead to low blood sugar and cravings for food. To modify the association between emotions and food, develop alternative reactions that are incompatible with eating. For example, you can learn to relax in emotion-provoking situations by engaging in certain breathing and muscle exercises (Jacobson, 1934).

Notice that the preceding techniques involve interrupting or eliminating problematic stimulus-response sequences—sequences such as watching a football game on television and drinking beer and crunching pretzels. When the cue is separated from the habitual behavior, an old and inappropriate pattern is terminated. Similarly, when appropriate responses are attached to new and more desirable cues, improved patterns are established—patterns such as eating low-calorie foods while seated at the dining-room table. The underlying premise in all of this, of course, is that eating behaviors are developed according to basic learning principles and may be altered by learning new patterns of behavior. The consistent successes reported by Stuart and the other researchers in this field seem to indicate that the premise is a well-founded one.

Although somewhat less research has been done on the modification of smoking behavior through stimulus-control strategies, preliminary findings are promising. A pair of case studies by Nolan (1968) and Roberts (1969) restricted smoking to arbitrary and unreinforcing situations—for example, to a special "smoking chair." In these cases, the reformed smoker was instructed to smoke only while in a special situation that was appropriately chosen to be nonentertaining. Some serious methodological problems complicated interpretation of the successful results reported by Nolan and Roberts. However, subsequent studies have suggested that stimulus-control applications can be useful in smoking reduction. Upper and Meredith (1970, 1971) and Shapiro, Schwartz, Tursky, and Shnidman (Article Thirteen) have reported some promising findings with an ingenious stimulus-control strategy. This technique, which was described in Chapter Two, involves establishing the buzz of a timer as an artificial self-regulated smoking cue. The existing evidence suggests that, if this strategy is conscientiously adhered to for a sufficient length of time, it can be a successful component in the elimination of smoking (see Shapiro et al., Article Thirteen).

Other stimulus-control strategies have been employed for the self-regulation of study habits, marital problems, and fears. As mentioned earlier, a student may arrange his studying environment so that distracting cues are absent and study-enhancing cues are present. A clean, well-lighted desk equipped with all the necessary tools (pens, felt markers, and so on) may be set up as the studying situation. A self-regulated contingency may be established such that, while the student is seated at the desk, he will do nothing but study—that is, he will not listen to the stereo, make phone calls, write letters, or daydream. If he begins to engage in any behavior incompatible with studying, he will immediately leave the desk so that he will not associate being at the desk with these other behaviors. Small blocks of study time (for example, 15 minutes) or content goals (for example, five text pages) may be used and subsequently increased to ensure initial maintenance of the stimulus-control program.

Self-regulated exposure to feared situations can also be used to gradually extinguish fear responses (Chapter One). For example, an individual who fears storms may play a sound-effects record album containing storm sounds at gradually increasing volumes to approximate actual storm cues. In these strategies, the feared stimulus must be presented in an initially weak form and then *very gradually* intensified. (Initial exposure to the problem stimulus at full intensity might increase fear and encourage the person to escape from the situation.) To increase the "tolerability" of the self-regulated stimuli, we might pair them with pleasant situations or responses (such as deep-muscle relaxation). This type of self-change strategy will be discussed further in the next chapter.

Note that up until this point our discussion of stimulus control has emphasized external cues. Recent research has shown that significant behavior-controlling cues also occur in a person's "internal" environment—that is, in his thoughts, images, and physiological sensations. Meichenbaum and Cameron (Article Eleven) discuss the modification of private self-generated cues in altering problem behaviors. This approach involves a type of "personal ecology" in which the individual is trained to improve his internal environment—that is, what he says to himself, his reactions to previously arousing cues, and so forth. As Meichenbaum's research demonstrates, a sizable portion of complex human behavior may be under "private" stimulus control. By evaluating and altering the nature of these stimuli, the behavioral designer can exhibit finer degrees of accuracy and therapeutic effectiveness.

Earlier in the chapter, we noted that an individual can prearrange the occurrence of cues that increase the chances that a behavior will occur. An alarm clock was one example. Other applications of this cueing strategy have also been investigated. For example, by using cards attached to a client's cigarette package, Mahoney (1971) cued the occurrence of positive self-statements (see Chapter Two). A similar strategy was employed by Hannum, Thoresen, and Hubbard (Article Five) with elementary-school teachers who wanted to alter their self-critical thoughts. In their study, a "smiley face" was placed near the classroom clock as a cue for the teachers to engage in positive self-thoughts. Other stimulus-control techniques have included placing a piece of tape over the face of one's watch to cue desired performances (for example, self-praise, covert recitation of to-be-memorized course content, or relaxation). An infinite variety of environmental cues may be arbitrarily chosen to elicit an almost equally long list of behaviors. For example, traffic signals can become cues for brief isometric exercises.

Cues may also be prearranged to decrease behaviors. A weight chart or pig poster on the refrigerator can discourage between-meal snacking. Similarly, a "skull" ashtray and a noncomplimentary smoking poster can act as cues that discourage smoking.

Before going on to our discussion of prearranged response consequences, we should note that strategies that simply alter behavior-eliciting cues may not be sufficient for long-term behavior change. As we pointed out in Chapter One, a given behavior is "sandwiched" between its cues and its consequences, both of which may play a significant role in maintaining it. Depending on the relative importance of antecedent cues and consequences in any particular instance, effective self-control may require changing both of these factors.

B. PREARRANGEMENT OF RESPONSE CONSEQUENCES

Many people have difficulty in understanding the role of self-control processes in the prearrangement of response consequences. However, as the Goldiamond and Bandura equations (presented in Chapter One) point out, the systematic altering of one's environment is perhaps the simplest example of self-control.

A person can prearrange consequences in several ways. Researchers have developed various physical and chemical devices that can be used for such purposes. A popular drug in the treatment of excessive alcohol consumption is Disulfiram (commercially known as Antabuse). This chemical produces extreme nausea when it is mixed with even small quantities of alcohol. The reforming drinker can take the drug at a nonproblematic point in the day (for example, early in the morning), thereby prearranging the consequences of drinking behavior for the next 24 hours—that is, subsequent intake of alcohol will result in severe nausea and vomiting. In this manner, the temptation to drink at a party that evening is significantly reduced. Although a similar chemical compound for smokers has yet to be perfected, Powell and Azrin (1968) developed a special cigarette box that delivers a painful electric shock when it is opened. By conscientiously employing such a device, the reforming smoker can prearrange the consequences of reaching for a cigarette. Unfortunately, preliminary research has suggested that additional measures are needed to increase the chances that a person will consistently use such a device.

Response consequences can also be prearranged through social contracts. This method has been referred to by researchers as "contingency contracting," since it involves a fairly formal agreement regarding personal contingencies. For example, one individual may deposit money or valuables with a second individual (or therapist) and sign an agreement prearranging the fate of these reinforcers. (For example, "For every week that I lose one pound, Fred will return one of my record albums. If I fail to lose a pound, the album for that week will be destroyed or given to an anonymous recipient.") An interesting case history involving contingency contracting was recently reported by Boudin (1972), who treated a college student for excessive use of amphetamines. In addition to arranging systematic feedback on her progress (self-monitoring), the client, a black female, deposited $500 with the therapist and signed a contract instructing him to send a $50 check to the Ku Klux Klan for every time she violated her contract. Only one violation occurred during the three-month period, and a two-year follow-up revealed no relapse to amphetamine use. Contingency contracts have also been used with adults in the treatment of smoking, alcoholism, and obesity as well as by parents and teachers with a variety of child behaviors (see Krumboltz & Thoresen, 1969; Thoresen & Mahoney, 1974). One of the problems with contracts requiring initial deposits of money or material goods is that the individual may never enter the agreement because of an inability or unwillingness to risk the loss of valuable personal possessions.

An alternative to the contingency contract is one that prearranges the occurrence of social rewards, such as attention. The dieting woman can request that her husband ignore (extinguish) or criticize (punish) her overeating responses and praise (reinforce) her appropriate eating behaviors. In marital therapies, it is often feasible and desirable that husband and wife contract with each other for their individual behavior improvements. (For example, the wife may request that her husband praise her for positive self-statements, and the husband may request that his wife praise his personal hygiene.)

A recent example of social-contingency contracting combined with stimulus control was reported by Neisworth (1972) in the modification of his own smoking behavior. After determining those situations in which smoking control was most difficult, he gradually limited the situations in which he could smoke. In addition to self-monitoring and some monetary reinforcers, Neisworth arranged for systematic social praise for his progress in reducing smoking. After the eighth week of this self-control program, he smoked no cigarettes (although urges to smoke continued for four months). A four-year follow-up revealed no recurrence of smoking behavior. Neisworth concluded his report as follows: "Truly, the road to (smoking) Hell is paved with good intentions, but the road to (nonsmoking) Heaven is paved with good cues and consequences" (p. 3). Amen.

Another means of enlisting social-environmental support for a self-change enterprise is the use of public self-monitoring. As we pointed out in the last chapter, simply recording a behavior often affects its occurrence. There is also some evidence indicating that publicly displaying self-recorded data may enhance behavior change by increasing the likelihood of social praise for progress (Thoresen, 1973b). Thus, the person can display his chart on an office door or send copies of it to friends and relatives.

There are, of course, many other techniques for prearranging the consequences of a person's behavior (for example, by placing a lock on the refrigerator). However, the ones outlined above have received the most research interest and support. The other major strategy in self-regulation—behavioral programming—involves alterations of response consequences *after* the response has occurred. Although the contingency may be set up in advance (for example, "For every cigarette I smoke I'm going to tear up a dollar bill"), the actual implementation of response consequences occurs after the fact. We shall now turn our attention to the behavioral-programming strategies.

SUPPLEMENTARY SOURCES

Stuart, R. B., & Davis, B. *Slim chance in a fat world: Behavioral control of obesity.* Champaign, Ill.: Research Press, 1972.

Thoresen, C. E., & Mahoney, M. J. *Behavioral self-control.* New York: Holt, Rinehart & Winston, 1974.

SUGGESTED READING

Meichenbaum & Cameron (Article Eleven)
Penick, Filion, Fox, & Stunkard (Article Twelve)
Shapiro, Schwartz, Tursky, & Shnidman (Article Thirteen)

SELF-CONTROL APPLICATIONS: BEHAVIORAL PROGRAMMING

There are many self-controlling actions that a person can perform *after* a certain behavior takes place. These actions are actually self-regulated consequences. Self-rewarding consequences are intended to increase behavior, while self-punishing consequences are designed to reduce behavior. Jeffrey (Article Seven) provides examples of several possible combinations of self-regulated consequences for a behavior.

The behavior to be changed can be covert (unobservable to others) or overt (observable). Covert behaviors are often thoughts, images, and feelings (for example, a recurring, nagging worry or an unpleasant image). Overt behaviors are all activities that are observable by others (for example, the rate at which a person speaks, the number of cigarettes he smokes, and the amount of time he spends studying).

Self-control techniques involve an important assumption—namely, that internal actions obey the same laws or principles as external actions do. Thus, a person can reward himself either covertly (by engaging in a very positive self-thought) or overtly (by drinking a beer or listening to a favorite record). The assumption of a correspondence between internal and external actions opens the door to a great variety of covert self-rewards and self-punishments. Bandura (1969) and others have reviewed many research studies that generally support this assumption. Meichenbaum and Cameron (Article Eleven) point to the significance of what we say to ourselves as a determinant of our actions. Although many people realize that they frequently talk to themselves, few appreciate the importance of these "internal monologues" in their everyday adjustment and happiness.

In this chapter, some self-reward, self-punishment, and combination techniques are presented. We have divided reward and punishment into two types: positive and negative. Table 5-1 illustrates the relationships between positive and negative reward and punishment.

TABLE 5-1. Positive and Negative Reward and Punishment.

	Positive ("Pleasant") Stimulus	Negative ("Aversive") Stimulus
Presentation	Positive reward	Negative punishment
Removal	Positive punishment	Negative reward

Reward (or reinforcement)—both positive and negative—*increases the frequency of a behavior.* In positive reward, the response is strengthened by a *positive* consequence. In negative reward, the response is strengthened by the removal or avoidance of a *negative* (aversive) consequence. These are sometimes called *positive* and *negative reinforcement.*

Punishment—both positive and negative—*decreases the frequency of a behavior.* In positive punishment, a response is suppressed or weakened by the removal or avoidance of a positive (pleasant) consequence. This procedure is sometimes called response cost, since the occurrence of the response "costs" the individual a valued consequence. (*Time out* from positive consequences is another term for positive punishment.) Negative punishment, on the other hand, suppresses a response by providing negative (aversive) consequences after the behavior.

In reward and punishment procedures, the consequence is *contingent* on the response (that is, if the response occurs, then a consequence occurs). This differentiates these procedures from the extinction procedures described in Chapter One. In extinction, formerly existing contingencies are discontinued, and the response no longer results in any change in stimulation (that is, the response neither produces nor removes positive or negative stimuli).

Consequences can, of course, be self-administered—that is, an individual can reward or punish himself for certain actions. Table 5-2 presents some examples of positive and negative self-reward and self-punishment techniques. Combination techniques often employ both positive and negative consequences. In addition, environmental planning (arranging cues and consequences in advance) is frequently combined with behavioral programming. Table 5-2 cites such combination procedures as self-desensitization and self-modeling. These techniques will be discussed later in this chapter.

TABLE 5-2.   Some Behavioral-Programming Methods.

Self-Reward Techniques (To Increase a Behavior)	Self-Punishment Techniques (To Decrease a Behavior)	Combination Techniques
Positive reward	*Positive punishment*	*Covert sensitization*
1. giving oneself a point or token that may be "redeemed" for a special purchase or for other pleasant activity	1. destroying or giving away a valued possession (such as tearing up a dollar bill)	1. imagining oneself feeling very nauseous
2. thinking a positive self-thought	2. foregoing a pleasant activity (such as a television program or movie)	2. imagining oneself undergoing surgery for lung cancer
3. watching a favorite television program		*Self-desensitization*
Negative reward	*Negative punishment*	1. relaxing while imagining taking an exam
1. removing pieces of an unattractive photo of oneself	1. self-inflicting pain (such as snapping a rubber band on one's wrist)	2. relaxing while imagining talking to girls
2. crossing out items on a list of one's negative behaviors	2. subvocalizing "I'm really stupid"	*Self-instruction*
3. storing a bag of ugly fat (representing one's own obesity) in the refrigerator and removing pieces as one loses weight	3. engaging in an unpleasant activity (such as eating a disliked food or wearing the button of a despised political candidate)	1. telling oneself to pay attention
		2. telling oneself to work slowly
		Covert self-modeling
		1. imagining oneself being assertive with a parent
		2. imagining oneself giving a speech before a large audience

As we suggested in Chapter Three, systematic self-observation may sometimes be effective in changing behavior. Although the reasons why self-observation works are not entirely clear, it seems probable that the systematic recording of information about one's own actions provides a basis for self-evaluation and, as a result, provides self-reinforcement. Obviously, this would be the case if the person were making progress in the desired direction. For example, Figure 3-1 in Chapter Three presented a daily weight chart showing a gradual yet steady loss of weight. Looking at such a chart certainly might make a person feel very good about himself and his progress.

Self-reward requires some kind of systematic gathering of information about a person's actions. In a way, self-observation "sets the stage" for self-reward by providing a basis upon which rewards can be made. Self-reward or any other behavioral-programming method involves self-observation of some kind. Hence, the success of self-change is affected by the accuracy and effects of self-observation.

A. SELF-REWARD

The major task in self-reward is carefully planning the circumstances in which specified rewards will be provided. In order to maximize the success of any self-reward program, we must consider several components of the process: what rewards to use, how to administer them, when to engage in self-reward, and how to ensure that self-change will be maintained.

Earlier an important distinction was made between *behavior to be controlled* (such as studying or smoking) and *self-controlling actions*. These two types of behavior must be separated if change is to occur and be maintained. It has been amply demonstrated that human behavior is influenced by its consequences. Self-controlling actions, like any other behavior, will be influenced by what happens when they are used. A beleaguered college freshman struggling to maintain a passing grade-point average will not continue to use self-observation and a study schedule if the consequences of these self-controlling actions are not sufficiently positive.

Many of the theoretical and research issues in self-reward are discussed by Bandura (Article Two) and Mahoney (Article Ten). One rather consistent research finding suggests that self-reward may be more effective if some form of external-reward training precedes it (Thoresen & Mahoney, 1974). Thus, chronic smokers planning to use self-reward techniques to reduce their smoking behavior may be more successful if they initially receive rewards from others. Further, the opportunity to observe someone else successfully using self-reward may also help. The continuity and interdependence of self-control and external control, discussed in Chapter One, bear this out. For their initial efforts, some people need a structured environment that "teaches" self-control with ample demonstrations and social reinforcement.

   1. Self-Contracting.   In many ways, the heart of any self-change program lies in systematic planning—that is, in specifying the details of its implementation and evaluation. This is what differentiates methods of behavioral self-control from the common-sense rationale of New Year's resolutions. Contracts are agreements that specify the responsibilities of all parties concerned, especially if the agreed-upon action is *not* carried out. In making an agreement with himself—that is, in a self-contract—the person is attempting to reduce confusion and inconsistency. In a way, it is an effort to take the things that a person says to himself (but often fails to act upon) out of the private or covert areas and make them public and thus more susceptible to the actions of others. A self-contract is thus a type of environmental planning, since it involves the prearrangement of stimulus cues and consequences to influence a behavior.

   A sample self-contract form is presented in Figure 5-1. A written form, of course, is not always needed. However, putting the contract in writing eliminates inconsistencies. The contract should specify that actions, not promises to take action, will be rewarded (see Kanfer & Karoly, Article Eight). The self-contract should also indicate what actions the person will take—that is, what he is agreeing to do relative to the goal. Other persons may be involved in the self-contract; they can agree to do certain things as well as to provide particular consequences. The contract should further indicate what will happen when the person carries out the agreement or fails to do so. It is at this point that self-reward (as well as self-punishment) is involved. Arranging for consequences to be provided by other persons is consistent with the notion that self-control represents a broad continuum of actions taken by a person and others in his environment. Since any personal decision of this type is subject to change, the contract should specify a review date when the person may reconsider the behaviors to be performed and the consequences provided. Both may need changing.

   Table 5-3 lists some of the important characteristics of self-change contracts. A more complete discussion of behavior contracts is found in Homme and Tosti (1971). As Table 5-3 suggests, rewards should immediately follow the desired behavior and should be provided in small amounts on a frequent basis. Rewards should also be tailored to the individual person. Of course, there will be exceptions to these suggestions, but, in general, these rules should promote successful self-change.

SELF-CONTRACT

Date *September 18, 1973*

Self: *Mary Baxter*

Other: *Jane Paulson*

Goal: *to reduce my smoking*

Agreement

Self: *I agree to smoke only during the first 15 minutes of any hour (1:00 to 1:15, 2:00 to 2:15, etc.). If I do not want a cigarette during an interval, I will wait for the next hour interval before I smoke.*

Others: *Jane Paulson (my roommate) agrees to praise me whenever she sees me not smoking and to refuse to talk to me while I am smoking.*

Consequences

Provided by Self:
(if contract is kept) *If I stick to the above agreement, at the end of each week (ending Sat at 6:00 P.M.) I will reward myself with a movie.*

(if contract is broken) *If I do not keep the above agreement during a particular week, I will do my roommate's laundry that Saturday evening (no movie).*

Provided by Other:
(if contract is kept) *Jane will (1) praise me for not smoking, (2) ignore me when I am smoking, and (3) do my laundry each week that I keep the contract.*

(if contract is broken) *For each week that I fail to keep the contract, Jane is authorized to (1) insist that I do her laundry and (2) limit my access to her stereo albums.*

Signed *Mary Baxter*

October 18, 1973

Review Date

Jane Paulson

Witness

FIGURE 5-1. Self-Contract.

TABLE 5-3. Characteristics of Self-Contracts.

Contract Conditions

1. Contract should be fair.
2. Terms of contract should be very clear.
3. Contract should be generally positive.
4. Procedures should be systematic and consistent.
5. At least one other person should participate.

Rules for Consequences

1. Self-reward (self-punishment) must be immediate and contingent on certain actions.
2. Small steps or approximations of the overall goal should be used.
3. Self-reward (self-punishment) should be provided frequently in small amounts.
4. Self-reward (self-punishment) should follow performance, not verbal promises.
5. Self-reward (self-punishment) should be provided after performance occurs (not before).
6. Type of self-rewards (self-punishments) should be individualized when possible.

(Adapted from Homme et al., 1968.)

2. Types of Rewards. The saying "Different strokes for different folks" captures an important point in the selection and use of rewards—namely, that individuals may vary greatly in what they consider rewarding. Premack (1965) suggested that any actions that a person engages in frequently (high-probability behaviors) can serve as rewards to increase infrequent behaviors (low-probability behaviors). This generalization is called the Premack Principle. Thus, a college professor who enjoys reading the *New York Times* (a highly probable behavior) could arrange a contingency to help himself complete his correspondence (something he constantly neglects). Five minutes of reading the *Times* could be "earned" for every letter answered.

The reward should be such that it is readily available and can be used immediately after a certain action takes place. Because of this, the use of high-probability behaviors is ideally suited for self-reward programs. Homme (1965), picking up on Premack's probability view of rewards, suggested a combination of rewards for helping persons to reduce chronic behaviors such as smoking and overeating. Actually, he proposed a combination of self-punishment and self-reward procedures. To reduce smoking, for example, the person is asked first to think a very aversive or negative thought about the problem behavior (such as "smoking kills") whenever he notices an urge to smoke. Then he engages in a positive thought about not smoking (such as "I will breathe more easily without coughing"). Immediately after this appropriate thought, the person engages in some high-probability behavior (such as drinking a cup of coffee).

Homme's work has stimulated a number of efforts to apply this kind of self-reward sequence in programs of self-change (see Thoresen & Mahoney, 1974). As cited earlier, Hannum, Thoresen, and Hubbard (Article Five) used high-probability behaviors (for example, looking at the wall clock) to increase the frequency of teachers' positive self-thoughts. Similarly, a depressed housewife was instructed to write six positive thoughts about herself on cards trimmed to fit inside the cellophane wrapper of her cigarette pack. She was told to read a positive thought from the card whenever she was depressed and then to reward herself with a cigarette, a high-probability behavior. In both cases, positive self-thoughts were greatly increased and feelings of depression and despair were reduced. Another example involved a college dropout who complained of severe depression and excessive use of drugs (Flannery, 1972). This individual increased positive self-statements by rewarding herself for practicing them with pleasure reading. This procedure, in combination with others, was effective in eliminating depression and drug-taking as well as in improving communications with family and friends.

To use frequent actions as rewards, we must take note of two things: (1) these actions should be not only frequent but also desirable (that is, watching a favorite program is a reward but cleaning chores are not) and (2) the person must not engage in the high-probability behavior if the action to be increased is not performed. (For example, no beer and burger at the 10 p.m. study break unless two chapters have been read.)

Sometimes a point system is very effective in satisfying the rules for self-reward. A person can provide himself with a point immediately after a response, and that point in turn can be exchanged for a variety of reinforcing events. In Article Three, Bolstad and Johnson demonstrate that disruptive schoolchildren can learn to reward themselves for *not* acting inappropriately (for example, for not talking, running around, or being physically aggressive). In this study, points could be exchanged for a variety of school materials, such as pencils, erasers, and note pads. This self-reward strategy was very effective in improving classroom behavior. Other researchers have shown that self-reward procedures can be successfully used for weight reduction, study-habit improvement, and the development of appropriate social skills (Thoresen & Mahoney, 1974).

Little is known at this point about how effective a covert consequence is compared with a more tangible consequence such as drinking a cup of coffee or rewarding oneself with money. Clinical case
studies seem to indicate that, when a person first imagines the behavior
he wishes to increase (such as volunteering comments in class discussions) and then immediately follows that image with a very positive
(self-rewarding) image (such as lying on the beach in the warm sun),
change does occur (Cautela, 1971). However, it is also clear that, if
progress is to continue, covert rewards must at some point involve other
kinds of positive consequences. At present, combinations of overt and
covert self-reward appear quite promising.

3. Positive or Negative Reward?   Earlier we distinguished between a positive and a negative reward. In the case of negative reward,
a person removes himself from an aversive situation only when a certain action takes place. As a result, the behavior that removes the negative event is strengthened. In Article Twelve, Penick et al. present an
ingenious example of negative self-reward. In their study, obese persons placed plastic bags of suet (animal fat) in their refrigerators.
These persons were asked to imagine that this suet represented the
excess fat on their own bodies, and they were allowed to remove one
piece for every pound they lost. When a person emptied the entire bag,
he received social reward from the other members of the group. Other
techniques such as stimulus control and a point system also were used
in this study to change eating habits and reduce weight. However, participants reported that the negative self-reward procedure contributed
significantly to their progress.
One reason why little use has been made of negative self-reward
is the aversive situation itself. It is understandably difficult for a person
to deliberately do something aversive. People tend to avoid such situations. However, the self-contract method does provide a structure within
which the details of aversive thoughts, images, and physical situations
can be planned to help eliminate problem behaviors. Examples of negative self-reward were suggested in Table 5-1.
In clinical settings, some work has been done in which the client
is asked to first imagine a very aversive scene (such as being sharply
criticized by an angry father) and then to follow that scene by imagining
himself engaging in the desired behavior (such as walking into a room
full of people and feeling comfortable) (Cautela, 1971). At this point,
however, we do not know if such a sequence actually brings about
change.
Negative self-reward offers a very promising method of self-

control, and we have been highlighting this method because it deserves attention. In terms of research evidence, however, positive self-reward is probably the most powerful and effective method. But a combination of positive and negative self-reward may offer an even better arrangement.

4. Self-Evaluation. One of the major obstacles in using self-reward is the fact that many individuals set excessively high standards for themselves. For such people, a performance is "never good enough" to merit self-reward. Bandura (Article Two) and others have identified defective self-evaluation as one of the most prevalent characteristics of persons experiencing severe emotional problems. One of the major contributions of a self-contract is to specify very concretely what performance will merit self-reward (and self-punishment).

As we mentioned earlier, self-evaluation is also related to self-observation. By gathering information on his action and by considering what constitutes "good" behavior, a person can help clarify for himself what merits self-reward (see Kanfer & Karoly, Article Eight).

5. Other Considerations. Several other features of self-reward, such as type, intensity, and magnitude of rewards, as well as the frequency of their use, can also be considered. In addition, there is the problem of potential versus current rewards. Is it more effective to use a new reward, such as a long-awaited trip, or a current activity, such as a favorite television program? Ongoing research in self-reward will help provide more information on these issues.

B. SELF-PUNISHMENT

A second major behavioral-programming method is self-punishment. Specified contingencies and behavioral goals are employed in self-punishment as well as in self-reward. The major difference between the two methods is in their intended effects: self-reward *increases* a behavior, while self-punishment decreases it. There are, of course, considerable individual differences as to what is in fact rewarding and punishing. Common forms of punishment include electric shock, nausea-producing drugs, and verbal criticism. As in the case of rewards, punishers can also be "internal" (for example, imagining a painful experience).

Employing the Premack Principle, a college senior can use something he does quite often and that he finds enjoyable (a high-probability behavior) to reward studying for graduate school entrance exams (an action he would like to increase). Likewise a low-probability behavior can be used to "punish" (that is, to reduce) a highly frequent behavior. Thus, a reformed smoker might punish his smoking urges by engaging in a low-probability (unpleasant) response (such as imagining a lung operation or having emphysema). As in the case of self-reward, the most important factor in self-punishment is the contingency of "if this, then that." Mahoney (Article Ten) discusses some of the issues relevant to punishment. Thoresen and Mahoney (1974) also discuss these issues.

A good deal of behavior is controlled by *aversive self-stimulation*—that is, by the person engaging in painful or negative actions in response to certain behavior. These self-punishing actions are learned largely by observing others. The study by Herbert, Gelfand, and Hartmann (Article Six) illustrates how self-critical statements (a kind of self-punishment) are learned. In everyday life, many individuals learn to avoid or reduce punishment from others by making self-critical and sometimes "confessional" statements.

Self-criticism illustrates the close relationship between the reward and punishment processes. A person often learns to be excessively self-critical because such action is rewarded by others and because it tends to reduce negative feelings such as guilt. A combination of excessive self-criticism and excessively high standards for self-reward constitutes a major clinical problem. Our culture is unfortunately one that discourages positive self-evaluation ("bragging") and encourages stoic self-denial and excessive self-criticism. Meichenbaum and Cameron (Article Eleven) discuss examples of negative self-talk and ways in which this kind of aversive experience can be reduced.

Self-contracts play an important role in effective self-punishment. If a punishing action is to reduce a behavior, it must be provided in a very systematic and consistent fashion immediately following the behavior. In addition, the intensity or strength of the aversive action should be strong enough to cause some discomfort. Self-punishment may be more effective if an alternative, and perhaps incompatible, positive behavior is also involved. In Chapter One, we mentioned that an effective way of reducing behavior is to reward incompatible actions; a technique of punishing negative behavior *and* rewarding positive behavior thus offers a very powerful combination. This method overcomes a major problem in using punishment—that is, that the accent is too much on what not to do instead of on what to do. Thus, an overweight businessman can use aversive images and loss of points when he eats certain fatty foods and, at the same time, can engage in self-reward when he resists the temptation to eat these foods.

1. Types of Punishers.   At present, we do not know what types of punishment (aversive stimuli) work best. Considerable effort has been made to use mild electric shock and nausea-producing drugs with chronic problems such as excessive drinking and smoking. However, the results have been meager and often inconsistent. More recently, efforts have been made to have persons self-administer shock using portable devices. McGuire and Vallance (1964) reported considerable success with smoking, alcoholism, and sexual deviation. Persons were asked to engage in the problem behavior or merely to imagine engaging in it and then were shocked. Gradually, each person was given the responsibility of using a portable device with which to self-administer shock immediately following the problem behavior.

In another study, Bucher and Fabricatore (1970) assisted a hospital patient in reducing hallucinations by using a portable shock device. The person was instructed to punish himself immediately after hearing voices. Within two weeks, the patient reported marked improvement. As noted earlier, in Mahoney's (1971) study, a young man used a heavy-gauge rubber band as the punishing stimulus to reduce his negative self-thoughts. He snapped the rubber band on his wrist immediately after engaging in critical thoughts. Such thoughts were completely eliminated in less than three weeks. However, positive self-thoughts did not increase as a result of this procedure; they had to be encouraged through self-reward using smoking as a high-probability behavior. Thus, combining self-reward and self-punishment strategies seems more effective than using either strategy alone.

Studies have indicated that imagined aversive consequences may be as effective as physical punishment in reducing the frequency of behaviors (Bandura, Article Two). Aversive imagery has been successfully used as self-punishment for problems of overeating, drinking, smoking, and sexual deviation. In one case (Davison, 1969), a young boy was taught to imagine his father acting in an extremely aggressive fashion. The boy then successfully used this aversive image as a punishing stimulus to reduce confrontations with his father. Covert sensitization is perhaps the most commonly used self-punishment technique of this type. In this procedure, the person first imagines the behavior to be reduced and then vividly imagines a very negative experience, such as feeling extremely nauseous and vomiting.

A variation of aversive imagery is called "ultimate aversive consequences" (Ferster, Nurnberger, & Levitt, 1962). Because so many undesirable behaviors have consequences that are immediately rewarding (for example, eating a piece of apple pie with whipped cream, having a fourth martini, and avoiding a feared social situation), Ferster and his colleagues suggested that the person use his imagination to collapse time and bring the long-term consequences of the problem behavior forward. A chronic smoker is thus asked to imagine himself in the hospital undergoing a major lung operation, and an obese person is asked to imagine himself dying of coronary heart disease. In a recent study, smokers used touching a pack of cigarettes as a cue for an image of some ultimate aversive consequence of smoking (Gordon & Sachs, 1971).

Thought-stopping is a variation of negative self-punishment. Instead of using shock or aversive imagery, the person is trained to shout the word "stop," first aloud, then softly, and finally quietly to himself, immediately after having an undesirable thought. A frantic college freshman who is constantly worrying about midterm exams could use thought-stopping to reduce such worries. Thoresen recently observed that a young intern teacher completely eliminated his "spiraling worries" (that sometimes continued for hours) and his migraine headaches and feelings of nausea by using thought-stopping combined with self-observation.

Other self-control techniques could be used simultaneously to increase appropriate behaviors such as studying. In the Hannum, Thoresen, and Hubbard (Article Five) study, teachers were briefly trained in thought-stopping to help them reduce negative self-thoughts.

Unfortunately, very little is known about what types of aversive consequences are most effective when self-administered. At this point, it seems reasonable to recommend that persons select aversive consequences that can be readily applied immediately after the problem behavior occurs (for example, aversive imagery and point fines). Further, self-punishment seems more likely to succeed if it is combined with other self-regulatory strategies (such as environmental planning and self-reward procedures).

2. Positive or Negative Punishment? Although positive self-punishment has been less examined than negative self-punishment, it seems especially promising as a self-control method. In positive self-punishment, the person voluntarily removes some positive event in response to the problem behavior. Thus, positive self-punishment is a type of "time out" from reward. This method of self-control is closely related to the "response-cost" method, in which a person fines himself for engaging in the behavior to be reduced. (For example, "Every time I eat dessert, I lose 30 minutes of free time to read for pleasure or watch pro football on television.") Axelrod and his colleagues (Article One) developed a clever self-punishment procedure to reduce smoking. After using self-monitoring to find out the average number of cigarettes smoked per day, they established a limit of 15 cigarettes (the person's average) with a goal of reducing that limit by one cigarette every five days. The agreement was made that, for every cigarette he smoked over the limit, the person would tear up a dollar bill. This contingency was never used because the person was completely successful in remaining within the limits. A second smoker agreed to fine herself 25 cents (to go to her favorite charity) for every cigarette exceeding the limit.

Support for the effectiveness of positive and negative self-punishment procedures remains limited. Preliminary studies, however, have suggested that these procedures can be effective *if* detailed arrangements in the form of a contract are used. Further, there is evidence to support the inclusion of some kind of social monitoring to make sure that the individual sticks to his self-contract.

C. COMBINATION TECHNIQUES

Self-control is often more effective when several procedures are combined. In Chapter Four, for example, a number of techniques for weight reduction were presented, including self-monitoring, environmental-planning (stimulus control), and behavioral-programming methods. It is, of course, quite reasonable that many behaviors might require combinations of these techniques. Behavior, after all, is a function of many environments—including the private environment within the skin—and, therefore, it may require a variety of self-controlling actions.

We will now discuss a few of the existing combination methods. Thoresen and Mahoney (1974) provide a more thorough discussion.

1. Systematic Self-Desensitization. Many persons suffer from unreasonable fears and anxieties that prevent them from doing what they want to do. Fears of taking examinations, giving public speeches, meeting new persons, and speaking out for one's rights are a few common examples. Over a decade ago, Joseph Wolpe (1958) developed a procedure to help a person take specific steps in a certain sequence to become less aroused and sensitive to problem situations—that is, a procedure of systematic desensitization. We previewed this procedure in Chapter One. Three basic steps are involved: (1) the person learns how to relax deeply, usually by tensing and relaxing muscles; (2) the person designates very specific situations related to his fear, listing them in order from the least to the most anxiety producing; and

(3) the person imagines himself experiencing situations from the list (hierarchy) while feeling calm and relaxed. He begins with the least arousing situation (for example, being given a speech assignment). When the individual can vividly imagine that situation and remain relaxed, he moves on to the next hierarchy scene. If an imagined situation produces anxiety, the individual stops thinking about it and concentrates on relaxing. Very small steps are made from one hierarchy scene to the next so that the person can comfortably "ease" himself into imaginary situations that are progressively more similar to the feared situation. Eventually he can comfortably imagine himself in situations that would have previously elicited anxiety (for example, giving a speech). This imaginary practice of calmly performing the feared behavior improves actual performance. The individual is also instructed to use his newly acquired relaxation skills in the actual feared situation so that formerly arousing cues become associated with nonanxious behaviors. A large number of studies have demonstrated that this treatment program works; persons are actually able to give a speech or take an exam without having to avoid the situation and without experiencing tremendous anxiety.

Several variations on this theme have been developed, one of which involves the self-administration of the treatment—that is, systematic self-desensitization. Training manuals (for example, Marquis & Morgan, 1968) have been written to help persons conduct their own desensitization. An extremely "test-anxious" college student thus can teach himself to physically relax by using tape-recorded instructions. He then can construct a list of very specific problem situations, from "It's the first day of my Chem 38 class, and the professor has announced the first midterm in three weeks" to "I am sitting in room 214 taking my chem midterm, and, in reading question 3 I realize I don't know the answer." Finally, the student can imagine himself in each situation on his list while feeling very calm and physically relaxed.

Successful variations of desensitization have included some in which the person actually experiences the situation (in vivo) instead of just imagining it but in which he still uses relaxation to reduce stress and tension. Bandura (1969) and Thoresen and Mahoney (1974) provide further discussion of variations of desensitization techniques.

One important variation of systematic desensitization has recently been developed. Instead of immediately terminating imagery of a particular situation when he feels stress or tension (the usual procedure), the person deliberately continues to imagine the scene and "relaxes away" his tension. Goldfried (1973) reported a case involving a college student who had a variety of fears and anxieties, ranging from certain insects to arguments with her father. After instruction in deep relaxation, the girl was taught to identify certain internal and external responses (such as a tightening of the stomach) as antecedents or cues to feeling anxious. As soon as she detected any cues, she immediately started to relax by using deep breathing and positive imagery—procedures designed to combat stress and tension. The young lady employed this technique in real-life situations with great success. Note that, in this form of desensitization (as well as others), a variety of cues and consequences are involved. In effect, the person is rearranging his internal environment so that physiological stimuli (such as a pounding heart and sweaty palms) become cues for self-relaxation.

The biggest problem with various forms of self-desensitization is staying with it. A recent study, for example, showed that a substantial number of persons simply did not carry on with the procedure after a few weeks (Phillip, Johnson, & Geyer, 1972). Establishing a behavioral contract and building in some additional self-reward for using the procedure may help considerably, especially in the beginning stages. Arranging the environment so that another person is involved may also facilitate staying with the contract, since such a person might provide praise and encouragement for progress. While the learning processes involved in desensitization remain to be clarified, substantial evidence supports the effectiveness of this strategy in eliminating a variety of undesirable avoidance behaviors.

2. Self-Instructions. We all, of course, talk to ourselves—sometimes incessantly—and some of us have elaborate fantasies about our personal performances. Until recently little research had been performed on the importance of these internal monologues. It is now believed that they play a critical role in personal adjustment. For example, there is evidence to suggest that debilitating fears and anxieties may be developed and maintained by self-arousal mechanisms (Bandura, 1969). The sounds outside a camp tent and the vibrations of an airborne jetliner are not inherently frightening; it is the labels and arousing embellishments we give these stimuli that cause distress. Individuals respond to "stimuli as perceived." By labeling a burning sensation in the chest as an impending heart attack instead of the consequence of a spicy meal, an individual can bring about extensive and even dangerous self-arousal. Phenomena such as paranoid delusions and voodoo deaths attest to the power of thoughts and perceived contingencies in the behavior of individuals.

Self-instruction involves the systematic use of certain self-verbalizations (talking to oneself). Reminders to "keep cool, relax, and stay calm" in a stressful situation may serve as a kind of stimulus control that directs action. We have already discussed self-praise and positive imagery as one kind of self-reward (see Hannum, Thoresen, & Hubbard, Article Five). Self-instruction, however, is usually used before and during an event instead of afterward.

An interesting self-instruction procedure called "stress inoculation" is described by Meichenbaum and Cameron (Article Eleven). These authors reasoned that persons need help in managing their physical *as well as* their psychological arousal. Individuals were told that anxiety is caused by a combination of events, including how a person explains problem situations to himself and how he "labels" his experience. After training in relaxation and the use of deep breathing to reduce physiological arousal, subjects were helped in developing appropriate self-instructions, such as "I'll just think about what I can do about it; That's better than getting anxious" and "I won't think about fear—just about what I have to do. I'll stay relevant." In one study, individuals found these skills very helpful in coping with fearful situations involving rats and snakes. Other studies by Meichenbaum and Cameron have demonstrated that hospitalized schizophrenics can be taught self-instructions to control their own verbal and nonverbal behavior. In addition, young children classified as extremely impulsive learned to increase their attention spans and improve their performances on intellectual tasks when they were given practice in relevant self-talk.

The value of self-instructions is not surprising when we consider that a large number of personal problems involve illogical thinking and confused conversations with oneself (Ellis, 1963). Indeed, many popular writers, such as Dale Carnegie and Norman Vincent Peale, have admonished individuals to think more positively and to reduce self-critical thoughts. Systematic training methods to teach individuals how to engage in more appropriate self-talk have been lacking until recently. In a very promising method presented by Meichenbaum and Cameron (Article Eleven), persons are first given the opportunity to observe others "thinking aloud" in problem situations and then practice adaptive self-instructions themselves, first aloud and then covertly.

The use of self-instructions comes very close to various forms of meditation and focused-attention methods that are sometimes referred to as self-hypnosis or autosuggestion. In meditation, a person often repeats a meaningless phrase continuously or counts the number of breaths he takes, usually while he is in a quiet and serene physical setting. Self-instruction methods (as discussed by Meichenbaum and Cameron), however, involve actions taken just prior to and during problem situations themselves. Still, self-hypnosis and various meditation techniques can be viewed in part as types of self-instruction in which the person uses certain covert statements to direct his attention and reduce stress and tension.

Careful research and training in self-instruction are only now getting under way. It seems clear that using certain comments to oneself in a variety of situations can be a powerful method of self-controlling a broad range of actions. Sometimes the best place to start in dealing with a problem is to turn off the "static"—that is, the self-critical, anxious, negative comments that a person makes to himself—and to turn on talk that is positive and task relevant.

3. Self-Modeling. Self-modeling can be viewed as a kind of cognitive rehearsal in which a person imagines himself engaging in certain behavior. This, of course, is very close to self-desensitization, in which the person constructs a list of problem situations and imagines himself in those situations. Indeed, if the problem situation is divided into a number of specific steps and relaxation training is introduced, there is no major difference between self-modeling and self-desensitization (Thoresen & Mahoney, 1974). Unfortunately, evidence on the effects of self-modeling techniques is still very sketchy (Kazdin, 1973). There is reason to believe, however, that this procedure contributes significantly to the effectiveness of other techniques (for example, self-desensitization and self-instructions) (see Thoresen & Mahoney, 1974).

4. Covert Sensitization. We saved a combination technique called covert sensitization for the last—possibly because it is so aversive. This procedure involves pairing an image of the problem behavior (such as seeing oneself eating a piece of banana cream pie) with another image that is very negative (such as getting sick and vomiting). These *covert* responses are used to make a person very *sensitive* to the problem—so much so that he'll avoid the behavior. Although we could have discussed this procedure as a negative self-punishment procedure, the method actually involves a number of other steps, such as practicing relaxation training, making a list of problem situations, and using negative self-reward. In the covert-sensitization procedure, the person first imagines a problem situation (such as reaching for a cigarette) and immediately follows it with a very nauseous image (such as starting to feel sick and upset and beginning to vomit). The person then imagines himself turning away from the cigarette and feeling much better (negative self-reward). In a fashion similar to that of desensitization, the person makes a detailed list of the elements of the problem situation, breaking it down into a number of specific actions (from first thinking about a cigarette to actually imagining the taste of a cigarette in his mouth). Sometimes the person also uses positive self-modeling by imagining himself acting appropriately in the problem situation.

This combination procedure has been successfully used with problems of alcoholism, drug taking, smoking, sexual deviation, and overeating. In one study (Ashem & Donner, 1968) a majority of longtime alcoholics were able to abstain from drinking for several months after using covert sensitization. In another case, a young man with a history of sexually molesting very young girls was able to eliminate that behavior (Barlow, Leitenberg, & Agras, 1969). Covert sensitization seems to be a very promising self-control method to use with chronic, hard-to-change behaviors such as drinking and smoking. Combining it with other self-control strategies may facilitate the development and maintenance of desired behavior change.

We have discussed a range of behavioral programming methods, each of which has demonstrated promise as a self-control technique. Two important points about the procedures discussed in this chapter seem to stand out: (1) environmental planning in the form of behavioral contracts can greatly increase the effectiveness and facilitate the maintenance of behavioral programming, and (2) a combination of procedures may increase the likelihood of success. It also seems that self-reward is one of the most consistently effective strategies and that covert procedures may also offer substantial assistance in the development and maintenance of a self-change program.

SUPPLEMENTARY SOURCES

Bandura, A. *Principles of behavior modification.* New York: Holt, Rinehart & Winston, 1969.

Goldfried, M. R., & Merbaum, M. (Eds.) *Behavior change through self-control.* New York: Holt, Rinehart & Winston, 1973.

Homme, L., & Tosti, D. *Behavior technology: Motivation and contingency management.* San Rafael, Calif.: Instruction Learning Systems, 1971.

Thoresen, C. E., & Mahoney, M. J. *Behavioral self control.* New York: Holt, Rinehart & Winston, 1974.

Watson, J., & Tharp, R. *Self-directed behavior: Self-modification for personal adjustment.* Monterey, Calif.: Brooks/Cole, 1972.

SUGGESTED READING

Axelrod, Hall, Weis, & Rohrer (Article One)
Bandura (Article Two)
Hannum, Thoresen, & Hubbard (Article Five)
Herbert, Gelfand, & Hartmann (Article Six)
Jeffrey (Article Seven)
Kanfer & Karoly (Article Eight)
Mahoney (Article Ten)
Meichenbaum & Cameron (Article Eleven)
Penick, Filion, Fox, & Stunkard (Article Twelve)

SELF-CONTROL: BEHAVIORAL
MEANS FOR HUMANISTIC ENDS

In presenting a behavioral approach to self-control, we have been underscoring a need to take action—that is, to carefully gather information through self-observation of behavior and to use environmental planning and behavioral-programming methods to produce change. The painfully shy college freshman can help himself become more outgoing and involved. The depressed and anxious housewife can take steps to become calmer and happier. The obese adolescent, failing in school and heavily into drugs, can bring about change. Accurate information must be gathered to assess progress. In effect, the person must function as a personal scientist, committed to taking action, yet tentative and flexible in terms of what to do. This scientific approach is crucial for the refinements and innovations that may be critical in adapting a self-control regimen to individual needs; the person must explore for himself what works best in his own case.

The scientific approach has often been maligned as something impersonal and dehumanizing, as something antithetical to basic human values. Roszak (1969), a leading antiscience spokesman, deplores science because it has failed to personalize man's experience and has relied on a very limited concept of objectivity and reality. We have presented the view that science can be very personal. An individual can systematically look at his own actions and at the variables that influence them. A personalized science of self-control can provide, evaluate, and refine techniques for individual adjustment and growth. Dealing, for example, with fearful self-doubts can be "objective" without being cold or sterile. This notion of objectivity is, of course, not exactly identical to the detached-observer concept of the physical scientist. A person can, however, be quite rigorous and systematic about his own actions and, at the same time, be thoroughly personal and intimately involved (Tart, 1972). It is here—in the process of examining the environment and refining techniques of self-control—that the perspective of a personal scientist is much in need.

A. SELF-ENGINEERING

We have highlighted the interdependence of behavior and environment, pointing out that each influences the other in a continuous reciprocal process. We are controlled and we control. Thus, in order to effect self-change, we must keep an eye on the many environments (including our internal environment) that influence behavior. We must then "engineer" those environments in ways that provide the needed cues and consequences for desired actions. There is nothing necessarily dehumanizing or impersonal in an "engineering mentality." Any kind of technology can be used to promote good or bad ends. We are concerned here with designing and redesigning physical, social, and cognitive environments in ways that encourage more positive and meaningful experiences. Talk of the personal and social engineering of environments leads us to an important point: any kind of effective self-control requires the involvement of others—that is, of the social environment—and often also requires the involvement of the physical environment. An individual will not be motivated to initiate or maintain effortful self-controlling behaviors unless his environment offers sufficient support for such an undertaking. Self-control requires environmental control.

As a culture, we have been extremely reluctant to use social engineering to prevent or solve problems. Traditionally, the "best" way to solve problems has been to talk them over with someone else—often a professional therapist—for a long period of time. Out of this talk, insight and self-understanding, especially of past experiences—the assumed prerequisites for change—are thought to emerge. Undoubtedly, some people have been helped by these procedures. More often than not, however, the change is nothing more than verbal insight—that is, a new way of talking about the problem. Yet the problem behaviors remain. We believe that meaningful change must go beyond insight. The individual must also develop "outsight" to understand how certain environments influence his behavior (Thoresen, 1973).

Etzioni and Remp (1972) provide a penetrating analysis of how social-engineering technologies have been all but ignored as means of helping individuals solve problems. Their discussion of problems such as drunk driving, birth control, drugs, and criminal behavior suggests that we often remain enamored with insightful talk and verbal persuasion (the "Enlightenment" approach) as ways to solve problems rather than use existing physical and social techniques. Thoresen (Article Fourteen) suggests that if we are genuinely committed to enhancing individual dignity and to promoting personal freedom, we must move beyond the humanistic-sounding rhetoric and toward environmentally based action programs. With the aid of sufficient "outsights," people can learn to engineer influential environments in ways that foster meaningful change.

B.   ENCOURAGING SELF-ACTUALIZATION

Abraham Maslow, the founder of the humanistic psychology movement, observed that our first and most pressing concern is "making the Good Person" (Maslow, 1969). For Maslow and many others, the good person is someone who experiences a sense of unity in life; who is very much aware and awakened to his behavior, especially in terms of thoughts, images, and physiological responses; who is compassionate and empathic with others; who can transcend the immediate external environment and create new ones with a personal meaning; and who is self-determining and personally responsible for his own actions. Humanistic educators (for example, Brown, 1972) have also expressed concern for the need to combine cognitive (academic) learning with social and emotional learning. What goes on in the body is every bit as important as what happens in the mind. The holistic perspective of humanistic psychologists and educators highlights the intimate relationship among what a person thinks, how a person feels, and what a person learns. The physical senses—touch, sight, sound, smell, and taste—and the imagination merit planned educational experiences, just as the "three Rs" do.

The history and the contemporary concerns of humanists, as well as of many behavioral psychologists who view themselves as humanists, are discussed by Thoresen (Article Fourteen). These concerns can be satisfied through methods of behavioral self-control. The skills of self-observation, environmental planning, and behavioral programming are especially well suited to providing the individual with the ability to act in more harmonious, compassionate, and responsible ways. The key to these self-actualizing concerns lies in viewing them as actions —that is, as human behavior—and in changing environments to encourage more self-actualizing behavior.

There are, of course, many paths to becoming a good person. A variety of Eastern cultural methods associated with yoga and Zen (for example, transcendental meditation) have gained popular support among those concerned with enhancing self-actualization. Recently, physical technology has been used to provide "biofeedback" so that persons can learn to alter several internal processes such as brain-wave patterns (alpha waves) and heart rate. In addition, a large number of what may be termed "Gestalt encounter sensitivity experiences" have been developed to promote self-actualization (for example, Gustaitus, 1969). However, a major barrier to fully understanding what constitutes the good person and self-actualization has persisted. This barrier involves ambiguity about what self-actualization is and how it is achieved. It is hard to know how to get there when you're confused about where you're going. Yet, it should be possible to take these important human concerns and talk about them in action terms—for example, what a more compassionate person would *do* or how a person would *act* if he were experiencing a greater sense of harmony and integration. By conceptualizing self-actualization in terms of human actions, we may be able to arrange physical and social environments to promote humanistic behavior. In Article Fourteen, Thoresen offers an analysis of the humanistic literature translated into behavioral terms. He speaks of self-knowledge and understanding in terms of self-observing internal and external responses, such as thoughts, images, and positive verbal comments. Compassion and empathy are seen, in part, as positive verbal and nonverbal interactions with others. This effort, while preliminary, suggests the possibility and promise of moving from the highly abstract and ambiguous to the more tangible and concrete. This may be the first step in helping individuals attain humanistic ends through behavioral means.

C. INDIVIDUAL FREEDOM AS PERSONAL POWER

Words such as "freedom," "autonomy," "dignity," and "personal growth" are revered and cherished because they connote something positive and personally relevant. They are what one semanticist has called "purr words"; they convey warm and positive meanings (Hayakawa, 1964). It has been our contention that the truly "free" individual is one who is in intimate contact with himself and his environment (both internal and external). He knows "where he's at" in terms of the factors influencing both his actions and his surroundings. Moreover, he has acquired technical skills that enable him to take an active role in his own growth and adjustment. He is no mechanical automaton passively responding to environmental forces. He is a personal scientist—a skilled engineer capable of investigating and altering the determinants of his actions. He is free to exert countercontrol on his environment, free from the resignation and inadequacies of a totalitarian existence, and free to draw upon a repertoire of effective behaviors. His happiness and development are not restricted by incapacitating fears or disabilities. Hence, the person with more freedom is one with skills of behavioral self-control.

One of the appealing and more humanistic aspects of behavioral self-control is its emphasis on the individual as a responsible agent in his own growth and development. He realizes that his actions are influenced by cues and consequences—both private and external —and that he can be actively involved in the direction and enhancement of his own adjustment. Where does this leave us in terms of the "source" of self-control? Does it come from within or from technical advice in a text such as this one? The answer, of course, is neither. Self-control is a complex learned skill that is influenced by both private and public factors (such as personal aspirations, learning history, peergroup influences, and authority figures).

The issue is not "who controls whom?" Applying the principles of behavioral self-control does not produce a more controlled person. Rather, it channels the influences of control. The obese housewife, the straight-F student, and the Caspar Milquetoast salesman are just as controlled as their slimmer or more successful counterparts. The latter, however, may have been more effective in directing and altering the factors that influence their performances.

Behavioral self-control places considerable responsibility on the individual in identifying and regulating significant elements in his own everyday adjustment. This "personal-scientist" view presumes a familiarity with the principles involved and a willingness to dignify self-change endeavors through scientific analysis and experimentation.

The case studies and research reports we have discussed represent some of the exciting contemporary developments in the area of self-control. As evidenced by the articles reprinted in this book, self-regulation has enlisted the research talents and conceptual skills of an ever-increasing group of professionals. The decades to come will undoubtedly witness expanding developments and controlled investigations of self-control processes.

We have presented a brief introduction to what may well be the most promising frontier in modern behavioral science. We believe that self-control skills—developed and refined through careful empirical methods—offer an excitingly effective means for the attainment of personally meaningful goals. In this sense, behavioral self-control represents an "applied humanism"—that is, a humane and long-awaited technology for giving power to the person.

SUPPLEMENTARY SOURCES

London, P. *Behavior control.* New York: Harper & Row, 1969.

Maslow, A. Towards a humanistic biology. *American Psychologist,* 1969, 24, 724-735.

Tart, C. T. States of consciousness and state-specific sciences. *Science,* 1972, 176, 1203-1210.

Thoresen, C. E. Behavioral humanism. In C. E. Thoresen (Ed.), *Behavior modification in education.* 72nd Yearbook of the National Society for the Study of Education, Part I. Chicago: University of Chicago Press, 1973. Pp. 385-421.

Thoresen, C. E., & Mahoney, M. J. *Behavioral self-control.* New York: Holt, Rinehart & Winston, 1974.

SUGGESTED READING

Thoresen (Article Fourteen)

SELECTED READINGS

USE OF SELF-IMPOSED CONTINGENCIES TO REDUCE THE FREQUENCY OF SMOKING BEHAVIOR[1]

Saul Axelrod, R. Vance Hall, Lynn Weis,
Sheila Rohrer

Self-punishment represents one form of behavioral programming (Chapter Five). In positive self-punishment, the individual removes some positive (pleasant) stimulus after the occurrence of an undesired behavior. This is equivalent to "fining" oneself for infractions.

Axelrod, Hall, Weis, and Rohrer present two case studies of positive self-punishment. In both studies, the undesirable behavior was cigarette smoking. For one subject, the self-punishment was tearing up a dollar bill for each cigarette that he smoked beyond a daily limit. The second subject punished herself by contributing 25 cents to charity for each cigarette that she smoked. In this second case, an additional strategy—not buying cigarettes—was in-

[1]This research was supported in part by the National Institute of Child Health and Human Development (HD-03144, Bureau of Child Research and Department of Human Development and Family Life, University of Kansas) and by the U.S. Office of Education (OEG-0-9-167016-3573, University of Connecticut). Reprints may be obtained from Saul Axelrod, Department of Special Education, Temple University, Philadelphia, Pa. 19122.

troduced. As we saw in Chapter Four, this is a form of environmental planning—that is, limiting the available responses before they occur.

Several aspects of these two case studies merit attention. First, both
utilized baselines and lengthy follow-up periods. Moreover, the first study used
a relatively innovative experimental design—the *changing-criterion* design
—which allows one to evaluate treatment effectiveness by looking at the correspondence between varying treatment components and actual behavior
change. Finally, in the first study, a total suppression of smoking behavior was
effected without a single instance of self-punishment. The subject never
exceeded his daily limit and was therefore never required to tear up a dollar
bill. This finding suggests that factors other than anticipated self-punishment
may have been operative (see Jeffrey, Article Seven). Self-monitoring and
gradual goal setting, for example, may have accounted for part of the success.

This article is a good illustration of single-subject research in self-control.
Its intensive analysis of two cases demonstrates both the clinical promise and
possible limitations of empirical case-study research.

The success of many behavior-modification procedures has been
dependent on a considerable amount of control over the consequences
that an individual receives. The settings for such studies have frequently involved classrooms, institutions, or home environments in
which teachers, ward attendants, or parents could apply contingencies
with a considerable amount of freedom. When a behavior problem is
exhibited by a noninstitutionalized adult, however, the degree of control
that can be exercised over his behavior is often quite limited. In such
cases, the approach has frequently been to treat the problem behavior
in tightly controlled therapy sessions for a period of time. The intentions
of these sessions are that the subject will first cease performing the
maladaptive behavior during therapy and that the effect will later
generalize to other parts of the subject's environment, in which the
therapist does not have control over contingencies. For a behavior such
as cigarette smoking, the procedure might involve pairing smoking with
an aversive event, such as electric shock (Carlin & Armstrong, 1968),
aversive noise (Greene, 1964), or hot smoke blown in the subject's face
(Franks, Fried, & Ashem, 1966). Once this aversive association has
been established in the therapy sessions, it is hoped that the association will be maintained outside of therapy.

A difficulty that might be encountered with such procedures is that
the associations that are developed in therapy sessions are not always
verified by the natural environment. The subject might learn that if
he smokes a cigarette in therapy, he will receive an electric shock but
that, when he is outside the therapy sessions, smoking a cigarette does
not result in shock. Thus, the aversive associations that an individual

has toward smoking might either be extinguished or become discriminative.

There is, therefore, a need for developing techniques that affect an individual's behavior when he is in his natural environment. One approach might be to have the contingencies applied by many of the subject's associates. The difficulty of organizing sufficient personnel, however, would often make such a tactic unreasonable. An alternative is to have the procedure constantly acting on the person in such a manner that it does not depend on the actions of a second party. Examples of such a tactic were provided by Azrin, Rubin, O'Brien, Ayllon, and Roll (1968) and by Azrin and Powell (1968) in an approach that was termed *behavioral engineering* (Azrin et al., 1968, p. 100). The procedure involves using a portable device that detects the undesirable behavior and delivers a stimulus to the individual after the behavior occurs. Behavioral engineering has been effective for decreasing slouching (Azrin et al., 1968) and for reducing smoking frequency (Azrin & Powell, 1968).

A problem with the behavioral-engineering approach is that the devices necessary for detecting a behavior and delivering a consequence may be difficult or expensive to obtain. Such a limitation is a serious one—if widespread use of behavioral principles is to become a reality. In the two studies that follow, the frequency of cigarette smoking was diminished by using procedures that the individuals applied to their own behavior and that did not necessitate the use of any electrical or mechanical apparatus. In both cases, the reliability of self-observation of smoking frequency was corroborated by associates of the subject, and experimental designs that verified the relationship between the operations and the reduction in smoking were employed.

EXPERIMENT ONE[1]

Subject

The subject, Lynn, who also served as the experimenter, was a 23-year-old graduate student who claimed that he had been smoking 20 to 30 cigarettes a day for approximately two years. He indicated that television commercials aired by the American Cancer Society and the American Heart Association had convinced him that he should stop smoking.

[1]Taken from Weis and Hall, 1970.

Definition of Smoking

Lynn carried a piece of paper with him and made a tally of each time he placed a cigarette in his mouth and lit it. For recording purposes, it did not matter how much of the cigarette was smoked. A record was kept during all of his waking hours (approximately 16 hours a day). On 14 occasions, reliability checks were made by Lynn's classmates, parents, or girl friend. In each instance, reliability was 100 percent.

Experimental Phases and Results

Baseline. The number of cigarettes Lynn smoked before experimental procedures were implemented was tallied for a 17-day baseline period. Figure 1 indicates that, during this phase, he smoked 16.6 cigarettes a day. From Days 8 to 13, Lynn also smoked a pipe. The pipe smoking, which is not included in the data, may have produced some decrease in cigarette smoking. During the final four days of the baseline period (Days 14 to 17), he smoked 16 cigarettes each day.

Tearing Up a Dollar Bill for Excessive Smoking. Beginning with Day 18, Lynn imposed a response-cost procedure (Weiner, 1962), in which he was required to tear a dollar bill into small pieces each time he smoked more than 15 cigarettes a day. The contingency was such that one dollar was to be ripped for each cigarette that exceeded the limit. The 15-cigarette criterion was in effect for five days and then was lowered to 14 cigarettes for five days, then to 13, to 12, and so on, until the criterion ceiling became 0. Figure 1 indicates that the subject never exceeded the maximum line criterion. After the response-cost contingency was in effect for 50 days, Lynn ceased smoking entirely. This observation was verified during a post-checks period, in which the response-cost procedure was employed, and again two years after the study was terminated. Lynn's friends also corroborated the fact that he had stopped smoking.

EXPERIMENT TWO

Subject

The subject, Sheila, was a 37-year-old teacher who also served as the experimenter. She had been smoking for 20 years before the study began and had previously made several unsuccessful efforts to

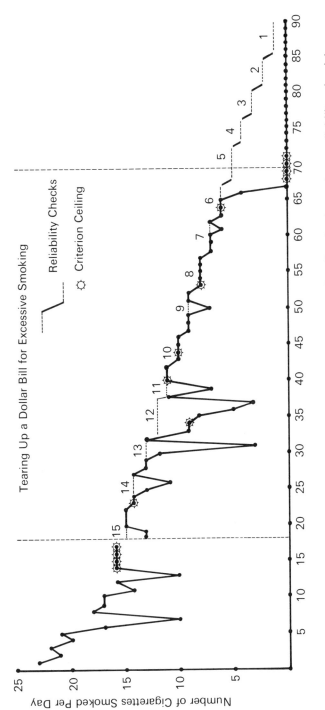

FIGURE 1. Record of the Number of Cigarettes Smoked Per Day by Lynn. (x = reliability check.)

stop smoking. She estimated that she had averaged 15 cigarettes a day before the study began.

Measurement of Behavior

Sheila obtained a record of the number of cigarettes she smoked either by counting the number of cigarettes in a package at the beginning and at the end of a day or by noting the number of cigarettes in an ashtray that was empty before she began to smoke. On 14 occasions, associates performed reliability checks, and, in each instance, there was 100 percent agreement in their records.

Experimental Phases and Results

Baseline$_1$.   Sheila obtained a record of the number of cigarettes she smoked for a 27-day period, during which no contingencies were applied to her behavior. Figure 2 indicates that, during the Baseline$_1$ stage, she smoked an average of 8.4 cigarettes a day, with a range of 0 to 20.

Twenty-five Cents Per Cigarette to Charity.   In the second stage of the study, Sheila contributed 25 cents to charity for each cigarette she smoked. Her average number of cigarettes per day dropped to 4.0 with a range of 0 to 8.

Twenty-five Cents Per Cigarette to Charity Plus No Purchase. During the third phase of the study, Sheila continued to contribute 25 cents for each cigarette she smoked and added the procedure of not purchasing cigarettes. In order to smoke, she therefore had to "bum" cigarettes from her associates. During the 16 days in which these procedures were in effect, she smoked no cigarettes on 13 days and averaged 0.37 cigarettes for the entire stage.

Baseline$_2$.   For three days, Baseline$_1$ conditions were reinstated. During this period, Sheila allowed herself to purchase cigarettes and did not contribute to charity after smoking a cigarette. The mean for the phase was 6.0 cigarettes a day.

Not Purchasing Cigarettes.   In the fifth stage of the experiment, she used the previous procedure of not buying cigarettes but did not contribute to her favorite charity after smoking. Under these conditions, Sheila smoked no cigarettes on 12 days and five cigarettes during one day.

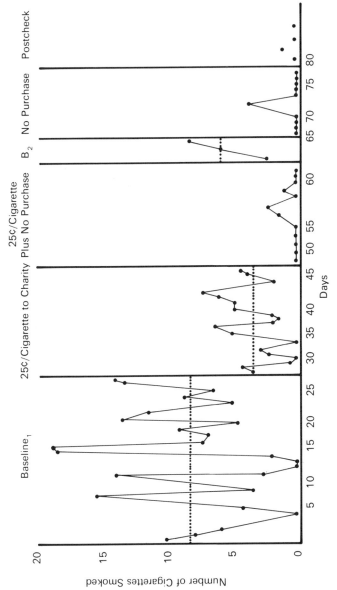

FIGURE 2. Record of the Number of Cigarettes Smoked Per Day by Sheila. The chart indicates the number of cigarettes the subject smoked each day during the following stages: *Baseline₁*—a period in which no contingencies were applied to smoking; *25 cents per cigarette to charity*—a phase in which the subject donated 25 cents to charity for each cigarette she smoked; *25 cents per cigarette to charity plus no purchase*—a phase in which the procedure of not buying cigarettes was added to the charity contingency; *Baseline₂*—a stage of reinstatement of *Baseline₁* conditions; and *Postcheck*—a stage of periodic checks on smoking behavior when the practice of not purchasing cigarettes was still in effect. (x = reliability check.)

Postcheck.   In the final stage of the study, measurements were conducted periodically, and the procedure of not buying cigarettes was still applied. During the four days on which the postcheck was made, Sheila smoked a total of only one cigarette.

One year after the study was formally terminated, Sheila indicated that she was smoking only in "stressful" situations, such as at the beginning of the school term and during university examinations. Unfortunately, she did not have data to indicate the frequency of her latest smoking behavior.

DISCUSSION

In both of these studies, procedures were employed that could be applied to noninstitutionalized adults without using expensive apparatus or therapy sessions. It was unnecessary to use second parties to implement the contingencies, although associates of the subjects were needed to perform reliability checks. Whereas other smoking studies have been concerned about generalization from the therapy environment to the natural environment, such a consideration was irrelevant in the present cases, since the therapy and natural environments were identical.

It should be noted that, in both experiments, the subject's estimate of the number of cigarettes he or she smoked was greater than the number that was actually recorded during the initial baseline phase. A possible explanation for this finding is that simply recording a certain behavior sometimes leads to an improvement. The feasibility of such an interpretation was demonstrated in a classroom experiment by Broden, Hall, and Mitts (1971), in which the study behavior of two children improved when self-recording techniques were instituted.

It is difficult to state why Lynn, the subject in Experiment 1, has not smoked since the study ended, but Sheila, the subject in Experiment 2, has exhibited some return to her former smoking behavior. Until the problem is solved, perhaps the best means of proceeding is to devise techniques that are sufficiently simple that, when reinstitution of the procedures becomes necessary, implementation can be achieved with a minimal amount of difficulty. Both procedures in this report satisfy this criterion. In fact, Sheila has indicated that she will reapply the experimental procedures if she decides that smoking has again become a problem for her.

The experimental design used in the first study provides an alternative to the reversal and multiple-baseline procedures used in most behavior-modification investigations. (Baer, Wolf, and Risley [1968] give a thorough description of these designs.) The design that we have termed the *changing-criterion* design consists of comparing the changing criterion for administering a consequence with the actual performance of the subject. When the correspondence between the two is high, one can have confidence that the criterion and its associated consequence are controlling the subject's behavior. In Experiment 1, it was found that Lynn exactly matched the maximum line criterion on 33 out of 50 days between the time the 15-cigarette criterion was used and the time the 6-cigarette maximum was employed. In addition, the correlation between the criterion ceiling and the number of cigarettes the subject smoked was $r=0.73$ ($p<.001$), indicating that as the criterion changed, there was a strong tendency for the smoking frequency to change in the same direction. (See Hall, Fox, Weis, and Quinn [in preparation] for more details on the changing-criterion design.)

Baer et al. (1968) pointed out the importance of intersubject reliability on the frequency of the problem behavior when instrumented recording is not possible; Simkins (1971) emphasized the importance of such reliability procedures for self-recorded behaviors. We would like to suggest another type of reliability technique that can be used when an individual applies consequences to his own behavior. The procedure, termed *reliability of operations,* refers to determining the degree to which the subject actually carries out the contract that he has made with himself. Such a tactic is desirable, since an individual might record his behavior accurately but might fail to apply a consequence to himself, particularly when aversive conditioning is involved. Thus, in Experiment 2, Sheila could fail to contribute 25 cents to charity for some of the cigarettes she smoked. Although a few violations of the contract might not affect the results, information on the degree to which the subject actually carried out the operations might be useful.

SELF-REINFORCEMENT
PROCESSES

Albert Bandura

Albert Bandura has been one of the leading researchers in self-control for many years. His conceptual analyses and laboratory experiments have been influential landmarks in the investigation of self-regulation processes. In this article, Bandura summarizes much of the laboratory research on self-reinforcement and discusses its implications for psychopathology and personal adjustment.

Bandura analyzes two separate approaches to research in self-control: (1) an approach dealing with the *development* of self-controlling responses (for example, through modeling, direct training, and instructions), and (2) an approach dealing with the actual *effects* of self-controlling responses (for example, self-reward and self-punishment). He describes several of his own experiments, which highlight the significance of social learning processes in human self-regulation.

Several points in this article merit specific attention. First, the preponderance of self-regulatory processes in complex human behavior is noteworthy. Bandura points out that most human performances are mediated by self-reactions and self-presented consequences. A second important point is that laboratory and applied research support the notion that self-administered rewards can, in fact, strengthen and maintain behavior. Finally, the significance of performance standards and thought processes in self-control deserves attention. Bandura points out that self-criticism and unrealistic personal goals characterize many forms of classical behavior pathology. He also indicates the clinical promise of recent research aimed at the modification of maladaptive thought patterns (see Meichenbaum & Cameron, Article Eleven).

Most human behavior is altered and maintained in the absence of immediate external reinforcement. It is generally assumed that people can, and indeed, do, exercise some degree of control over their own actions by utilizing self-generated stimulation. Experimental investigations of self-regulatory processes have primarily focused on the manner in which self-produced verbal and imaginal representations of events serve a performance-guiding function. Another major aspect of self-control is concerned with whether people can regulate their own behavior through self-produced consequences. Until recently, self-reinforcement phenomena have been virtually ignored in psychological theorizing and experimentation, perhaps due to the strong set established by studies conducted with infrahuman subjects. Unlike humans, who generally respond to their own behavior in self-approving or self-criticizing ways, rats and chimpanzees are disinclined to pat themselves on the back for commendable performances, or to berate themselves for getting lost in cul-de-sacs. By contrast, people typically set themselves certain standards of behavior and self-administer rewarding or punishing consequences depending on whether their performances fall short of, match, or exceed their self-prescribed demands.

A self-reinforcing event includes several subsidiary processes, some of which have been extensively investigated in their own right. First, it involves a self-prescribed standard of behavior which serves as the criterion for evaluating the adequacy of one's performances. The standard-setting component has been explored in some detail in studies of aspiration level. Most performances do not provide objective feedback of adequacy, and consequently, the attainments of other persons must be utilized as the norm against which meaningful self-evaluation can be made. Thus, for example, a student who achieves a score of 160 points on a given examination, and who aspires to exceed modal performances, would have no basis for either self-approving or self-disparaging reactions without knowing the accomplishments of others who are selected as the appropriate comparison group. As a second feature, a self-reinforcing event, therefore, often entails social-comparison processes. Third, the reinforcers are under the person's own control, and fourth, he serves as his own reinforcing agent. The significance of the two latter defining characteristics should be underscored because in some studies designed to investigate self-reinforcement processes, subjects do not have free access to the rewards; hence, the procedures essentially represent variations on externally managed reinforcement systems. Johnson and Martin (1972), for example, report a study in which subjects activated a reward signal after making responses they judged correct, but only a small proportion of the signaled correct responses was actually reinforced by the experimenter. Although subjects in this study judged when their performances deserved to be rewarded, the reinforcement was, nevertheless, externally controlled.

Investigations of self-reinforcement processes involve two separate lines of research. One set of studies is primarily designed to identify the conditions under which self-reinforcing responses are acquired and modified. In these experiments, self-rewarding and self-punishing responses constitute the dependent variables. The second line of research is principally concerned with whether self-administered rewards and punishments serve a reinforcing function in controlling the person's own behavior. In testing for reinforcing effects, self-reinforcement serves as the independent variable that is measured in terms of its power to influence performance.

DETERMINANTS OF SELF-REINFORCING RESPONSES

Several paradigms have been used to explore the acquisition of self-reinforcing responses. In the procedure typically employed by Kanfer and Marston, subjects perform a task in which their performances remain ill-defined; they are instructed to press a button that flashes a light or dispenses a token whenever they think their responses are correct. These accuracy judgments are interpreted as self-reinforcing responses.

In some of the studies conducted within this approach (Kanfer and Marston, 1963a; Marston, 1969) subjects were presented with a pseudo-subliminal perception task in which the same unrecognizable nonsense syllable was flashed on the screen on each trial, and subjects were required to guess which of several designated words they saw; in other studies (Kanfer and Marston, 1963b; Marston, 1964a) subjects selected what they considered to be the correct nonsense syllable from among alternatives that were randomly chosen as right; in other experiments (Marston, 1967), subjects took tokens when they believed that they had hit the bull's-eye with darts tossed while blindfolded, when they assumed that they had judged the length of lines correctly, or when they judged their responses to projective-test stimuli as accurate or popular (Marston, 1964b); and in still other investigations

(Kanfer, 1966), the number of times that children claimed they guessed correctly the number ranging from 0 to 100 that the experimenter would pick on each trial was used as an index of self-reward. Considering the extremely low probability of correct matches, high responses on the latter task more likely reflect fabrication than positive self-evaluation.

Certain interpretive problems arise when self-reinforcing responses are defined in terms of accuracy judgments. The major difficulties stem from the fact that correctness evaluations and self-commendations may be only partially correlated. There are many occasions when people evaluate their performances as accurate but not deserving of self-praise. The lack of relationship between these two sets of responses is most likely to obtain when individuals are required to perform tasks that they regard as simple or trivial, or that they personally devalue. Similarly, people may designate their responses on a particular task as inaccurate, but these judgments are unaccompanied by self-disparagement if the assignment is viewed as excessively difficult, irrelevant, or inappropriate to their background training. A mathematician, for example, who is asked to solve elementary arithmetic problems would undoubtedly judge his calculations to be accurate but hardly worthy of self-reward; conversely, a humanities enthusiast might rate most of his responses on tests of engineering competence inaccurate without engaging in any self-condemnation.

The necessity for distinguishing between the two types of responses would readily become evident if the experimental procedures previously described included two sets of response buttons, one signifying accuracy judgments and the second measuring self-approving reactions. The mathematician solving elementary arithmetic problems would frequently press the "accurate" button, but he might rarely, if ever, press the "commendable" button. The dual-response arrangement would also provide information on whether procedures in which subjects' performances remain ill-defined produce an adequate amount of self-reinforcing behavior. Under conditions of performance ambiguity, people may be willing to make tentative guesses about their responses but view the situation as providing insufficient basis for engaging in self-reward.

The foregoing comments, while questioning the substitution of accuracy estimates for direct measures of self-reinforcing behavior, are not meant to imply that categorization of one's responses on an accuracy dimension under low-feedback conditions is irrelevant to self-reinforcement processes. Performance designation serves as one of several factors determining whether individuals will respond with self-praise or self-reproof. Research conducted within this general paradigm (Kanfer, 1970a) has identified many variables that influence the incidence with which ambiguous performances are self-defined as accurate.

Ordinarily, self-reinforcement occurs in response to performances that are clearly discernible. That is, golfers see the distance and direction of their drives; students receive explicit scores on their academic tests; and authors can recognize the amount of material that they have written within a given period. In investigating the determinants of self-reinforcing responses, one must, of course, avoid performances that either produce distinct evaluative feedback or for which there are pre-existing norms. When self-evaluative responses are already linked to differential performance levels, subjects' covert self-reinforcement may obscure the influence of experimentally manipulated variables. It is therefore advantageous to choose tasks which produce performances that have no pre-established, self-evaluative significance. In other words, subjects can observe their attainments, but they have no basis for judging their adequacy. A person who receives a score of thirty on an unfamiliar motor task, for example, cannot determine whether it represents a mediocre, an adequate, or a superior achievement. By eliminating evaluative feedback, it is possible to study the conditions under which self-reinforcing responses can be established to particular performances. The paradigm originally employed by Bandura and Kupers (1964) was selected with the above requirements in mind.

Establishment of Self-Reinforcing Responses through Differential Reinforcement

Self-reinforcing responses are undoubtedly developed to some extent through selective reinforcement. In this learning process, an agent adopts a criterion of what constitutes a worthy performance and consistently rewards persons for matching or exceeding the adopted criterion level, but nonrewards or punishes performances that fall short of the minimum standard. When persons subsequently respond to their own behavior they are likely to reinforce themselves in a similarly selective manner. The effects of differential reinforcement of qualitative variations in performance on patterns of self-reward have not as yet been investigated experimentally. Kanfer and Marston (1963a) have shown that miserly and indulgent pretraining can influence the rate at which subjects administer tokens to themselves for responses they judge to be correct. The performances of some adults were generously rewarded with token reinforcers accompanied by an approving attitude toward self-reward, whereas with others the experimenter parted grudg-ingly with a few tokens and cautioned subjects against requesting rewards for performances of questionable accuracy. Those who re-ceived lenient training later rewarded themselves more frequently on a different task than subjects who were stringently trained, even though the achievements for both groups were comparable.

Establishment of Self-Reinforcing Responses through Modeling

There exists a substantial body of evidence that modeling proces-ses play a highly influential role in the transmission of self-rein-forcement patterns. In the standard paradigm (Bandura and Kupers, 1964; Bandura, Grusec, and Menlove, 1967), subjects observe a model performing a bowling task in which he adopts either a high-performance standard or a relatively low criterion of self-reinforcement. On trials in which the model attains or exceeds the self-imposed demand, he rewards himself with candy or exchangeable tokens and expresses positive self-evaluations, but when his attainments fall short of the adopted requirement he denies himself available rewards and reacts in a self-derogatory manner. Later, observers perform the task alone, during which time they receive a predetermined set of scores and the performances for which they reward themselves are recorded. The results show that people tend to adopt standards for self-reinforcement displayed by exemplary models, they evaluate their own performances relative to that standard, and then they serve as their own reinforcing agents. In the study by Bandura and Kupers (1964), children who observed a model setting a high standard of self-reinforcement later rewarded themselves sparingly and only when they achieved superior performances, whereas children exposed to models who con-sidered low achievements deserving of self-reward later tended to rein-force themselves generously for mediocre performances (Figure 1). A control group of children, who had no exposure to models, did not reward themselves selectively for differential levels of achievement. Subjects in the experimental conditions not only adopted the modeled standards of self-reinforcement, but they also matched variations in the magnitude with which the models rewarded their own performances.

In laboratory studies, a self-reinforcing response typically com-bines self-administration or self-denial of available tangible rewards with verbal self-praise or self-criticism. The verbal self-evaluation is an important defining component of a self-reinforcing event. The fact that a person passes up available edibles or exchangeable tokens does

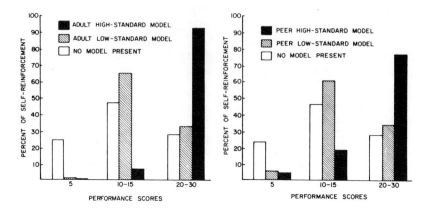

FIGURE 1. *Frequency with which children rewarded themselves at three performance levels after observing models reinforce themselves either according to a high standard (score
of 20 points) or a low criterion (10-point score) of achievement.*
Control subjects had no prior exposure to models. The figure on
the left depicts the patterns of self-reward for children who
observed adult models; the figure on the right presents the distribution of self-reward for children who were exposed to peer
models. (Bandura and Kupers, 1964.)

not by itself signify a self-punishing response. The absence of a response may be due to satiation, to disinterest in the material objects,
or to any number of extraneous factors. However, when a model refrains
from taking rewards and derogates his performances, there is no question that he is engaging in self-punitive behavior. Some investigators
have either deleted (Colle and Bee, 1968) or varied (Liebert, Hanratty,
and Hill, 1969) the verbal self-evaluation component on the assumption
that it represents a "rule structure."

Verbal self-commendation and self-derogation following differential attainment provide the basis for inferring the guiding standard, but
the specific modeled examples do not constitute the rule. In fact, in
experiments in which performances vary over a relatively wide range,
post-experimental interviews disclose that the standard of self-
reinforcement children derive from the models' performances does not
always correspond to the one that was actually modeled. One must
distinguish between a rule statement that defines the minimum criterion
for self-reinforcement from self-critical and self-approving verbalizations accompanying specific performances. There is a marked difference between derogating oneself for a particular performance (e.g.,

"That's poor; it doesn't deserve a treat") and verbalizing a rule for self-reinforcement that applies to all instances (e.g., "I reward myself only when I get a score of twenty points or above"). To delete the verbal self-reinforcing reactions is to remove an important feature of the very phenomena being studied. As might be expected, matching self-rewarding behavior is more effectively established when verbal self-evaluative responses are modeled than when they are not.

Manipulation of verbal self-reinforcement also tends to introduce other unintended variations in treatment conditions. It is difficult to make changes in verbal self-reinforcement without producing corresponding variations in the emotional intensity with which self-reinforcing responses are modeled. Results are therefore not easily interpretable from studies where self-reinforcing responses are performed enthusiastically when accompanied by verbal self-evaluations and perfunctorily when verbal self-reinforcers are omitted (Liebert, Hanratty, and Hill, 1969).

It will be recalled that social-comparison processes were assigned a prominent role in self-reinforcement. In the preceding experiment by Bandura and Kupers (1964), both the model and the subjects obtained a wide and overlapping range of scores; consequently, subjects had no reliable basis for judging their ability level. Ordinarily, social groups contain models of clearly differing abilities so that a given individual must select the modeled standards against which to evaluate his own performances. According to social-comparison theory (Festinger, 1954), persons tend to choose reference models who are similar in ability, and to reject those who are too divergent from themselves. One might also expect a history of negative reinforcement of achievement behavior to lower people's evaluation of their own performances (Stotland and Zander, 1958) and hence reduce the frequency and generosity with which they reward themselves.

To test the above propositions, an experiment was conducted (Bandura and Whalen, 1966) in which children underwent a series of success or failure experiences, following which they were exposed to either a superior model adopting a high criterion for self-reward, an inferior model displaying a very low standard of self-reinforcement, an equally competent model exhibiting a moderately high self-reward criterion, or they observed no models. Children who witnessed the inferior model subsequently rewarded themselves more frequently at low-performance levels and more generously than subjects who observed competent models adopting higher criteria of self-reinforcement. Upward discrepancies from adult models thus enhanced children's evaluation of their attainments. In accord with social-comparison theory, children rejected the self-imposed reinforcement contingencies of the superior model and adopted a lower standard commensurate with their achievements. Experimental subjects who had undergone failure experiences generally rewarded themselves less frequently than their successful counterparts. However, superior attainments outweighed the effect of reinforcement history so that subjects in all modeling conditions exhibited equally high rates of self-reward for outstanding performances regardless of whether they had previously met with repeated success or failure.

Although the exacting norms of highly divergent models tend to be rejected, nevertheless it is not uncommon for people to adopt stringent standards of self-reinforcement. An experiment by Bandura, Grusec and Menlove (1967) investigated some of the social conditions under which persons emulate austere standards of self-reinforcement even though the self-imposition of such contingencies produces negative self-evaluative consequences. Children were exposed to an adult model who performed the bowling task at a consistently superior level and adopted a high criterion of self-reward. Half the subjects experienced a prior rewarding interaction with the model, whereas with a second group of children the same model behaved in a nonnurturant manner. This relationship variable was selected on the assumption that the rewarding quality of the model, which tends to increase interpersonal attraction, would facilitate emulation of the model's norms. Adherence to high standards of achievement is generally rewarded and publicly recognized. Therefore, with half the subjects in each of the two levels of nurturance, the adult model was praised for adopting stringent standards of self-reinforcement, but with the remaining children the model received no social recognition for high standard-setting behavior.

Ordinarily, individuals are exposed to a multiplicity of modeling influences, many of which operate in opposing directions. Speculations about the influence of multiple modeling on social learning generally assign importance to conflicting identification with adult and peer models. In order to determine the effects of simultaneous exposure to antagonistic modeling influences, half the children in each subgroup observed both the stringent adult and a peer model who displayed a low standard of self-reward. When faced with a conflict between adult and peer standards, children would be predisposed toward peer modeling because emulation of high aspirations results in frequent negative self-reinforcement of one's performances. It was assumed, however, that the tendency for peer modeling to reduce the impact of adult modeling might be counteracted by the operation of opposing influences arising from positive ties to the adult model, and from vicarious positive reinforcement of high standard-setting behavior.

Figure 2 presents the per cent of trials in which children rewarded themselves for performances below the minimum criterion adopted by the adult model. As shown graphically, children exposed to conflicting modeling influences were more inclined to reward themselves for low achievements than children who had observed only the adult model consistently adhere to a high standard of self-reinforcement. Children were also more likely to impose severe criteria of self-reward on themselves when the adult model received social recognition for his high standard-setting behavior than when the model's stringent achievement demands went unrewarded. However, contrary to expectation, subjects who had experienced a highly nurturant interaction with the adult model were more likely to accept the low-performance standard set by the peer than if the adult model was less beneficent. Apparently, a nurturant relationship was interpreted by the children as permissiveness for lenient self-demands.

Comparison of subgroups containing various combinations of variables revealed that the influence of the peer's liberal self-reward was effectively negated by social reinforcement of the adult's high standard-setting behavior. The most austere pattern of self-reinforcement was displayed by children who experienced a relatively nonnurturant relationship with the adult model, who had no exposure to conflicting peer norms, and who witnessed the adult receive social recognition for adhering to high standards (see Figure 2). These children, who rarely considered performances that fell below the adult's criterion worthy of self-reward, displayed unyielding self-denial. The adoption and continued adherence to unrealistically high self-evaluative standards is especially striking, considering that the self-imposition of rigorous performance demands occurred in the absence of any social surveillance, under high permissiveness for self-gratification, and the modeled standards resulted in considerable self-devaluation and self-forbiddance of freely available rewards.

Comparative studies (Liebert and Allen, 1967; Liebert and Ora, 1968) disclose that modeling and direct training, in which experimenters judge which of the performer's attainments are deserving of reward, are equally effective in transmitting high standards of self-reinforcement. Under naturally occurring conditions, modeling and reinforcement practices often operate concurrently in ways that either supplement or counteract each other. Findings of research in which both of these sources of influence are varied simultaneously (McMains and Liebert, 1968; Mischel and Liebert, 1966; Rosenhan, Frederick, and

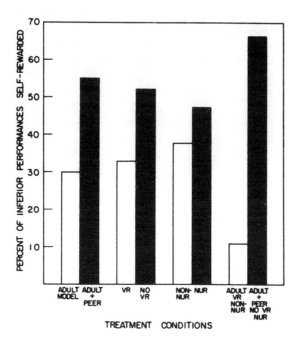

FIGURE 2.   Percent of trials in which subjects rewarded themselves for performances below the minimum standard adopted
by the adult model as a function of model nurturance, vicarious reinforcement of high standard-setting behavior, and
exposure to conflicting peer-modeling influences. (Bandura,
Grusec, and Menlove, 1967a.)

Burrowes, 1968) show that rewards are most sparingly self-administered when stringent standards have been consistently modeled and
imposed, whereas social-learning conditions in which persons both
model and reinforce lenient performance demands produce generous
self-reward patterns of behavior. Discrepant practices, on the other
hand, in which models prescribe stringent standards for others but
impose lenient ones upon themselves, or who impose austere demands
on themselves and lenient ones on others, reduce the likelihood that
high standards will be adopted.

The transmission of self-reward patterns through a succession of
models has been demonstrated by Mischel and Liebert (1966). Children who adopted the standards of reinforcement of adults subsequently both modeled the same self-rewarding behavior with peers

and applied the same reinforcement contingency to their performances. Marston (1965a) has likewise shown in an experiment with adults that witnessing models reinforcing their own performances at either high or low rates not only affected the self-reinforcing behavior of the observers, but also influenced the frequency with which they later reinforced another person performing the same task. Results of these laboratory experiments are in accord with field studies demonstrating that, in cultures where austerity is consistently modeled and reinforced as the dominant social norm, not only are positive reinforcements sparingly self-administered, but because of the emphasis on personal responsibility for high standards of conduct, self-denying, self-punitive, and depressive reactions occur with high frequency (Eaton and Weil, 1955). By contrast, in societies in which generous self-gratification patterns predominate, self-rewards are usually made contingent upon minimal performances (Hughes, Tremblay, Rapoport, and Leighton, 1960).

SELF-REINFORCEMENT, SELF-CONCEPT, AND ACHIEVEMENT BEHAVIOR

In the aforementioned laboratory studies, individuals who had been exposed to models favoring lenient standards of self-reinforcement were highly self-rewarding and self-approving for comparatively mediocre performances. By contrast, persons who observed models adhering to stringent performance demands later displayed self-denial and self-dissatisfaction for objectively identical accomplishments. These contrasting self-reactions illustrate how self-esteem, self-concept, and related self-evaluative processes can be conceptualized within a social-learning framework. From this perspective, self-esteem is the result of discrepancies between a person's behavior and the standards that he has selected as indices of personal merit. When behavior falls short of one's evaluative standards, the person judges himself negatively or holds himself in low self-esteem. On the other hand, when performances coincide with, or exceed, a person's standards, he evaluates himself positively, which is considered indicative of high self-esteem.

The self-concept, which is assigned a prominent role in some theories of personality, also reflects the phenomenon of self-reinforcement. Self-concept usually signifies a person's disposition toward positive and negative self-evaluation of different aspects of his behavior. In measuring this personality characteristic, individuals are presented with a set of evaluative statements in adjective check lists, Q-sorts, or inventories, and asked to rate which statements apply to them. The individual responses are then summed to provide a global index of self-evaluation. Within a social-learning approach, a negative self-concept is defined in terms of a high frequency of negative self-reinforcement of one's behavior and, conversely, a favorable self-concept is reflected in a relatively high incidence of positive self-reinforcement (Marston, 1965b).

Dysfunctions in self-reinforcement systems often assume major importance in psychopathology through their capacity to create excessive self-punishment and aversive conditions that can maintain other forms of deviant behavior. Many of the people who seek psychotherapy are highly competent and free of debilitating anxiety, but they experience a great deal of personal distress stemming from excessively high standards of self-evaluation that are often supported by unfavorable comparisons with models noted for their extraordinary achievements. Talented individuals who have high aspirations that are possible but difficult to realize are especially vulnerable to self-dissatisfaction despite their notable achievements. As Boyd (1969) graphically describes this phenomenon, "Each violinist in any second chair started out as a prodigy in velvet knickers who expected one day to solo exquisitely amid flowers flung by dazzled devotees. The 45-year-old violinist with spectacles on his nose and a bald spot in the middle of his hair is the most disappointed man on earth."

In its more extreme forms, an austere system of self-reinforcement gives rise to depressive reactions, chronic discouragement, and feelings of worthlessness and lack of purposefulness. Excessive self-disparagement, in fact, is one of the defining characteristics of psychotic depression. As Loeb, Beck, Diggory, and Tuthill (1967) have shown, depressed adults evaluate their performances as significantly poorer than do nondepressed subjects, even though their actual achievements are the same. People also suffer from considerable self-devaluation when they experience loss in ability due to age or physical injury but continue to adhere to their original standards of achievement. In the latter instances, most of their performances are negatively self-reinforced to the point where eventually they become apathetic and abandon significant aspects of their behavioral repertoire. When a person's behavior produces self-punishing consequences, any activities that avert or reduce these aversive outcomes are thereby strengthened and maintained. Many forms of deviant behavior, such as alcoholic self-anesthetization, grandiose ideation, and reluctance to engage in activities that may have self-evaluative implications, serve as means of escaping or avoiding self-generated aversive stimulation

The discussion thus far has emphasized the personal negative by-products of stringent self-reinforcement. Social problems can arise from deficient or deviant self-reinforcement systems. Individuals who have failed to develop well-defined standards necessary for adequate self-regulating reinforcement, and those who make self-reward contingent upon skillful performance of antisocial behavior, readily engage in transgressive behavior unless deterred by externally imposed controls. Similarly, individuals who set lax behavioral standards for themselves are inclined to display low achievement strivings.

There is reason to assume, from findings reported later, that self-reinforcement serves both a motivating and a reinforcing function with respect to achievement behavior. It has been repeatedly demonstrated (Locke, Cartledge, and Koeppel, 1968) that performance standards are a major determinant of level of productivity. The higher the standards that people set for themselves, the higher their attainments. Setting performance goals by itself does not automatically produce achievement behavior. Rather, the motivational effects of goal-setting are most likely mediated by self-reinforcement. After a person has committed himself to a specified level of performance, his self-approval becomes contingent upon goal attainment. This leads him to intensify his efforts in order to exceed self-disappointing performances. Having achieved a given performance, people are usually no longer content with it and make self-reward contingent upon progressively more difficult accomplishments. In the present interpretation, motivational effects derive not from the goals themselves but from the fact that people respond evaluatively to their own achievements and, therefore, regulate their level of effort accordingly.

CONDITIONS MAINTAINING SELF-REINFORCING RESPONSES

In preceding sections, processes have been examined whereby evaluative and reinforcing functions performed by others are transferred to the individual himself so that he serves as the reinforcer of his own actions. An interesting, but inadequately explored, question is what maintains discriminative self-reinforcing responses after they have been acquired through modeling and direct training. No elaborate theory is needed to explain why people engage in self-rewarding behavior. The more challenging question requiring explanation is why people deny themselves available rewards over which they have full control, and why they punish themselves.

Conditioned Relief

One possible interpretation is that self-evaluative responses acquire secondary reinforcing properties through repeated association with primary or social reinforcement. According to this classical-conditioning view, which has been advanced by Aronfreed (1964), transgressive behavior arouses anticipatory anxiety as a result of past association with punishment. Under conditions where social disapproval occurs contiguously with termination of anxiety or punishment, verbal criticism attains anxiety-attenuating value. The subject therefore applies critical labels to his own behavior because they serve as automatic anxiety reducers. To test this notion, Aronfreed (1964) conducted an experiment in which children performed an ambiguous task; on designated trials a buzzer sounded, signifying a transgression, following which the children were verbally reprimanded for behaving the "blue" way and deprived of some candy. For one group of subjects, the critical label "blue" was expressed when the buzzer and punishment were terminated; for a second group the label coincided with the onset of buzzer and punishment; while with control children the blue label was verbalized as the buzzer was turned off, without any accompanying punishment. On two test trials, during which the buzzer signaled a transgression, children who experienced labeling at the termination of punishment were more inclined to verbalize the critical label than either the controls or the children receiving labeling at the onset of punishment, who did not differ from each other.

The above findings are consistent with a conditioned-reinforcement view, although interpretation of the data is complicated by the fact that children rarely uttered the critical label on their own and did so only after being verbally prompted by the punishing agent through a series of questions concerning their actions. Given anxiety arousal, one would expect an anxiety reducer to be performed rapidly and spontaneously. An alternative interpretation of the data is that the verbal response was performed because of its anticipated functional value rather than for its conditioned mollifying effects. That is, by uttering the critical label, the children could terminate the experimenter's verbal probing. Subjects who had earlier learned that a particular verbalization discontinues punishment by the experimenter should be more willing to produce it when prompted to do so than children for whom the verbal response brought on the punishing experiences. The differential expectations established through prior training might be expected to persist over more than two trials. The conditioned-reinforcement theory of self-punishment would also require several complicated assumptions to explain how children adopt self-punishing responses by observing punishments self-administered by a model for devalued behavior without observers experiencing any direct aversive consequences.

Self-Arousals

There is a growing body of evidence (Bandura, 1969) that in humans the effects of paired stimulation are largely governed by an intervening self-stimulation mechanism. These findings indicate that a stimulus is not automatically endowed with emotion-arousing or emotion-reducing properties through association with primary reinforcement. Rather, as a result of paired experiences, a conditioned stimulus assumes informative value that is capable of activating emotion-provoking or calming thoughts. The self-stimulation view of conditioning based on thought-produced arousal suggests a somewhat different mode of operation of self-punishment than is assumed in the conditioned-reinforcement explanation.

In everyday situations, the performance of punishable behavior creates anticipatory arousal that is likely to persist in varying degrees until the person is reprimanded. Punishment not only terminates distressing thoughts about impending discovery of the transgression and possible social condemnation, but it also tends to restore the favor of others. Thus, punishment can provide relief from self-generated aversive stimulation that is enduring and often more painful than the actual reprimand itself. This phenomenon is most vividly illustrated in extreme cases where people torment themselves for years over relatively minor transgressions and do not achieve equanimity until after making reparations of some type. Self-punishment may serve a similar distress-relief function. Having criticized or punished themselves for undesirable actions, individuals are likely to discontinue further upsetting ruminations about their behavior.

The way in which self-punishing responses can be maintained by averting anticipated punishing consequences is strikingly demonstrated by Sandler and Quagliano (1964). After monkeys learned to press a lever to avoid being shocked, a second contingency involving self-administered painful stimulation was introduced. A lever-press prevented the occurrence of the original shock, but it also produced an electric shock of lesser magnitude. As the experiment progressed, the self-administered shock was gradually increased in intensity until it equalled the aversive stimulation being avoided. However, the animals showed no reduction in the frequency of self-punishing responses although this behavior no longer served as a "lesser of two evils." Even more interesting, after the avoided shock was permanently discontinued but lever-pressing responses (which had now become objectively functionless) still produced painful consequences, the animals continued to punish themselves needlessly with shock intensities that they had previously worked hard to avoid. This experiment reveals how self-punishment can become autonomous of contemporaneous conditions of reinforcement and be maintained through its capacity to forestall anticipated aversive experiences.

Further support for the emotion-reducing function of self-punitive behavior is furnished by Stone and Hokanson (1969). When adults could avoid painful shocks by administering to themselves shocks of lesser intensity, self-punitive responses not only increased but they were accompanied by reduction in autonomic arousal. Self-punishing responses continued to be performed at an undiminished rate, though with increased autonomic arousal, after conditions were altered so that self-administered punishment was only partially effective in avoiding painful stimulation.

The preceding analysis of self-punishment can be applied as well to self-disappointing performances as to transgressive behavior. The valuation of performances which fall short of, match, or exceed a reference norm is partly achieved through differential reinforcement. For example, parents who expect their children to exceed the average performance of their group in whatever tasks they undertake will selectively reward superior achievements and find fault with average and lower-level attainments. Differential achievement levels thus take on positive and negative value, and the performance standard common to the various activities is eventually abstracted and applied to new endeavors. That is, a person for whom average performances have been repeatedly devalued will come to regard modal achievements on new tasks as inadequate and attainments that surpass modal levels as commendable. It is assumed that, like transgressive behavior, inferior performances can be a source of disconcerting thoughts and social disapproval that individuals will strive to reduce by criticizing or punishing themselves.

As shown earlier, specific patterns of self-reinforcement can be acquired observationally without the mediation of direct external reinforcement. Once the evaluative properties of differential accomplishments are well established, favorable or inadequate matches with adopted standards are likely to elicit self-reactions that, in turn, give rise to self-rewarding or self-punishing behavior. At this stage the whole process becomes relatively independent of external reinforcement, but remains dependent upon cognitive evaluations based on the match between self-prescribed standards, performance, and the attainments of reference models.

External Reinforcement

Although self-punishment can operate autonomously to some extent by reducing self-generated aversive stimulation, self-reinforcing responses are partly sustained by periodic external reinforcement. Adherence to high standards of self-reinforcement is actively supported through a vast system of rewards involving praise, social recognition, and a variety of awards and honors, whereas few accolades are bestowed on people for rewarding themselves on the basis of mediocre performances. To the extent that people choose a reference group whose members share similar behavioral norms for self-reinforcement, a given individual's self-evaluations are undoubtedly influenced by the actual or anticipated reactions of members whose judgments he values highly. Once established, patterns of self-reinforcement are thus intermittently reinforced and upheld through selective association.

In everyday life, high evaluative standards are not only favored, but negative sanctions are frequently applied to discourage inappropriate positive self-reinforcement. Rewarding oneself for inadequate or undeserving performances is more likely than not to evoke critical reactions from others. Similarly, lowering one's performance standards is rarely considered praiseworthy. As a result of extensive social training, performances that are self-defined as failures come to elicit self-devaluative reactions that are incompatible with self-rewarding behavior and thus reduce its occurrence.

Finally, it should be noted that self-punishment often serves as an effective means not only of lessening negative consequences administered by others, but in eliciting commendations from them as well. By criticizing and belittling themselves, people can predictably get others to enumerate their noteworthy accomplishments and abilities, and to issue reassuring predictions that continued effort will produce future triumphs.

REINFORCING FUNCTION OF SELF-ADMINISTERED CONSEQUENCES

The studies reported earlier were designed primarily to identify some of the variables governing the acquisition of self-rewarding and self-punishing responses. Given that individuals can be influenced to engage in self-reinforcing activities, the basic question remains whether self-generated consequences serve a reinforcing function in regulating behavior. Demonstrations of the behavioral effects of self-produced response consequences require experimental situations in which self-reinforcing events serve as the controlling variables in relation to other forms of behavior.

To test the relative efficacy of self-monitored and externally imposed systems of reinforcement, Bandura and Perloff (1967) conducted an experiment that proceeded in the following manner: Children worked at a manual task in which they could achieve progressively higher scores by performing increasingly more effortful responses. Eight complete rotations of a wheel were required to advance 5 points so that, for example, a total of 16 cranking responses was necessary to achieve a 10-point score, 24 responses to attain a 15-point score, and so on. Children in the self-reinforcement condition selected their own achievement standards and rewarded themselves with tokens whenever they attained their self-prescribed level of performance. Children assigned to an externally imposed reinforcement condition were individually matched with partners in the self-reward group so that the same performance standard was externally set for them and the reinforcers were automatically delivered whenever they reached the predetermined level. To ascertain whether subjects' behavioral productivity was due to the operation of contingent reinforcement or to gratitude for the rewards that were made available, children in an incentive control group performed the task after they had received the supply of rewards on a noncontingent basis. A fourth group worked without any incentives to estimate the amount of behavior generated by the characteristics of the task itself. Because the capacity to maintain effortful behavior over time is one of the most important attributes of a reinforcement operation, the dependent measure was the number of responses the children performed until they no longer wished to continue the activity.

As shown graphically in Figure 3, both self-monitored and externally imposed reinforcement systems sustained substantially more behavior than either the contingent reward or the nonreward condition, which did not differ from each other. In the case of boys, externally administered rewards generated more behavior than self-reinforcement, but otherwise the two systems of reinforcement proved equally efficacious. Of even greater interest is the prevalence with which children in the self-monitored condition imposed upon themselves highly unfavorable schedules of reinforcement. Not a single child chose the lowest score which required the least effort, while approximately half of them selected the highest achievement level as the minimal perfor-

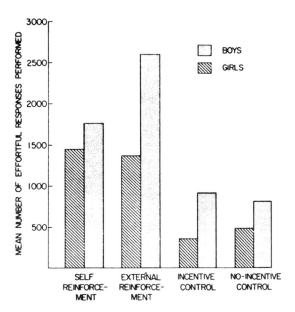

FIGURE 3. *Mean number of responses maintained by self-monitored, externally imposed, and noncontingent systems of reinforcement. (Bandura and Perloff, 1967.)*

mance meriting self-reward. Moreover, a third of the children subsequently altered their initial standard to a higher level, without a commensurate increase in amount of self-reward, thereby imposing upon themselves a more unfavorable work-to-reinforcement requirement. This behavior is all the more striking because the self-imposition of stringent performance demands occurred in the absence of any social surveillance and under high permissiveness for self-reward.

It can be reasonably assumed that most older children have acquired standards of achievement through modeling and differential reinforcement, and that they have undergone experiences in which rewarding oneself for performances judged to be unworthy has been socially disapproved. Hence, under conditions where persons are provided with opportunities to optimize their material outcomes by engaging in behavior which has low self-regard value, conflicting tendencies are likely to be aroused. On the one hand, individuals are tempted to maximize rewards at minimum-effort costs to themselves; they can achieve this by simply lowering their performance standards. On the other hand, low-quality performances produce negative self-evaluative consequences, which, if sufficiently strong, may inhibit undeserving self-compensation. Apparently, subjects were willing to deny themselves rewards over which they had full control rather than risk self-disapproval for unmerited self-reward. Many of the children, in fact, set themselves performance requirements that incurred high-effort costs at minimum material recompense. These findings are at variance with what one might expect on the basis of reward-cost theories, unless these formulations include the self-esteem costs of rewarding devalued behavior. The desire to avoid aversive self-devaluative consequences may also partly explain why children willingly give up rewards they possess in response to substandard performances after having observed models relinquish rewards and criticize themselves for behavior they judged inadequate (Herbert, Gelfand, and Hartmann, 1969).

In recent years, self-reinforcement procedures have begun to be employed to modify and to maintain response patterns in treatment programs. These studies usually measure the frequency with which deviant responses occur during baseline conditions and after self-administered consequences are made explicitly contingent upon selected behaviors. Goodlet and Goodlet (1969), for example, compared the incidence of aggressively disruptive behavior in boys during a baseline period, when teachers rewarded the children with exchangeable tokens for reductions in aggressiveness, and when the boys evaluated their own performances and reinforced their own behavior accordingly. The mean amount of disruptive behavior displayed by the boys under these three conditions was 35.33, 8.92, and 9.95, respectively. These findings indicate that self-administered consequences can aid in controlling one's own behavior; but the comparative data should be accepted with reservation because the sample size is small and the two systems of reinforcement were not administered in counterbalanced order. Lovitt and Curtiss (1969) and Glynn (1970) also provide evidence that when behavioral objectives and contingency systems are clearly specified, children are able to manage their own behavior as well as or more effectively by self-reinforcement than is achieved through similar externally administered consequences.

Several studies have been reported in which self-administered, aversive consequences were used with some degree of success to reduce disfluencies (Goldiamond, 1965), obsessional ruminations (McGuire and Vallance, 1964), craving for addictive drugs (Wolpe, 1965), and deviant sexual behavior (McGuire and Vallance, 1964). The preliminary findings of these studies, while most interesting, require further validation through systematic manipulation of self-reinforcement procedures.

Recent investigations of techniques of self-control also assign a principal role to self-managed reinforcement. In these treatment programs (Ferster, Nurnberger, and Levitt, 1962; Harris, 1969; Stuart, 1967), changes in highly refractory behavior are induced by having subjects regulate the stimulus conditions that ordinarily control undesired and competing response patterns. However, unless positive consequences for self-controlling behavior are also arranged, the well-intentioned practices are usually short-lived. Self-controlling behavior is difficult to maintain because it tends to be associated, at least initially, with relatively unfavorable conditions of reinforcement. Prepotent activities such as heavy drinking by alcoholics and excessive eating by obese people are immediately rewarding, whereas their detrimental consequences are not experienced for some time. Conversely, self-control measures usually produce immediate unpleasant effects while the personal benefits are considerably delayed. Self-reinforcement practices are, therefore, employed to provide immediate support for self-controlling behavior until the benefits that eventually accrue take over the reinforcing function. This is achieved by having individuals select a variety of activities that they find rewarding and make them contingent upon the performance of self-controlling behavior. Successful results have been achieved with self-managed programs of behavioral change. However, self-reinforcement is only one component in a multiple method, and its relative contribution to the measured outcomes has not been adequately assessed.

COVERT SELF-REINFORCEMENT

All of the preceding studies involved self-administration of tangible reinforcers. Of considerable interest is the question of whether symbolically produced consequences can serve a reinforcing function in regulating overt behavior. Weiner (1965) reports some evidence that symbolized outcomes may possess reinforcing properties that are similar to their physical equivalents. Inappropriate motor responses by adults were either punished by withdrawal of monetary points or by having the subjects imagine the same loss of monetary points, or their performances had no consequences. Weiner found that imagined aversive consequences and the actual occurrence of the same negative outcomes both reduced responding compared to the condition involving no feedback. Covert self-punishment, however, produced somewhat weaker reductive effects. These findings suggest that overt behavior can be partly regulated by covert self-reinforcement operations.

To the extent that covert self-reinforcement can substitute for, supplement, or reduce the effects of extrinsic consequences (Kanfer, 1968), this factor may partly account for intersubject variability in the degree of control exercised over human behavior by external reinforcement. It is also likely that covert self-reinforcement mediates the effects of many extrinsic events that are attributed reinforcing properties. For example, informative feedback of performance can enhance and maintain responding even when the information signifies level of attainment rather than accuracy which can improve performance through its response-guidance functions. Confirmation of correctness by itself does not have inherent rewarding value. Performance knowledge assumes positive or negative qualities only when evaluated by the performer in relation to his intrinsic standards. In other words, it is not the lights or the tones signifying correct responses that are reinforcing; rather, they serve as cues for subjects to apply to themselves positive or negative self-evaluations which function as the critical reinforcing events. Hence, correctness feedback on tasks that are personally devalued or regarded as trifling is unlikely to operate as a reward. On the other hand, confirmation of attainments that exceed personal standards of what constitutes a worthy performance will tend to activate positive self-reinforcement. Knowledge of past achievements may also lead subjects to raise their performance standards for positive self-evaluation, thus increasing their level of effort on the task. The motivational and goal-setting effects of knowledge of results are well documented by Locke, Cartledge, and Koeppel (1968).

Possible applications of covert self-reinforcement are discussed by Homme (1965) in a paper concerned with implicit psychological activities. In reducing detrimental behaviors that produce immediate and automatic reinforcing effects, the individual selects numerous aversive consequences of the behavior which can be employed as covert negative reinforcers. Whenever he is instigated to perform the undesired behavior, he immediately symbolizes the aversive effects or revivifies other unpleasant experiences. Miller (1951) and Grose (1952) have shown that negatively valenced thoughts generate strong emotional responses. In fact, imagined painful stimulation can produce subjective distress and physiological arousal similar to those responses induced by actual painful stimulation (Barber and Hahn, 1964). To the extent that sufficiently strong affective consequences can be symbolically produced contingent upon undesired behavior, its occurrence may be significantly reduced. Covert self-reinforcement is likely to exert greatest controlling power when applied to weaker incipient forms of the behavior than when the response tendency is quite compelling, or after the undesired behavior and its attendant reinforcement have already occurred.

Thought-induced affective experiences have been most extensively employed in aversive counterconditioning for the purpose of controlling injurious addictive behavior or intractable response patterns that can create serious social consequences (Bandura, 1969). In the application of this procedure, the objects to which individuals are markedly attracted are repeatedly paired with aversive reactions that are symbolically induced. The negative contents are usually drawn from disagreeable, painful, or revolting experiences that the individuals have previously undergone either in connection with the pleasurable objects and activities or in other contexts. Preliminary results based upon clinical applications reveal that aversions can be established in this manner for modifying alcoholism (Anant, 1967; Ashem and Donner, 1968; Miller, 1959); obesity (Cautela, 1966); deviant sexual behavior (Davison, 1968b; Miller, 1963); and drug addiction (Kolvin, 1967).

The foregoing procedure gains support from experimental investigations of classical conditioning that rely upon symbolically induced emotional responses. Subjects are informed that the CS will sometimes be followed by shock; they are given a sample shock or a single confirmation trial during the acquisition series, but otherwise the CS is never paired with any externally administered aversive stimulation. Subjects develop conditioned autonomic responses in the absence of an external UCS by generating fear-producing thoughts in conjunction with the occurrence of the CS (Dawson and Grings, 1968; Grings, 1965). Bridger and Mandel (1964), in fact, report that autonomic conditioning was similar regardless of whether the CS was associated with threat of shock alone, or with threat and actual shock stimulation. Some suggestive evidence for the influential role of self-stimulation in symbolic conditioning is provided by Dawson (1966) who found that the degree to which subjects believed that shock would follow a certain signal and the severity of the shock they anticipated were positively correlated with the extent of autonomic conditioning.

MODIFICATION OF THOUGHT PROCESSES THROUGH SELF-REINFORCEMENT

The preceding section discussed how symbolically produced effects can be employed as reinforcing events to control overt behavior. Often, certain trains of thought produce strong emotional responses that are subjectively distressing or behaviorally disruptive, in which case the problem becomes one of controlling the covert events themselves.

Assuming that symbolic activities obey the same psychological laws as overt behavior, it should be possible to significantly influence the nature, incidence, and potency of covert events. The difficulties in detecting the presence of implicit responses present a major obstacle to their control by reinforcement practices if one adheres to the conventional paradigm in which an external agent monitors the occurrence of the desired behavior, imposes the contingencies on subjects, and administers the reinforcers to them. However, as Homme (1965) points out, the occurrence or absence of covert events can be easily and reliably detected by the person doing the thinking. Consequently, such responses can be most easily influenced through self-reinforcement. In this type of approach, implicit events are self-monitored, the contingencies are self-prescribed, and the consequences are self-produced.

Homme suggests that Premack's (1965) differential-probability principle (i.e., any highly preferred activity has reinforcing capabilities) might be utilized in the contingency arrangement and selection of self-reinforcers. In this approach, the strength and incidence of certain classes of thoughts are modified by making preferred activities contingent upon their occurrence. If thought processes are controllable by this means, then depressive, infuriating, and other vexatious ruminations could be reduced by self-reinforcement of more constructive lines of thought. The results of both clinical and laboratory studies are sufficiently promising to warrant further investigation of self-reinforcement processes and their role in the self-regulation of behavior.

SELF-REGULATION IN THE MODIFICATION OF DISRUPTIVE CLASSROOM BEHAVIOR

Orin D. Bolstad and Stephen M. Johnson

Bolstad and Johnson present a well-designed and well-analyzed field experiment on the effects of self-reinforcement and external reinforcement. They studied first- and second-grade children who frequently engaged in disruptive behavior—for example, talking without permission, hitting other children, and leaving their desks. At the outset, these children averaged over one disruptive behavior per minute. After a baseline period, all the children—except those in the control group—received points for reducing their disruptive behavior Following this, two groups of children were trained to self-observe their disruptive actions, and they were awarded points if their counts were close to those made by an external observer. The children also lost points if there were major differences between the two counts. Some children then observed their own behavior, without having to agree with the external observer, and rewarded themselves for acting less disruptively.

The study illustrates some important points: (1) young children can readily learn to observe and reward their own actions; (2) self-management techniques can be just as effective as procedures controlled by others; and (3) well-designed experimental group studies of self-control are possible in natural settings such as the classroom.

Interestingly, there was considerable variability within each treatment group—that is, some children reduced their disruptive behavior much more than others did. Why this occurred is unclear. Further, the self-regulation group that continued self-observation during the final phase, when no points were given, was somewhat less disruptive than the others. Systematic self-observation may set the stage for evaluative self-reactions (see Articles Two and Nine).

Disruptive classroom behavior has often been the target of behavior modification technology. Many studies have demonstrated that rates of disruptive behavior can be substantially reduced by the systematic application of externally managed contingencies (e.g., Allen, Hart, Buell, Harris, and Wolf, 1964; Patterson, 1965; Homme, C'deBaca, Devine, Steinhorst, and Rickert, 1963; Schmidt and Ulrich, 1969; Wasik, Senn, Welch, and Cooper, 1969; O'Leary, Becker, Evans, and Saudargas, 1969; Thomas, Becker, and Armstrong, 1968). However, few attempts have been made to explore the utility of self-managed contingencies in affecting desirable behavior changes in the classroom setting.

Lovitt and Curtiss (1969) demonstrated the potential of self-regulation for increasing a student's academic response rate. They found that higher academic rates occurred when the pupil arranged the contingency requirements than when the teacher specified them. In another classroom study, Glynn (1970) found that self-determined reinforcement was as effective as experimenter-determined reinforcement in increasing academic response rate and that differential token reinforcement experience influenced subsequent rates of self-determined reinforcement. Several other studies conducted in laboratory settings have further suggested the potential utility of self-monitoring and self-reinforcement in the modification of behavior. The results of studies on self-administered reinforcement have consistently demonstrated that behavior may be modified and maintained as well with a self-administered token reinforcement system as with an externally managed reinforcement system. Marston and Kanfer (1963) found that self-reinforcement procedures were effective in maintaining previously learned verbal discriminations. Also, Bandura and Perloff (1967) demonstrated that self-managed reinforcement was as effective as externally managed reinforcement in maintaining effortful motor behavior with children. Furthermore, there is evidence that suggests that behaviors maintained by self-reinforcement may be more resistant to extinction than those maintained by external reinforcement (Kanfer and

Duerfeldt, 1967; Johnson, 1970; Johnson and Martin, 1972). Johnson and Martin (1972) have suggested that these results may be a result of the conditioning of self-evaluative responses as secondary reinforcers. These authors proposed that the secondary reinforcing properties of positive self-evaluation served to maintain children's attention to task in the absence of token reinforcers.

The present study attempted to apply self-regulation procedures to reduce disruptive behavior in the classroom. Within this context, the study was designed to test the relative effectiveness of self- and externally managed reinforcement systems during reinforcement and extinction.

Baseline observations on the frequency of three disruptive behaviors (talking out, aggression, and out-of-seat behaviors) were collected on the four most disruptive children in each of 10 classrooms. Following baseline, three of the four most disruptive children in each class received reinforcement for achieving low rates of disruptive behavior (external regulation). The fourth child served as a no-regulation (NR) control subject. Two of the three experimental subjects were then taught to self-observe their own disruptive behavior accurately. In the final reinforcement period, these subjects were given complete control over dispensing reinforcers to themselves (self-regulation, SR), based on their self-collected data. Subjects in the other experimental group (ER) continued with the externally managed reinforcement system. In extinction, reinforcement was discontinued for all subjects, but one of the self-regulation subjects in each of the classrooms continued overtly to self-observe.

Based upon the research cited above, it was hypothesized that self-regulation procedures would be as effective as externally managed procedures in maintaining low rates of disruptive behavior. It was also predicted, in light of Johnson (1970) and Johnson and Martin (1972), that the reduction in disruptive behaviors achieved through self-regulation procedures would be more resistant to extinction than that achieved through external regulation. The act of recording disruptive behaviors in the self-regulation procedure might be expected to have acquired conditioned aversive properties because rates above criteria levels have been previously consequated by response cost punishment (see Weiner, 1962), or the loss of a token reinforcer. On the other hand, recording rates below criteria levels might set the occasion for positive self-evaluation by virtue of its association with the receipt of token reinforcers. In extinction, the conditioned aversive or reinforcing properties of self-monitoring and self-evaluation were presumed to continue in the absence of primary reinforcement. These conditioned properties (aversive or reinforcing) were assumed to provide the mechanism by which the self-regulation procedures would retard extinction.

In order to increase the likelihood that self-monitoring and self-evaluation would occur during extinction, one of the two SR subjects in each class was asked overtly to self-observe during extinction. It was predicted that this group of subjects (Group SR_1) would demonstrate even greater resistance to extinction than the other SR subjects (Group SR_2) who were not required overtly to self-monitor in this phase. Without previous training in self-observation, it was expected that the ER group would show the least resistance to extinction of the three experimental groups. The predicted direction, then, of resistance to extinction was $SR_1>SR_2>ER$. All three groups were expected to have lower rates of disruptive behavior than the NR control group.

METHOD

Subjects

This experiment required the initial selection of disruptive students. Ten teachers of combination first- and second-grade classes in two schools were asked to pre-select six to eight of their students who typically emitted high rates of disruptive behavior. This group was observed for six days of pre-baseline and, on the basis of the resulting data, the four most disruptive students in each class were selected. The four subjects in each classroom were assigned to one of four groups. Restricted randomization procedures were used in assigning subjects to conditions in order to maximize the similarity of baseline averages. The experiment thus began with 40 subjects, 10 in each group. Any subject who did not emit 0.4 disruptive behaviors per minute or more during the subsequent baseline phase was dropped from the study. Also, subjects who were absent four or more successive days or for more than a total of six days during the study were not included. As a result of these a priori decision rules, seven subjects were dropped from the experiment, leaving nine subjects in the ER group and eight subjects in each of the SR and NR groups. Five subjects were later added in a new NR control group. The total number of subjects in the experiment was 38.

Experimental Setting

This experiment was conducted in five classrooms in each of two elementary schools of similar middle class socio-economic representation. A single observer was situated in each classroom in a position from which he could clearly see and hear each subject. An additional observer rotated among the five classes at each school to obtain observer-agreement data. All observers were uninformed regarding the hypotheses of the study and the assignment of subjects to conditions.

The experimental setting was defined by the situation in which the student was sitting in his desk and working independently on his assignment. Periods during which subjects were receiving individual attention from the teacher, or were involved in assigned activities that deviated from the experimental setting as defined, were not included in the sample. The experiment was conducted for one 30-min session per day for a period of eight weeks.

Procedure

An initial pre-baseline period of six sessions served both as a subject-selecting device and as a period of adaptation to the observers' presence. Immediately before baseline data were collected, teachers informed their classes that four named students would be involved in a university experiment and that the remainder of the class would not be included or involved. Phase I of the experiment constituted the measure of a baseline of disruptive behavior for subjects in all four groups. Before the five baseline sessions, all subjects were informed that observers would be counting the frequency of certain of their behaviors, which were then specified to them. Disruptive behaviors included:

1. Talking-out or making inappropriate noise without the permission of the teacher.
2. Hitting or physically annoying other students.
3. Leaving desk to do unassigned or inappropriate activities.

Pre-baseline analyses revealed that observers were capable of both simultaneously and continuously observing each of the four subjects in their classrooms on these salient categories of behavior with respectable observer agreement. Observers continued to count the frequency of disruptive behaviors for all subjects throughout the experiment. Observers recorded all occurrences of each disruptive category in 5-min time blocks. Given the above restrictions on the experimental setting, the average number of minutes each child was observed per day was 22 min. The total frequency of disruptive behaviors per day was divided by the total number of minutes observed on that day for each subject. The dependent variable was thus measured in terms of disruptive behaviors per minute.

The present experiment involved four phases beyond the baseline period. Some part of the treatment program was systematically changed in each phase for one or more groups. An outline of procedures for each phase is presented in Table 1.

Phase II of the experiment, lasting six sessions, immediately followed the baseline period and involved external regulation procedures for all three experimental groups. External regulation was defined as an external source evaluating behavior and dispensing reinforcement contingent upon that evaluation. In this ER condition, three arbitrary levels of disruptive behavior were designated:

1. Fewer than five disruptive behaviors.
2. Fewer than 10 disruptive behaviors.
3. More than 10 disruptive behaviors.

Subjects were instructed that if their behavior were at Level 1 during the session, they would receive eight points; if their behavior were at Level 2, they would receive four points; if their behavior were at Level 3, they would receive no points. Points were redeemable for reinforcements dispensed by the experimenter. Reinforcers were of a school-related nature and included pencils, erasers, notepads, *etc.* These reinforcers were placed in three boxes. With four points, a subject was allowed to choose out of a box labelled "4", which contained the least expensive reinforcers (less than 7¢). Eight points earned the choice of a prize from a box labelled "8", with slightly more expensive prizes (7¢ to 15¢). Subjects were also allowed to save points to earn children's readers (25¢) from a "12"-point box. Experimental subjects received points and chose prizes immediately after each session in the counselor's office to avoid jealousy of control subjects and classroom peers. All prizes were picked up by subjects at the end of the school day.

In Phase III, lasting seven sessions, two of the three experimental groups began training in self-regulation procedures. Self-regulation is here defined as the case in which the individual evaluates his own behavior and dispenses his own reinforcers contingent with previously learned criteria. The two SR groups were given self-observation cards and instructed in recording their own behavior within the three disruptive behavior categories. At the end of each session in Phase III, the SR groups' subjects' observation cards were matched against the observers' data to check on the subjects' accuracy. If a subject's self-observation rating was within a range of three disruptive behaviors above or below the observer's score, the subject received the equivalent number of points as dispensed in Phase II under the ER condition. If, however, a subject rated himself beyond the range of three disruptive behaviors above or below the observer's rating, the subject received two points less than he would have received for the coder's rating. These measures were added to improve the accuracy of self-observation. The ER and NR groups continued in Phase III with the same treatment as in Phase II.

In Phase IV, lasting seven sessions, both SR groups self-regulated independently, without checking accuracy with the observers. In this phase, the self-observation data constituted the sole determinant of the number of points SR subjects received, irrespective of the observers' ratings. The criteria for the dispensing of points were the same as in Phase II. Both ER and NR groups continued as before.

In Phase V, lasting seven sessions, subjects in all groups underwent extinction. Subjects in the experimental groups were informed by the experimenter that prizes were no longer obtainable. One SR group (SR₁) was asked to continue to self-observe their frequency of disruptive behaviors on the self-observation cards.

TABLE 1. Experiment Design: Treatment by Groups and Phases.

Groups	I	II	III	IV	V
ER	Baseline	ER	ER	ER	EXT
SR₁	Baseline	ER	SR*	SR	EXT**
SR₂	Baseline	ER	SR*	SR	EXT
NR	Baseline	NR	NR	NR	EXT

*Monitored
**Self-observation continued

An additional control group (Group 5) was added to the study when the experiment was conducted in the second school. This group was distinguished from the initial control group by having all its subjects in a single classroom. That is, there were no experimental subjects present in the Group 5 classroom.

RESULTS

The dependent variable in this study was the frequency of disruptive behaviors per minute. Observer agreement on this variable was measured by the correlation between the daily recorded frequencies of the regular observers and the observers who alternated between classes. The average Pearson Product Moment correlation over all five phases was 0.93. Figure 1 shows the mean number of disruptive

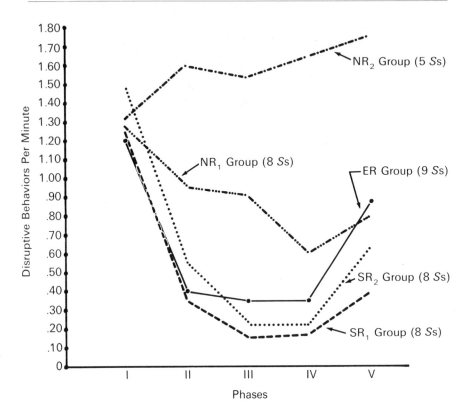

FIGURE 1. *Average Disruptive Behavior Per Minute of Groups.* During Phase I (baseline), disruptive behaviors were observed in class. During Phase II (external regulation), children in all experimental groups (ER, SR₁ and SR₂) were awarded points after class for fewer disruptions. During Phase III, ER group remained on external regulation while the self-regulation groups (SR₁ and SR₂) were trained to record and report their own behavior and were given points for accurate reports of fewer disruptions. Phase IV was the same as Phase III, except that points were given for children reporting few disruptions regardless of the accuracy of their reports. In Phase V (extinction), no points were given and only the SR₁ group was still required to record and report on their disruptive behavior.

behaviors per minute for each group in each of the five phases.[1] As will be clear from the ensuing presentation of these results, the group data reflect rather well the direction of change for the individual case.

[1]Individual subject data can be obtained from the authors on request.

Results were analyzed separately for each phase. In all phases beyond baseline, one-way analyses of variance were performed on the raw scores for that phase. Orthogonal comparisons were made between the three experimental and two control groups and between the two self-regulation groups and the one external regulation group, where appropriate. Summaries of individual subject data are also presented that provide a perspective on the magnitude and breadth of change.

Phase I: Baseline

A one-way analysis of variance on the mean rates of disruptive behaviors per minute across all five days of baseline revealed no significant differences between groups ($F < 1$, $df = 4,33$). Thus, all groups were essentially the same in their display of disruptive behavior before the experimental procedures were introduced.

Phase II: External Regulation

Analysis of raw score data in this phase showed a significant groups effect ($F = 6.35$, $df = 4,33$, $p < 0.01$). The orthogonal comparison between the three experimental and two control groups revealed a significant difference in favor of the experimental groups ($t = 4.75$, $df = 33$, $p < 0.01$). In this phase, 96% of the experimental subjects reduced their rate of disruptive behavior and 76% reduced their rate to less than one-half of their baseline level.

There was a noticeable reduction from the baseline in the number of disruptive behaviors for Control Group 4 in this and all subsequent treatment phases (see Figure 1). In Phases II, III, and IV, the frequency of disruptive behavior for Group 4 was reduced from baseline by 28%, 38%, and 54% respectively. This finding might partially be accounted for by the fact that 23% of the disruptive behaviors of these control subjects during baseline involved interactions with the experimental subjects in the same classroom. In the subsequent phases, however, only 7% of the disruptive behaviors in Group 4 involved interaction with subjects in the experimental groups. The subjects in Group 5 were all in a separate classroom in which no experimental subjects were present. This group did not show the same reduction from baseline level as did subjects in Control Group 4. Multiple comparisons using Duncan's New Multiple Range Test showed that Group 4 emitted a significantly lower rate of disruptive behaviors than Group 5 ($p < 0.05$) in this phase. There were no significant differences between these two groups in the previous baseline phase.

Phase III: Self-Regulation and External Regulation

One-way analysis of variance revealed a significant groups effect in Phase III ($F=12.49$, $df=4,33$, $p<0.01$). Again, an orthogonal contrast demonstrated that the three experimental groups had significantly lower rates of disruptive behavior than the two control groups ($t=6.88$, $df=33$, $p<0.001$). In this phase, 96% of the experimental subjects decreased their rate of disruptive behavior to less than one-half of their baseline level. And, 84% reduced their rates to less than one-third of baseline level.

An orthogonal comparison of the self-regulation and external regulation groups yielded no significant difference ($t=0.88$, $df=33$). That is, in Phase III, subjects who continued to receive ER treatment did not differ significantly in the raw score analysis from subjects who, in this phase, received training in SR procedures. Nonetheless, it was found that only 33% of the subjects in the ER condition decreased their disruptive rate from their Phase II level, whereas 88% of the subjects in the SR condition decreased their rate from the previous phase. Also, the SR groups averaged 42% less disruptive behavior in this phase than the ER group.

The subjects who received SR training were checked as to the accuracy of recording their frequency of disruptive behaviors. In Phase III, it was found that 75% of the subjects' self-observation ratings fell within the permissible range of plus or minus three disruptive behaviors as recorded by the experimenter. The median discrepancy between the subjects' ratings and the experimenter's was 2.07 disruptive behaviors. Forty-four per cent of the discrepancies were in the direction of underestimation by the subjects; 28% of the discrepancies represented overestimation; and 27% of the accuracy checks showed the subjects and the experimenter to be in perfect agreement.

Subjects in the SR condition in Phase III were fined two points for inaccuracy of ratings that did not fall within the permissible range of plus or minus three disruptive behaviors as recorded by the observer. An average of 6.1 points per day was obtained by SR subjects in this phase, which is contrasted by an average figure of 6.4 points that could have been earned had fines not been imposed. As such, the subjects in the SR groups received only 5% less points than they would have without the two-point fine for inaccuracy. The ER group in

Phase III earned an average of 5.3 points per day. There were no significant differences between the ER and SR groups in terms of number of points received in Phase III ($t=1.04$, $df=23$), in spite of slightly lower rates of disruptive behavior and fines for inaccuracy for the SR groups.

Group 4 continued to emit a significantly lower rate of disruptive behaviors than Group 5 in this phase ($p<0.01$), as revealed by Duncan's New Multiple Range Test.

Phase IV: Self-Regulation and External Regulation

Analysis of variance for means in Phase IV revealed a significant groups effect ($F=17.73$, $df=4,33$, $p<.01$). As in the previous two phases, an orthogonal comparison indicated that the three experimental groups differed significantly from the two control groups ($t=7.22$, $df=33$, $p<0.001$). An orthogonal contrast comparing raw score means of self-regulation and external regulation groups revealed no significant difference ($t=0.98$, $df=33$).

It can readily be seen from Figure 1 that all three experimental groups maintained the same rates of disruptive behavior in Phase IV as they had in Phase III. Again, 96% of the experimental subjects continued to maintain their rate of disruptive behavior in Phase IV at a level less than one-half of their baseline rate; and 80% maintained at a level less than one-third of their baseline rate. The breakdown of these experimental groups in Phase IV revealed that 89% of the ER subjects reduced their rate of disruptive behavior to less than one-half of baseline level; 67% reduced their rate to less than one-third of baseline level. In the SR groups, 100% of the subjects reduced their rate to less than one-half of baseline levels and 92% less than one-third baseline levels. In this phase, the SR groups averaged 39% fewer disruptive behaviors than the ER group.

Although the subjects in the two SR groups were neither informed of nor rewarded for self-observation accuracy in this phase, 71% of the subjects' self-observation ratings fell within the range of plus or minus three disruptive behaviors as recorded by the experimenter. The median discrepancy between the subjects' ratings and the experimenter's was 1.75 disruptive behaviors. As in the previous phase, the majority of the discrepancies were in the direction of underestimation of disruptive behavior by the subjects. Forty-five per cent of the discrepancies represented underestimation, 21% represented overestimation, and 34% of the accuracy checks showed perfect agreement between observers and subjects.

In Phase IV, subjects in the ER condition earned and received an average of 5.7 points per daily session. It was found that the SR subjects awarded themselves an average of 7.4 points per session, whereas their corresponding rates of disruptive behavior merited only 6.4 points. That is, SR subjects received an average of 16% more points than they deserved. An examination of the individual subject data indicates that this discrepancy between points awarded and deserved was accounted for by fewer than half of the subjects involved. More specifically, nine of the 16 SR subjects consistently awarded themselves veridically. Two subjects tended to over-reward themselves by approximately one point per day, while five others awarded themselves considerably more points per day than were earned (2.5 points or more). The nine accurate SR subjects obtained significantly lower rates of disruptive behavior than the seven inaccurate subjects ($t=2.61$, $df=14$). It should also be pointed out that these nine subjects were not significantly lower in disruptive rates at baseline ($t=1.14$, $df=14$) than the seven inaccurate subjects.

Multiple comparisons using Duncan's New Multiple Range Test again revealed that control Group 4 emitted significantly fewer disruptive behaviors than control Group 5 ($p<0.001$).

Phase V: Extinction

An additional observer was introduced in each school in this phase. This observer also alternated between classes to provide additional observer agreement data. This observer was totally naive as to the previous four phases and thereby had no opportunity to infer hypotheses or establish bias. The average Pearson Product Moment correlation between the daily rates obtained by the naive observers and the regular observers was 0.93 in Phase V. An average correlation between the regular alternating observers and the observers who remained in the same class was 0.98 in this phase.

During Phase V, the predicted direction of resistance to extinction was $SR_1>SR_2>ER$ and, it was predicted that all three experimental groups would have lower rates of disruptive behavior than the NR control condition. A trend analysis on this predicted direction obtained significance ($t=3.17$, $df=33$, $p<0.01$).

A significant main effect for groups was obtained in Phase V in the raw score analysis ($F=4.11$, $df=4,33$, $p<0.01$). Three orthogonal comparisons were performed on these Phase V raw score results. The first comparison revealed that the three experimental groups continued to be lower in rate of disruptive behavior than the two control groups even in the absence of reinforcement ($t=2.99$, $df=33$, $p<0.01$). The second comparison indicated that the two SR groups were not significantly lower in raw score disruptive rates than the ER group during extinction ($t=1.31$, $df=33$). The third comparison showed that Group 2 (SR_1), whose subjects continued to self-observe during extinction, was not significantly lower ($t=0.50$, $df=33$) than Group 3 (SR_2).

While the analyses given above test the significance of observed differences in the extinction period, they do not test differences in resistance to extinction. The following analyses were performed to analyze that question.

Two orthogonal comparisons were performed on the difference scores derived by Phase IV subtracted from Phase V. These analyses revealed that there were no significant differences between the ER group and the two SR groups in terms of increased rate of disruptive behaviors from the last phase of treatment to extinction ($t=0.85$, $df=33$) and that there were no significant differences between the two SR groups ($t=0.80$, $df=33$).

Repeated measures analysis of variance performed across the seven days of Phase V, with the mean of Phase IV as the starting point, provided a measure of resistance to extinction for the three experimental groups. This analysis revealed a significant trials effect ($F=2.39$, $df=7,154$, $p<0.05$), reflecting extinction over trials but no main effects for groups ($F=1.18$, $df=2,22$) or for the groups by trials interaction ($F=0.74$, $df=14,154$). The three experimental groups, then, did not extinguish differentially during this period.

During extinction, 56% of the ER subjects maintained their reduced rate of disruptive behavior at less than one-half of their baseline level whereas, for the subjects in the two SR groups, 69% maintained at or below one-half of their baseline level. Only 22% of the subjects in the ER group maintained their reduced rate at less than one-third their baseline level, while 56% of the subjects in the two SR groups maintained at or below one-third of their baseline level. As in the previous phase, the SR groups averaged 39% fewer disruptive behaviors than the ER group, even in the absence of reinforcement. And, the SR_1 group, which continued to self-observe during extinction, averaged 53% fewer disruptive behaviors than the ER group.

The superiority of control Group 4 over Group 5 was maintained at a significant level ($p<0.01$) in this phase (Duncan's New Multiple Range Test).

An examination of Figure 1 reveals that the two SR groups consistently averaged less disruptive behavior than the ER group in Phases III, IV, and V. Summaries of individual data also indicate that the SR groups reduced their rate of disruptive behavior from baseline more than the ER groups in all three of these phases. Nevertheless, orthogonal comparisons on the raw scores analyses of variance do not reflect any superiority of the SR condition. Because of the large within-group variability in rates of disruptive behavior evidenced in these comparisons, difference score analyses were also conducted. Between-subject (within groups) .variability is reduced by difference scores analyses in that difference scores can control for initial baseline differences.

Orthogonal comparisons on the difference score analyses of variance reveals that the SR groups did not reduce their rate of disruptive behavior significantly more than the ER group in Phase II ($t=1.17$, $df=33$). This is as expected because both conditions received the same external reinforcement treatment in this phase. But, in the next two phases, representing different treatment conditions, the SR groups were found to have reduced their disruptive behavior rate significantly more from baseline than the ER group (Phase III: $t=2.50$, $df=33$, $p<0.05$; Phase IV: $t=2.32$, $df=33$, $p<0.05$). This greater reduction for SR groups persisted in Phase V, extinction ($t=2.49$, $df=33$, $p<0.05$). These findings should be qualified by acknowledging that there are a number of important problems with difference scores, two of the most critical being the reliability of the differences and possible correlation of differences with pre-treatment scores (Lord, 1967).

DISCUSSION

In all phases after baseline, the experimental groups exhibited significantly lower rates of disruptive behavior than the control groups. Clearly, both the external and self-regulation procedures were effective in establishing and maintaining reductions in disruptive behavior.

It was hypothesized that self-regulation procedures would be as effective as externally managed procedures in maintaining low rates of disruptive behavior. Figure 1 indicates that not only were the self-regulation procedures as effective as externally managed procedures but that they were slightly more effective in producing consistently lower rates from their introduction in Phase III through extinction in Phase V. Throughout each of these three phases, the two self-regulation groups evidenced an average of roughly 40% fewer disruptive behaviors than the externally managed group. In spite of this apparent superiority of the self-regulation procedures, significant differences between this condition and the external management condition were not obtained upon direct comparison of raw score data. Large within-group or between-subject variability characterizes these group comparisons. Difference-score analyses, which control for this variability problem, demonstrate a significant superiority for the self-regulation procedures over the external regulation procedures in terms of greater reductions from baseline levels. As previously indicated, however, difference scores are difficult to interpret in group comparisons, due to a number of inherent problems in their analysis. Thus, while a slight superiority for the self-regulation procedures is indicated by the data, differences between the two conditions were not found to be significant upon direct comparison. Therefore, the hypothesis that self- and externally managed procedures would be equally effective in maintaining low rates of disruptive behavior was essentially supported.

Crucial to the effectiveness of any self-regulation procedure is the accuracy of self-observation. It is an encouraging finding in this study that most of the first- and second-grade children deemed disruptive by their teachers and a screening procedure, were capable of self-observing their frequency of disruptive behavior with respectable accuracy. This is especially noteworthy in that the SR subjects did not receive immediate feedback as to their accuracy in training and no feedback during Phase IV and extinction. This relatively high degree of accuracy in self-observation for young children is congruent with other findings (Johnson, 1970; Johnson and Martin, 1972).

It is also crucial to the effectiveness of any self-regulation procedure that subjects reward themselves appropriately. In Phase IV of this study, subjects in the SR condition exercised control over dispensing points to themselves, independent of the observers' data. These subjects had the opportunity to receive more points than they deserved, simply by not recording all occurrences of their disruptive behavior. The previous literature on self-reinforcement suggests that when subjects take over the task of dispensing their own reinforcements, only minimal average increases in reinforcement delivery occur (Kanfer and Duerfeldt, 1967; Johnson, 1970; Johnson and Martin, 1972). The present study revealed that the SR subjects received an average of 7.4 points per session, whereas their rates of disruptive behavior merited only 6.4 points, representing an average daily discrepancy of one point. The results indicate that this discrepancy was accounted for primarily by seven SR subjects who reported inaccurate self-observation data. The remaining nine subjects recorded accurately in this phase and consistently awarded themselves exactly the number of points they deserved. It is obvious that discrepancies in points received *vs* deserved are not consistent across subjects. It is also obvious that this average one-point per day error in reinforcement delivery is inconsequential for purposes of application.

The fact that SR subjects in Phase IV had the opportunity to receive more points than their actual behavior merited has important implications for considering differences in the SR condition *vs* the ER condition. As long as subjects in the SR condition accurately observe and thereby reinforce their behavior contingently, consistent with the same criteria as the ER group, there is no differential advantage for the SR condition. However, when an SR subject awards himself more points than he deserves, a magnitude of reinforcement confound exists in that this subject receives more than his counterpart in the ER condition. This potential confound is problematic for the ER *vs* SR comparison in Phase IV, particularly for the seven inaccurate SR subjects. An important consideration for the application of self-regulation procedures is whether or not this potential discrepancy in points received *vs* merited results in increments in disruptive behavior rate. It is interesting that the SR subjects did not evidence higher rates of disruptive behavior in Phase IV, relative to Phase II or relative to the ER group, when they had the opportunity to receive points independent of their actual behavior.

The second hypothesis predicted that the reduction in disruptive behaviors achieved through self-regulation procedures would be more resistant to extinction than that achieved through external regulation. Even though the groups were aligned in the predicted direction in the extinction period with $SR_1 < SR_2 < ER$, greater resistance to extinction was not clearly evident from these data. It appears that the slight superiority of the SR groups in extinction, previously described, can be accounted for almost entirely by their superiority in the two former periods. This interpretation is substantiated by the nonsignificant findings in the repeated measures analysis of the extinction data. It should also be pointed out that the resistance to extinction comparison between the two procedures was confounded by different magnitudes of reinforcement received by SR and ER groups. This confounding could have been averted by yoking or matching the amount of reinforcement delivered to the ER subjects with the amount that SR subjects dispensed to themselves. However, ER subjects, receiving yoked reinforcement, might learn that the amount of reinforcement they received was unrelated to their actual behavior. The confounding influence of this operation was viewed as far more serious than the anticipated minor differences in receipt of token points.

The resistance to extinction predictions were based on assumptions about the conditioned aversive and reinforcing properties of both overt and covert self-observation and self-evaluation during extinction. It was believed that children in the self-regulation groups would continue more overt (SR$_1$) and covert (SR$_2$) self-observation and self-evaluation than would children in the ER group and that these behaviors would retard extinction. While there appears to be no support for this line of reasoning in the direct comparison of the ER groups with the combined SR groups, there may be some weak support for it in the comparisons of the two SR groups. The SR children who continued overtly to self-monitor in extinction displayed 23% less deviant behavior in extinction than those who were not asked to continue self-monitoring. This superiority does not appear to be due to any appreciable prior advantage (see Figure 1) nor is it related to different magnitudes of reinforcement. The significance of the directional prediction also lends weak support to the superiority of the SR group, whose members continued to self-monitor during extinction. Another possible explanation for these differences in extinction might be that the continuing presence of the observers served as a cue to remain well-behaved for the SR$_1$ subjects. The earlier accuracy checking in Phase III may have had some continuing effect on the subjects' behavior. However, this seems unlikely given that SR subjects were not checked for inaccuracy in the intervening seven days of Phase IV. While the SR$_1$ vs SR$_2$ differences were not of great magnitude nor statistically significant on direct comparison, it appears to be a noteworthy finding consistent with the conditioned reinforcement hypothesis.

An unexpected finding in this study was the marked decline in disruptive behavior for the control subjects who were present in the same classrooms as the experimental subjects. One possible explanation is that when the disruptive behavior of three of the four most disruptive students in a class is substantially reduced, this will have a dampening or a spread effect on the fourth student. Some evidence for this explanation was provided in that control subjects had fewer disruptive interactions with the experimental subjects during the treatment phases than they did during baseline. An alternative explanation is that the control subjects may have discovered that the other subjects in their classrooms were getting reinforcers at the end of the school day for low rates of disruptive behavior. This knowledge may have set the occasion for vicarious reinforcement or fruitless attempts also to earn reinforcement by emitting low rates of disruptive behavior. The interpretation that the reduction in Group 4 had something to do with the presence of treatment in the classrooms is borne out by the comparison of Group 4 with Group 5 in which no such reduction was observed. The significantly lower rate of disruptive behavior for Group 4 represents an important finding in suggesting that the modification of disruptive children in the classroom may have suppressive effects on other disruptive children in the same classroom. Indeed, it is possible that the whole social system in the classroom is affected by intervention with selected children.

The findings of this investigation have important implications for the applied use of self-regulation in the classroom. It appears that self-regulation procedures can be as effective, if not slightly more effective, than external regulation procedures for this population. Disruptive children in the first and second grade have been determined to be quite capable of self-observing and recording their own disruptive behavior with impressive accuracy. Perhaps the simple act of self-recording disruptive behaviors accounted for the slight superiority of the self-regulation groups. The act of self-recording would seem to have the advantage of more immediate loss of reinforcement signals with greater consistency than would the recording of an observer or teacher with external regulation procedures. Furthermore, most children in self-regulation appear capable of self-observing their own behavior, and thereby applying designated contingencies, without the monitoring of an external agent.

In terms of teacher time and effort, self-regulation procedures have the advantage of being more practical and less expensive. Although these procedures might initially require as much teacher involvement as externally managed procedures, it is apparent that a good deal of the responsibility of monitoring a child's disruptive behavior can be turned over to the child, without substantial increases in disruptive rate. It may be necessary for the teacher occasionally to check the accuracy of a child's monitoring, but it is apparent that this procedure would, nevertheless, require less time and effort than the continuous monitoring of a child with external procedures.

In general, the results of this and other investigations (Johnson, 1970; Johnson and Martin, 1972; Lovitt and Curtiss, 1969; Glynn, 1970) are clear. Self-regulation procedures appear to be either equally effective or more effective than external regulation procedures in both establishing and maintaining desired changes in behavior. Furthermore, it appears that most children of this age are capable of self-monitoring their own behavior and applying designated contingencies. It is concluded that self-regulation procedures provide a practical, inexpensive, and powerful alternative to external procedures.

THE EFFECT OF SELF-RECORDING ON THE CLASSROOM BEHAVIOR OF TWO EIGHTH-GRADE STUDENTS

Marcia Broden, R. Vance Hall, Brenda Mitts

One of the most interesting studies of self-observation was reported by Broden, Hall, and Mitts. These investigators, working with two eighth-grade students in a "real-life" setting, demonstrated that systematic self-monitoring could dramatically alter behavior. The study carefully examined what happened when a person was asked to observe certain actions over a relatively long time period. The study is noteworthy for several reasons: (1) it used an intensive $(N=1)$ research design with a "reversal" procedure—that is, a procedure in which the influence of a factor is investigated by systematically presenting and withdrawing that factor (see Chapter Three); (2) it illustrated the indirect relationship of self-observation reliability to observed behavior change; (3) it suggested the power of systematic self-observation to alter the person's environment and thereby to support the changed behavior; and (4) it clearly demonstrated the short-lived effects of self-observation on behavior *without* other changes in the environment.

One of the interesting findings was that a simple recording proce-

From *Journal of Applied Behavior Analysis,* 1971, **4**(3), 191-199. Copyright 1971 by the Society for the Experimental Analysis of Behavior, Inc. Reprinted by permission.

dure—making a mark on a slip of paper—gradually became a "cue" for the person to engage in the desired behavior without actually having to mark the slip. However, when the slip of paper was not used, the person's behavior tended to return to the level that it was at before self-observation was started. The study suggests that highly accurate and reliable self-observation may not be essential in changing behavior. Additional studies employing the type of design used by these investigators are needed if the processes of self-observation are to be more fully understood.

Helping a student acquire appropriate study behaviors has probably been a problem since schools began. Various techniques, including counseling, special classes, and use of the leather strap have been tried. Very often these approaches have been ineffective and parents, teachers, and students have resigned themselves to a year of problems and frustration.

Since the 1960s, a concerted effort has been exerted to apply systematically behavior modification principles in the public school classroom. A number of studies have shown that giving attention for a behavior immediately after it occurred caused this behavior to increase in strength, while consistently ignoring a behavior frequently resulted in a decrease in strength. Hall and Broden (1967), Hall, Lund, and Jackson (1968), and Thomas, Becker, and Armstrong (1968) successfully used this technique to affect study behavior in the classroom by having teachers attend only to study or non-disruptive behaviors while ignoring non-study or disruptive ones. Hall, Fox, Willard, Goldsmith, Emerson, Owen, Davis, and Porcia (1971) used teacher attention, feedback, praise, and other available reinforcers to control disputing and talking-out behaviors in various classrooms.

The use of behavior modification principles was expanded to include varied techniques by other experimenters. Madsen, Becker, and Thomas (1968) assessed the effect of rules as well as ignoring and praising behaviors. Peer control of arithmetic and spelling scores was demonstrated in a study by Evans and Oswalt (1967). Barrish, Saunders, and Wolf (1969) used a loss of classroom privileges to reduce out-of-seat and talking-out behaviors in a fourth grade class. Hall, Panyan, Rabon, and Broden (1968) showed that teacher attention, a study game, and loss of time for a between-period break were effective in increasing an entire class's study behavior.

McKenzie, Clark, Wolf, Kothera, and Benson (1968) used a token system backed by privileges and allowances to increase academic performance in a special education classroom. Broden, Hall, Dunlap, and Clark (1970) increased study behavior in a junior high special education class using a point system in which points were redeemable for privileges available in the class and school. They demonstrated that while praise was effective in modifying behaviors, praise coupled with points issued contingently for acceptable behaviors seemed more effective at the junior high level.

Each of the methods listed, while successful, involved a relatively systematic effort on the part of the teacher to initiate the behavior change or to monitor and reinforce the desired behaviors. None of these studies dealt with the problem of what to do with a student in a room where the teacher does not want to or "cannot" work with a specific student. Such situations are often found in secondary level classrooms where teacher lectures are a primary form of instruction.

The method used in the present study was self-recording. It was initially an effort to assess whether a subject's recording of his own behavior would help increase or decrease its occurrence, and whether someone not in the classroom could modify classroom behavior. It was also an attempt to assess a procedure whereby self-recording could be withdrawn with no significant decrease in study once higher study rates had been established.

EXPERIMENT I

Subject and Setting.   Liza was an eighth-grade girl enrolled in a history class at Bonner Springs Junior High, Bonner Springs, Kansas. She was doing poorly in history (her grade was a D−) and had told the counselor she was interested in doing better in school. The counselor set up weekly counseling sessions with Liza but found that according to the teacher and to Liza, just talking over a problem had not carried over into the class setting.

Liza's history class met daily immediately after lunch for 40 min. The teacher, a young man, stood near the front of the room throughout most of the period. Liza sat toward the back of the room. Classes were primarily lecture sessions in which the teacher talked as he stood in the front of the class. There was some class discussion when the teacher interspersed questions within the lecture.

The counselor and the experimenter had approached the teacher about giving increased attention to Liza for study. The teacher expressed a willingness to cooperate but felt that due to the lecture format of the class and the amount of material he had to cover each day he could not consistently attend to Liza for studying. For this reason it was decided to use self-recording with the counselor as the agent for initiating and carrying out the experimental procedures.

Observation.   An observer entered the classroom during a 5-min break before the class and took a seat at the back of the room. She observed for 30 min of the 40-min session, beginning when the bell rang to signify the start of class. She left during a break at the end of the class session. Pupil behaviors were recorded at the end of each 10 sec of observation. Teacher attention to Liza was recorded whenever it occurred. Liza was not told that she was being observed.

Pupil behaviors were dichotomized into study and non-study behaviors. "Study" was defined as attending to a teacher-assigned task and meant that when it was appropriate, Liza should be facing the teacher, writing down lecture notes, facing a child who was responding to a teacher question, or reciting when called upon by the teacher. "Non-study" behaviors meant that Liza was out of her seat without permission, talking out without being recognized by the teacher, facing the window, fingering non-academic objects such as her makeup, comb, purse, or working on an assignment for another class.

Data were recorded on sheets composed of double rows of squares with each square representing the passage of 10 sec of time. (See Hall, *et al.*, 1968). The top row was used to record teacher attention which was recorded whenever the teacher called on or spoke to Liza. The bottom row was used to record Liza's study or non-study behaviors.

Reliability checks were made at least once during each phase of the study. During these checks, another observer made simultaneous and independent observations. After the observation the sheets were compared and scored interval by interval for the number of intervals of agreement. The total number of intervals of agreement were divided by the total number of intervals observed and this figure was multiplied by 100 to obtain a percentage figure. Agreement of the records for this study ranged from 87 to 96% for study behavior and 100% for teacher attention.

Method

Baseline.   Baseline data were recorded for seven days before experimental procedures began. The counselor saw the subject twice during this time for a weekly conference (a procedure followed before recording data and continued throughout the study).

Self-Recording[1].   On the eighth day of observation, the counselor met the subject in conference and gave her a slip containing three rows of 10 squares (see Fig. 1) and directed her to record her study behavior "when she thought of it" during her history class

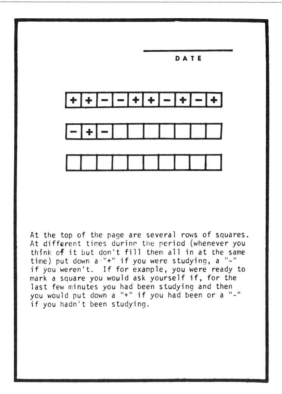

FIGURE 1.   Sample of Self-Recording Sheet Used by Liza.

sessions. Some aspects of study behavior were discussed at this time, including a definition of what constituted studying.

Liza was instructed to take the slip to class each day and to record a "+" in the square if she was studying or had been doing so for the last few minutes, and a "—" if she was not studying at the time she thought to record. Sometime before the end of the school day she was to turn it in to the counselor. The slips were available each day from the counselor and could be obtained during breaks between classes. At the weekly pupil-counselor conference, the self-recording slips were discussed and the counselor praised Liza's reports of study behavior, emphasizing the days when the per cent of plus marks was high.

Baseline2.   Slips were not issued for five days (Days 14 through 18). When, on the second day of Baseline2, Liza requested one, the counselor stated that she was out of slips and would tell her when she got more.

Self-Recording₂.   Slips were once again handed to the subject by the counselor at some time before history period and Liza was instructed to record her study and non-study behavior.

Self-Recording Plus Praise.   The teacher was asked to attend to Liza "whenever he could" and to praise her for study whenever possible. Slips for self-recording continued to be available to Liza and counselor praise continued to be issued for plus marks on the self-recording slips during the weekly conference.

Praise Only.   No slips were issued to Liza. Teacher attention continued at a higher rate than during Baseline.

Baseline₃.   Increased teacher attention was withdrawn.

Results

Baseline.   Figure 2 presents a record of Liza's study behavior and of teacher verbal attention. During baseline conditions, Liza had a low rate of study (30%) despite two conferences with the counselor and promises to "really try." The mean rate of teacher attention was two times per session.

Self-Recording₁.   During the Self-Recording₁ phase, when Liza began to record her classroom behavior, a significant change in study behavior was noted. It increased to 78% and remained at that approximate level for the next six days. Teacher attention remained at a mean level of two times per session.

Baseline₂.   On the fourteenth day of observation, Liza was told by the counselor that no more recording slips were available. The first day under these conditions the rate of study was 70%. It then dropped to an average of 27% for the next four days. Teacher attention averaged 2.5 times per session.

Self-Recording₂.   When recording slips were again issued to Liza her study rate increased to an average of 80%. However, when on two days no slips were issued (Days 20 and 27) the rate declined to 30% and 22% respectively. During this phase, the teacher gave Liza attention approximately 1.7 times per class session.

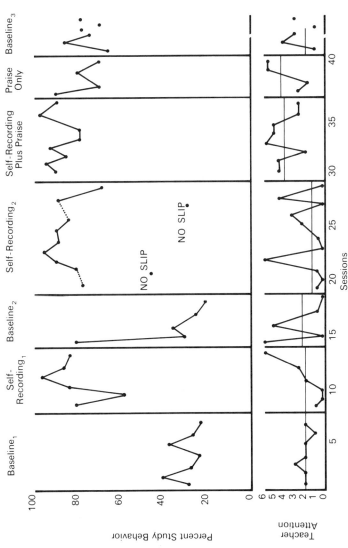

FIGURE 2. A record of Liza's study behavior and/or teacher attention for study during: Baseline₁—before experimental procedures; Self-Recording₁—Liza recorded study or non-study on slips provided by counselor; Baseline₂—Self-recording slips withdrawn; Self-Recording₂—Self-recording slips reinstated; Self-Recording Plus Praise—Self-recording slips continued and teacher praise for study increased; Praise Only—Increased teacher praise maintained and self-recording withdrawn. Baseline₃—Teacher praise decreased to baseline levels.

Self-Recording Plus Praise.   On Day 30, the teacher was again asked to praise Liza or give her increased attention when she studied. At this point the teacher agreed to do so because Liza was now engaging in a higher rate of study and he felt it would be easy and justifiable to do so. In this phase, teacher attention increased to 3.5 times per session. Liza continued to carry slips to class, sometimes filling them out and sometimes not. Under these conditions study increased to 88%.

Praise Only.   On Day 38 the Praise Only phase was begun and slips discontinued. Teacher attention was observed to be at a mean rate of 3.7 times per session. Liza's study rate averaged 77%.

Baseline₃.   The teacher was then asked to decrease the amount of attention to Liza. During this Baseline₃ phase, no marked decrease in study rate was evident, though there was some decline. The first three joined points of the Baseline₃ phase represent consecutive days following the Praise Only phase. The three separated points represent post-check days with approximately one-week intervals between observations, which further indicates increased study was being maintained.

Subject's Record Vs. Observer's Record.   Table I presents the levels of study recorded by Liza and the observer during the Self-Recording phases. During the Self-Recording₁ phase, Liza recorded study or nonstudy on the average of 12 times per session. There was very little correlation between Liza's and the observer's estimates of the per cent of study on a day-to-day basis. Variations between records ranged up to 29%. However, the means of the overall subject-observer records were similar. For example, the mean of Liza's estimate of her study behavior during Baseline was 76%. The observer's record revealed that Liza actually studied an average of 78% of the time.

During the Self-Recording₂ phase, the number of times Liza recorded decreased to 11 marks per class. On four days she did not record at all. Liza's mean estimate of her study was 81%, the observer's was 80%. Again, there was little correlation between Liza's record and the observer's record on a day-to-day basis.

The number of times Liza recorded during the Self-Recording Plus Praise condition declined markedly to 2.3 times per session and Liza recorded on only three of the nine days during this experimental phase. Liza's mean estimate of study was 89%, that of the observer was 88%.

There was, of course, no self-recording during the other phases of the experiment.

TABLE 1.   A Record of Per Cent of Study Recorded by the Observer and by Liza during Self-Recording Phases of Exp. I.

Experimental Phase	Observer	Liza
Self-Recording$_1$	78%	80%
	54%	70%
	79%	—
	92%	63%
	82%	79%
	80%	90%
Mean	**78%**	**76%**
Self-Recording$_2$	75%	60%
	Probe "A"	
	78%	100%
	87%	80%
	90%	FORGOT
	84%	FORGOT
	84%	FORGOT
	79%	75%
	Probe "B"	
	83%	90%
	59%	FORGOT
Mean	**80%**	**81%**
Self-Recording$_3$ Plus Praise	89%	FORGOT
	93%	FORGOT
	83%	FORGOT
	92%	FORGOT
	81%	66%
	81%	100%
	96%	FORGOT
	88%	100%
Mean	**88%**	**89%**

EXPERIMENT II

Subject and Setting.   The second subject, Stu, was an eighth-grade boy enrolled in a fifth-period math class at the same school. He was referred by his teacher, a man, who expressed a desire to find some means to "shut Stu up." He reportedly talked out in class continually, disturbing both the teacher and his classmates. The class was composed of 28 "low" achieving students. It met for 25 min and then students went to lunch, returning afterward for another 20 min of class.

Observation.   Observation records of Stu's behavior were made on sheets identical to those used in the previous experiment. The category of "talking out" was added, however, to the observation code. A talk out was defined as any verbalization that occurred during class which had not been recognized by the teacher and was recorded if it occurred at any time within each 10-sec interval. Since some of Stu's talk outs were not audible to the observer, both audible talk outs and instances when Stu's lips moved while facing another student and while another student was facing him were considered as talk outs. Study behavior and teacher attention to the subject were also recorded. Reliability of observation during each experimental phase was assessed in a manner similar to that used in the first study. Agreement of the records on the number of talk outs ranged from 84 to 100%.

Method

Baseline[1].   For nine days before experimental procedures were initiated, data were recorded during the first half (Session A) of the period. On Days 1, 4, 5, 6, and 8 data were recorded during the second half of the period (Session B) as well.

Self-Recording, Session A.   During the first experimental phase, the teacher handed a slip of paper to Stu at the beginning of class with the instructions to use it and that it would be collected during lunch. A facsimile of the slip is shown in Fig. 3. On it was printed a rectangular box about 2 by 5 in. (5 by 12.5 cm) and the statement "record a mark every time you talk out without permission." At the top of the slip was a place for the subject's name and the date. No further instructions were given.

Self-Recording, Session B.   Slips were not issued during Session A but were given to Stu just before Session B. No contingencies were in effect during Session A.

Self-Recording (Sessions A and B)[1].   Stu was given the slip at the beginning of class and told to record all period (both Session A and Session B). He was told the slip would be collected at the end of class.

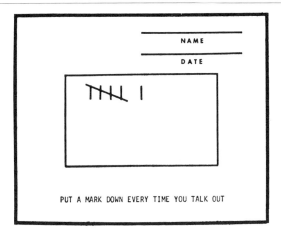

FIGURE 3. Sample of Self-Recording Sheet Used by Stu.

Baseline₂. Self-recording slips were not issued for any part of the math period.

Self-Recording (Sessions A and B)₂. Self-recording slips were issued and Stu was told to record talk outs for the entire period and that the slips would be collected at the end of class.

Results

Baseline₁. During the Baseline phase, Stu talked out on the average of 1.1 times per minute for the first half of the period and 1.6 times a minute during Session B. (See Fig. 4.)

Self-Recording, Session A. When the teacher began issuing slips to Stu for Session A, the frequency of his talk outs declined during Session A to 0.3 times a minute. The frequency of these talk outs during Session B, however, remained at 1.6 times a minute.

Self-Recording, Session B. After giving Stu the sheet seven days for Session A the teacher commented that "it is the second half of the period which has always been the problem," so contingencies were reversed. Slips were issued only during the second half of the period. The rate of verbalizing without permission during Session B declined to 0.5 times a minute. However, the rate of talking out during Session A, which was not under self-recording contingencies, increased to 1.2 times a minute.

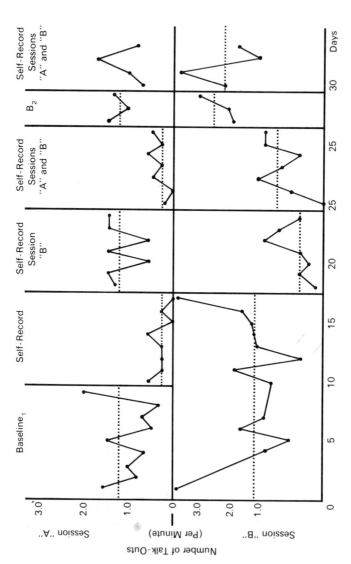

FIGURE 4. A Record of Stu's Talking-Out Behavior during Sessions A and B of Fifth-Period Math Class. Baseline₁ —Before experimental procedures; Self-Record, Session A— Stu recorded his talk outs during Session A only; Self-Record, Session B—Stu recorded his talk outs during Session B only; Self-Record, Sessions (A and B)₁—Stu recorded his talk outs during both math class sessions; Baseline₂—Return to Baseline conditions, self-recording slips withdrawn; Self-Record (A and B)₂—Stu recorded his talk outs for both A and B Sessions.

*Self-Recording (Sessions A and B)*₁. When slips were issued for both A and B Sessions, the mean talk-out rate during A was 0.3 times per minute while that for B was 1.0 per minute, both well below baseline rates that were recorded.

*Baseline*₂. When slips were no longer furnished Stu during a second baseline phase, the rate of talk outs increased to a mean of 1.3 during Session A and 2.3 per minute during Session B.

*Self-Recording (Sessions A and B)*₂. When self-recording slips were again issued for the entire period, there was a slight but not significant decrease in the number of talk outs to a mean rate of 1.0 per minute in Session A and 2.2 per minute in Session B.

DISCUSSION

These studies indicated that it is possible to use self-recording procedures to modify behaviors of pupils in secondary-level public school classrooms. In Liza's case, self-recording was used to increase an appropriate behavior (study) while in Stu's case self-recording proved effective in decreasing an inappropriate behavior (talking out).

In the experiment with Liza, someone outside the classroom, a counselor, was able to institute procedures that brought about an increase in study to a point that the teacher was able to maintain it with his attention and/or the other reinforcers already available in the classroom. Previous research had shown that systematic teacher attention can be used to increase study rates of elementary pupils (Hall, *et al.*, 1968; Hall, *et al.*, 1968). Broden and Hall (1968) demonstrated that teacher attention was also effective at the junior high school level. There were indications, however, that secondary level teachers were sometimes reluctant to carry out procedures that did not seem to fit their teaching style.

In Liza's case, initially the teacher did not feel that he could systematically increase his attention for study due to the lecture-discussion format he used. On the first day of Baseline₂, however, when the self-recording slips had been withdrawn, Liza's study behavior had remained at a high level. An analysis of the data showed that she had received an uncharacteristically high rate of attention from the teacher on that day (five times). This indicated that it might eventually be possible to withdraw the slips and maintain high study rates and that the teacher might willingly increase his attention to Liza for study if her study rate was already at a high level. The drop in study rate on the second day and subsequent days of Baseline₂ indicated that Liza was still very much under the control of self-recording.

The effect of issuing self-recording slips was further confirmed in the Self-Recording₂ phase. When probes were inserted and she was given no slips on Days 20 and 27 there were accompanying drops in study rates on those days. It is of interest to note that study dropped on Day 27 despite the fact that by this second probe, Liza had begun "forgetting" to record her study and non-study behavior on some days. This would indicate the possibility that the slip itself had become a cue or discriminative stimulus (S) for study whether or not it was used for self-recording. Liza's record of her study behavior did not correlate with the observer's record. However, it is important to note that correlation between Liza's estimate and her actual behavior was not necessary to achieve or maintain high study rates.

When the slips were withdrawn in the Praise Only phase, study was maintained at an acceptable level. Even when increased praise was withdrawn in the Baseline₃ phase, study remained at acceptable levels. Although it would have been interesting to have continued the Baseline₃ phase for a longer period the experiment was terminated due to the close of the school term. Even so, the data indicated that once higher study levels were achieved and maintained for a period of time, slips and high rates of teacher attention could be withdrawn without significant reductions in study. There was some subjective evidence that Liza's increased study may have resulted in increased academic performance because her report card grade in history increased from D− to C.

Although the experiment with Stu was in many ways a replication of the first study there were several important differences. Liza had expressed a desire, in fact had requested help, to improve her study behavior. Her counselor praised her when she reported high study rates on the self-recording slips. Later, her teacher began attending to her and praising her for study once higher rates were achieved.

Stu, on the other hand, had not expressed concern or asked for help in decreasing his talking-out behavior. The teacher rather than a counselor was the agent for dispensing the self-recording slips to Stu. Another difference was that no attempt was made to differentially reinforce Stu with praise or attention for the decreases in talking out that were observed. Previous research (Hall, Fox, Willard, Goldsmith, Emerson, Owen, Davis, and Porcia, 1971) indicates that doing so would have increased the effectiveness of the procedures used. In spite of these factors it seems that initially issuing slips and having Stu record on them did affect his talking-out behavior. As in Liza's case, this was true even though there was very little correlation between the number of talk outs recorded by Stu and the observer's record. This is illustrated by the fact that on Days 10, 11, and 12 the observer's record showed that Stu's talk outs were occurring at 0.4, 0.3, and 0.3 times per minute. On the same days, however, Stu recorded 1.5, 0.5, and 0.8 talk outs per minute. That self-recording had little effect during the final phase of the experiment may have been due to the fact that no contingencies were ever applied to differential rates of talking out and the slips thus lost their effectiveness. Further research will be necessary to determine if this is the case. Furthermore, the records kept of his study behavior indicated that initially self-recording of talk outs may have affected his overall study rate. This effect was not conclusive or lasting, however. When self-recording was instituted for Session A, study increased from 30% to 55%. When self-recording was instituted for Session B, study increased from 24% to 42% while it decreased to 32% in Session A. When self-recording was instituted for the entire period, however, study decreased to 24%.

Perhaps the most promising feature of self-recording will be to use it as a procedure for initiating desirable levels of appropriate behavior to a point where the teacher can more easily reinforce the desired behavior with attention, praise, grades, or other reinforcers available in the classroom.

A BEHAVIORAL STUDY OF SELF-ESTEEM WITH ELEMENTARY TEACHERS[1]

James W. Hannum, Carl E. Thoresen,
David R. Hubbard, Jr.

Self-esteem has generally been viewed as an enduring personality trait or construct that influences how a person thinks and feels. Many would suggest, for example, that if a person is very depressed, it is because of low self-esteem or a negative self-concept. However, behavioral investigators (for example, Homme, 1965; Marston, 1965b) have argued that self-esteem is influenced by what a person says to himself. Thus, a person with high self-esteem is someone who talks to himself in a positive way—that is, he frequently engages in positive self-evaluations and has a low frequency of negative self-evaluations. In effect, we can say that self-esteem is made up in part of a variety of covert actions—thoughts, feelings, and images about oneself. Further, these internal actions are changeable; thus, a person can directly alter his self-esteem. Of course, many experiences outside of the person influence how he thinks and

This is the first publication of this article. All rights reserved. Permission to reprint must be obtained from the authors and publisher.

[1]This research was supported by the Stanford Center for Research and Development in Teaching, School of Education, Stanford University as part of the Personal Competencies Project directed by the second author.

feels about himself. Yet, for some persons, directly reducing negative self-thoughts may be an important step in improving self-esteem.

Hannum, Thoresen, and Hubbard report a preliminary field experiment in which three elementary teachers who complained of being too self-critical tried to improve their self-esteem. Self-monitoring, discussed in Chapter Three, was first employed to establish a baseline frequency of their positive and negative self-thoughts. After several days, a thought-stopping technique was used to reduce negative self-thoughts, followed by a procedure that employed high-frequency behaviors (such as looking at the clock) to cue or remind the teachers to think positive self-thoughts. Classroom observers also recorded certain external behaviors of the teachers, such as positive or negative verbal statements and positive or negative nonverbal responses to students (for example, a smile or a frown). In addition, certain student behavior was also observed.

The results of this preliminary study raise an important question: were the teachers in fact experiencing an increase in their self-esteem? Since positive self-thoughts could not be observed by anyone else, it is difficult to know if the data are valid. Perhaps the teachers were simply reporting what they thought the investigators wanted them to report. Two of the three teachers were extremely enthusiastic about the results, reporting that they felt more positively about themselves. However, the failure to find marked changes in observed *overt* behaviors leaves the question open. Self-thoughts, of course, may change without any immediate change in external behavior.

The study does suggest that a person can systematically observe his evaluative self-thoughts in an everyday situation without major difficulties. The direct relationship (if one exists) between overt and covert behavior merits further study. Perhaps the relationship is more indirect, especially in timing—that is, changes in positive self-thoughts may occur a considerable length of time after any notable changes in external actions. In addition, in order to improve self-esteem, it may be necessary for an individual to alter internal events other than evaluative self-thoughts (see Article Eleven) as well as certain external events. For example, a teacher may find that efforts aimed at reducing stress and tension responses coupled with participation in an ongoing counseling group markedly increase her self-esteem.

Evidence suggests that internal events, such as thoughts and images, may follow the same principles of behavior as do external events (Bandura, 1969; Mahoney, 1970). Thus, the modification of internal, or covert, behavior should logically proceed similarly to that of external behavior. Concern with what may be termed *covert-* or *cognitive-behavior modification* has recently increased with efforts to examine a number of covert techniques (for example, Thoresen & Mahoney, 1974). A growing number of studies have suggested that such modifications are possible (for example, Mahoney, 1971; Todd, 1972; Meichenbaum & Goodman, 1971) and that covert changes may lead to changes in overt behavior (Meichenbaum & Cameron, Article Eleven).

A personality construct long considered a significant determinant of a person's overt behavior is that of self-esteem. A person's "attitude" toward himself has been correlated with numerous other variables, such as birth order, religious background, school achievement, and parental self-esteem (Rosenberg, 1965; Coopersmith, 1967). If self-esteem is viewed as a class of covert behaviors concerned with a person's self-evaluations, then these self-evaluations may be altered by utilizing behavioral principles. Further changes in internal behavior should presumably lead to identifiable changes in overt behavior. Clinical evidence (for example, Rogers, 1961) suggests that changes in self-esteem may cause behavioral change, although some investigators have argued that internal change—that is, change in self-esteem—probably follows rather than precedes overt change (for example, Hobbs, 1962).

In this study, a behavioral definition of self-esteem was developed by drawing from the work of Marston (1965a) and Homme, C'deBaca, Devine, Steinhorst, and Rickert (1963). A positive self-concept was defined as a high frequency of positive (reinforcing) self-evaluations combined with a low frequency of negative (punishing) self-evaluations; a negative self-concept was viewed as the obverse—that is, as many negative evaluations and few positive ones. Hence, changes in self-esteem could occur if self-thoughts (self-verbalizations) were modified directly. Self-esteem, of course, could also be changed by altering the person's external environment. This study, however, examined methods for modifying self-thoughts directly.

Thought stopping (Wolpe & Lazarus, 1966; Cautela, 1969) was selected to reduce the frequency of negative self-thoughts ($-ST$), and a derivation of Premack's (1965) differential-probability principle, termed *positive intervention,* was used to increase positive self-thoughts ($+ST$). The effect of these interventions on other self-esteem indices and on selected overt behaviors in the classroom was also explored.

METHOD

Subjects

The subjects were three elementary school teachers from the Stanford University area who volunteered to participate following presentations at various teachers' meetings. These teachers complained of being excessively critical of themselves and indicated that they wanted to change this behavior. Two teachers (S1 and S3) were female, and one (S2) was male; each teacher was between 52 and 56 years old and had at least 16 years of teaching experience.

Procedure

The study was based on an intensive clinical design that involved making repeated measures of each subject during each phase (Sidman, 1960; Chassan, 1967) and comparing these measures to the subject's own baseline. Causality was investigated by using a stable baseline prior to intervention. The experiment involved four separate phases: baseline, thought stopping, positive intervention, and follow-up.

Baseline.   Each teacher was provided with two wrist counters and was asked to self-observe positive and negative self-thoughts during a specified hour each day. A list of common self-thoughts was generated for each teacher during an initial interview to aid in the self-observation. The scope and quality of each teacher's self-evaluations were also discussed during this interview. An example of a positive self-thought was "I'm patient with the children." A negative self-thought might have been "I'm just too old for teaching." At the end of each day, the teachers recorded the frequency of thoughts in a special notebook and completed a short daily report form, listing positive and negative events (outside of their classroom activities) that they may have been thinking about that day. Classroom observers recorded four categories of teacher behavior during this same hour throughout the study (40 to 43 days). The overt behaviors observed were positive verbal responses (such as "That's good"), negative verbal responses (such as "Stop doing that"), positive nonverbal responses (such as smiling), and negative nonverbal responses (such as shaking one's hand at a student). Single instances of each behavior were recorded for each 10-second period, and the daily totals were converted to rates by dividing by the total time periods observed. Interobserver reliability was assessed on 16 separate days throughout the study. The reliabilities for the four variables were .65, .98, .98, and .93, respectively. The lower reliability for positive verbal responses was due to one day's discrepancies. With this day deleted, the reliability of this variable increased to .90. The Gough Adjective Check List (Gough & Heilbrun, 1965) was also administered to each teacher at the beginning of the study; two scales derived from this measure were used as indications of self-acceptance and self-criticism. The baseline phase continued for a minimum of two weeks.

Thought Stopping.   Two teachers (S1 and S2) participated in this intervention, which began immediately following the baseline phase. S3 was called out of town for a family emergency; her baseline was therefore extended, and thought stopping was not used. In thought stopping, the person learns to subvocalize the word *stop* to reduce unwanted thoughts. Success in reducing the frequency of unwanted obsessive thoughts has been reported by Yamagami (1971), Cautela (1969), and others (see Wolpe & Lazarus, 1966). The two teachers received one thought-stopping session with a trainer on the first day of the phase and a short check-up contact several days later. The teachers were asked to use the technique on their negative self-thoughts for a two-week period. Both teachers also continued monitoring the frequency of their positive self-thoughts.

Positive Intervention.   All teachers participated in this intervention, which was designed to increase positive self-thoughts. The intervention was based in part on Premack's (1965) differential-probability principle as outlined by Homme (1965). High-frequency behaviors that each teacher performed in the classroom were identified (for example, looking at the wall clock). In addition, a recognizable stimulus cue (a small blue decal) was developed to remind the teacher to think a positive self-thought. This sequence of engaging a high-probability response and cueing a positive self-thought should have reinforced positive self-thoughts. Clinical success in using variations of these procedures to increase positive self-thoughts has been reported (for example, Jackson, 1972; Mahoney, 1971; Todd, 1972). Each teacher received one session of instruction on the first day of this phase and a short check-up several days later. This technique was used over a two-week period. During this time, teachers continued to monitor negative self-thoughts.

Follow-Up.   Positive intervention was withdrawn, and teachers continued to self-observe for a three- to six-day period. Following this period, several interviews were held with each teacher to assess his or her reactions to the study. The Gough Adjective Check List was also readministered.

RESULTS

The positive and negative self-thought data for the three teachers are presented in Figure 1, plotted against days of observation. The

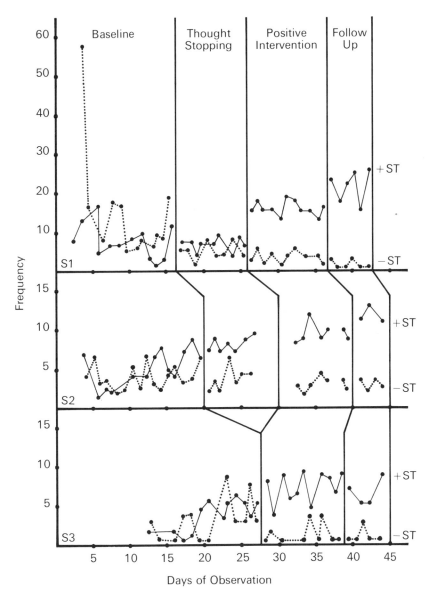

FIGURE 1. Positive Self-Thoughts (+ST) and Negative Self-Thoughts (−ST) for S1, S2, and S3 Plotted against Days of Observation.

daily thought frequencies and daily rates for the four overt behaviors were analyzed for between-phase mean changes using a one-way analysis of variance. A planned contrast was also computed for each variable between the two phases in which change was predicted. For the positive variables, this planned contrast was between the thought-stopping (TS) and positive-intervention (PI) phases; for negative variables, the contrast was between the baseline and TS phases. All variables with significant analysis-of-variance results were subsequently tested for the presence of a significant linear trend and lag 1 autocorrelation within each phase (Rao, 1967). A lag 1 autocorrelation test indicates if the data from one day is significantly related to the data from the next day. These tests were performed on the data from each teacher's reports to determine if the nonindependence of the data (autocorrelation) was a factor. The analysis-of-variance procedure assumes independence between data points.

The data from each teacher's positive and negative daily reports were dichotomized into days on which a report was made and days on which no report was made. A comparison of the changes in these daily reports between phases was done using the Fisher Exact Probability Test (Siegel, 1956). The pre- and post-treatment scores on the Gough Adjective Check List were converted to self-acceptance scores (total favorable adjectives checked over total adjectives checked) and self-criticism scores (total unfavorable adjectives checked over total adjectives checked). These raw scores were then converted to percentile scores using the population values provided by Crowne, Stephens, and Kelly (1961).

Teacher One (S1)

Teacher One showed significant increases in positive self-thoughts (+ST), with a major increase during the positive-intervention phase (see Table 1). Negative self-thoughts (−ST) decreased significantly, with a major decrease during the TS phase. The first day's data for −ST were omitted from the analysis because they clearly represented an extreme point. A log transformation of the data was conducted to help equalize the interphase variances. The teacher's *observed* negative verbal responses (also log transformation) decreased significantly ($F=4.43, p<.01$), as did positive verbal responses ($F=4.27, p<.025$). However, positive and negative nonverbal responses did not change significantly across the four phases. Tests for linear trend and lag 1 autocorrelation were insignificant on the four variables for which significant changes were found.

TABLE 1. Analysis of Variance for Positive Self-Thoughts (+ST) and Negative Self-Thoughts (−ST) between Intervention Phases with Planned Contrast.

	Variable	Source	d.f.	MS	F	P
S1	+ST	Between phases	3	520.1	43.46	<.001
		TS/PI contrast	1	648.2	53.78	<.001
		error	36	12.0		
	−ST(log)	Between phases	3	7.0	23.59	<.001
		Base/TS contrast	1	5.1	17.36	<.001
		error	35	.3		
S2	+ST	Between phases	3	63.77	29.62	<.001
		TS/PI contrast	1	16.07	7.47	<.025
		error	30	2.15		
	−ST	Between phases	3	3.73	2.18	n.s.
		Base/TS contrast	1	.50	.29	n.s.
		error	30	1.71		
S3	+ST	Between phases	2	13.88	5.12	<.025
		Base/PI contrast	1	25.80	9.52	<.01
		error	22	2.71		
	−ST	Between phases	2	25.70	6.02	<.01
		Base/PI contrast	1	40.91	9.60	<.005
		error	24	4.26		

Teacher One's positive daily reports showed a significant increase ($p<.01$) during the PI phase and a nonsignificant increase in general. Negative daily reports showed a near-significant decrease during TS and a nonsignificant decrease overall. On the adjective check list, the self-acceptance score increased (pre-post) from the 83rd to the 88th percentile, while the self-criticism score decreased from the 33rd to the 11th percentile.

Teacher One indicated improvement in self-esteem with significant changes in positive and negative self-thoughts. These self-thought changes were supported by two other self-report measures, but there were conflicting results with regard to overt-behavior changes.

Teacher Two (S2)

Teacher Two demonstrated a significant increase in positive self-thoughts (+ST) ($p<.01$) and a slight decrease in negative self-thoughts (−ST). However, as Figure 1 suggests, positive self-thoughts increased significantly during the baseline—that is, self-observation led to a sig-nificant increase in positive self-thoughts during the baseline phase. This accelerating trend was statistically significant ($p<.01$). However, when the trend effect was removed and the remaining deviations analyzed, no significant changes were found between any of the treat-ment phases. It is important to note that Teacher Two objected to the thought-stopping technique—that is, he did not think it would work. Thus, his use of thought stopping was limited. None of Teacher Two's overt behaviors showed significant mean changes; tests for phase trends and lag 1 autocorrelation were also insignificant.

Positive daily reports showed a near-significant increase during PI; however, a near-significant *decrease* occurred during the follow-up. Negative daily reports did show a significant decrease ($p<.05$) during PI and a nonsignificant decrease overall. Teacher Two's self-accep-tance score from the adjective check list increased from the 87th to the 93rd percentile, and his self-criticism score decreased from the 18th to the 12th percentile.

In contrast to the Teacher One's self-report data, Teacher Two's data indicated fewer significant changes. Self-observation had a sig-nificant effect on +ST during the baseline phase, and that effect con-tinued during all the phases. At best, thought stopping and positive intervention may have maintained the gains made during the baseline phase. Negative self-thoughts diminished slightly. Moreover, there was little change in observed overt behaviors.

Teacher Three (S3)

For Teacher Three, both positive self-thoughts and negative self-thoughts increased during the baseline. Inspection of the frequency graph (Figure 1) indicates that these increases were due to the extremely low frequencies reported during the initial four to six days of self-observation. After this period, the frequencies stabilized at somewhat higher rates. It was assumed that this observed shift was the result of adaptation to the self-observation procedures. Therefore, these first few days were dropped from the analysis (the first six days for +ST and first four days for −ST). This reduced the baseline slopes for these two variables and provided a more stable indication of pre-intervention frequencies. The analysis of variance on the remaining data demonstrated significant changes in both positive and negative self-thoughts, with the major change occurring during PI (see Table 1). None of the overt behavior variables showed significant mean shifts.

The frequency of observed positive nonverbal responses and

negative verbal responses in the classroom had significant negative (decelerating) trends during the baseline. This decelerating trend continued during PI for negative verbal responses. None of the variables produced a significant lag 1 autocorrelation.

Since negative nonverbal responses showed a major *shift* in slope between the three phases, F-tests for parallelism of regression $(B_1 - B_2 = 0)$ were conducted between baseline and PI and between PI and follow-up. The results indicated a near-significant decreasing slope shift $(F=3.47)$ between the baseline and PI phases; however, negative nonverbal responses showed a significant increasing shift between PI and follow-up $(F=5.37, p<.05)$. Hence, observed negative nonverbal responses diminished during the positive intervention but quickly increased after the treatment stopped.

Positive daily reports significantly increased during PI $(p<.01)$ and also overall $(p<.01)$. Negative daily reports showed nonsignificant decreases during PI and overall. Teacher Three's self-acceptance score remained at the 99th percentile due to a ceiling effect; her self-criticism score remained unchanged at the 16th percentile.

In general, Teacher Three showed increased positive self-thoughts and decreased negative self-thoughts. Positive daily reports also increased. While observed negative nonverbal actions changed during the positive intervention, the change was not maintained.

Post-treatment interviews indicated that two teachers (S1 and S3) were profoundly influenced by the interventions; both referred to their participation as among the most significant events of their lives. An important component of the strategies seemed to be the experience of self-control—that is, demonstrating that they themselves could change the ways in which they thought. The remaining teacher felt that the treatments "sort of helped, but not much."

DISCUSSION

The following conclusions seem warranted:

1. Positive intervention was effective in increasing positive thoughts.
2. Thought-stopping intervention was less effective than positive intervention in reducing negative self-thoughts; limited training in thought stopping and the noncooperation of one subject restricted its effectiveness.
3. The treatments generally did not produce changes in observed external behaviors; however, anecdotal post-treatment interview data suggested that overt-behavior changes had occurred.
4. The techniques of self-observation employed in this study were feasible for teachers to use in the classroom during ongoing activities.

A problem with this research was that corroboration of changes in broad categories of self-thoughts was sought in similarly broad categories of positive and negative overt behavior. Had changes in more *specific* self-thoughts been compared with changes in the *specific* behaviors that the thoughts encompassed, a more direct relationship may have been found. The relatively imprecise groupings of this study may have obscured relationships between the covert and overt variables.

Thought stopping resulted in negative *and* positive thought reductions for S1 (see Figure 1), although only negative self-thoughts were the focus of intervention. In the follow-up interviews, the subject provided a possible explanation. She reported thinking negative self-thoughts, using the *stop* procedure, and then switching to a positive self-thought. Thus, she may have inadvertently made a negative self-thought the dominant cue for a positive self-thought, thereby reducing positive self-thoughts as negative self-thoughts decreased. With S2, thought stopping was ineffective. This teacher voiced objections to the procedure in the final interviews. Additional training sessions may have increased the effectiveness of thought stopping (see Thoresen & Mahoney, 1974). Clearly, additional studies are needed to evaluate the effectiveness of thought stopping as a covert control strategy.

There is some indication that positive intervention may have inadvertently employed high-probability behaviors (HPB) as stimulus cues (discriminative stimuli) for positive self-thoughts rather than as reinforcing stimuli. The sequence reversal—that is, engaging in the high-probability response before engaging in the target behavior—however, appeared effective. Teachers reported the self-reinforcing effects of engaging in positive self-thoughts; using the wrist counter to record a +ST may have also functioned as a reinforcing event. Thus, the temporal sequence of a low-probability behavior followed by a high-probability response may not be essential in all conditions of human learning (see Ashem & Donner, 1968). Use of a high-probability response as a discriminative stimulus may be sufficient without a provision for overt reinforcement, since covert self-reinforcement may occur (as was suggested in the interview data).

A limitation of the present study involves the problem of experimenter-demand factors as an alternative explanation of the results (see Jeffrey, Article Seven). Conceivably, changes in positive self-thoughts may have covaried with the nonspecific effects of engaging in a "treatment" per se and not necessarily with the positive-intervention treatment. This rival hypothesis can be examined in subsequent studies in which (1) some subjects are misled about the possible effects of treatment (for example, Barlow, Leitenberg, & Agras, 1969), (2) a reversal or multiple-baseline design is employed (Thoresen, in press), or (3) a comparative-group design is used. While comparison of each subject with his own baseline performance does answer the question of relative change for that person, it fails to fully explain why change occurred. Additional studies seem warranted in order to examine how interventions can be used to alter covert actions that relate to positive self-esteem and self-concept.

The reactive effect of self-observation was evident with S2 and, to a lesser extent, with S1. Since reliability checks on self-observation were impossible due to the covert nature of self-thoughts, changes due to self-observation reactivity could not be separated from changes due to inaccurate observation and to possible shifts in the teacher's response-category definitions. However, the continual rise of positive self-thoughts with S2, irrespective of intervention phase, seems a likely case of reactivity. The immediate decrease in negative self-thoughts for S1 after the first day was also likely a reactive effect. In this latter case, the teacher reported being "shocked" at the number of negative self-thoughts that she had on the first day. This reaction suggested that some form of self-punishment may have operated to reduce negative self-thoughts. In contrast, the increases in negative and positive self-thoughts for S3 after the first four to six days were probably *not* due to reactivity but to increases in the accuracy of the self-observation. This teacher reported taking the first week to arrive at a stable definition of what thoughts she was to observe. Further studies should aim at separating the reactivity and reliability effects of self-observation primarily dealing with overt behavior (Kazdin, Article Nine). The reliability of covert self-observation is more difficult; concurrent observation of overt actions that are related to internal actions provides an indirect method. However, as indicated earlier, both types of behavior should be more specifically identified.

This study, in general, indicates that covert events are both observable and modifiable and thus need not remain outside the realm of effective intervention and self-control. Further work is needed, however, to establish the functional relationships between overt and covert behaviors.

IMITATION AND SELF-ESTEEM AS DETERMINANTS OF SELF-CRITICAL BEHAVIOR

Emily W. Herbert, Donna M. Gelfand,
Donald P. Hartmann

Self-criticism represents a form of negative self-punishment (Chapter 5) in which the individual presents himself with a negative verbal statement following the occurrence of undesired behavior. The voluntary self-removal of valued possessions is a form of positive self-punishment—"positive" because it involves the withdrawal of a positive stimulus, and "punishment" because it is designed to decrease the frequency of a behavior. In the following article, Herbert, Gelfand, and Hartmann investigate the development of both positive and negative self-punishment. Children in an experimental group observed an adult model who played a miniature bowling game, criticized his performance, and fined himself valuable tokens. When the children were subsequently allowed to play the game themselves, those who had observed the self-critical model were much more self-punitive than those who had not seen the model. These findings support the notion that self-punitive response patterns may be learned and maintained through modeling (see Bandura, Article Two).

From *Child Development*, 1969, **40**, 421-430. © 1969 by The Society for Research in Child Development, Inc. Reprinted by permission.

It is difficult to explain the development of self-critical behavior since self-criticism would appear aversive and unlikely to have any intrinsic reinforcing properties. Most theories of personality development have asserted that the child learns to evaluate his performance as "good" or "bad" by adopting the performance standards that his parents and other socialization agents have imposed upon him (Maccoby, 1959; Sears, 1957). Thus, a child verbally criticized by his parents for a substandard performance may in their absence criticize himself for failing to meet that standard. Behaving like the parent is assumed to produce conditioned reinforcers even when the parent's behavior has resulted in withdrawal of approval. Maccoby (1959) has suggested that parental behavior is attended to, rehearsed, and then reproduced by the child under conditions similar to those which originally evoked the parental response (e.g., following a deviant act). Research findings have generally substantiated Maccoby's formulation; for example, Aronfreed (1963, 1964) has demonstrated that children reproduce an adult's criticism of their behavior if the critical comments have been paired with the termination of an aversive event. Grusec (1966) has found that withdrawal of love or material reinforcers contingent upon transgression in a game would also facilitate children's verbal self-criticism. In addition, research by Kanfer and Duerfeldt (1967) indicated that when objective criteria for self-evaluations are absent, adult subjects may apply to themselves the same sanctions imposed upon them by a model.

It is also possible, however, that the child learns to evaluate his performance by imitating directly the standards and evaluations the parents apply to themselves. Self-criticism might then be acquired through imitation of a self-critical model.

This latter hypothesis seems especially reasonable in view of the well-documented evidence that children readily imitate a model's performance standards for self-reinforcement (Bandura, Grusec, & Menlove, 1967; Bandura & Kupers, 1964; Bandura & Whalen, 1966; Mischel & Liebert, 1966; Ofstad, 1967). Recently Gewirtz and Stingle (1968) suggested that self-criticism may be learned through direct imitation of a model when other imitative responses have been intermittently reinforced or when imitation removes or avoids a noxious stimulus. The study reported here was an attempt to investigate the possibility that self-critical behavior can be acquired through imitation of a self-critical model without the observer's having had any prior interaction with the model.

If self-critical behavior is to be meaningfully used to designate a response class, then individuals who characteristically rate themselves as inferior to their peers in social and academic skills (those with low-rated self-esteem) will more readily make self-derogatory responses for sub-standard game performance than will subjects rating their skills as high. The basis for this expected relation is further strengthened by the frequently reported finding that susceptibility to social influence is an inverse monotonic function of self-esteem (Hovland, Janis, & Kelley, 1953; Janis, 1954). That this relation is a linear one has recently been seriously questioned by Nisbett and Gordon (1967). Variables, such as sex and age of the subject and comprehensibility and plausibility of the communication, may drastically alter the relation between self-esteem and persuasibility (Janis & Field, 1959; Lesser & Abelson, 1959; Nisbett & Gordon, 1967). Moreover, research in the area of imitative learning also suggests that no simple relation exists between self-esteem and social influence (Bandura & Whalen, 1966; Gelfand, 1962). Nevertheless, self-esteem may be negatively related to a smaller and logically closely related class of imitative behavior such as imitation of self-criticism.

The present study investigated imitation by children of an adult's self-critical comments and performance-contingent relinquishing of rewards, as well as the relation among three measures of self-esteem and self-criticism displayed while playing a bowling game. It was predicted that (1) children would imitate a model's voluntary forgoing of reinforcement and self-critical comments following substandard scores, and (2) a negative relation would be found between children's rated esteem and both the frequency of relinquishing tokens and of making self-critical comments.

METHOD

Subjects

The subjects were 40 fourth-grade students, 20 boys and 20 girls, selected from two classes totaling 52 students, from a public elementary school serving a middle-class residential area.

Self-Concept Inventories

The self-concept inventory developed by P. S. Sears (1960) was used to assess self-esteem prior to experimental manipulations. This self-concept inventory is currently in an experimental stage (P. S. Sears, mimeographed paper, 1966). Tabachnick (1962) reported a split-half reliability for the inventory of .94. The Kuder-Richardson reliability in the present study was .91 for the entire scale. Spaulding (1964) found that children scoring high on this measure of self-concept were in the classrooms of teachers rated high in degree of communication with students and low in degree of negative evaluation of students. The inventory consisted of 100 items covering 10 areas of competence presumed important in children's self-evaluations. Each item was rated on a five-point scale for comparison of the rater with his classmates. Scores were the average of the five-point ratings excluding ratings on the 10 items dealing with social relations with the opposite sex. These items were excluded because of their depressing effect on Kuder-Richardson item homogeneity.

A second measure of self-esteem, the Bledsoe-Garrison (1962) self-concept inventory, was also administered to the subjects. This questionnaire included 30 trait-descriptive adjectives individually rated on a three-point scale as characteristic of the rater. Only ratings for the portion labeled "this is the way I am now" were used. Bledsoe (1964) reported (1) negative correlations of self-esteem scores and scores on the Taylor Manifest Anxiety Scale for boys and girls and (2) low positive correlations of self-esteem scores and measures of intelligence and academic achievement for boys but not for girls.

A final esteem measure was the subject's rating on a five-point scale of how well he thought he would do on the bowling game in relation to children his own age both (1) before he played the game (how well I think I will do), and (2) after he played (how well I think I did).

The performance ratings were included to establish the appropriateness of a comparison of behavior on the bowling task with the other self-esteem measures. The postperformance rating was added to provide a measure of systematic changes, due to the game or the modeling, on the subjects' perception of the adequacy of their performance.

Bowling Task Apparatus

A miniature bowling alley modified from the one developed by Gelfand (1962) was used for the performance task. The 36 X 12-inch runway was partially screened by a 6-inch plywood shield to conceal the target area. Three lights were horizontally mounted at 3-inch intervals on an 11 X 12-inch display panel positioned behind the plywood shield and slanted at 45 degrees to the runway. The display panel extended back 6 inches and housed the necessary equipment to enable semiautomatic programming of game scores. The apparatus was painted red, and 3-inch yellow numbers, 5, 10, and 15, were painted above the display lights to indicate scores. When the steel bowling ball broke a photobeam crossing the alley, a preselected-score light controlled by the experimenter from a hand-sized switching panel was illuminated for 3 seconds. To help make the apparatus appear appropriate for both boys and girls, sex-appropriate cutouts approximately 2 X 2 inches in size were taken from Whitman Preschool Puzzles and fixed below the display lights with tape. A coffee can labeled "Bad" was used as the receptacle for poker-chip tokens given up for poor performance. Assorted wrapped candies, pencils, and pennies which could be exchanged for tokens were available in a basket on top of the display panel.

Experimental Conditions

A point-biserial correlation computed between Sears self-esteem scores and sex indicated that boys had higher scores than did girls ($r_{pb}=.38$, $p<.003$). Before assigning subjects to experimental conditions, sex groups were further divided at their median esteem scores to form high and low esteem groups (Median=333, $N=24$ for boys; Median=261, $N=27$ for girls). Forty subjects were then quasi-randomly assigned to eight experimental conditions: (1) two esteem levels, high and low, (2) model and no-model conditions, and (3) boys and girl subjects.

Bowling Task

At least 1 week after administration of the Sears test each subject was taken from the classroom to a small room by the experimenter. Here, subjects in the model condition were introduced by name to the model who was in the room when the subject arrived. In all conditions, an observer seated near the game recorded scores, tokens given up, and subjects' comments. Two adults, a man and woman, served as observers and models, the same-sex adult as model and the opposite-sex adult as observer. The control panel was hidden from view behind the bowling apparatus and the female experimenter sat to the right of the display panel, with eyes directed to the instrument housing while controlling scores.

Subjects in the model condition were told that the purpose of the experiment was to develop a new game and to assess the performance of both adults and children. The adults were purportedly asked to come to the school so the game wouldn't have to be moved. Subjects were told that the possible scores of 0, 5, 10, and 15 were obtained by the ball's triggering hidden switches. The observer demonstrated how the game worked by carefully rolling the ball for each possible score. Both subject and model then privately rated their expected performance in the game on the five-point rating scale. Next, each was given 20 tokens and the token exchange value was explained. Tokens left at the end of each player's turn could be exchanged for an equal number of assorted candies, pencils, and pennies. The "Bad" container was indicated as a receptacle used by some people for giving up tokens when they threw bad scores. The child was then asked to call out the adult's scores while he or she played. The adult model, who played the game first, supposedly because he had little time off from work, then threw 20 balls. He relinquished a token for each score of 0 and 5, thereby giving up 10 tokens, and made one of five predetermined self-critical comments following each low score (e.g., "boy, that was a stupid thing for me to do"). The model then privately rated his performance before exchanging his tokens and leaving. The subject called out his own scores when he played and also rated his performance after playing.

Subjects in the no-model conditions were given identical instructions except that no references were made to a model, and they were told that no adults came to play that day.

The experimenter and the observer made no comments and avoided eye contact with the model and the subject while the game was played. All subjects and models obtained the same scores in the same randomly determined order; 10, 0, 5, 15, 15, 5, 0, 10, 0, 15, 5, 10, 5, 5, 10, 10, 5, 10, 5, 10.

A month after completion of the bowling game procedure, the Bledsoe-Garrison self-concept inventory was administered.

RESULTS

Relinquishing Tokens

The results of an analysis of variance performed on the total number of tokens given up in a 2-sex X 2-model conditions X 2 Sears self-esteem groups design appear in Table 1. The only reliable source of variance was model versus no-model condition. Only three subjects in the no-model condition relinquished any tokens, and these were all given up following scores of 0. All 20 subjects observing a model gave up some tokens ($M=5.25$, $SD=2.79$). Sex differences were potentially confounded with sex differences in self-esteem on the Sears test; however, an analysis of co-variance performed on the number of tokens given up indicated that sex groups were not different when subjects were equated for self-esteem ($F=2.24$, $df=1/35$).

TABLE 1.   Analysis of Variance on Total Number of Tokens Given Up.

Source	df	MS	F
Sex (A)..	1	8.10	1.99
Model vs. no-model (B).....................	1	250.00	61.58*
Self-esteem group (C)......................	1	0.40	0.09
A × B...	1	10.00	2.46
A × C...	1	1.60	0.39
B × C...	1	2.50	0.61
A × B × C....................................	1	4.90	1.20
Error...	32	4.06	

* $p < .001$.

Additional analyses computed on the number of tokens given up using three divisions of self-esteem (high, medium, and low) again did not indicate differential effects due to self-esteem ($F=0.466$, $df=2/17$, $p>.25$). Thus the repeated failure to demonstrate an effect due to self-esteem cannot be considered a spurious result from using only two divisions of self-esteem and thereby obscuring a potential curvilinear relation.

Because sex or self-esteem could have differentially affected the number of tokens given up for individual scores, an analysis of variance was performed on the percentage of imitation for scores of 0 and 5 (the proportion of tokens given up per opportunity). The only significant effect was that due to score, that is, porportionately more tokens were forgone following scores of 0 than scores of 5 ($F=6.02$, $df=1/16$, $p<.05$). This may have resulted from the subjects' expectations regarding differences between the skill of adults and children despite the equivalence of their game performance.

Self-Critical Comments

Though the model made self-critical comments following each low score (10 during each game) only a total of 7 imitative comments were made, 1 by each of seven subjects. While a few imitative comments were made, no comments were made by subjects in the no-model condition. The Fisher exact probability for the number of subjects who made self-critical comments in the model versus no-model conditions was $p=.004$. Apparently, the experimental setting discouraged any talking, and the modeled comments partially counteracted the suppressive effect of the setting.

Self-Esteem Ratings

Analysis of variance on the five-point pre- and postperformance ratings indicated no change in rating from pre to post ($F=1.88$, $df=1/32$, $p>.05$), so neither the game nor the modeling systematically affected the subjects' perceptions of the adequacy of their performance. Girls had reliably lower ratings than boys, a result congruent with sex differences that appeared on the Sears test ($F=8.36$, $df=1/32$, $p<.01$). Also, as expected from Sears self-esteem scores, subjects in the low-esteem group rated their performance lower than did subjects in the high-esteem group ($F=6.06$, $df=1/32$, $p<.05$). In spite of the low pre-post correlation for the subjects' self-ratings on the five-point scale ($r=.17$, $N=40$, $p>.05$), Sears scores were moderately related to both pre- and post-performance ratings ($r=.49$ with pre and .51 with post, $N=40$, $p<.05$).

As a check for a potential relation between performance ratings and self-critical behavior, the distribution of tokens given up when self-esteem groupings were based on high, medium, and low preperformance ratings for each sex group was examined. This distribution indicated, as did results based on Sears scores, that there was no relation between self-ratings and self-denial of reinforcers.

Although neither Sears scores nor performance ratings were found to be related to the subjects' self-critical behavior while playing the bowling game, the Bledsoe-Garrison test was included to provide an additional check. Inspection of the distribution of tokens given up when self-esteem groupings were based on trifurcating the scores indicated no relation. Nor was the Bledsoe-Garrison test related to any other measure of self-esteem used in the present study ($r=.15$ with the Sears test, $r=.02$ with preperformance ratings, and $r=.15$ with postperformance ratings). Unlike the Sears test and the performance ratings, no sex differences were found on the Bledsoe-Garrison test.

DISCUSSION

The results indicate that children do imitate a model's behavior even when imitation results in a loss of material rewards. While only 3 subjects in the no-model condition gave up tokens, all 20 subjects who observed a self-denying model relinquished rewards. One possible explanation for the subjects' willingness to deny themselves attractive rewards is suggested by Hill's (1960) theory that children may engage in self-punitive responses in order to terminate aversive events, such as punishment from parents, and to regain parental approval through renunciation of wrongdoing. Hill thus views self-criticism as instrumental in bringing about cessation of punishment and the return of positive reinforcement. If Hill's theory is correct, the children in the present study may have engaged in self-critical responses because they expected the experimenter's overt or implicit approval for doing so. Grusec (1966) also attributed her findings that nonreinforcement failed to extinguish verbal self-criticism to her subjects' expectations of experimenter approval for their self-critical remarks. Grusec suggested that the children's inferences regarding the experimenter's pleasure could have been sufficiently reinforcing to maintain self-critical behavior so long as these expectations were not directly disconfirmed. A similar effect may have been responsible for the self-critical performance of children in the present experiment.

Surprisingly, none of the three self-esteem measures differentiated subjects on the number of tokens given up. One possible explanation for the failure to find the hypothesized relation between self-esteem and self-denial of reinforcement is that the power of the modeling manipulation may have left little room for individual differences. However, although the modeling conditions account for a substantial portion of the variance in token relinquishment (66 per cent; $eta = .81$), the relation is far from perfect. Furthermore, the internal consistency of the Sears test and the reliable but low intercorrelations among the performance ratings and Sears scores indicated that self-esteem as measured on the Sears test was appropriately compared with behavior on the bowling task. Unexpectedly, scores on another test purportedly measuring self-esteem, the Bledsoe-Garrison test, were neither related to the dependent variables nor to the other self-esteem tests.

The low intercorrelations between the various measures of self-esteem (Median $r = .16$; Range from .02 to .51), despite the similarity of measurement method, indicated a striking lack of convergent validity (Campbell & Fiske, 1959). These findings again highlight the need for use of operational definitions in personality measurement (Bechtoldt, 1959).

Although the virtual absence of imitation of self-critical labels is not unique to this study (Bandura & Kupers, 1964; Bandura & Whalen, 1966), it appears that the experimental setting discouraged any talking. In other studies of self-criticism, extensive verbal probes have been used to elicit reproduction of the critical label (Aronfreed, 1963, 1964; Grusec, 1966). Certainly further research is needed to isolate the variables controlling imitation of different types of behavior.

It is concluded that children may learn self-critical behavior, specifically self-denial of rewards following substandard performance, through observation of adult models. In addition, it appears that self-esteem as measured on questionnaires is virtually independent of self-denial of rewards in the experimental setting used in this study. This finding suggests that specific self-evaluations may have little predictive value for evaluative behaviors in other settings.

SELF-CONTROL: METHODOLOGICAL ISSUES AND RESEARCH TRENDS[1]

D. Balfour Jeffrey

In Chapter Three, some problems involved in assessing the processes and outcomes of self-control research and practice were briefly discussed. For example, the need to measure the frequency of a problem behavior in the presence of a self-control technique as well as in its absence was stressed. The relative value of intensive ($N=1$) research designs and empirical group experiments was also discussed, and the difficulties of self-observation, as an assessment procedure and as a self-control technique in itself, were considered.

Jeffrey discusses several factors of importance in improving research in self-control. He focuses on a variety of methodological issues, such as the use of between-subject (comparative-group) and within-subject ($N=1$) research

[1]This article was prepared especially for this volume. I particularly wish to thank Donald P. Hartmann, Roger C. Katz, and Michael J. Mahoney for their suggestions and encouragement. I also wish to thank Donna M. Gelfand, Emily W. Herbert, Rashel Jeffrey, David A. Shaw, and Carl E. Thoresen for their critical readings of earlier drafts of this paper.

designs and the need for studies of self-control that use many different methods. He raises questions about the reliability—that is, the consistency and stability—of the data reported in many self-control studies and expresses concern for the validity of such data. Are most research results actually brought about by the self-control methods? Could other factors, such as experimental bias or the subject's (client's) expectancy of change, account for the results?

Jeffrey's concerns reflect a problem in self-control research—that is, that assessment and techniques are often confounded. For example, a person may self-monitor his urges to smoke and the number of cigarettes that he smokes, but the process of monitoring may subsequently influence urges and smoking. This article offers suggestions for disentangling assessment and self-control techniques.

Jeffrey raises two crucial questions: (1) "will self-control changes be maintained?" and (2) "how costly (cost-effective) are self-control methods?" Little is known about these points at present; neither is much information available on the efficacy of control techniques for complex human problems. Helping people develop problem-solving skills so that they can become their own therapists seems to be a promising strategy.

Self-control research and its clinical applications have grown rapidly in the last decade. During this time, there has been some confusion in the use of the terms *self-control, self-regulation, self-management,* and *self-directed behavior.*[2] For present purposes, *self-control* (SC) will be used as a generic term to mean any response made by an organism to change or maintain his own behavior.

Recently, a number of authors have summarized the self-control research and its clinical applications (Bandura, 1969; Cautela, 1969; Goldfried & Merbaum, 1973; Kanfer, 1970a; Kanfer & Phillips, 1970; Mahoney, 1972a; Thoresen & Mahoney, 1974; Watson & Tharp, 1972), while others have discussed experimental design and methodological issues that pertain to psychotherapy investigations in general (Bergin & Garfield, 1971; Campbell & Stanley, 1963; Goldstein, Heller, & Sechrest, 1966; McNamara & MacDonough, 1972; Paul, 1969; Stollak, Guerney, & Rothberg, 1966).

The primary focus of this article is on methodological issues that are particularly germane to self-control research. These issues include: (1) research strategies and significance, (2) operational definitions and theory construction, (3) reliability and validity of external monitoring and self-monitoring, (4) patient and therapist variables, (5) artifacts such as demand characteristics and evaluation apprehension, (6) generalization and follow-up, and (7) cost-effectiveness. A secondary aim is to delineate some of the emerging research trends in self-control.

[2]See Goldfried and Merbaum (1973), Marston and Feldman (1970), and Thoresen and Mahoney (1974) for discussions of the various definitions of *self-control.*

I.   RESEARCH STRATEGIES AND SIGNIFICANCE

Various research strategies and experimental designs have been used in clinical inquiries. The differences in the approaches of several authors to clinical research will be examined first, and their similarities will then be related specifically to SC research. A discussion will follow on research significance, internal and external validity, and within- and between-subject designs.

Kanfer and Phillips (1970) identify three frames of reference from which clinical and SC research can be viewed: (1) basic research on behavioral mechanisms versus applied research on therapy effectiveness; (2) research in laboratory settings versus research in clinical settings; (3) nomothetic research (the study of a few behaviors in many subjects) versus idiographic research (the study of individual subjects in detail)—a traditional dispute that is currently reflected in the controversy of the between-subject group design versus the within-subject operant design.

Paul (1969), in discussing research tactics, recommends the following sequence for behavior-modification research: (1) developing treatment procedures in the laboratory, (2) testing procedures in case studies and single-group experiments, (3) evaluating systematically controlled group studies, and (4) conducting comprehensive factorially designed experiments.

Bergin (1971), however, takes exception to Paul and others (for example, Edwards & Cronbach, 1952) who place a strong emphasis on comprehensive factorial designs. According to Bergin, factorial designs have not been conducted because they are expensive, because they assume a level of precision that has not yet been developed, and because they may not be appropriate for studying the practice of therapy. Bergin goes on to offer two alternative strategies for developing new techniques and for testing their effects. One is the experimental laboratory approach, and the other is an elaborate objective case-study approach. Lazarus and Davison (1971) also encourage the use of innovative clinical case studies. They argue that our greatest advances in therapeutic theory and practice often come through clinical case studies rather than through tightly controlled laboratory or factorial field studies.

Although these authors have emphasized different approaches, they all have one thing in common—they clearly recognize the importance and interrelationship of a variety of approaches in the development of a scientific field and in its clinical applications. Paul (1969) summarized a perspective for behavior-modification research that is directly applicable to and recommended for SC research.

Since research training does not ensure ability or acquaintance with the range of problems and issues existent in the clinical situation, and clinical "savvy" does not ensure ability or acquaintance with the problems and issues of research, this state of affairs may not be an unfortunate one. Thus, as the field of behavior modification enters the experimental era, all levels and approaches to the ultimate question may be expected to continue. It is to be hoped, however, that each approach will be seen in perspective, in its relationships both to other approaches and to the actual level of product obtained, so that future generations may view the field as a composition of "artisans" or "scientists," whether research or applied, rather than as cultists bound by historical inheritance [p. 61].

Similarly, Goldfried and Merbaum (1973) argue that self-control, like any other psychological phenomenon, can best be understood within the framework of general psychology and that the advancement of the self-control field is most facilitated by the interplay among theory, research, and actual clinical application.

A flow chart might help to clarify some of the relationships between the substantive areas and research strategies of general psychology and self-control research. Some of the content areas of psychology that are relevant to SC phenomena are listed under general psychology. Areas such as animal-experimental psychology, human-learning psychology, developmental psychology, and social psychology provide the fundamental empirical and theoretical foundations on which SC investigations rest. Research strategies in psychology that are most used in clinical investigations are listed in the right-hand column. Either within-subject or between-subject designs can be employed in laboratory studies, clinical case studies, and experimental field studies. Both the substantive areas and research strategies of general psychology have a direct influence on SC research. (The arrows represent the interactions and feedback among all the parts.)

Several recent investigations illustrate these influences on SC research. Mahoney and Bandura (1972) employed animal-experimental developments with pigeons and a within-subject, laboratory-research strategy to investigate the mechanisms of self-reinforcement. Others (Jeffrey, 1973; Leak & Fraser, 1972) have employed social-psychology findings from the attribution-theory literature and a between-subject, experimental-field-study research strategy to investigate the effectiveness of SC treatment procedures.

The implications of this total-systems approach to SC research are clear. Although statistical significance and methodological rigor are important criteria, by themselves they are insufficient criteria to evaluate the total significance of a study (Lykken, 1968). The ultimate criterion is whether an investigation contributes to the scientific development of the self-control field. For example, an SC case study

TABLE 1. A Flow Chart of the Research Strategies and the
Areas of General Psychology as They Relate to Self-Control
Research.

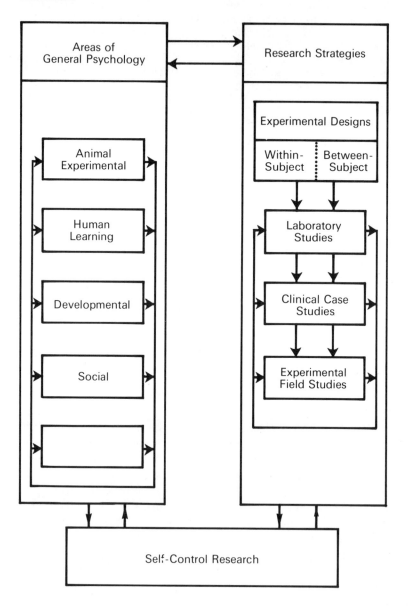

may be methodologically or theoretically weak, but it may generate invaluable hypotheses that later can be confirmed or disconfirmed under more tightly controlled experimental conditions. Other investigations may be clinically weak, but they may offer some empirical methodological or theoretical advances that will generate later applications for practice. The important point is for SC researchers to keep a perspective on what they are doing and on how their work can contribute to the progress of the self-control field.

Internal and External Validity

From whatever frame of reference SC research is approached—pure or applied, laboratory or field, nomothetic or idiographic—the same basic principles of experimental design are used for the discovery of phenomena and the establishment of cause-effect relationships (Paul, 1969; Underwood, 1957). In discussing general principles of experimental design, Campbell and Stanley (1963) identified 12 factors that can jeopardize the internal and external validity of an experiment. For a study to have internal validity, its particular set of results must be due to the treatment variables under study rather than to extraneous influences. Factors that threaten the internal validity of an experiment include the following: history, maturation, testing, instrumentation, statistical regression, biases, experimental mortality, and selection-maturation interactions. Underwood calls these factors "lethal errors" because no specific cause-effect relationships can be established unless these threats are controlled. Internal validity is the basic minimum without which any experiment is confounded.

External validity refers to the extent to which experimental results can be generalized to different populations, treatments, procedures, and measures. Factors jeopardizing external validity include reactive effects of testing, interaction effects of selection biases and experimental variables, reactive effects of experimental arrangements, and multiple-treatment interference. Since all SC research is eventually directed toward application, it must establish external validity in addition to internal validity. Without external validity, no SC theory, experiment, or treatment can be generalized to real-life situations.

Since both internal and external validity are essential to SC research, the ideal approach is to select designs strong in both types of validity. However, in practice, increasing one type of validity may jeopardize the other. For example, an SC laboratory experiment may have good internal validity but may lack external, or an SC field study may attempt to establish external validity but may lack internal validity on some factor. Since it is rarely possible to satisfy the requirements of both internal and external validity within the same experiment, the limits of an experiment should be noted, and a series of systematic replications should be conducted to establish both internal and external validity.

Within-Subject and Between-Subject Designs

In recent years, there have been arguments about the superiority of the newer within-subject designs over the traditional between-subject group designs (Gelfand & Hartmann, 1968; Honig, 1966; McNamara & MacDonough, 1972; Paul, 1969; Sidman, 1960). This article will not go into the details of these arguments but will highlight a perspective that SC investigators should keep in mind when choosing an appropriate design. Unfortunately, arguments of the superiority of one design over the other have clouded the more fundamental issues of the questions that are being asked in a study and the factors that must be considered in order to demonstrate a causal relationship. Both the between- and within-subject designs should be evaluated in terms of whether they are appropriate for the questions being asked (McNamara & MacDonough, 1972; Thoresen, 1969).

Before looking at some of the conditions under which one design is preferred over the other, it might be helpful to briefly review the basic characteristics of each design. In the between-subject design, a different experimental manipulation is made on each group of subjects. The causal relationship is inferred from the differences between the groups. Usually, statistical methods are used to determine whether there were significant differences between the groups.

In the within-subject design, all the experimental manipulations and observations are made on the same subject. The causal relationship is inferred from the effects of the different experimental conditions on the subject. Usually, the results are graphed to determine whether there were differences between the various experimental conditions.

The two most common types of the within-subject design are the ABAB reversal and the multiple baseline. The essential characteristics of the ABAB reversal are the following: (1) during the first phase (A_1), baseline observations are collected on the target behavior; (2) during the second phase (B_1), the treatment is instituted, along with continual data collection of the target behavior; (3) during the third phase (A_2), there is a return to baseline—that is, a removal of the treatment manipulation; (4) during the fourth phase (B_2), the treatment is reinstituted. If the behavior under investigation is controlled by the experimental manipulations, it will change in a systematic manner with each introduction and removal of the treatment manipulations (Sidman, 1960).

The essential characteristics of the multiple-baseline design are as follows: (1) data must be kept on three or more independent behaviors—that is, behaviors two and three are unaffected when behavior one is changed by an experimental manipulation; (2) the treatment procedure is applied to target behavior one until a change is shown in that behavior; (3) the treatment is applied to target behavior two and later to additional target behaviors. If the target behaviors change substantially at the point at which the treatment is introduced, then a cause-effect relationship can be inferred. Hall, Cristler, Cranston, and Tucker (1970) present an excellent description of the multiple-baseline procedures along with illustrations of three variant designs (across situations, across individuals, and across behaviors).

A number of methodological, practical, and ethical considerations need to be taken into account in deciding whether to use a within-subject or a between-subject design in a particular investigation. The following are some of the situations in which a within-subject design is preferred to the between-subject design: (1) when it is the most convincing means of demonstrating the causal or functional relationship between a behavior and its controlling variables (Bandura, 1969; Sidman, 1960); (2) when reversals are possible and acceptable and the ABAB design can be used, or when three or more behaviors are independent and the multiple-baseline design can be used; (3) when enough subjects are not available for a between-subject group design; (4) when the subjects available for an experiment are not homogeneous—that is, they do not have common characteristics on which they can be compared across groups; (5) when statistical assumptions for a group design cannot be adequately fulfilled; (6) when therapists, teachers, or parents are being trained in empirically based procedures for managing an individual's behavior (Risley, 1969). Illustrations of the within-subject design can be found in an increasing number of SC studies (for example, Broden, Hall, & Mitts, 1971; Fixsen, Phillips, & Wolf, 1972; Herbert & Baer, 1972; Lovitt & Curtiss, 1969).

Some of the situations in which the between-subject design is preferred over the within-subject design are the following: (1) when the relative effectiveness of different treatment procedures is examined (Baer, 1971; Bandura, 1969)—for example, between-subject designs have been employed to investigate the relative effectiveness of self-reinforcement versus external reinforcement with children in a laboratory setting (Bandura & Perloff, 1967), the effectiveness of various SC procedures in the modification of weight (Mahoney, 1972b), and the relative effectiveness of self-control therapy versus external-control therapy (Jeffrey, 1973); (2) when a researcher is interested in establishing normative data on large populations; (3) when it is impossible or undesirable to reverse a behavior and, consequently, an ABAB-reversal design cannot be used or when three or more behaviors are not independent of one another and, consequently, a multiple baseline cannot be used; (4) when subjects are available to participate in an experiment for only a short time—that is, they are not available for an investigation that might take weeks or months, as is often the requirement in a within-subject design; (5) when it is impossible or impractical to take the nonreactive, repeated measurements necessary in a within-subject design; (6) when complex phenomena are being investigated and there is a great deal of "noise" or uncontrolled variability. In the latter case, statistical methods can be used to help isolate the experimental manipulation from the uncontrolled variability.

Although there are often clear advantages to using either a within- or between-subject design, there are also situations in which there are advantages to using both designs. Increased confidence in the validity of both the designs and the findings can be achieved by conducting systematic replications across designs. For example, similar results have been found in the use of contingency-management procedures for weight loss in both a within-subject design (Mann, 1971) and a between-subject group design (Jeffrey & Christensen, 1972).

There may also be cases in which some combination of the between- and within-subject design features would be better than either design used separately. Glynn's (1970) experiment on the classroom applications of self-determined reinforcement and Mahoney, Thoresen, and Danaher's (1972) study on covert-behavior modification illustrate the utility of combining both designs. Regardless of the design chosen for a particular study, all designs need to control for the same factors that jeopardize internal and external validity (Campbell & Stanley, 1963).

In SC research, as in any research, the development of the area is uneven. At any point in time, one part may need more emphasis than another. Recent reviews of SC literature indicate that current research might profit most if it emphasized experimental investigations (Mahoney, 1972a). Particular attention should be directed toward controlled experimental field studies in order to test the external validity of laboratory findings and toward analogue studies in order to explore some of the basic mechanisms of SC phenomena. However, the development of field and analogue research is dependent to a large

extent on the development and use of sound methodological procedures (Hempel, 1966; Underwood, 1957). Since many SC studies are
lacking in methodological sophistication, there needs to be methodological improvement before advances can be achieved in substantive
areas of the SC field. Many of the problems, such as that of devising
adequate and acceptable definitions of SC, artifacts, and so on, can
be solved by the application of existing methodological developments
in fields such as experimental, developmental, and social psychology.
Some of the more important problems for SC research will be examined
in greater detail in the following sections.

II. OPERATIONAL DEFINITIONS AND THEORY
CONSTRUCTION

Any scientific endeavor in its beginning is beset with confusion
about terms, and the SC area is no exception. But if any field is to
advance scientifically, the definitional and theoretical foundations must
be clarified (Bergmann, 1957; Marx, 1951; Underwood, 1957).

A survey of the definitions of *self-control* (see Thoresen & Mahoney, 1974) indicates that there are some differences in the ways in
which the term is used. Because there is no common agreement at
this time, it seems essential that all SC investigations should include
clear, explicit, operational definitions of *self-control* and other self-
hyphenated terms (such as *self-reinforcement* and *self-monitoring*).

Gewirtz (1971) and Stuart (1972) are critical of the use of self-
hyphenated terms because they are usually poorly defined, the descriptive and explanatory functions of the terms are often confused, and
the role of environmental causative factors is often de-emphasized or
forgotten. Their arguments are valid, but their conclusion that self-
hyphenated terms should be avoided is not valid. Self-hyphenated
terms are useful for describing experimental or treatment procedures.
This descriptive function must at all times be kept separate from an
explanatory function of terms, for the latter involves a statement of
cause and effect that requires sound experimental evidence.

The Role of Theory in Self-Control Phenomena

The assumptions, characteristics, and role of theory construction
are extensively covered in the philosophy-of-science literature (for

example, Bergmann, 1957; Danto & Morgenbesser, 1960; Hempel, 1966; Marx, 1951). Commenting on theory, Underwood (1957) states:

> For although we couldn't arrive at any acceptable specific use of the word "theory," it nevertheless always implies an attempt to bring order to the world of empirical facts by abstracting out the commonalities underlying the facts. All this means is that we are searching for generalizations, and this *is* science [p. 268].

Underwood's viewpoint is recommended for SC inquiries; theory construction should play an essential role in both basic and applied SC research, because it can help abstract and integrate the commonalities underlying the facts.

An excellent example of an initial attempt at theory construction is Kanfer's (1971) model of self-regulation. This model is only tentative, but its heuristic value is that it summarizes many empirical studies and generates some theoretical and clinical generalizations that can be subsequently investigated. According to Kanfer, self-regulation has three stages: self-monitoring, self-evaluation, and self-reinforcement. The first stage, self-monitoring, starts with the input that follows the execution of a response. The sources of the inputs are external environmental consequences and internal response-produced cues (that is, verbal-symbolic, proprioceptive, and autonomic cues) triggered by the response. The next stage, self-evaluation, is viewed as a conditional discrimination in which the content of the previous step (the inputs from a response plus current situation and inputs from prior experiences) serves as the stimulus determining the self-evaluative response. The outcome of this discrimination is the person's "judgment" that his performance exceeds, equals, or falls below his comparison criteria. Within a certain range of motivational conditions set by the situational demands and the person's history, the "judgment" serves as a discriminative stimulus for positive or negative reinforcement. The third stage is the actual delivery of self-reinforcement, either covertly or overtly. The self-reinforcing operations are assumed to rest on the outcome of a discrimination in which the person evaluates the adequacy of his actions.

As an illustration of Kanfer's model, consider the following. A student studies hard for an exam, and this behavior results in self-monitoring of (1) external consequences—that is, his grade on the exam and social response from the class—and (2) internal consequences—that is, autonomic over-activity and physical exhaustion. Next, the student compares his actual performance with his learned performance criteria. If he "judges" his recent performance to be superior to his performance criteria, he might positively reinforce himself —covertly by saying to himself that he has done a good job and overtly by going to the local pub to have a few drinks.

III. RELIABILITY AND VALIDITY OF EXTERNAL MONITORING, SELF-MONITORING, AND BEHAVIORAL QUESTIONNAIRES

Behavior modification has emphasized an empirically based orientation more than any other school of therapy has. Nevertheless, behavior-modification research in general and self-control research in particular have not given adequate consideration to some of the essential components of psychometric theory. This section will discuss two cardinal features of psychometric theory, reliability and validity, in terms of the measurement procedures that are most germane to SC research—namely, external monitoring, self-monitoring, and behavioral questionnaires. A brief discussion of the utility of the three types of measurement follows.

Reliability

Since reliability is a complex topic, this section will highlight some areas pertinent to SC investigations. It will consider the importance of reliability, suggest some cautions in using mechanical recording devices, and offer guidelines for estimating interobserver reliability.

The Importance of Reliability.   The general concept of reliability refers to the consistency of measurement procedures (Cronbach, 1960; Nunnally, 1967). Without reliable or consistent measurement procedures, any study is confounded. For example, if an experimenter's measure of the number of self-reinforcements children administered to themselves was inconsistent, one would not know at the end of the experiment whether any "changes" in the children's behavior were due to the treatment or due to the inadequate data-collection procedures. Therefore, it is very important that adequate reliabilities be obtained and reported.

Regardless of whether the data-collection procedures involve external monitoring, self-monitoring, or both, interobserver reliability estimates should be calculated routinely on the pertinent variables. Unfortunately, the reliability of self-monitoring has not yet been adequately demonstrated, as has been noted by a number of authors (Kanfer, 1970b; Nelson & McReynolds, 1971; Simkins, 1971a; Tighe &

Elliott, 1968). Many early studies that employed self-monitoring did not report reliability (for example, Cautela, 1966; Fox, 1962; Goldiamond, 1965; Stuart, 1967). In order to more adequately assess the reliability of self-monitoring, recent experiments have employed independent observers in addition to the subjects monitoring their own behavior (Broden, Hall, & Mitts, 1971; Fixsen, Phillips, & Wolf, 1972; Herbert & Baer, 1972). Hopefully, experiments such as these will encourage more SC investigators to deal with the important issue of reliability.

Recording Devices.   In recent years, mechanical recording devices have assisted in efficient and reliable data collection (Schwitzgebel, 1968). These recording devices range from simple wrist counters (Katz, in press; Lindsley, 1969) to complicated electromechanical instruments. For example, Azrin and his associates have developed portable, semi-automated instruments that count the number of cigarettes taken from a special pack (Azrin & Powell, 1968) or that count the number of times a subject assumes an inappropriate posture (Azrin, Rubin, O'Brien, Ayllon, & Roll, 1968).

Although these measurement devices provide convenient and precise ways to record behavior, they do *not* guarantee reliability (Simkins, 1971a). The monitor may unintentionally or intentionally push the wrist counters incorrectly, take cigarettes from packs other than the special counter pack, or forget to wear the posture harness. Portable recording devices offer a practical and economical way of measuring behaviors. However, the reliability of the recording device should be separated from the reliability of the person using the device. The consistency of both the recording device and the operator must be assessed to determine the reliability of the total measurement system.

Estimating Interobserver Reliability.[3]   Percent-of-agreement procedures are normally used for estimating interobserver reliability (Bijou, Peterson, & Ault, 1968). Although not usually reported, correlation coefficients can also be calculated for the same types of observation data.

The advantages of the percent-of-agreement method for estimating reliability are that (1) it is easy to calculate, and (2) it is useful for training raters, since the responses can be tied to specific time intervals and errors can be detected. Some of the main disadvantages of the percent-of-agreement method are that (1) it can give deceptively high estimates of interobserver reliability when the proportion of either

[3]The material on estimating interobserver reliability is based on a longer paper by Hartmann (1972a). See his paper for details on the calculation of reliability estimates and the advantages of the correlation procedure.

occurrence or nonoccurrence is high; (2) it is highly sensitive to an observer's "dropping" a single trial, so that all subsequent trials are mismatched—for example, Observer A is marking Trial 5 while Observer B is marking Trial 6; and (3) it does not lend itself to additional mathematical analyses.

A major advantage of using correlation coefficients, as is done in classical psychometric theory, is that further mathematical analyses can be performed on the descriptive statistics. For example, correction for attenuation, true- and error-score variances, and the limiting effect of reliability on validity can be estimated with great precision. In addition, the correlation coefficient handles extreme base rates (high or low) more effectively than the percent-of-agreement procedure. Some disadvantages are that the correlation coefficient may be more difficult to calculate than the percent-of-agreement procedures and that it does not pinpoint specific agreements or disagreements.

Although each procedure has merits, for most SC experimental inquiries, the correlation-coefficient procedure is clearly *preferred* over the typical percent-of-agreement procedure for estimating interobserver reliability.

Validity

Measurement validity refers to the degree to which an assessment procedure estimates what it is designed to measure (Cronbach, 1960; Nunnally, 1967). In psychometric theory, high reliability (such as inter-observer reliability) does not necessarily ensure high validity. For example, two observers obtain 100 percent interobserver agreement when they purportedly count the number of reinforcements a child administers to himself; in actuality, the observers inadvertently count the number of reinforcements the experimenter administers to the child. In this case, there would be perfect reliability, no validity, and a totally meaningless study. Therefore, it is essential in SC inquiries that both the reliability *and* validity be ascertained.

When observational procedures are employed, conditions can arise that can undermine validity. Four conditions that are of particular concern to SC investigations are drift, reactivity, bias, and generality. Definitions and examples of each are presented.

1. Drift refers to whether or not the target behavior being measured begins to change or deviate across time from the original operational definition of the target behavior. For example, Patterson and Harris (1968) and Reid (1970) have found that, in external-monitoring, even well-trained observers may in time begin to redefine the initial

target behavior in their own terms. Thus, the behavior that is actually measured drifts farther and farther away from the behavior as it was originally defined. Patterson and Harris controlled for this drift by recalibrating (retraining) their raters each week with the original criterion measure.

The same problem can occur in self-monitoring. For example, Thoresen, Hubbard, Hannum, Hendricks, and Shapiro (1973) encountered the self-observer drift problem with a nursery-school teacher in a within-subject-design study. After an initial high level of interobserver agreement, the teacher tended to "redefine" positive verbal responses such that the percentage of agreement dropped after two weeks. If subjects are assigned to monitor their own behavior, they should be trained initially in self-monitoring, and, then, calibration checks should be made at appropriate intervals to assess whether they have drifted from the original operational definition.

2. Reactivity refers to whether or not a measurement procedure itself caused a change in the behavior being monitored. There is ample evidence that observers can be obtrusive (Johnson & Bolstad, 1972; Patterson & Harris, 1968; Webb, Campbell, Schwartz, & Sechrest, 1966). An excellent example of the reactive effects of an observer is seen in a study by Surratt, Ulrich, and Hawkins (1969). They investigated the effects of a fifth-grade student's modifying the maladaptive study behaviors of four first-grade students. A concealed, post-treatment TV observation indicated that the behavioral changes effected during the treatment phases were partially maintained by the regular classroom environment. However, a replication of the baseline phase with the observer in the classroom produced an increase in the rate of study behavior. This indicated that the observer's presence acted as a discriminative stimulus for studying. Similarly, other experiments show that self-monitoring can also be a reactive measure (Broden, Hall, & Mitts, 1971; Johnson & White, 1971; McFall, 1970). For example, in one study, McFall (1970) first unobtrusively recorded all students' smoking rates during class periods; some students were then instructed to record their own smoking frequency and others to record the number of occasions on which they considered smoking but did not do so. The results showed that self-monitoring caused a change in their smoking rate, thus indicating that self-monitoring was a reactive data-collection procedure.

Several strategies can be used to control for reactive effects in external monitoring and self-monitoring. In the case of external monitoring, nonobtrusive measures can be developed, as advocated by Webb, Campbell, Schwartz, and Sechrest (1966). Archival data, such as grades, can serve as direct or indirect unobtrusive dependent measures (Gottman & McFall, 1972; Johnson & White, 1971). Furthermore, it would seem, with our present technology and a little ingenuity, that more unobtrusive measures could be developed than are presently employed in SC research. For example, a concealed TV camera, such as the one used in the Surratt, Ulrich, and Hawkins (1969) study, can be used in conjunction with or in place of both external monitoring and self-monitoring. However, when any concealed measurement device is contemplated, ethical considerations must be taken into account in deciding whether it should be used.

Another strategy of reducing reactive effects is to let an independent observer monitor for a period of time to allow the person who is being observed to habituate to the observer (Gottman & McFall, 1972). After the habituation to the observer has occurred, relevant data can then be collected, including data on how reliably the individual monitors himself.

Since self-monitoring is inherently an obtrusive measure, steps should be taken to control for its possible reactive effects. The simplest way is to use an unobtrusive measure in place of self-monitoring. If this is neither possible nor desirable, the effects, if any, of self-monitoring on the dependent variable can be allowed to stabilize before instituting the treatment. (The section on self-monitoring discusses additional means of controlling for these possible reactive effects.)

3. Bias refers to whether or not the observer has some systematic tendency to measure responses in ways that deviate from the initially defined behavior. For example, experimenter biases or expectancies may have strong effects on the observer's tendency to measure the results in a way favoring the experimenter's hypotheses (Johnson & Bolstad, 1972; Rosenthal, 1969).

High interobserver reliability does not necessarily control for bias. An obvious example of high interobserver reliability with bias occurs when two observers are informed of experimental hypotheses and distort the data to conform to these hypotheses. Observers' biases can be controlled by keeping observers unaware of the hypotheses of the experiment and by having independent observers occasionally check the regular observers. For example, Patterson (1970) keeps his observers unaware of the purpose of his experiments and even has some observers work in a separate building so that they have no contact with the experimenter. These "outside" observers act as independent checks on the "inhouse" observers.

The problem of bias validity may be even more acute in self-monitoring when both the therapist and patient have strong expectancies and investments in positive results. Consequently, it is particularly important to gather independent assessments of the subject's self-monitoring.

4. Generality refers to the representativeness of the behavior sampled in terms of the total population of target behaviors. For example, if external monitoring were used to assess an individual's smoking behavior and if the data were collected only while he was at school, then serious questions could be raised about whether the data were representative of his smoking, since the sampling procedure did not include significant smoking situations other than at school. The ideal solution to the lack of generality is to have continuous monitoring of all relevant behaviors. However, this is usually not feasible. When behavior is sampled rather than monitored continuously, Patterson and Harris (1968) recommend checking the various settings in which the target behavior occurs and then collecting representative data from each relevant setting.

In self-monitoring, the problem and solution are the same. Whenever the target response can be continuously self-monitored, then such a strategy is clearly preferred. For example, it is easy for a person to wear a wrist counter and self-record all the cigarettes he smokes. However, it is often unrealistic to have a person continuously record all relevant behavior.

For example, if an experimenter asks a patient to record all the food he eats for six months, the patient may comply for a week or so and then understandably extinguish self-recording as it becomes a burdensome chore. In general, it is advisable for the experimenter and the patient to work together to specify the target behavior. They should also decide on a method of data collection that will ensure representativeness but will not be burdensome. Finally, an independent check should be made to ensure that the patient has self-monitored correctly.

Self-Monitoring

There are some problems in the use of self-monitoring that warrant special attention. First, it should be determined whether self-monitoring is being used as a measurement procedure—that is, to collect data on some dependent variable, whether it is being used as the independent variable, or whether it is being used for both purposes. If self-monitoring is being used to collect data, then all the previous comments about reliability and validity are applicable.

However, if self-monitoring is being used as an independent variable, then its effects must be clearly isolated and controlled. The reactivity of self-monitoring has raised substantial interest in the use of self-monitoring as a treatment component of SC programs (for example, Herbert & Baer, 1972; Johnson & White, 1971; Kanfer, 1970b; McFall & Hammen, 1971). Furthermore, since self-monitoring is an inextricable component of any self-control model (Buckley, 1968; Kanfer, 1971), it is unrealistic to try to program an SC treatment in the absence of some self-monitoring.

A feasible strategy to isolate the effects of self-monitoring is to use an experimental design that separates the relative contribution of self-monitoring from other aspects of the treatment. A between-subject group design with a no-treatment control group, a self-monitoring group only, and a self-monitoring-plus-some-treatment group could be used to isolate the relative contributions of self-monitoring to behavior change. An experiment by Mahoney (1972b) illustrates the use of this paradigm. He investigated, among other things, the effects on weight reduction of a no-treatment control, of self-monitoring of weight, and of self-monitoring plus self-reinforcement for weight loss.

An ABCABC within-subject design—in which A is baseline (independently assessed), B is self-monitoring, and C is self-monitoring plus treatment—might be used to isolate the relative contributions of self-monitoring to behavior change. Independent measurement of the target behavior is necessary throughout all conditions of a within-subject design study (see Table 2B). A multiple baseline might be used when an ABCABC-reversal paradigm is impractical or unethical (see Table 2C). Examples of both of these within-subject paradigms, with slight modifications, are reported in two experiments by Fixsen, Phillips, and Wolf (1972) in which they investigated the reliability and the effects of self-reporting and of peer reporting.

Other designs, such as a multiple-time-series design, may be used to isolate the effects of self-monitoring in the natural environment (Gottman & McFall, 1972). Earlier comments about research strategies and design should be taken into account in selecting an appropriate design.

A second problem associated with self-monitoring occurs when the variables (independent or dependent) are covert rather than overt, since it is difficult to estimate the reliability of covert responses. The problem can perhaps be better understood by crossing the type of response (overt or covert) with the use of self-monitoring as a dependent or an independent variable. The four combinations of independent-dependent variables and over-covert responses are summarized in Table 3. It is assumed that, in each case, the therapist-experimenter will initiate some overt intervention but that, within the SC paradigm,

TABLE 2. Designs to Isolate the Effects of Self-Monitoring.

2A Between-Subject Group Design

Groups	Measurement		
	Pre	Post	Follow-up
No treatment control			
Self-monitoring only			
Self-monitoring + treatment			

2B Within-Subject Design/ABCABC Reversal

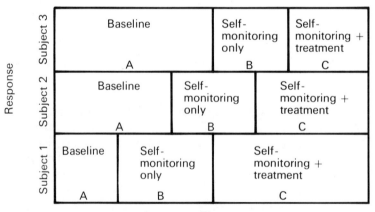

Response	Baseline (independently assessed)	Self-monitoring only	Self-monitoring + treatment	Baseline	Self-monitoring only	Self-monitoring + Treatment
	A	B	C	A	B	C

Time/Units

2C Within-Subject Design/Multiple Baseline

the patient-subject will initiate some independent variable (the controlling response) to control some dependent variable (the controlled response). In Case 1, there is obviously no major problem in determining reliability, since all responses are overt. But in Cases 2, 3, and 4, which involve covert responding, problems can occur. Several partial solutions are recommended for dealing with these cases.

TABLE 3.   Different Combinations of Independent-Dependent Variables and Overt-Covert Responses.

Experimenter-Therapist	Case Number	Schemata		Subject-Patient Examples	
		Independent Variable	Dependent Variable	Independent Variable	Dependent Variable
Experimenter-Therapist initiates overt independent manipulation	1	Overt I	Overt D	S overtly rewards himself for losing weight by going to a movie.	S loses weight.
	2	Overt I	Covert D	S overtly rewards himself with a cigarette each time he has a positive self-thought.	S increases rate of positive self-thoughts.
	3	Covert I	Overt D	S covertly goes through systematic desensitization hierarchy for a car phobia.	S terminates overt avoidance of cars.
	4	Covert I	Covert D	S covertly reinforces himself with positive imagery for self-confident thoughts.	S increases frequency of self-confident thoughts.

One tactic is to have a subject report orally to an experimenter what he does covertly (Mahoney, 1970). This approach is simple and convenient; however, it does have its difficulties. As Simkins (1971a) has noted, a distinction must be made between the initial covert response and the act of overtly reporting the covert response. The latter can be influenced by demand characteristics, experimenter biases, and the therapist's verbal and nonverbal contingencies. If a subject's oral report of his covert responses is used, precautions should be taken not to put pressure on the subject to report his covert responses in a particular way.

A second tactic is to externalize what are typically covert responses so that they become overt responses. The covert independent variable (Case 2) can be externalized and performed in the experimental setting so that it can be measured. For example, some studies on obesity have had covert self-reinforcement lists read out loud in the presence of the therapist to ensure a reliable manipulation of the independent variable (Jeffrey, Christensen, & Pappas, 1973). A variant of this is to have covert self-reinforcers (for example, subjects saying to themselves "I'm a good person when I lose weight") transformed to overt, tangible reinforcers. Mahoney (1972b) has had subjects deposit money with the therapist at the beginning of their treatment program. They could later use this money to reward themselves for desired performances (for example, "I'm a good person for losing weight this week, so I'll reward myself"). The amount of money used can be easily and reliably measured.

A third tactic is to use the intervening-variable approach (Marx, 1951). This tactic involves (1) specifying a theory of self-regulation that has some testable hypotheses, (2) specifying an overt response that is functionally related to the manipulation of the intervening variables, and (3) performing experiments that confirm or disconfirm the hypotheses. Schematically the model would look like this:

(1)	(2)	(3)
Overt		Overt
independent →	Intervening →	dependent
variable	variable	variable

Bandura's (1971) model of SC and the problem of depression is one illustration of this schematic paradigm. Bandura states that depression may be due to a lack of sufficient self-reinforcements. Furthermore, others (for example, Ferster, 1965; Jackson, 1972; Lewinsohn, Weinstein, & Shaw, 1969) have posited that people who are depressed display a low rate of behavior in general (low activity level). One might reason, therefore, that an increase in covert positive self-thought should produce an increase in overt behaviors. Finally, a series of experiments could be conducted to test (1) if the experimenter's and subject's overt manipulations lead to (2) an increase in the subject's covert self-reinforcements, which subsequently lead to an increase in his covert positive self-thoughts, resulting in (3) an increase in his overt activity level. Although link 2 cannot be reliably measured, the initial link (the experimenter's and subject's overt manipulation) and the final link in the chain (the subject's overt behavior) can be reliably measured.

Similarly, Mischel and his associates have used the same tactic in the investigation of basic mechanisms of SC (Mischel & Ebbesen, 1970; Mischel, Ebbesen, & Zeiss, 1972). In their experiments on cognitive and attentional mechanisms in delay of gratification, they have tested (1) whether different experimenter manipulations lead to (2) different covert activities in children and subsequently to different frustration levels, resulting in (3) predicted differential durations of children's waiting to ring a bell. Again, link 2 cannot be directly measured, but the initial and final links can be reliably assessed.

Even though covert processes cannot be directly measured, sound methodological procedures can be employed that allow for the inclusion of covert processes—which are important aspects of human behavior—in inquiries of the basic mechanisms and clinical applications of self-control (Nelson & McReynolds, 1971; Proctor & Malloy, 1971).

Behavioral-Assessment Questionnaires

A behavioral-assessment questionnaire is a straightforward approach that simply asks a person to describe his behavior in a specific situation. Since behavioral questionnaires provide an efficient way to quickly collect a great deal of information and since they involve a person in the assessment of his own behaviors, it would seem advantageous for SC investigators to use behavioral questionnaires whenever they are appropriate. However, caution should be taken to use behavioral questionnaires as a supplement to, *not* as a substitute for, self-monitoring and external monitoring.

Some examples of existing behavioral questionnaires follow: (1) Cautela and Kastenbaum (1967) have reported the use of a reinforcement-survey schedule in therapy training and research; (2) Wolpe (1969) has developed a life-history questionnaire and fear inventory; (3) Jeffrey (1970) has reported the use of a study-reinforcement questionnaire; (4) Gelfand and Hartmann (1972) have developed a reinforcer-identification list for children that can be filled out by teachers and parents; (5) Tasto and Suinn (1972) have constructed a fear-survey schedule. Only Tasto and Suinn's report has dealt with the problems of reliability and validity; nevertheless, the behavioral-questionnaire approach to assessment seems to have much potential utility and should be further explored in SC investigations.

Utility of the Measurement Procedures

The collection of data is dependent on the questions asked and the design used in a study. Often, unreliable, invalid, or insufficient data are collected in a study. No matter how good a design may be, without reliable and relevant information, no study can be interpreted unambiguously. External monitoring or self-monitoring plus external reliability monitoring can be expensive, but, in conducting an experiment, one needs to look at the expense of the measurement procedures in terms of a larger cost-benefit model.

Consider, for example, an elaborate field study that will investigate some SC program to modify the drinking behavior of alcoholics in an outpatient setting. Furthermore, assume that part of the treatment involves subjects in monitoring their own drinking. To hire observers to monitor the subjects would obviously be more expensive than to have them monitor their own drinking. But it could be even more expensive and harmful in the long run to conclude that some SC treatment was "successful" when in fact the subjects may have biased or falsified their self-monitored data. On the other hand, an *exploratory* SC case study of the use of covert self-reinforcement may not need an elaborate, independently verified data-collection procedure. The main point is to aim for judicious procedures that will provide appropriate information regarding the questions under investigation.

IV. PATIENT AND THERAPIST VARIABLES

Traditional psychotherapy research has emphasized the importance of patient and therapist variables, sometimes to the extent of ignoring treatment variables (Bergin & Garfield, 1971; Goldstein, Heller, & Sechrest, 1966). However, the focus of behavior-therapy research has been just the opposite. The initial emphasis on treatment procedures may have been needed in the early stages of behavior therapy, but it is now time to include relevant patient and therapist variables in the domain of behavior modification in general and self-control research in particular. Paul (1969), for example, recommends including the relatively stable personal-social characteristics and physical life-environmental characteristics of both clients and therapists as appropriate domains of behavior-modification inquiries. Research indicates that important patient variables are motivation, expectancy, and socio-economic status; important therapist variables are expectancy and interpersonal skills (Fiske, Hunt, Luborsky, Orne, Parloff, Reiser, & Tuma, 1970; Kiesler, 1971).

Although most behavior-modification and SC clinical case studies allude to patient and therapist characteristics, the primary emphasis is on the learning-based treatment procedure. In some SC studies (for example, Johnson, 1971; Stuart, 1967; Todd; 1972), a plausible rival hypothesis for the outcome might have been that it was not the treatment procedure per se but the patient's motivation and expectancy and the therapist's interpersonal skill and expectancy that accounted for most of the positive results. In the final analysis, the issue of patient and therapist variables can best be answered empirically by the inclusion of these variables in SC research.

In surveying the traditional therapy-outcome research, Bergin (1971) generally found that patients exposed to a treatment condition showed greater variability on the post-treatment measure than patients "exposed" to a no-treatment condition. He also found that some patients in "successful" treatment groups did not improve and that some even grew worse. Similar findings are now appearing in the SC literature (Mahoney, 1972c). For example, an analysis of the results of some SC studies that report significant differences between the treatment group and the control group also reveals that some patients in the "superior" treatment groups did not improve and that some even grew worse (Harris & Bruner, 1971; Penick, Ross, Fox, & Stunkard, 1971). It would seem prudent for SC investigators to report individual results in addition to group results and to note if there are "unsuccessful" individuals in "successful" treatments.

V. ARTIFACTS: DEMAND CHARACTERISTICS AND EVALUATION APPREHENSION

Of the many possible artifacts in behavioral research (see Rosenthal & Rosnow, 1969), demand characteristics and evaluation apprehension seem particularly relevant to SC research and therefore warrant further elaboration.

Demand Characteristics

Orne (1969) refers to demand characteristics as those cues of an experiment that govern the subject's perception of his role in the experiment. These cues include the experimental setting, instructions, and equipment and the experimenter's role and behavior. Since SC research deals with a social-influence process in which the experimenter tries to influence the subject to change his behavior, SC investigations need to control for social-influence processes that go beyond the therapeutic techniques being studied.

Orne (1969) suggests several quasi-control procedures that can be used to "control" for demand characteristics. By quasi-controls, he means design procedures that facilitate inferences about the experimental manipulations. Two types of quasi-controls are postexperimental inquiry and the nonexperiment.

Orne notes that human subjects think and talk and that a great deal can be learned about an investigation by simply interviewing the subjects after the experiment is over. Debriefing of this type is so easy that it seems incredible that it has not been employed more frequently. There are some obvious problems in conducting postexperimental interviews, but the information obtained would seem to warrant this routine usage by SC researchers.

In a nonexperiment, the subject is presented with all the experimental procedures except the actual treatment. The dependent variable is still measured, and the experimental subjects are compared with the nonexperimental subjects. If there is no difference between the experimental and nonexperimental subjects, there is suggestive evidence that demand characteristics have a significant effect on the results.

Evaluation Apprehension

Evaluation apprehension refers to the subject's concern that he receive a positive evaluation from the experimenter, or at least that he provide no grounds for a negative one (Rosenberg, 1969). Evaluation apprehension is important to the extent that the subject's initial concern that he will be evaluated positively is confirmed by the investigation and that his concern affects the results of the study. In an extensive review of subject effects in experimental research, Weber and Cook (1972) concluded, among other things, (1) that there is widespread evidence for the construct of evaluation apprehension and (2) that evaluation apprehension can seriously restrict both the internal and external validity of an experiment.

The possible confounding effects of evaluation apprehension exist in SC research. For example, when self-reinforcement is used, the subject's apprehension that he will be evaluated by the experimenter on how he uses self-reinforcement may affect his performance. Several studies with children in school have demonstrated that self-administered reinforcement systems can change and maintain behavior as well as externally administered reinforcement systems can (Glynn, 1970; Lovitt & Curtiss, 1969). From a careful analysis of the self-reinforcement manipulation, it appears that the subjects knew that they were being monitored and evaluated by the experimenter. The fact that the experimenter evaluated the subjects and that the subjects knew they were being monitored may have affected their behavior. Unfortunately, these studies neither controlled nor discussed the issue of evaluation apprehension.

Two tactics might be used to control for evaluation-apprehension effects. First, these effects can be minimized by changing experimenters, reducing continuous feedback, providing no cues of what is expected, and reducing the power of the experimenter over the subject (Rosenberg, 1969). Another tactic is to isolate any effects of evaluation apprehension by including them as part of the treatment. For example, a between-subject group design that included a control group, a self-reinforcement group in which subjects were told that the experimenter would evaluate how they reinforced themselves, and a self-reinforcement group in which the subjects were told that the experimenter would not evaluate how they reinforced themselves would allow any effects of evaluation apprehension to be separated out.

VI.   GENERALIZATION AND FOLLOW-UP

Two of the fundamental assumptions of the behavior modification of the 1950s and 1960s were that behavior could be changed and that, once changes were instituted, naturally occurring contingencies would maintain the new behavior. Presently, there are sound experimental data to substantiate the former assumption but a paucity of data to substantiate the latter.

In a review of token-reinforcement programs, O'Leary and Drabman (1971) and Kazdin and Bootzin (1972) have concluded that there were little data indicating that generalization had occurred in token programs. Bernstein (1969) concluded, in a review of smoking research, that neither behavior modification nor traditional therapy programs could maintain nonsmoking behavior. Patterson, Ray, and Shaw (1968) found in their early work with families that much of the behavior changed during treatment was not maintained during follow-up. After two decades of discouraging data, behavior modifiers are now recommending that "generalization should be programmed rather than expected or lamented" (Baer, Wolf, & Risley, 1968, p. 97).

One of the fundamental assumptions and purported advantages

of an SC approach is that the probability of generalization and maintenance of behavior is dramatically increased (Bandura, 1969; Cautela,
1969; Thoresen & Mahoney, 1974). However, there is a paucity of data
to substantiate this SC assumption. Often studies employing an SC
procedure by itself or in combination with other procedures have
reported "success" at the end of treatment but have not conducted
adequate follow-ups to test whether the behavior change was maintained (for example, Gygi & Saslow, 1971; Johnson, 1971). Other
studies have conducted adequate follow-ups but have then found that
the behavioral changes were *not* maintained (for example, Harris &
Bruner, 1971). Still others have proposed using an SC problem-solving
model that in essence should increase generalization, or the ability of
a person to deal with new problems across new situations or behaviors
(for example, D'Zurilla & Goldfried, 1971). Although this problem-
solving model looks promising, there are insufficient data to evaluate
the effectiveness of the approach.

VII.   COST-EFFECTIVENESS

Patterson, Ray, and Shaw (1968) recently wrote: ". . . it seems
important for social engineers not only to assess the relative perma-
nence of their efforts but also to provide data describing the amounts
of time required as an investment to produce these effects" (p. 54).
They further state that intervention techniques that effect change but
do not persist may be of interest but have little utility; intervention
techniques that have effects and persist but cost inordinate amounts
may also have little utility. Thus, there is a clear need to develop intervention techniques that have effects and persist and that are feasible
in terms of cost.

Another assumption and purported major advantage of an SC
approach is that it is "efficient" and cheaper than traditional therapies
(Cautela, 1969). Again, there are little data to substantiate this fundamental SC assumption. In fact, as of this writing, I have not seen a
single study comparing the cost-effectiveness of an SC treatment with
that of any other treatment approach.

There are presently no clear guidelines on how to proceed in
assessing cost factors. Some of the factors that might be considered
are the following. First, there should be a regular tabular reporting of
the number of contacts, the therapist's time, the amount of money spent
for therapist-client interactions, and the client's work on his own, as
suggested by Stuart (1967) and Patterson (1969). Second, the social
cost of the maladaptive behaviors of the patients needs to be more

adequately assessed. For example, the cost in terms of increased health problems and medical expense might be assessed for smokers versus nonsmokers. Some of the work being pioneered in human-resources accounting (Pyle, 1970) may have useful implications in this regard. Third, a comprehensive decision-making model for evaluating the cost of inappropriate behaviors versus the cost of alternative treatment programs might be utilized. In this way, more rational, humane decisions can be made about which treatment programs to implement (Arthur, 1969; Edwards, 1954).

To increase the rate of reporting, and hence the gathering, of systematic follow-up and cost-effectiveness data, it would seem advisable for editors of behavior-modification and clinical journals to determine minimum standards for reporting follow-up and cost-effectiveness data.

RESEARCH TRENDS

Recent studies, reviews, and books dealing with SC phenomena indicate a number of emerging research trends. The purpose here is not to present an exhaustive review but rather to highlight some of the more important trends. The aim is to present a perspective on the ideas that are beginning to have a creative, catalytic effect on both basic and applied SC investigations. Some of the trends are the following: (1) using an environment-self interdependence model; (2) shifting the locus of control from the therapist to the patient; (3) training the patient in self-observation, self-evaluation, and self-reinforcement; (4) programming strategies on how to control behavior rather than just changing a specific behavior; and (5) applying systems theory to SC research.

Environment-Self Interdependence Model

For centuries, there have been theological and philosophical arguments about whether the self or the environment controls one's behavior. Only recently has experimental research been conducted on the origins and mechanisms of SC. Current data indicate that the origins of SC lie in the biological and social environment (Bandura & Walters, 1963; Gewirtz, 1971; Kanfer & Phillips, 1970; Skinner, 1953). However, in the process of learning self-regulatory behaviors, the individual is not just shaped by the environment, but he also becomes an active shaper of the environment. Skinner (1971), writing about the design of a culture, states: "The relation between the controller and controlled is reciprocal" (p. 169). Bandura (1969) describes the relationship between the individual and the environment as a continuous reciprocal-influence process. A human being is controlled by the environment, and he also controls part of the environment that affects him and others. Thus, the old polemics of whether "willpower" or the environment totally controls a person's behavior are antiquated. Traditional conceptions of "willpower" are inadequate, since they do not take into account the continuous influence of the environment on the individual. On the other hand, "traditional" behavior-modification notions about the totally controlling environment are inadequate, since they do not take into account the continuous influence of the individual on the environment. In essence, there is an inseparable interdependence between the environment and the self—between being controlled and controlling—and this interdependence should be taken into account in our research and clinical applications.

Locus of Control

The programming of self-regulation requires a fundamental shift in the control of behavior from external change agents to the individual himself. The implication for clinical applications is that the external change agent must train the subject to be his own change agent.

Although O'Leary and Drabman (1971) and Patterson, Ray, and Shaw (1968) never talk specifically about self-control, they make similar suggestions for facilitating generalization effects from behavior-modification programs—that is, for programming the treatment so that the objects of change have responsibility for changing and maintaining their behavior. Discussing variables that promote generalization effects in token economies with children, O'Leary and Drabman (1971) recommend giving children the expectation that they are able to do well, having children aid in the specification of the terminal behaviors (goals) and the contingencies to be used, and teaching children to evaluate their own behavior. Similarly, Patterson et al. (1968) wrote: "Our current efforts have been toward developing more systematic training programs in which the parents *participate* in solving a more extended series of child problem behaviors" (p. 52).

Research on the internal-external control-of-reinforcement construct also seems relevant to the problem of shifting control from external change agents to the individual himself. Rotter (1954) theorizes that the potential for any behavior to occur is a function of the individual's *expectancy* of obtaining a reward for a given behavior and the *value* of the reward for that behavior to the individual. That is,

$$BP = f\ (Exp + RV),$$

where BP = behavior potential, Exp = expectancy, and RV = reward value. In terms of this theory, a useful construct known as the internal-external control of reinforcement (IE) was developed as a generalized expectancy that relates to whether the individual possesses or lacks power over what happens to him. Rotter, Seeman, and Liverant (1962) define more precisely what they mean by IE:

> As a general principle, then, internal control refers to the perception of positive and/or negative events as being a consequence of one's own actions and thereby under personal control. Whereas external control refers to the perception of positive and/or negative events as being unrelated to one's own behaviors in certain situations and therefore beyond personal control [p. 499].

Several recent reviews of the IE research (for example, Lefcourt, 1966; Rotter, 1966) have concluded that the IE construct has sufficient reliability and validity to warrant further use. A major interpretation of these studies is that research in human learning should take into account the subject's perception of the degree of control he has over the experimental task. Furthermore, these studies provide support for the hypotheses that the individual who is internally controlled (that is, the individual who has a strong belief that he can control his own destiny), in contrast to the individual who is externally controlled, is likely (1) to be alert to those aspects of the environment that provide useful information for his future behavior; (2) to take steps to improve his environmental condition; (3) to place greater value on skill or achievement reinforcements and to be generally more concerned with his ability; (4) to be resistive to subtle attempts to influence him (Rotter, 1966).

Several areas of interest that have not been investigated sufficiently are the origins of internal- or external-control expectancies, the specific operations necessary to modify an external-control expectancy (Lefcourt, 1967), and the ways in which these IE beliefs are related to SC behavior. A possible relationship between IE beliefs and SC behavior can be seen in Patterson, Ray, and Shaw's (1968) operant work on programming generalization. Their efforts to generalize overt behaviors may have resulted in a more internalized orientation that helped subjects maintain their behavior in future situations, since the subjects had the "expectation" that they could control their own behavior. It may be fruitful to attempt to integrate theoretically and empirically the traditional "trait" work on IE and the more recent operant work on programming generalizations with SC research.

Training in Self-Monitoring, Self-Evaluation, and Self-Reinforcement

Bandura's (1971) and Kanfer's (1971) theoretical formulations indicate that self-monitoring, self-evaluation, and self-reinforcement are crucial components in establishing functional self-control behaviors. This suggests that it is important to train the individual in accurate self-monitoring, realistic self-standard setting and self-evaluation, and appropriate self-reinforcement.

Bandura (1971) points out the importance of dysfunctions in self-evaluations and self-reinforcement in psychopathology. Unrealistically high standards lead to poor self-evaluations, little positive self-reinforcement, and much negative self-reinforcement. This in turn gives rise to depressive reactions, chronic discouragement, and feelings of worthlessness. Furthermore, behavior patterns such as alcoholism and grandiose ideation, which are used to avert or reduce self-punishing consequences, are thereby strengthened. Individuals who lack well-defined prosocial self-evaluative standards (for example, psychopaths) often engage in transgressive behavior unless deterred by externally imposed controls. Other individuals who have adopted low self-evaluative standards are inclined to display low achievement striving.

General Strategies of Controlling Behavior

Behavior modification in its infancy (1960s) rightly focused on specific, well-defined problems—such as tics, stuttering, bed-wetting, and phobias—and achieved remarkable success (Grossberg, 1964). But as behavior therapy moves into its adolescence in the 1970s, there will be an increasing focus on the treatment of more complex problems, such as career choices, family conflict, and juvenile delinquency (Hartmann, 1970, 1972b; Krasner, 1971).

The treatment of only specific problems may not be the best way to program self-regulation of multiple, complex problems; rather, it may be better to teach a general strategy of controlling problem behaviors. Already, there is a trend in the direction of teaching strategies of controlling behavior. For example, Patterson, Ray, and Shaw (1968), in their work with families, wrote: "Part of the success at follow-up will hinge upon the ability of the professional to train the family in the use of general intervention strategies for handling new problems as they arise . . ." (p. 50). D'Zurilla and Goldfried (1971) have developed the general-intervention-strategy notion even further in their proposed SC problem-solving model. They recommend teaching a person a general strategy of problem solving that he can, then apply to the specific problem being encountered *and* to future problems as well. Krumboltz and Thoresen (1969) also advocate teaching clients decision-making and problem-solving skills as a way of providing SC competencies.

Systems Theory

In the past few years, a growing number of scientists have advocated the application of systems theory to the behavioral sciences (Boulding, 1956; Buckley, 1968; Heimstra & Ellingstad, 1972). A number of systems-theory developments, such as cybernetics, feedback theory, decision theory, and operations research, all have application to SC phenomena. For example, Cannon (1968) talks about cybernetics and self-regulation of the body; Notterman and Trumbull (1950) write about self-regulating systems and stress. In developing his model of self-regulation, Kanfer (1971) has borrowed extensively from systems theory. Zifferblatt (1973) has combined operant techniques with operations research to develop a complex treatment strategy for complex behavioral problems. Already, a comprehensive behavioral-systems training program in counseling therapy has been developed that trains a counselor to teach clients SC skills, such as personal decision-making, career-problem solving, and anxiety-stress reduction (Thoresen, 1972b). The contribution of systems theory to basic and applied SC research has only begun to be realized. There are many exciting possibilities that should be systematically explored in the years ahead.

SUMMARY

This article has attempted to present some of the methodological issues that should be considered in SC research. A broad perspective was recommended for conducting and evaluating SC research. Since there has been some confusion in the use of SC terms, it was urged that clear, explicit, operational definitions be employed in all SC investigations.

On the issue of experimental design, it was pointed out that, since all SC research is eventually directed toward application, SC research must establish *both* internal and external validity. Furthermore, it was seen that both the between- and within-subject designs have their advantages and disadvantages; SC investigators should carefully define the problem to be studied and then select a design that can best answer the problem. Regardless of the design chosen for a particular study, SC inquiries always need to control for factors that jeopardize internal and external validity. However, since not every study can control for all factors, direct and systematic replications are needed.

Two major features of measurement theory, reliability and validity, were discussed in terms of measurement procedures most germane to SC research—namely, external-monitoring, self-monitoring, and behavioral assessment questionnaires. It was concluded (1) that reliability should always be determined, for without it SC research may be confounded, and (2) that, in most SC experiments, the correlation-coefficient procedure should be used instead of the typical percent-of-agreement procedure for estimating interobserver reliability. Definitions and examples of drift, bias, reactivity, and general validities were presented as they relate to both external monitoring and self-monitoring. Further discussion focused on self-monitoring as a measurement procedure, as an independent variable, or as both. An additional problem occurs when the self-monitoring variable (independent or dependent) is covert rather than overt. Behavioral-assessment questionnaires, which simply ask what a person's behavior is in specific situations, would seem to have much potential utility in SC investigations. Regardless of whether external monitoring, self-monitoring, behavioral questionnaires, or some combination of procedures is used, the main point is to aim for judicious measurement procedures that will provide reliable and valid data to answer the questions under investigation.

Patient and therapist variables were discussed, and recommendations were made to include them in future SC research. Some of the more important patient variables are motivation, expectancy, and socio-economic status. Finally, some of the more important therapist variables are theoretical biases, expectancies, experiences, and interpersonal skills.

Of the many possible artifacts in behavioral research, demand characteristics and evaluation apprehension seem particularly relevant to SC research. Demand characteristics are those cues that may influence the subject's perception of his role in the experiment and may also implicitly communicate the experimental hypotheses. The postexperimental inquiry and the nonexperiment were suggested as two ways to control for possible confounding in SC research. Evaluation apprehension refers to the subject's concern that he receive a positive evaluation from the experimenter or at least that he provide no grounds for a negative one. Both demand characteristics and evaluation apprehension raise important questions about possible confounding of SC research and will, therefore, require future attention from SC investigators.

Some of the purported advantages of an SC approach are that the generalization (across time, situations, behavior, or all three) and the efficiency are better than in other treatment approaches. However, at the present time, there is a paucity of data to support these SC assumptions. Hopefully, SC investigators will begin to include systematic follow-up and cost-effectiveness analyses in future studies to evaluate their assumptions empirically.

A second purpose of this chapter was to delineate some of the emerging trends in SC research. In the process of learning self-control behaviors, the individual is not just shaped by the environment, but he also becomes an active shaper of the environment. Thus, there is an inseparable interdependence between the environment and the self, between being controlled and controlling. The programming of self-regulation requires a fundamental shift in the control of behavior from external change agents to the individual himself. The implications for clinical applications are that the external change agent trains the subject to be his own change agent.

Present SC research and theoretical formulations suggest that, in training self-regulation, it is important to train the individual in accurate self-monitoring, realistic self-standard setting and self-evaluation, and appropriate self-reinforcement. In addition, research on the internal-external control-of-reinforcement construct (IE) also seems relevant to SC work. Suggestions were made for integrating the IE research with SC research. Furthermore, it seems that the treatment of a specific problem may not be the best way to program SC of multiple, complex problems; rather, it may be better to teach general strategies for controlling problem behaviors. Finally, a survey of the literature indicates that systems theory has many potential applications to SC research and should be explored in the years ahead.

SELF-CONTROL: A
BEHAVIORISTIC EXCURSION
INTO THE LION'S DEN

Frederick H. Kanfer and Paul Karoly

The theory and research of Frederick H. Kanfer have had a tremendous influence on the field of self-control. In this article, Kanfer and Karoly analyze the concept of "self-control" and relate it to social-learning principles. Their discussion of the concept of "self" and its historical perspective highlights the significance of this research area for contemporary psychology.

One of the many interesting points made by Kanfer and Karoly has to do with the concept of "freedom." Although the existence of free will has been debated by philosophers for many centuries, the authors point out that the reality of personal freedom may not be so important as its illusion. That is, whether or not an individual actually is "free," he acts as if he were—he perceives himself as a free agent.

The environmental and cultural aspects of human self-regulation are discussed at length by Kanfer and Karoly. In an attempt to avoid the traditional connotations of the word "self," they suggest the labels *alpha-* and *beta-control*. A working model of self-regulation is then presented. In addition to incorporating significant individual factors (such as personal learning history, motivation for success, and so on), their model divides self-regulation into three basic

From *Behavior Therapy*, 1972, **3**, 398-416. Copyright © 1972 by Academic Press, Inc. Reprinted by permission.

processes: (1) self-monitoring, (2) self-evaluation, and (3) self-reinforcement. Kanfer and Karoly point out that most instances of human self-control involve "conflicting consequences." That is, responses to be increased (for example, physical exercise) often involve *immediately unpleasant but ultimately positive consequences*. Responses to be decreased (for example, smoking and over-eating), on the other hand, frequently involve *immediately pleasant but ultimately negative consequences*. Many self-controlling strategies attempt to bring the delayed consequence closer to the occurrence of the to-be-controlled behavior.

A final issue that is discussed by Kanfer and Karoly has to do with the role of *contracts* (see Chapter Five) and verbal promises in self-regulation. Their intriguing analysis of "intention statements" represents a significant and innovative approach to this topic. Many of their hypotheses and recommendations have already received support from laboratory experimentation.

Historically, clinical psychology and personality theory have been oriented around conceptions of internal causation; the origins of action being localized, first within the *soul*, then the *psyche*, the *instincts*, and the *mind*. In contemporary theory, the *self* has been viewed as the pilot of individual behavior. These internal agencies have been characterized as multileveled, hierarchically organized structures, relatively free of the influence of situational determinants (Levy, 1970; Maddi, 1968). Self-determinism and the doctrine of free will and individual responsibility are direct descendants of the internal causation hypothesis. An active, directive, and aware mental apparatus knows the environment, represents it symbolically, and relates to it dispositionally (e.g., Heider, 1958). By contrast, experimental psychologists from Watson (1919) to Skinner (1971) have advocated an environmentalist position. They have questioned the intrapsychic view, arguing that a person's momentary behavior is best understood as a result of the continuously acting influence of setting characteristics, learning history, and transient organismic states rather than of the inferred actions of indwelling agents. Within clinical psychology, the latter conceptual position characterizes the foundation of the behavior therapies.

At the core of the view proposed here is a recognition of the existence of a subtle dualism that presumes the dignity and inherent morality of man to *precede* his social development, and to give order to cultural and individual growth. Almost 50 years ago, Kantor (1924) argued eloquently against the use in psychology of metaphysical abstractions, which find extreme representations in the "bodyless mind" of the psychists and the "mindless body" of the mechanists. His analysis retains its timeliness.

A scientific view need not deny the importance of self-awareness, individual responsibility, and purposefulness of one's life. However, such a view maintains that the behavioral events to which these terms sometimes refer are the *product* of acculturation, the response to the existing social order and social demands. Thus, what are commonly labeled as man's purposiveness, self-actualization or morality are not innate characteristics of a newborn infant. They are learned behaviors maintained over generations because of their utility in maintaining the prescribed relationship between an individual and his social unit. It is conceivable that the total social repertoire of persons, their self-attitudes, perceptions of the "nature" of man and the essential purposes of life can be altered by appropriate arrangement of the cultural milieu (cf., Skinner, 1971).

PURPOSE

This paper is divided into four parts. (1) We briefly discuss some divergent views of the image of man, especially as related to the concept of self, and the variables that are presumed to control man's behavior. (2) We attempt to show why a reexamination of the relative contributions of environmental and individual influences is especially relevant in the context of current rapid social and technological changes. (3) We attempt to show how a critical aspect of the self-reflective dimension of man, that of self-control, can be treated with the aid of a closed-loop learning model and how this viewpoint can affect further research. This analysis also questions the trait conception of self-control and suggests a probabilistic approach that deals with assessment of controlling variables of multiply determined phenomena. It proposes that self-control phenomena (involving behaviors that have conflicting outcomes) can be analyzed as a function of the integrated actions of (a) current environmental variables, and (b) self-generated variables that have been brought into a person's repertoire by earlier training. (4) The proposed point of view is extended to suggest some specific applications for the practice of behavior therapy.

SOURCES OF CONTROL

The concept of *self* is found in the early writings of the Greek philosophers, and to this day refers to a consistent, unitary structure or force that differentiates individuals and guides their thought and action. Formal theoretical statements, such as those of James, Freud, Sullivan, Allport and others, represent the contemporary view of the processes by which man's self-awareness influences his social adaptation.

On the other hand, for the environmentalist such terms as *self, ego,* or *intrapsychic structure* represent mental way stations, superfluous by-products of a labeling process. Environmentalists assert that the scientific analysis of behavior can only be impeded by systems that emphasize the inaccessible and the complex. Skinner (1953, 1971), Lundin (1969), and McGinnies (1970) are among many writers who have attempted to cover the broad range of human events from a behavioral perspective. For the strict behaviorist, control is a matter of specification of relevant antecedents and consequences of a given behavior. Thus, Skinner argues: "When all relevant variables have been arranged, an organism will or will not respond. If it does not, it cannot. If it can, it will" (1953, p. 122).

Predictably, extreme positions elicit extreme counter-arguments. Although it has been repeatedly asserted that the term "control" in psychological terminology is equivalent to such "neutral" terms as determine, titrate, or order, its negative overtones of restraint, inhibition, and restrictive regulation have not been omitted by contemporary critics of behavioral views. Recently, Portes (1971) has taken up the behaviorist challenge on logical and epistomological grounds. His major criticisms are that:

> There are two crucial elements missing in the behavioristic image of man: (a) a systematic understanding of meanings, and (b) an explicit recognition of self-reflectiveness in human beings (page 306).

The first point addresses itself to the understanding of the genesis and organization of language, an area that has puzzled men of all theoretical persuasions. The second point suggests that the contemporary behaviorist, in blissful ignorance, operates on the assumption that man is a linear, input-output system, a simple mechanistic device that is not affected by its own output.

Recent efforts to expand the behavioristic model have included the substantive aspects of phenomena that have traditionally been emphasized by nonbehavioral theories. Behavioral analysis and research methods have been applied to the phenomena *in vivo* or in laboratory analogies. For example, the areas of observational learning, of aggression, of group interaction, of achievement, of thinking and perceiving have been increasingly drawn into descriptions of the psychological processes from a behavioral or social learning framework.

The cognitivist critique of the behavioral image of man (e.g., Breger, 1969) is constructive only insofar as it points to the dangers of philosophical narrowness that fosters a *rejection of events* (phenomena). Most critics, however, tend to confuse contemporary *behavioris-*

tics (Skinner, 1953, 1969) with Watsonian behaviorism (1919). While the former emphasizes functional relationships between measurable events, the latter (essentially a surgical solution to the mind-body problem) tends to rule out psychological phenomena from investigation when the methodology runs into difficulty (e.g., the measurability of "private events"). Thus, in Watsonian behaviorism the person is viewed as a behaving organism *minus* mind, rather than simply as a behaving, interacting organism. Skinner (1971) rejects concepts such as freedom, dignity, responsibility and autonomy along with other mentalistic myths as being unnecessary for adequately describing and/or improving the conditions of human life. But by concentrating on life as it *ought to be,* Skinner minimizes current critical social realities in his recent book. Freedom may be a myth, but wars are fought and lives lost because of this fanciful *attribution.* It behooves the behaviorist, then, to analyze the functional significance of (i.e., the momentous results of the beliefs in) this construct in contemporary society, even while questioning its independent existence. Similarly, those who hold an intrapsychic image of man, and deride the token economy approach in the treatment of psychotic or retarded patients as dehumanizing and simplistic, should also recognize that this technique has demonstrated its utility in helping to change these patients' behavior toward more "human" status (cf., Ayllon & Azrin, 1968; Weisberg, 1971).

The issue of control has centered about the definition of a vague boundary between acceptable and unacceptable social (external) influences on individual behavior. It is asserted that our society should allow the individual to express himself and to maximize his range of choices, while minimizing the negative consequences of individual expression as it encroaches on the "freedom" of others and the stability of the social order. But, what is the proper measure of excessive control? Some object only to the pervasiveness of control, while others reject altogether the use of some means of control for any purpose (cf., discussions in London, 1969; Delgado, 1969; Ehrlich, 1968; Ferkiss, 1969; Taylor, 1968). Those who deplore control by social agencies have usually appealed to an inner sense of righteousness (morality, conscience, ":superego") to provide for regulation from within. This interiorized sense of right and the structures which support it are believed to act as a safeguard against undue or unnatural constraint from without (Fromm, 1941).

From a radical perspective it is possible to visualize a society in which environmental control (supplemented by genetic and pharmacological engineering) would extend over most of a person's behavior. However, three factors would appear to mitigate against such total control: the ultimate biological separateness of organisms, the continuity of their unique histories, and the inaccessibility of patterned "within-the-skin" stimuli and responses to the observation of others. Some of the current influences on behavior thus might be best sorted out into those that originate in the immediate environment and those that stem from a person's application of previously learned techniques of behavior control. The remaining problem lies in the fact that even clear external controls are frequently inconsistent, thus setting up both positive and aversive consequences for the same behavior. The cigarette smoker is reassured by tobacco company ads, but frightened by American Cancer Society pamphlets. Restaurants and weight-watcher clubs vie for control of the obese person. And guardians of morality and pornographers attempt to hold out diametrically opposed reinforcers for exposure to sexual material. A behavioral theorist would speculate that these conflicting external controlling stimuli, acting at different occasions and over a long time, create the same problems that "self-control" is intended to solve.

CULTURAL IMPLICATIONS OF SELF-CONTROL

The relative success of behavioral approaches in relating action to external variables has overshadowed the attempts to explicate individual behavior that is relatively independent of momentary environmental influences. Personality theorists who have used introspective analysis as the basic datum for their constructions have also obfuscated this area by contaminating the method with the content (e.g., in interviews or some personality tests). While psychologists have related self-regulation either to the axiomatic statements in their image of man as inherently self-directing or have ignored this feature of men altogether, social anthropologists and futurologists have dealt more directly with the concept in a manner that suggests the need for its reappraisal in psychology. Consistent with the speculations and prophecies of futurologists (e.g., Ferkiss, 1969; Taylor, 1968; Toffler, 1970; and many others) it is believed that the rapid rate of changes in life settings associated with sociological, cultural and technological innovations and experimentation call for a reconsideration of the role that individual self-determination can play. The transience of interpersonal relationships, of the dominant social influences and of the social demands in the late twentieth century western world and the probability of an increasing rate of such changes calls for reconsideration of the entire concept of adjustment and the relevance of self-regulation as a process that orders individual behavior in the social surrounding. Personality theories that presume a central role for enduring traits, structures, individual responsibility and free choice may have appeared less inadequate for social situations in which contextual determinants were quite constant. The increasing change pattern calls for a more realistic recognition of the critical importance of the situation-person *interaction* in the understanding of individual behavior. In fact, it raises the possibility that the self, as a critical organization of individual behaviors, is only a transitory behavioral organization, subject to alteration by the large changes in models, available satisfactions, environmental demands and other features associated with our rapid cultural changes (cf., Gergen, 1969). Thus, for the self, as for so many other physical and psychological phenomena, perhaps the statement may be appropriate that nothing is as constant as change itself.

In the personality assessment domain, a similar argument has been raised by Mischel (1968) and others who reject approaches that emphasize the importance and persistence of enduring behavioral characteristics. In clinical psychology, practitioners find that it is no longer necessary to view adjustment of a patient to his environment as the only desirable end state. Rather, that it is also possible to help patients to choose among environments that match their behavioral repertoire and their motivational history. In brief, it is assumed that there is under way a decreasing consistency of behavior among socializing agents, and an increasing availability of models (e.g., via television, physical mobility, expanded knowledge, and extended exposure to different life styles and significant people). These factors have led to a loosening both of specific and uniform institutional controls and of informal customs and traditional modes of behavioral influence. As the latter are often cited as the most salient influence on individual conduct (e.g., Nadel, 1953) and as customs seem to be changing most rapidly, the need for individual standard setting is highlighted. As western man is now exposed to many diverse environments, greater attention must be given to the conditions that permit a person to develop criteria for his own conduct that generalize across varied settings. Bennis (1968) has captured the essence of this view in a recent essay on our changing society:

> With all the mobility, chronic churning and unconnectedness we envisage, it will become more and more important to develop some permanent or abiding commitment . . . This means that as general commitments become diffused or modified, a greater *fidelity* to something or someone will be necessary to make us more fully human. For some the commitment may be derived from marriage . . . for others a profession, work, the church, or some group may emerge as a source of fidelity. Ultimately, the world will require us to rely most heavily on our own resources (p. 128).

A behavioral view suggests that, if at least some individual consistency is required for adaptive living, then the increased variability in situations will require more emphasis on and training in the individual's development of self-generated motivations and standards and means for maintaining such consistency across situations.[1] Implicit in these expectations is the necessity for working toward new values and rules for individual responsibility to replace the current emphasis on conformity to institutionally established rules and to modify our current yardsticks for judging self-regulation as adequate or deviant.[2] Many clinicians have already encountered indications of this change in the increase of problems of "impulse control," earlier regarded as signs of constitutionally determined deficiencies in self-control. The high frequency shoplifting, violent aggressive behaviors, or failures to tolerate aversive conditions for even brief time spans demand a reexamination of the origin of these acts.

TOWARD A CONCEPTUAL ANALYSIS

Reinforcement contingencies provided by social and natural events continuously modify a person's behavior. At times, conflicts arise, involving the presence of two responses with near equal consequences, or one response with both positive and aversive outcomes. Extensive studies of these phenomena (Dollard & Miller, 1950; Miller, 1944, 1959) have suggested numerous techniques for conflict-resolution. Among them are (1) altering reinforcing magnitude for one of the alternatives or the single conflictful response; (2) punishment; (3) removal of all discriminative stimuli. Given the inconsistencies of reinforcing practices in our culture and the impracticality of continuous monitoring by external agents, persons are expected to develop techniques for initiating controlling responses on their own. Generalized reinforcement is given for such achievement throughout a child's socialization. These observations have led behavioral writers to postulate that a person can be taught to control the variables that alter his own behavior and recent research has supported this assumption (e.g., Bem, 1967; Hartig & Kanfer, 1973; Meichenbaum & Goodman, 1969a,b, 1971). Nevertheless, some extreme environmentalists have maintained

[1]Of course, social control and technological programming also offer the alternative of increasing homogeneity by genetic engineering and environmental restrictions via education, mass media and biochemical or physical coercion.

[2]We are not suggesting that self-regulatory and self-control efforts are the *only* means of adaptation to the "accelerative thrust" of changing environments that men can or *should* employ. We will have to learn to tolerate change, to be more flexible, while at the same time, seeking to "tame" the runaway technology that threatens our ability to cope (cf., Toffler, 1970, Ch. 17 ff).

that self-control "really refers to certain forms of environmental control of behavior" (Rachlin, 1970, p. 185). What remains to be explained to make the transition from environmental to self-control is the process by which an individual breaks the chain of behaviors at a particular point, initiates controlling responses (learned earlier in similar situations) and maintains the new response chain, even though the controlled behavior has a high probability of occurrence and immediately reinforcing consequences. For pragmatic reasons, the ubiquity of self-generated controlling behavior and its "portability" makes it useful to distinguish it from cases in which behavior is directly dependent on external agents.

Alpha- and Beta-Regulation.   For expository purposes (and to avoid the established connotations of the term *self*), the label *alpha* will be assigned to that portion of multiple sources of behavior control that depend on the direct influence of the external environment, while the term *beta* will signify the moderating psychological processes that supplement a simple input-output relationship on the basis of the person's past history, biological constitution, and his pattern of generating "internal" stimulational processes (including sensory and proprioceptive feedbacks, discrimination, and response-produced stimulation). The degree to which internal stimulation and self-generated reinforcing events take on importance depends upon the magnitude and specificity of these variables, and on the richness and complexity of the person's available covert behaviors as they moderate and interact with the effects and directions of external controlling events. Further, since verbal, imaginal, and other forms of "inner" behaviors are postulated to have been established originally by external contingencies, these behaviors are presumed to follow the same rules of acquisition, maintenance and extinction as publicly accessible behaviors. Finally, it is assumed that these behaviors can be trained by systematic external regulation so as to provide the most effective augmentation of the behavioral input-output loop, constituting that which has been called the self-directing or self-reflective function of man.

In suggesting the use of response-centered cybernetic concepts we are borrowing a paradigm which has been employed fruitfully in other sciences and disciplines and whose psychological implications are increasingly evident in experimental areas of psychology (e.g., Adams, 1971; Miller, Galanter, & Pribram, 1960), in clinical psychology (Phillips & Wiener, 1966; Yates, 1970), and social learning (Miller, 1959). However, the system-analogy is not used to imply any further simile between man and machine, nor to reflect on the basic behavior units of which the system is composed.

Beta-Regulation. The concept of self- (now termed beta-) regulation is concerned with the processes by which an individual alters or maintains his behavioral chain in the absence of immediate external supports. Recently, a detailed componential analysis of this process has been outlined (Kanfer, 1971). In this approach beta-control is viewed as a special case of beta-regulation (Kanfer, 1970a) in which the goal is to alter the probability of executing a final response in the chain. It must be noted that individuals never cease to be affected by alpha variables. It is only the human potential for supplementing these effects that makes analysis of beta variables so critical. Recognition of these as "inner-life" determinants has been the hallmark of dynamic and phenomenological psychologies. In order to present our model of beta-control, we begin with a brief review of the three stage model of beta-regulation from which it is derived.

When conditions are such that behavior chains are not run off smoothly (for example, when a choice point is reached or an external event interrupts and refocuses attention, or if the activation level suddenly changes), *self-monitoring* is hypothesized to go into operation. Utilizing the input from the external environment as well as response-produced cues (verbal-symbolic, proprioceptive, or autonomic), the person is in a position to *self-evaluate*, i.e., to make a discrimination or judgment about the adequacy of his performance relative to a subjectively held *standard* or comparison criterion. Within the limits of an individual's social learning history and current situational factors, the judgment serves as an S^D either for positive self-reinforcement (SR+), if the outcome of the comparison is favorable, or for self-presented aversive stimulation (SR−), if the comparison is unfavorable. Thus, behavior is maintained or altered by self-reinforcements, relatively independent of current alpha variables. The foregoing closed-loop model is shown in Fig. 1.

In this model, beta-control is viewed as a process that involves the introduction by the individual of supplementary contingencies designed to enable a person to alter an ongoing behavioral chain. In order to make the unexpected happen, to act counter to the immediate contingencies, to move from automatization to de-automatization of behavior, a change in one pivotal regulatory operation in the beta-regulation model is required. Namely, the individual must set up an *ad hoc* performance standard to guide the direction of his behavior.

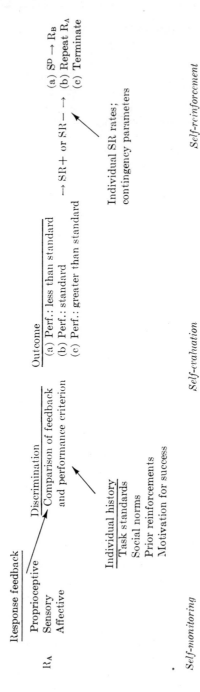

FIGURE 1.   A Working Model of Self-Regulation.

We call this central element a *performance promise* or *contract*.[3] In beta-control situations the individual is hypothesized to make a contract, i.e., to specify performance criteria. This process can be covert, or overtly made in interaction with another person. The antecedents of beta-control (self-control) lie in the discrepancy between self-observation and the performance promise, followed by self-reinforcement aimed at reducing the discrepancy.

THE SCOPE AND LIMITS OF BETA-CONTROL

Before proceeding with a discussion of beta-control contracts in therapy, further definitional elaboration of the concept is needed. Most descriptions of self-control have been anchored in the judgment of observers who note (a) sudden large changes in the probability of a behavior, or (b) responses that are infrequently made under the given conditions. Lacking information about variables effecting these changes or controlling the behavior, the term (self-control) has often been applied indiscriminatively in the labeling of insufficiently analyzed events. Fundamentally, beta-control always involves a situation in which it is possible to engage in behaviors that are judged to have a high probability (on the basis of the external antecedents and available reinforcers), but instead a response of lower probability occurs. Typically, we are concerned with *increasing* the probability of approach to or tolerance of an *immediately aversive* situation in order to achieve a *long-range positive outcome* (e.g., presenting phobic clients with feared objects, or keeping an uninterested student in school); or *decreasing* the probability of approaching an *immediately rewarding* situation in order to avoid long-term negative outcomes (e.g., inhibiting the alcoholic's drinking, the smoker's smoking, the obese individual's eating).

When the response to-be-controlled (e.g., smoking, drinking, tolerating a delay, etc.) loses its pleasurable or aversive consequences, then beta-control is no longer a relevant explanatory mechanism. Also, if the situation compels a change in the probability of a particular response, then beta-control is not involved. If, for example, a person remains in the presence of an aversive stimulus because there is no escape, or if he fails to partake of reward because the consum-

[3]The use of the term "contract" should not be construed to imply more than a convenient analogy. Its purpose is to facilitate a rudimentary conceptual organization and hypothesis generation by borrowing from an area that has already integrated the relationships between standards, performance criteria and payoff conditions for many social practices.

matory response also brings on strong situational punishment, he has *not*, at that moment, executed beta-control. Once an obese person has put a lock on the refrigerator or the alcoholic mixed an emetic in his drink, alpha variables are sufficient to account for the resulting behavior.

The utility of the conceptualization of beta-control can be demonstrated when the component processes proposed are deliberately altered in experimentally controlled situations, (i.e., those in which all external variables are held constant), and response changes are observed. Empirical evidence for the basic beta-regulation model has been summarized elsewhere (Bandura, 1969; Kanfer, 1971).

In addition, a highly probable but undesirable response could be countered by providing the person an even more probable response that is socially and personally acceptable. Thus, a smoker might be influenced to give up tobacco if (assuming he is also sexually oriented) sexual experiences would be offered in all situations that have previously led to smoking. This solution is obviously inadequate, especially if the response to be eliminated is at high strength and has a long history of occurrence in many settings. Also current extinction theories do not agree that opportunity for a stronger (competing) response would necessarily reduce the frequency of a lesser response once the now more potent reinforcer (e.g., the sexual response) is no longer available.[4]

Frequently outside observers have attached such labels as courage, stoicism, or self-denial to some behaviors. If these do not have conflicting contingencies associated with execution, then the phenomenon falls outside the definition of beta-control. Many a war "hero" has repudiated the intentions attributed to him regarding his behavior under fire. Some have even declined the honors (i.e., social reinforcement) bestowed upon them for their acts of heroism. General attributions of beta-control to the addict in withdrawal treatment, the alcoholic in hospital confinement or the obedient child in the principal's office are usually not appropriate on the basis of the present definition. The critical element in beta-control is the person's actions toward altering a strong externally determined pattern of present behavior to meet a criterion, often hidden from the observer, that the person has previously set.

[4]The repeated findings of temporary reduction in smoking with a wide variety of therapeutic techniques and the subsequent increases on follow-ups attest to the short-term nature of effects of external (alpha) control procedures (e.g., Bernstein, 1969; Hunt, 1970; Keutzer, Lichtenstein, & Mees, 1968).

BETA-CONTROL IN BEHAVIOR THERAPY

We are now prepared to consider the process of changing self-generated response-probability in a clinical setting. Some of the difficulties surrounding the clinical use of beta-control are easily inferred from the preceding discussion. For example, the clinician must take special care to analyze fully the relative contributions of alpha and beta variables to the client's behavior. For some maladaptive behavior patterns—such as alcohol or drug addiction—it may be necessary to induce first a contingency conflict, (i.e., to equalize positive and negative consequences of the behavior) rather than to assume such motivational underpinnings. Powerful external reinforcers (alpha variables) may then have to be used to strengthen the client's capacities for initiating beta-control. And, differences in the client's characteristic use of positive and negative self-reinforcement in supporting a self-change program must be taken into account.

Additionally, when *contractual negotiation* is seen as a component of beta-control (Kanfer & Karoly, 1972b), it becomes clear that a therapist cannot simply teach his client a set of techniques for behavioral changes. Whether the client makes use of this training will depend on the effects of the same variables that influence all interpersonal negotiations. Interest in contractual arrangements in the therapeutic setting is evident in the analytic model as classically viewed (Freud, 1913; Menninger, 1958), in Sullivan's (1953) interpersonal model, in a group-analytic model (Berne, 1961, 1964), and in a dyadic-interactional model based upon an integration of Sullivanian concepts with Thibaut and Kelley's (1959) social psychology (Carson, 1969). The contract is familiar within a behavioral paradigm (e.g., Pratt & Tooley, 1964; Sulzer, 1962) and has recently been proposed as a fundamental adjunct in an encounter or sensitivity-group context (Egan, 1970). In the present theoretical model the contract occupies a special position, reflecting the intention statement or performance promise, a central component in the beta-control process. It is deliberately used as a means for expediting change, and its role is scrutinized in a behavioral analysis.

Remaining within our expanded behavioral model, we can ask several related questions: What are the relevant antecedents of contract making (i.e., the uttering of *performance promises, commitments,* or *intention statements*)? Under what conditions are contract or intention statements *not* likely to be made? And, importantly, under what conditions are intention statements likely to lead to action, i.e., matching of behavior to stated intentions?

THE PROMISE AS VERBAL OPERANT

When an individual makes a contract covertly or with another person (his therapist), the *ad hoc* standard or performance promise emerges as a statement of intention. Such statements may be viewed as verbal operants. The dangers inherent in attempting to infer intentions from actions have been widely discussed; yet, less obvious are the various tactical errors that can result from ignoring the discriminative and reinforcement nexus within which overt and covert statements of intention may occur. The intention statement may be one of the critical components of a beta-control sequence, *or* it may be a terminal link in an alpha-controlled chain leading to a courageous-appearing declaration and social approval. Therefore, it behooves us to examine the alpha and beta variables that determine the probability of an individual's emission of a verbal operant of the *contract class*.

In the present paper, we can only list some of the factors which we have elsewhere suggested as *promoting intention-statement making* (cf., Kanfer & Karoly, 1972b). Among others, they include the following conditions:

a. When an individual responds to cues in his environment ("external" or "internal") that signal the conflictful nature of a current behavior pattern.
b. When a person is suffering from the aversive effects of the behavior to be controlled.
c. When the individual is satiated with respect to the undesirable behavior.
d. When contingent social approval for intention-statements is easily available.

Even in the absence of conditions conducive to intention-statement making, an individual with a positive history for their emission can be expected to show a relatively high probability of employing them. We have suggested several conditions that would *lower the probability of verbal intention operants*. These may be employed for therapeutic purposes. They include settings in which:

a. The probability of social disapproval for intention statements of a specific sort is high.
b. The probability of execution of the controlling response is generally known to be low.

c. The general expectancy for ultimate reinforcement (payoff) for executing the controlling response is low.
d. The person has a history of prior unsuccessful execution attempts and has developed what has been termed "learned helplessness" (Seligman, 1968).
e. Strong punishment is attached to the possible nonfulfillment (nonexecution) of the intent.

Finally, we have speculated on the conditions producing the all-important link between verbal operants and behavioral execution, i.e., the factors that facilitate the matching of actions to words. As we have pointed to the reasonableness of withholding gratuitous admiration for individuals who might not, in fact, be exercising beta-control, we have highlighted the absolute clinical *necessity* of refraining from rewarding performance promises lest we support "empty" verbalizations in lieu of the beneficial behavioral alterations implied by the beta-control sequence.

The probability of *initiating behavior that leads to fulfillment of a contract* can be viewed as a complex function of the following additional factors:

a. The explicitness or clarity of the contract (emphasizing the need for specifying the desired outcome in some detail, providing performance standards for facilitating self-evaluation, delineating consequences, and outlining methods for the achievement of the desired goal).
b. The mutuality of control in the helping relationship (i.e., relating to the therapist's ability to uphold "his end" of the contract via the judicious use of alpha-control).
c. The persistence of the aversive consequences of the undesirable behavior beyond the time at which the intention operant is emitted.
d. The individual's skill and experience in making the instrumental responses required for contract execution.
e. The continuous use of (and/or training in) self-monitoring that permits behavioral gains or losses to have their maximal motivational impact.
f. The past experience as a basis for the expectation of success or failure of a beta-control program.

We have suggested that the clinician be on guard against reinforcing performance promises if they undercut behavioral fulfillment and provide support for behaviors that obviate beta-control. We have also focused on the seemingly paradoxical suggestion that in order to assist a client in achieving beta-control, a therapist must initially exercise a large amount of social (alpha) control over his client's actions and choices.

IMPLICATIONS AND RESEARCH DIRECTIONS

Our efforts at analysis reflect a tentative set of hypotheses about the manner in which the phenomena subsumed under labels of will power, freedom of choice or similar alleged mental processes may be broken down into practical components and tested empirically. The components are integrated into an expanded S-R formulation (a closed-loop approach) and yet, the phenomena typically attributed to the intrapsychic domain are not ignored or sidestepped. Thus, the difficulty in accounting for all human behavior in terms of immediately apparent alpha variables does not force us to go to "cognitive" theory which postulates different mechanisms for private than for overt behaviors. Instead, the basic behavioral analysis (Skinner, 1953) can be extended to cover both public and private events.

Our analysis has suggested that the term self-control, originating in a dualistic image of man, does not offer a useful conceptualization of the phenomena it purports to describe. Recent behavioral approaches to other personality variables (e.g., dependency, aggression) suggest that a more fruitful attack would be to investigate the events in question by sorting out the component controlling variables, on the basis of their source. As the combination of immediate external influences and self-generated stimuli shifts toward the former, alpha-control describes the dominant sources of influence. With a shift toward self-generated processes beta-control takes on predominance. In human behavior, the occurrence of either extreme as a pure case is probably rare and surely limited in time. What should be emphasized is that at any moment the learning history (a product of alpha *and* beta variables) may be more or less influential than the controlling features of the immediate environment. When the degree of alpha control is reduced or the subject is given opportunity to exercise control over his behavior, changes in the controlled behavior have been reported (Kanfer & Seidner, 1973).

Several current research projects are available that test the various facets of the contract concept as related to beta-control. In our laboratories, in a recent master's thesis (1972), Cox has shown that the degree of explicitness of a contract and mutuality (or nonmutuality) of its observance can influence individuals' tolerance of a noxious situation (a cold pressor test). Marlatt and Kaplan (1972) examined a very common variety of intention statement, the New Year's resolution. They found that broken resolutions were more often *reported* within relatively specific categories than the more global (inexplicit) resolutions. Resolutions that are more difficult to *verify* externally tend to be more freely reported as successfully carried out. There is potentially less risk and greater immediate payoff involved in vowing to "be more in tune with the world" than in resolving to give up smoking today, or to lose 27 pounds in 10 weeks.

The present framework suggests that there is an important functional link between verbalization of intentions and motor responses. Theoretically, verbal mediation has been integrated with self-direction in the work of Bem (1967), Kohlberg, Yaeger, and Hjertholm (1968), Luria (1961), Piaget (1926), and others. Recently efforts at training children to modify ineffective (usually impulsive) behavior patterns via various self-instructional modes have demonstrated the utility of the present line of reasoning (cf., Hartig & Kanfer, 1973; Meichenbaum & Goodman, 1969a, b; 1971; Palkes, Stewart, & Kahana, 1968). Further research in the training of children and adults (with or without clinical problems) in the use of beta-control techniques and in the transfer of alpha- to beta-control is also needed (cf., Mahoney, 1970, for a discussion of methodological issues in the experimental analyses of covert processes).

Of importance, in light of the present emphasis, is continued research regarding the factors influencing the negotiation of contracts in interpersonal settings, especially the genesis of commitments. Contract psychology gives renewed importance to the patient-therapist relationship. Further, the examination of individual differences in such areas as skill in exercising beta-control, cross-situational beta-control, goal (standard) setting, self-monitoring, self-reinforcement (and self-punishment) patterns, and interpersonal styles would be helpful in explicating the beta-control process. Hopefully, investigators will find some new answers to old problems, and a more precise framework upon which to hang old answers.

SELF-MONITORING AND
BEHAVIOR CHANGE[1]

Alan E. Kazdin

Observing one's own behavior is a common event. Few persons, however, observe their own behavior in an organized, systematic fashion. More generally, they have a vague notion of their actions, often "selectively remembering" certain things and forgetting many others. Behavioral self-observation or self-monitoring, as discussed in Chapter Three, is one of the first and most important steps in self-control, because it provides the person with an ongoing record of the behavior to be controlled (or of related actions). The person not only notices certain behaviors but also keeps a written record of them. Without systematic data, the task of self-control is made extremely difficult, if not impossible.

Self-monitoring often has a "reactive" effect—that is, the behavior being observed is changed. In this way, self-observation may serve as a self-controlling technique. However, such changes cause problems in interpreting results when self-observation is used as an assessment method.

These issues and many others are thoroughly reviewed by Kazdin. After an extensive examination of several self-observation studies, he concludes that

[1]The author wishes to gratefully acknowledge Frederick H. Kanfer, Richard M. McFall, Michael J. Mahoney, Lee Sechrest, and Carl E. Thoresen for their generous comments and suggestions on an earlier draft.

the effects of self-observation on behavior are inconsistent. Sometimes the behavior in question is altered, but usually the change persists for a short time only. At other times, systematic self-observation by itself does not change the behavior being observed. Kazdin raises several important points: (1) studies to date have typically confounded self-observation with other techniques, making interpretation difficult; (2) future studies should control for many factors, such as experimenter bias, reactive effects of external observers, and the "demand characteristics" of being in a study, which can influence the behavior being studied; (3) the timing of self-observation (observing before or after) and the schedule of observing (continuously or intermittently) need to be studied; and (4) priority should be given to studies that show whether self-observation can alter behavior and under what conditions such changes occur.

Self-monitoring (SM) consists of observing one's own behavior. The monitoring of one's own public behavior or private events and the reporting of these events do not constitute a new topic in psychology. Indeed, we can trace its historical origins to aspects of classical psychophysics (Guilford, 1936) and, of course, to structuralism, which employs its own form of self-observation—introspection (Chaplin & Krawiec, 1960). The recent interest in self-observation has a different emphasis but, as will be evident later in the paper, shares a few of the problems of introspection. Increasing interest in various aspects of clients' everyday behaviors and in the use of new therapy techniques accounts for a great part for the burgeoning development of SM. A recent trend has been toward conducting therapeutic procedures in traditionally extra-treatment settings (such as the home and the classroom) and toward using nonprofessionals (such as parents and teachers) as therapeutic agents (Guerney, 1969). Numerous problems that have come under psychotherapeutic focus in the last few years require monitoring the subject's behavior in everyday situations. The subject himself is usually enlisted to provide data on his own behavior. For example, smoking cigarettes, overeating, engaging in homosexual activities, and experiencing fear or anxiety in certain situations have all been monitored by subjects. For a variety of problems, self-report data are easily obtainable. Presumably, if the data are reliable, self-monitoring provides access to the population of instances in which the behavior is performed rather than to the small sample of instances that could be obtained if an external agent conducted time-sampled observations. Thus, initial interest is, in part, in SM as an assessment technique. SM allows access to data that would otherwise not be readily available or, in the case of private events, perhaps would not be available at all.

In the area of psychological measurement, attention has recently focused on the reactive effects of assessment (Webb, Campbell,

Schwartz, & Sechrest, 1966). Reactivity, or awareness on the part of the subject of being assessed, can influence behavior (Moos, 1968). Tharp and Wetzel (1969, Chap. 6) have referred to "the intervention effects of assessment" to note that observation alone in behavior-modification programs may serve as an experimental intervention sufficient to effect therapeutic change. Reactive effects have been of concern in several areas of psychology. In industrial psychology, the Hawthorne studies revealed the dramatic effects that the subjects' awareness of assessment has in a field setting (Lana, 1969). In personality assessment, extensive research efforts have been devoted to combating response distortions, such as socially desirable responding (for example, Edwards, 1957), which are particularly evident on reactive self-report inventories. In the area of attitude change, elaborate precautions have been taken in experimental procedures to avoid reactive arrangements (Aronson & Carlsmith, 1968). The potential problems associated with the effects of reactive arrangements in laboratory research have been elaborated on by Weber and Cook (1972). Analogous influences of the act of observation have been discussed in both physics and the life sciences (Heisenberg, 1958). Suggestions for nonreactive and indirect psychological-assessment procedures have been advocated to overcome the influence of the subject's awareness on behavior (Kidder & Campbell, 1970; Webb & Salancik, 1970).

In psychological assessment, reactive procedures can alter the respondent's behavior in several ways, such as by determining the role the subject selects in the assessment situation or by sensitizing the subject to further experimental intervention (Webb et al., 1966). Of course, awareness of testing need not contaminate responses or delimit the external validity of the results (Campbell & Stanley, 1963). However, the probability of response contamination is increased when the subject is aware of assessment.

All of the problems of reactivity and obtrusive assessment become salient when an individual monitors his own behavior. The process of assessment may be particularly vulnerable to influence when the person serves as a subject and an observer. In these cases, the subject is placed squarely in the role of an evaluator of the behavior he performs and of the desirability of that performance. The reactive effects of SM are particularly interesting because behavior may change in a predictable direction. When SM is used in therapy studies, behavior change may be in the direction for which therapy was sought. In such cases, assessment itself becomes an intervention strategy that can effectively alter behavior (Tharp & Wetzel, 1969).

An additional impetus for interest in SM is broader than the assessment of behaviors in everyday situations but is related to that assessment. Over the past few years, the use of *instigation-therapy* techniques (Kanfer & Phillips, 1966) has proliferated. In this form of therapy, the patient is taught (by the therapist) to modify his extratherapeutic environment and to apply certain behavior-change techniques to himself. The person is trained to become his own therapist and to regulate his behaviors and the events that control them. Therapy is instigated by the therapist but executed and ultimately conducted entirely by the patient. These procedures require that the subject monitor his own behaviors in the daily situations in which the behavior-change technique is actually executed. The therapist usually has access only to the subject's self-report of the target behaviors rather than to the performance of the behaviors. The use of instigation-therapy techniques goes hand in hand with treatment of problems in therapy that are not easily accessible to the therapist (such as smoking, eating, and sexual responses). Examples of the use of instigation techniques have been reported by Fox (1962), Ferster, Nurnberger, and Levitt (1962), and Goldiamond (1965a). In each of these studies, the subjects were given some directives on how to regulate their environment to maximize behavior change. Typically, the subjects reported back to the therapist to relate how well the procedure worked.

In numerous studies using instigation techniques, persons have self-monitored responses to record change resulting from the manipulation of the environment. In certain situations, SM alone may effect the intended therapeutic change without invoking other regulatory contingencies. The present paper reviews studies examining the effect of SM on behavior change. Problems related to SM as an assessment technique will be discussed, since often they are inextricably bound with the evaluation of the efficacy of the procedure.

REVIEW OF SELF-MONITORING

Several studies have evaluated SM as a component of other behavior-change procedures. Ferster et al. (1962) trained overweight persons in self-control techniques. Developing stimulus control, applying aversive consequences to build avoidance, shaping appropriate eating responses, weakening the chain of eating responses, and self-monitoring daily food intake were combined to develop self-control. This initial study stressed the importance of careful monitoring as a basis from which therapeutic intervention could be designed.

Similarly, Fox (1962) developed stimulus-control procedures to promote efficient study behaviors in college students. Self-monitoring was used to determine when to continue or cease studying. However, carefully kept data records were not collected from the subjects.

Goldiamond (1965a) extended self-control procedures to a variety of behaviors. Individuals were trained to analyze conditions that controlled responses in several situations in order to effect desired behavior change. As part of the procedure, subjects self-monitored target behaviors. Stimulus-control and extinction procedures were used to alter behavior. In different cases, successes were noted in an increase in studying, a reduction in overeating, an elimination of sulking in a distressed spouse, and improved marital relationships. Thus, the therapeutic interventions were quite successful in altering the target behaviors. Self-monitored data provided useful feedback, but the role of self-monitoring in effecting behavior change independent of other procedures was not determined.

These three studies represent early use of behavioral-instigation techniques in which consultation was used to help the client plan how to restructure the environment according to principles of learning. As Homme (1965) has noted, if behavior is a function of its consequences, it does not matter who manipulates the consequences, even if it is the person himself. These three studies support this contention. Nevertheless, the interest in SM in these studies was primarily as a technique to assess the effects of other experimental interventions. The possible therapeutic benefits of SM were neglected or considered ancillary. Several subsequent case reports and investigations have explored these effects.

Rutner and Bugle (1969) used SM with a schizophrenic psychiatric inpatient who reported frequent auditory hallucinations. For several days, the patient recorded the frequency of her hallucinations. After the first three days of SM, the data collected by the patient were publicly displayed on the ward. Daily records of no hallucinations were praised by the staff. Reported frequency of hallucinations dramatically decreased (from 181 to 10) in the three days of SM alone. The reported hallucinations decreased to zero on the 16th day. Of course, after the first three days, it was not possible to distinguish the influence of reinforcement and public display from the influence of SM. Further, it is not clear that the data reflected actual instances of auditory hallucinations. This is a problem of considerable magnitude whenever self-report data are used for responses that are inaccessible to the experimenter. Social reinforcement in this case study was delivered for a *recording* of low rates of hallucinations, not for a reduction of them. Nevertheless, the results were sufficiently intriguing to suggest that SM might produce beneficial effects.

Other case reports have produced variable effects with SM. Thomas, Abrams, and Johnson (1971) used SM to reduce multiple tics (Gilles de la Tourette syndrome) in a young male adult. Since only one of the tics (vocal tic, vocal sound, or neck tic) could be reliably recorded at one time by an independent observer, each behavior was treated in sequence. The subject counted his vocal tics and reported them every 15 minutes to an observer who followed him. Praise was given for low rates. This procedure rapidly reduced the vocal tic. SM combined with reciprocal-inhibition therapy reduced the other two behaviors. Although the authors concluded that SM reduced tics, the effects of SM alone, independent of either praise or reciprocal-inhibition therapy, were not isolated. Either praise or desensitization alone might have effected behavior change.

In another case report, SM alone did not lead to behavior change. Jackson (1972) treated a case of depression using self-reinforcement. Each day the subject monitored housekeeping activities, rated her depression, and recorded the frequency of self-reward (that is, praising herself or engaging in desirable activities) for 10 days of baseline. Subsequent treatment consisted of setting delimited behavior goals (housekeeping activities) and programming self-reward after achieving a goal. Under this regime, both ratings of depression and frequency of self-reinforcement showed improvement. While the treatment was associated with beneficial changes, SM alone during baseline was not.

Mahoney (1971) described an adult male with obsessions who was treated with self-management techniques. As part of the procedures, the client self-monitored obsessions and, later on, positive self-thoughts. During baseline (for up to four weeks in the case of positive thoughts), SM did not result in behavior change.

Bayer (1972) reported no reduction in hair pulling for a subject who self-recorded this response daily. When social reinforcement was provided by the therapist for graphic records of low rates of the response, hair pulling decreased slightly. In the final phase, when the patient was required to bring the pulled hair to the therapist, the response decreased markedly. SM alone did not effect response reduction.

Aside from case demonstrations, several investigations have led to inconclusive results on the effects of SM independent of confounding influences. Rehm and Marston (1968) included SM as part of treatments to reduce social anxiety in males. Subjects received either self-reinforcement, nonspecific therapy, or no therapy. Self-reinforcement subjects monitored their social interactions with females and delivered points to themselves contingent upon their performance. In treatment sessions, the therapist praised previous social interactions (depending upon the number of self-administered points) and encouraged interactions. The other two groups were provided contact with the therapist without SM or reinforcement. Therapist and self-reinforcement along with SM led to greater changes on several measures than the other conditions did. The effects were maintained for up to seven to nine months of follow-up. Initially, SM might be considered to be a crucial ingredient in the effective treatment procedure since all groups had some form of therapist contact. However, SM was combined with self-reinforcement (administration of contingent points backed by therapist praise) and with therapist feedback. Thus, the specific causal agent of therapeutic change is unclear.

In other studies, SM was evaluated in the design independently of other procedures that might account for therapeutic effects. Stollak (1967) compared various experimental conditions for weight loss over an eight-week treatment period. One group kept a diary of foods eaten (amount and kind of food and time food was eaten) for the duration of treatment; another group kept a diary and met weekly with an experimenter who verbally reinforced reports of moderate eating and discussed unwise eating habits. In other groups, shock was added (delivered contingent upon statements related to fattening foods or delivered randomly).

SM with experimenter feedback led to a significant reduction in weight, whereas SM alone with no experimenter contact did not. No-contact control subjects were required to monitor their behavior and showed no weight reduction. During the follow-up interval (eight to ten weeks), the SM-plus-therapist-contact group gained weight and returned to the pretreatment weight level. Interestingly, experimenter contact was important. SM with experimenter contact did result in weight loss, whether the experimenter used contingent or noncontingent shock. SM alone (in the absence of experimenter contact) was insufficient to alter weight. This negative finding was replicated in two different groups.

In another weight-control study (Hall, 1972), the weights of TOPS (Take Off Pounds Sensibly) members for the previous three months were obtained prior to their participation in the study. Before implementing treatment (self-control or reinforcement), Hall conducted two SM phases. In the first SM phase, subjects monitored their own weight; in the second phase, weight and food intake were self-monitored. The previous records (before the SM periods) showed a weight change of −.01 pound per week over three months. Monitoring daily weight showed an average weekly change of +.04 pound per week, a slight weight *gain*. When both weight and food intake were monitored, the average weekly weight change was +.19 pound. Apparently, over a total of four weeks of SM, there was a negligible but consistent *increase* in weight. Individual-subject data were not presented, so it is not clear how representative these means are.

Mahoney, Moura, and Wade (1973) compared the effectiveness of self-reward, self-punishment, self-reward/self-punishment combined, SM, and no-SM in reducing weight. Money deposited by the subjects was used for self-consequation. All subjects except the controls monitored daily weight, "fat thoughts" (discouraging self-verbalizations), "thin thoughts" (encouraging self-verbalizations), overeating, and resistance of overeating. Subjects who used self-reward and self-reward/self-punishment combined showed greater weight loss at the end of four weeks of treatment and at the end of a four-week follow-up than the no-SM control group did. For our purposes, the most important finding is that SM and no-SM control subjects did not differ significantly in mean weight loss at the end of treatment (.8 and 1.4 pounds, respectively).

In these three studies, the effects of SM, independent of additional therapeutic procedures, failed to result in behavior change. An exception to these findings was reported in a study by Stuart (1971). The combination of several behavioral techniques (Stuart, 1967; Stuart & Davis, 1972) was compared with a self-control procedure for weight control. Prior to treatment, subjects self-monitored their eating habits for five weeks. For both groups, the collection of baseline data was associated with a weight loss of approximately 4½ pounds. The weight loss tended to attenuate as time progressed—that is, greatest losses occurred in the first week of SM.

Similarly, Mahoney (in press) found that three groups who self-monitored their weight and their eating habits significantly reduced their weight over a two-week baseline period. Subsequently, different self-reward strategies were implemented for two of these groups. The group that continued to self-monitor without additional contingencies did not change during the six-week treatment period. Apparently, the initial effects of self-monitoring attenuated over time.

Self-report data have constituted the primary dependent measure of the efficacy of treatments for cigarette smoking. Thus, SM is usually employed in both treatment and control groups within a given study. However, in the majority of studies, the presence of factors in the control groups that themselves can effect behavior change (for example, suggestions to reduce smoking or placebo drugs) precludes evaluation of SM alone (Keutzer, 1968; Nolan, 1968; Resnick, 1968; Wagner & Bragg, 1970; see Bernstein [1969] for review).

In a few studies, self-recorded baseline data have been compared with prebaseline estimates of smoking behavior. Usually, the pre-baseline estimates of cigarettes smoked daily are higher than the baseline data (Axelrod, Hall, Weis, & Rohrer, 1971; Berecz, 1972). As-suming that prebaseline estimates are reasonably accurate, this sug-gests a reduction of smoking that might be attributable to SM. However, prebaseline estimates may be spuriously inflated for various reasons. For example, in order to be accepted into a smoking study, the poten-tial subject may exaggerate the extent of his habit. Further, any reduc-tion in baseline may occur because of participation in a smoking study rather than because of recording per se. (See Bernstein [1969] for a discussion of related issues.)

Rutner (1967) compared five procedures in reducing cigarette smoking: covert sensitization, contingency management, response sub-stitution (breath-holding), contract management (gradual reduction by contract arrangement), and SM. The SM procedure required that, when subjects smoked, they had to ask someone who was present to initial their recordings on a card. All subjects recorded their smoking for three weeks after the single initial session. At the end of 21 days, all groups significantly reduced their reported smoking, with the greatest change shown in the contract-management group. Although SM was "not a smashing success" (p. 43) relative to other treatments, it did result in a significant reduction in smoking. The procedure of requiring someone to sign the card when the target response is made is a unique use of SM. This may augment the evaluative components that may be inherent in SM.

One of the most frequently cited studies demonstrating dramatic effects of SM was conducted by McFall (1970) during class sessions of a college course. College students monitored either the number of cigarettes smoked in class or the number of times they considered smoking but in fact did not smoke. Nonsmoking students in the class unobtrusively recorded the smoking frequency of the smokers over three experimental phases (baseline, SM, and return to baseline). Stu-dents who monitored cigarette smoking significantly *increased* their rate of smoking, whereas those who monitored their resistance to temp-tation tended to decrease in smoking (nonsignificant change). Both groups showed a mean decrease in time spent smoking per cigarette. The effect of SM was durable for the group that monitored smoking. When self-recording was discontinued, the frequency of smoking remained greater than the initial baseline. For the group that monitored resistance to temptation, there were no significant within-group differ-ences across phases. Apparently SM had an effect only on the monitor-ing of smoking, and the effect was on increasing operant rates. This study has been criticized in terms of "demand characteristics" implicit in the situation (Orne, 1970). These and other methodological issues will be taken up later.

McFall and Hammen (1971) evaluated several procedures to isolate nonspecific treatment factors that contribute to smoking reduction. All subjects were told to monitor their smoking and to quit on their own "cold turkey" during the three-week period of the study. Four different SM instructions were used. One group received no specific instructions and was told to hand in daily records of smoking. A negative-SM group recorded "negative points" on a wrist counter whenever smoking occurred. Positive-SM subjects recorded "positive points" on a wrist counter when they resisted the temptation to smoke. Both negative- and positive-SM subjects were told to say to themselves "I do not want to smoke" when they recorded data. A final group recorded positive points and was required to record 20 points per day.

At the end of three weeks, all groups showed a significant decrease in reported smoking. The specific effects of SM were not entirely clear, since additional nonspecific treatment accoutrements were included (for example, instructions to quit smoking, a requirement that all cigarettes be purchased at the clinic, and contact with the clinic and an experimenter two times per week). However, the authors note that, during the three days of baseline, self-monitored rates were significantly lower than prebaseline estimates of normal smoking. This suggests that SM led to change before other treatment factors were introduced. However, other factors may influence prebaseline estimates of smoking, as was discussed earlier. Despite the fact that this study has provided the greatest use of SM, the results are ambiguous, as the authors note, and cannot be interpreted as support for the efficacy of SM alone.

Participation in the study without SM may have led to changes. A group that did not self-monitor the target response would be required to separate the effects of participation in an experiment from the effects of SM. A recent study attempted to evaluate this problem. McNamara (1972) reported a study that evaluated different SM procedures to reduce nail biting. Some subjects were instructed to perform and monitor responses that were incompatible with nail biting (such as finger tapping or pulling one's hand away from one's mouth). Other subjects engaged in an incompatible response but did not monitor that response. Additional subjects recorded nail biting and either did or did not engage in competing activities. A final group did not self-monitor any behavior. Using nail length over four weeks of the study as the dependent measure, the experimenter found that all groups showed significant improvements over time, with no differences among groups. In short, SM did not result in greater change than a no-SM control did. This suggests that a reactive effect of participation in a therapy study and awareness of assessment, among other things, contributed to the change.

Other studies of SM of smoking have shown inconsistent results. Axelrod et al. (1971) used contingency contracting with two individuals to reduce smoking. In the first case, there was a gradual reduction of smoking over a 17-day period of baseline (SM). In the second case, no reduction of smoking was noted over the 27 days of recording. Powell and Azrin (1968) had subjects (and participant-observers) observe smoking behavior. After base recordings were taken, subjects were exposed to literature pointing out health hazards of smoking and then wore a shock apparatus (to adapt to the reactive arrangement before shock was connected). SM throughout these phases did not seem to alter reported frequency of smoking. Chapman, Smith, and Layden (1971) combined faradic aversion and self-management training. Prior to training, subjects monitored their smoking rates. SM did not decrease smoking over five days. However, treatment dramatically reduced smoking. Berecz (1972) compared minimal treatment and waiting control groups to various procedures for reducing smoking (covert imagery of smoking followed by either a painful or a subliminal shock). Predata estimates of smoking that were obtained on an initial questionnaire were significantly higher than actual data self-recorded during a baseline week. Of course, as the author noted, these results cannot be attributed to SM because of the possible initial overestimation of smoking on the questionnaire. A more crucial test of the SM inadvertently came from the waiting control group, which self-monitored smoking over the three-week delay period. From the data presented graphically (for males only), SM did not alter smoking rates over the four consecutive weeks of observation.

An interesting study demonstrating the effects of SM was conducted by Broden, Hall, and Mitts (1971). A trained observer monitored the behavior of two junior high school students to obtain a baseline rate of attentiveness for one student and a baseline rate of talking out for the other student. Subsequently, an SM procedure was implemented in which subjects were given sheets to keep data on the target behavior. One subject recorded attentive or inattentive behavior on the data sheet whenever she thought about recording. The other student monitored the frequency of talking out. With each subject, reversal conditions were included in the experimental design to demonstrate a functional relationship between SM and behavior. SM reliably altered behavior—that is, it increased attentiveness in one student and decreased talking out in the other student. These results are especially interesting because self-monitored data were not very reliable compared with records of an independent observer. (See the reliability discussion that follows.) This study provided an unambiguous demonstration of SM. Whenever SM was in effect, behavior changed dramatically.

Herbert and Baer (1972) instructed two mothers to count their episodes of attention to appropriate behavior in their deviant children. Observers also gathered data in the home to provide independent assessment of the self-monitored behavior. In a reversal design, several phases were evaluated. Consistent increases in maternal attention resulted from SM. When SM was discontinued temporarily, the amount of maternal attention stabilized at levels attained in the previous SM phase. When one mother monitored attention to inappropriate child behavior, the frequency of attention to appropriate behavior was not affected. For one mother, intermittent SM (SM on 3 days of the 21-day follow-up) maintained high levels of the target behavior. This study demonstrates strong effects of SM.

A point that should be mentioned is that instructions given to the mothers specified that keeping a record of behavior might change how they acted; the experimenters specified that they wanted to see if counting attention would alter the children's behavior. Indeed, in one phase, one mother was explicitly told to decrease her attention to inappropriate behavior. Instructions about the goals of the program may have augmented the reactive arrangement of SM. Even if instructions did not entirely account for behavior change, they may have interacted with the effects of SM. Collecting data can provide self-reinforcement when behavior changes in the desired direction. Instructions may have augmented the effect of reinforcement (see Ayllon & Azrin, 1964).

Recently, Fixsen, Phillips, and Wolf (1972) examined the effects of SM and peer monitoring on room-cleaning behavior of predelinquent boys. Independent observations of room cleaning were made by an observer. After the baseline (no SM), the boys kept records of room cleaning. A negligible effect of SM on room cleaning resulted, but this dissipated over time. According to the self-monitored data, which were grossly unreliable, however, room cleaning was markedly high during the SM period. A reversal and reinstatement of experimental conditions showed that actual room-cleaning behavior was not reliably changed over pre-SM rates. Notwithstanding self-reports of high levels of performance of the target response, actual behavior was unaffected by SM.

Using college students, Johnson and White (1971) examined the effects of SM on course grades. Students monitored either the time they spent studying or the time they spent dating. Demand characteristics for behavior change were controlled for by telling subjects that the purpose of the study was to examine "student life." The results showed that grades (accumulated points) in the course in which all subjects were enrolled were significantly higher for subjects who monitored study time than for control subjects who did not monitor any behavior. Yet, grades for students who monitored dating were not significantly different from grades of nonmonitoring controls or subjects who monitored study time. Study time showed moderate to high correlations with grades over weeks of the study. Time spent dating tended to correlate negatively with grades (low and nonsignificant correlations). The effects of SM on study behavior were demonstrated. No direct data were presented to indicate that observing the target behavior (dating or studying) increased performance of that behavior.

Mahoney, Moore, Wade, and Moura (1973) compared continuous SM (in which subjects recorded *each* correct response) plus accuracy feedback, intermittent SM (in which subjects self-recorded every *third* correct response) plus feedback, feedback alone, and no-SM or feedback on performance in a programmed-learning task designed to prepare college students for the Graduate Record Exam. SM groups recorded correct answers on the programmed material. SM subjects spent more time at the task and had greater accuracy in math (but not verbal) problems than did the subjects who received feedback alone and the subjects in the control group. Continuous SM was superior to intermittent SM in the time spent on task only.

Gottman and McFall (1972) had high school students from an inner-city school monitor either their verbal participation in class or their nonparticipation (desire to talk but a failure to talk, for whatever reason). Eventually, there was a crossover of these conditions. When subjects monitored participation, talking in class increased. However, when subjects monitored instances of nonparticipation, talking either decreased relative to baseline or remained at baseline levels of participation.

At the present time, one would have to conclude that the effect of SM in altering behavior has not been consistently found. Several studies reviewed here failed to find any behavior change when subjects recorded their own behavior. In many studies in which SM was effective, a variety of other procedures already known to influence behavior (for example, contingent praise, desensitization, therapist contact, and suggestion to alter the behavior) co-varied with SM. Few studies have attempted to dismantle therapeutic treatments of which SM is a part. McFall and Hammen (1971) demonstrated that the consistency of results obtained in studies on smoking reduction can be achieved with nonspecific-treatment factors, such as SM, therapist contact, and instructions to quit smoking. However, the nonspecific treatment itself requires further dismantling to isolate the effects of SM.

An excellent study of SM that ruled out the effects of therapist contact was done by Stollak (1967). Two no-contact control groups were used to evaluate weight-loss treatments; members of one of the groups monitored their eating behaviors. At the end of the eight weeks, there was no difference between these two groups. When the no-SM/no-contact control group members subsequently self-monitored their own eating, no weight loss was found over an additional eight- to ten-week period. Thus, for between- and within-group comparisons of the effect of SM, no behavior change occurred. The best evidence for the effects of SM derive from McFall (1970), Broden et al. (1971), Gottman and McFall (1972), Johnson and White (1971), and Mahoney, Moore et al. (1973).

Video-tape feedback has been used as part of behavior-modification programs with children to alter maladaptive behavior (Creer & Miklich, 1970; Schwartz & Hawkins, 1970). Apparently, passively observing one's own behavior via data collected by others can effectively alter that behavior. Thus, it is reasonable to conclude that SM, in which the subject is actively involved in the data-collection process, would lead to behavior change. In any case, the research on self-confrontation suggests that the feedback component contributes to behavior change.

RELIABILITY OF SELF-MONITORING

The importance of SM reliability varies with the purpose for which SM is employed. When SM is used as an assessment technique, reliability is exceedingly important; when it is used as a behavior-change technique, the consistency and accuracy of measurement are certainly less crucial and perhaps irrelevant.

Assessment

Recently, great concern has been expressed regarding the reliability of SM (Nelson & McReynolds, 1971; Simkins, 1971a, 1971b). Implicit in this concern for consistency and accuracy of measurement is the issue of validity. As Campbell and Fiske (1959) have noted, reliability and validity can be viewed as end points on a continuum. Reliability is the agreement between two measures when the methods of assessment are maximally similar. Validity is the agreement between measures when the methods of assessment are maximally dissimilar. Frequently, the checks on self-monitored data are made by comparing peer records or ratings (Fixsen et al., 1972; Goldstein, 1966) or records made by an external observer (Broden et al., 1971). Self- and peer measures are similar in that they are both frequency counts (or ratings) but differ in the method by which they are obtained—that is, the different agents who make the measurement. Most authors discuss this as reliability of agreement, or the degree to which observers (self and others) agree on the occurrence of the behavior. However, different observers may have somewhat different methods and these methods may affect the data obtained. As such, agreement comparisons are somewhere between reliability and validity estimates.

Several studies report findings on agreement between SM data and external criteria. Fixsen et al. (1972) found that self-monitored reports of room cleaning were strikingly disparate from data gathered by an independent observer. Peer and self-reports showed poor agreement with an observer's data (50 percent agreement). Peer and self-reports tended to agree with each other somewhat better (76 percent). Thus, although there was some agreement between self- and peer records, neither of these accurately reflected actual performance. Interestingly, both peer and self-reports showed consistent bias in a favorable direction—that is, the desirable responses were recorded as occurring more frequently in peer and self-reports than in data obtained by an independent observer. Providing token reinforcement for agreement between self- and peer reports improved agreement (86 percent agreement). However, the highest agreement obtained between self- and observer reports was 73 percent.

Broden et al. (1971) found large discrepancies between self-monitored data on classroom behavior and the records of independent observers stationed in the classrooms. For one student, mean attentive behavior self-recorded across three experimental phases corresponded closely with the means obtained by an independent observer (within two percentage points). However, on any given day, discrepancies were large (up to 29 percent difference in the amount of attentive behavior). Moreover, the student forgot to record her own behavior on 9 of 23 (or 39 percent) of the days. Risley and Hart (1968) noted a lack of correspondence between what preschool children reported doing and what they actually did. However, reinforcement for accurate self-report dramatically improved agreement between self-report and observational records of performance. Although these studies suggest that self-report data are often unreliable, the fact that children were the subjects in each case may account for the lack of agreement between self-reports and observations by others.

Evidence with adults employing different target behaviors shows greater agreement between self-monitored and independently monitored records. Azrin and Powell (1969) reported 98 percent agreement between self-report and observational records of pill taking of hospital employees. Ober (1968) found a correlation of .94 between self-reports of smoking and reports made by friends of the subjects. Mahoney, Moore et al. (1973) used an unobtrusive reliability measure of subjects' self-recording. As subjects recorded a correct response on a programmed learning task, a surgical needle punctured the answer sheet (on a roll that advanced with each response). There was a high percentage of agreement (93.8 percent) between SM records and the unobtrusive measure. In the study by Herbert and Baer (1972), agreement between SM responses and those collected by observers in the home averaged 46 percent and 43 percent for the two women. A product-moment correlation between totals of SM data and observers' data (computed for one of the subjects) approached zero. Goldstein (1966) reported only moderate correlations between self- and peer ratings of smoking ($r = .44$) and drinking (alcohol consumption) ($r = .65$). However, in Goldstein's report, ratings were used (Likert scale). Ratings may be less well agreed upon than frequency counts.

Reliability of self-report data needs to be given much more attention. Often self-report data are not validated against independent measures. In any given study, the behavior change evidenced in self-report measures cannot be considered necessarily to reflect actual change in nonverbal behavior in the absence of corroborative data.

In numerous cases, of course, reliability of self-monitored data cannot be objectively monitored, at least at the present time, because the subject's response is not available to independent observers. Studies on covert-behavior-modification techniques frequently require subjects to report on their private experiences. Mahoney, Thoresen, and Danaher (1972) had subjects observe the frequency of using imagery and covert repetition to mediate paired-associate learning. Rutner and Bugle (1969) had a psychotic patient record the frequency of auditory hallucinations. McFall (1970) had Ss record the number of times they felt like smoking but did not. In these instances, there is no behavioral referent that can be objectively monitored to assess the reliability of SM. Of course, these covert responses are not in principle unavailable to public assessment. Private events (such as urges, images, and hallucinations) may have some concomitant event that can be objectively measured (see Levine & Greenspoon, 1971). Along this line, a subject might self-monitor a private event, such as interest in a particular stimulus or set of stimuli. Self-report may correlate highly with a physiological response, such as pupil dilation, that can be independently assessed (Hess & Polt, 1960). Nevertheless, at the present time, SM is frequently used for private data that cannot be assessed independently.

As an *assessment* technique, SM cannot be evaluated in situations in which convergent measures are unavailable. When self-report measures alone are used to measure behavior, it is unclear that the reported behavior actually changed. For example, in the report of Rutner and Bugle (1969), only self-report data were available to show a change in the frequency of hallucinations. Yet, self-report is itself a behavior that may be controlled by contingencies (such as reinforcement or punishment) different from those used to control the target behavior. Unless there are additional data to support the behavior change suggested by self-report data, one should be cautious in assuming that actual behavior (nonverbal) has changed. It may be more parsimonious to assume that verbal report alone changed rather than that both verbal report and nonverbal behavior changed. Of course, several different studies provide corroborating data. For example, if private events (urges to smoke) are monitored, the self-report data can be corroborated partly by reliable reports of actual decreases in smoking. The credibility of a change in private events is greatly increased when public events predicted to be concomitant also change (Mahoney et al., 1972). The need to corroborate self-report data is great. Studies comparing independent assessment measures with self-report data have shown that subjects tend to underestimate their performance of undesirable behaviors (Bolstad & Johnson, 1971; Thomas et al., 1971) or toward overestimating their performance of desirable behaviors (Fixsen et al., 1972; Risley & Hart, 1968). An investigator should interpret self-report data cautiously, particularly when inferred change is in a socially desirable direction.

Behavior-Change Technique

If SM is employed because its reactive effects are anticipated to result in therapeutic change, it is not necessarily important that the data obtained via SM be reliable. The reactive effects of observation do not depend upon the reliability of the observation technique. Of course, to determine that there is in fact a change in behavior, a reliable independent assessment technique is presupposed (Simkins, 1971a). Nevertheless, reliable assessment need not come from the subject and the data he produces. For example, Broden et al. (1971) and Herbert and Baer (1972) found large discrepancies between SM data and independent checks by observers. Nevertheless, changes in the self-monitored behavior were dramatic. Thus, *reliably* observing one's own behavior is not essential in changing that behavior. When SM is considered as a behavior-change technique, reliability of SM data may be irrelevant.

Several factors need to be separated to determine what ingredients in SM contribute to behavior change. SM consists of several operations, including reactive assessment, instructions, and suggestions for change.

REACTIVITY

Self-observation is usually a reactive measurement technique, because the subject is aware that he is assessing his own behavior. Conceptually, SM consists of two procedures that go together: assessment by the subject himself (as opposed to an external agent or observer) and reactive measurement (awareness of the assessment). While these features go together in SM, they need not go together when assessment is conducted by an external agent. When an external agent observes behavior, assessment can be reactive or nonreactive. (That there may be degrees of reactivity is not crucial for this point.) From an assessment standpoint, it is interesting that SM constitutes a reactive arrangement. From a therapeutic standpoint, it is interesting that SM can lead to behavior change. However, from the behavior-change standpoint, separate features that account for the effects of SM can be partialed out. The therapeutic effects of SM can be attributed to the effects of reactive assessment (that is, the subject's awareness that particular responses are being monitored) or to the effects of *self*-observation (as opposed to observation by an external agent). Comparing the effects of unobtrusive nonreactive assessment conducted by an external agent with the effects of SM, which is reactive, does not clarify what may contribute to the effects of SM. Any differences in behavior change resulting from SM and from nonreactive assessment by an external observer can be attributed to the difference in agents conducting the assessment (self or other) or to the difference in reactivity.

For example, in the Broden et al. (1971) study, classroom behaviors of two children were monitored unobtrusively by observers in the classroom. There was no indication that the subjects knew they

were being observed or what particular behaviors were being monitored. Subsequently, these children observed themselves, and the self-
monitored behavior changed. Conclusions were made regarding the
effects of SM on behavior. Yet, it is unclear from this type of comparison
that the differences were not due to nonreactive versus reactive assessment procedures, independent of SM. A more interesting comparison
would be between reactive assessment conducted by an external agent
and SM. The relative contribution of the agent in assessment (self versus external observer) could be separated out in this fashion, since
both methods of assessment are reactive.

Reactive assessment alone can account for behavior change independently of SM. Surratt, Ulrich, and Hawkins (1969) evaluated the
effect of reinforcement on the behavior of elementary-school students.
An elementary-school student from another class was used as a behavioral engineer. This student operated a console that was used to cue
students as to their performances. During baseline (no reinforcement),
the equipment and observer were stationed in the room. The observer
wore sunglasses to avoid revealing who was being observed. Nevertheless, the presence of the observer and special equipment constituted
a reactive experimental arrangement. During baseline, all four students
observed showed a gradual reduction in the time spent working. This
suggests that the reactive effects accounted for some initial (undesirable) behavior change.

As mentioned earlier, McNamara (1972) compared several SM
techniques in reducing nail biting. A control group did not monitor this
or any related behavior but was assessed on the dependent measure
(nail length). All groups improved over the four weeks of the study.
This suggests that a reactive arrangement (participation in a treatment
project) contributed to the change. If a no-SM control group had not
been included in the design, the results might have been mistakenly
attributed to the effects of SM.

In several studies, the effects of SM are attributed to the reactivity
of the assessment procedure. It is significant that self-assessment can
be reactive and effect systematic behavior change. However, it is
important to determine if SM has an additional effect on behavior
beyond the effect of reactive assessment, which is present when assessment is made by an external agent.

INSTRUCTIONS, SUGGESTION, AND EXPERIMENTAL DEMAND

Implicit in the discussion of reactivity is the idea that, when subjects monitor their own behavior, they learn the experimenter's purpose

in assessment and the direction in which behavior is expected to change. The subjects can respond to the demand characteristics of the situation (that is, to the implicit suggestions for change). Of course, to determine the unique contribution of SM to behavior change, it is necessary to separately evaluate the effect of instructions to the subjects as to the goals of assessment and the effect of suggestions for change. In the majority of SM studies reviewed earlier, instructions or suggestions were explicitly given to SM groups. For example, Thomas et al. (1971, p. 167) informed the subject that SM would be valuable in changing the target response (reducing tics). Herbert and Baer (1972) told subjects that monitoring their behavior might change it. When such expectancies are explicitly planted, the role of SM is obfuscated.

In studies in which instructions and explicit suggestions are absent, the implicit experimental demand may be no less obvious. The demand for participating in a treatment study for cigarette smoking or weight control, for example, is rarely for an *increase* in the behaviors (smoking or eating) that make the clients seek treatment. Implicitly, the demand is for a reduction of smoking or eating. Similarly, when a child is told to record his classroom behavior (Broden et al., 1971), an implicit situational demand may be to alter the behavior in accord with normative expectations. In such cases, the role of SM per se is unclear. Another aspect of demand characteristics includes the demands the subject sets for himself under a particular situational condition.[2] Participation in a treatment study for a particular behavior may stem from demands the clients make upon themselves for a directional behavior change (for example, to reduce smoking). In cases in which the demands dictated by the situation or the client himself may be operative, the role of SM per se in changing behavior is unclear.

Orne (1970) has suggested that the effect of SM be evaluated against simple instructions to change the target behavior. If instructions alone can alter behavior to the same extent that SM can, this shows that SM subjects *could be* responding to demand characteristics. However, this does not tell us whether demand characteristics actually did determine the changes made through SM (Orne, 1969).

One way of assessing the potential role of demand characteristics in altering behavior is to use a preinquiry technique (Orne, 1969). For preinquiry, a group of subjects is asked to predict the experimental result without going through the experimental procedures. Preinquiry subjects are asked to perform on dependent measures as subjects who

[2]The author is grateful to Frederick H. Kanfer for emphasizing this point.

had actually participated in the procedures would. These results show, among other things, demand characteristics associated with experimental conditions. Orne (1969) suggests that only when preinquiry results are somewhat different from the data actually obtained from running subjects through the study can demand characteristics be ruled out. Quasi-controls, of which preinquiry is one example, cannot tell us what accounts for the results obtained from subjects who are actually participating in the procedure. However, such controls can increase or decrease the plausibility of experimental demand as a rival hypothesis.

Johnson and White (1971) attempted to reduce demand when evaluating SM. College students enrolled in a course observed either their studying or their dating behavior as part of a project to evaluate "student life" and to determine the amount of time and energy that students spend in certain activities. Grades obtained by subjects who self-monitored studying were significantly higher than those obtained by control subjects who did not monitor any behavior. Grades of subjects who monitored dating behavior were intermediate between, and not significantly different from, grades of control subjects and subjects who monitored studying. Apparently, monitoring either behavior in this study led to improvements over control subjects. The authors suggest that SM of any behavior may lead to evaluation of that behavior (for example, studying or dating) and consideration of the desirability of its performance.

In an investigation of "student life," there may be an implicit demand for increased studying because this is a socially desirable response (presumably) of students. Thus, this study does not totally exclude the possibility of experimental demand. In future studies, greater attention needs to be given to the demand characteristics in investigations of SM. Quasi-controls (Orne, 1969) may be particularly useful.

PARAMETERS OF SELF-MONITORING

In addition to instructions, suggestion, and demand characteristics, parameters of the SM process itself may influence the degrees of reactivity of assessment and concomitant behavior change. Three parameters—timing of SM, incompatible responses, and schedule of SM—will be discussed (although only briefly, since the literature bearing on the influence of such factors is sparse).

Timing of SM

The response chain performed by an individual may be monitored at any of several points before, during, or after the response of therapeutic focus. For example, with cigarette smoking, the individual can monitor the frequency of a specific behavior (overt or covert) leading up to smoking (for example, feeling an urge to smoke, reaching for a cigarette, or opening the package), the actual smoking behavior itself (for example, taking a puff or smoking the cigarette halfway), or acts following smoking (for example, throwing away the butt). The effect of SM may depend upon where in the chain of responses monitoring takes place relative to the target response. The effects of monitoring responses that precede or follow the target behavior remain to be carefully investigated. Drawing from related laboratory evidence in the area of punishment, we can hypothesize that, perhaps, monitoring responses early in the response chain may be more likely to suppress an undesirable target behavior than applying consequences later in the sequence (for example, Aronfreed & Reber, 1965; Walters, Parke, & Cane, 1965).

A related issue in the timing of SM concerns the delay between the target response and the recording of that response. Insofar as SM constitutes an aversive event (if the occurrence of an undesirable behavior is recorded) or positive event (if a desirable behavior is recorded), a delay in recording may reduce the efficacy of the procedure, as would the delay of punishment or of reinforcement. Moreover, the greater the delay between the response and the recording of the response, the less accuracy there may be in recording. Since the relationship between efficacy of SM in changing behavior and the accuracy of recording is not always high, it is unclear what effect a delay in recording would have.

Incompatible Responses

Besides monitoring responses in the sequence leading up to and following the target response, we can monitor behaviors incompatible with the target response. For example, McFall (1970) had some subjects monitor their failure to smoke after having considered smoking—a response that is incompatible with smoking. McNamara (1972) had some subjects monitor either tapping their fingers or pulling their hands away from their mouths—responses that are incompatible with nail biting, the target response.

The effects of monitoring the target behavior, as compared with monitoring incompatible behavior, have not been well studied. In McFall's (1970) study, individuals who recorded the number of cigarettes they smoked increased their smoking, whereas subjects who recorded their nonsmoking behavior tended to decrease in their smoking. Other studies have not shown differences attributed to whether smoking or the failure to smoke was monitored (see McFall & Hammen,

1971). Yet, Gottman and McFall (1972) showed that self-observing oral participation in a high school class increased student talking, whereas observing instances of nonparticipation resulted in less participation. McFall's work in these studies suggests that the self-monitored behavior will increase whether or not it is compatible with the target response (for example, the act of smoking) that the experimenter has selected. Determining generality of these results across behaviors will require further study.

Frequently, SM is used to suppress an undesirable target behavior. Conceivably, monitoring desirable, incompatible behaviors in addition to the undesirable target response could facilitate behavior change. Punishment studies suggest that, when response alternatives are available to an individual, punishment is more effective in suppressing the undesirable target behavior than it is when no alternative is available (see Azrin & Holz, 1966). Simultaneously monitoring target and incompatible responses may be more effective in facilitating behavior change than observing either response alone, since a response alternative is made salient. Observing two behaviors, the target behavior and an incompatible response, provides the opportunity for both self-reinforcement and self-punishment.

Schedule of SM

The reactivity of assessment may be a function of the frequency with which observations are made. Presumably, self-assessment that is very frequent makes the response more salient than infrequent self-assessment does. SM following performance of the target response may serve as positive reinforcement or as punishment, depending upon whether the goal is acceleration or deceleration of the response. Based on an extrapolation of laboratory work on reinforcement schedules, we can predict that continuous SM should be more effective than intermittent monitoring in altering behavior. In one study (Mahoney, Moore et al., 1973), continuous SM of correct responses in a learning task was superior to intermittent SM on the total time spent on the task. Yet, there were no differences in the number of academic problems completed or the accuracy of performance attributed to the different SM schedules.

The possibility exists that frequent assessment may lead to habituation of any aversive aspects or satiation of any reinforcing aspects that assessment provides. This might account for the attenuation of the effect of SM that some studies report with continuous SM (for example, Fixsen et al., 1972; Stuart, 1971).

Schedules of SM warrant investigation because their effects may bear relation to the maintenance of behaviors altered through SM (see Herbert & Baer, 1972). After behavior has been altered through SM (or through any other procedure), an increasingly intermittent SM schedule (for example, monitoring behaviors a few days a month and thinning the schedule further) might be sufficient to maintain performance. The effects of maintenance strategies using SM have not been investigated.

INTERPRETATION OF SM EFFECTS

To note that self-assessment is reactive does not provide insight as to why SM can result in systematic behavior change, what particular aspects of the procedure are crucial, and what mediates behavior change. Several theories of behavior change provide possible explanations of the reactive effects of SM. It is useful to briefly review two of these—the feedback theory and the operant-consequences theory —and to suggest areas within each theory that might provide guidelines for fruitful research.

Feedback and Self-Regulation

The feedback model of self-observation offers a parsimonious explanation of the effects of SM on behavior. The person monitoring his own behavior receives knowledge of the results of his performance. The motivational effects of knowledge of results (KR) have been reviewed by Locke, Cartledge, and Koeppel (1968). As these authors point out, KR alone is insufficient to change behavior or to initiate action. It is important to know how the subject evaluates or appraises that knowledge. In particular, the *goal* the subject sets for himself (or has imposed on him) determines how KR will affect performance. Across several studies using a variety of motor, visual, and cognitive tasks, the effects of KR on behavior depended upon the goals or standards set for the Ss (Locke et al., 1968). (Many of these studies used SM to provide KR.) Mace (1935, in Locke et al., 1968), in a KR study of motor learning, noted that KR may implicitly suggest to the subject an appropriate standard of performance that serves to regulate his behavior. Thus, feedback is important only in relation to standards for performance. Locke et al. concluded that there is no effect of KR over and above that which can be attributed to differential goal setting across subjects. KR effectively motivates performance to the extent that specific goal setting is facilitated.

Kanfer (1967, 1970b; Kanfer & Karoly, 1972a; Kanfer & Phillips, 1970) has elaborated on the role of feedback and goal setting in relation to SM and behavior change. He proposes that SM requires a person to deliberately attend to some aspect of his performance. As the data are collected, it becomes clear to the individual that his behavior does or does not depart from a range of consensually accepted behaviors, particularly in situations in which there may be aversive consequences for such behavior. Departure from a cultural (or self-imposed) standard triggers self-regulatory processes (including self-reinforcement or punishment), and behavior is brought back within the acceptable range. SM begins a feedback loop in which self-adjustive responses are made until the standard for performance is met. Kanfer and Phillips (1970) review several additional areas, to which the feedback loop, or servomechanism model, readily applies, including motivation and learning.

Considering the results of SM studies reviewed earlier, we find that the feedback explanation is quite applicable. In several studies, such as those on cigarette smoking and obesity, subjects who participated had defined their own behavior as deviating from some consensually or personally validated standard. When data are gathered on target behaviors, the goal is fairly explicit (for example, reduction in smoking or in overeating). Accurate self-recording may supply the required knowledge of performance (smoking or overeating) to motivate behavior change.

Of course, one need not participate in experiments to begin the SM process. In everyday life, there are several cues that can initiate SM (Kanfer & Phillips, 1970). These include the intervention by others who attempt to regulate behavior, the presence of extremes of affective activation (for example, excitement, hyperactivity, boredom, and depression), the failure to attain anticipated consequences, and the availability of different roles or ways of responding to a given situation. All these situations may occasion self-evaluation, self-observation, and behavior change.

Kanfer and Phillips (1970) suggest that recognition of behaviors that deviate from a norm and subsequent self-regulation (through self-reward and punishment patterns) may be developed in childhood. Parents and other adults typically monitor a child's behavior and may help him develop SM. Certain child behaviors become cues for reinforcing or punishing consequences. These behaviors themselves may become cues for regulating performance. Perhaps SM can be learned vicariously by adopting parental standards. Several studies have demonstrated that patterns of self-reinforcement or self-criticism can be learned, vicariously or directly, through reinforcement or punishment (for reviews see Aronfreed, 1964; Bandura, 1971). Self-regulation patterns *require* SM so that the child can compare his performance to some standard and can either reinforce or punish himself.

In light of this feedback-loop model of behavior change via self-regulation, Kanfer (1970a) has suggested that training in self-observation can enhance the effects of self-regulation. Presumably, if a person can accurately assess his own behavior, he can more readily determine how well it meets or falls short of the desired performance standard. Accurate SM seems essential if the self-regulation process is to be achieved. Yet some studies suggest that accuracy of feedback is not essential for behavior change through SM. However, there may be lower limits to the accuracy of SM, below which the reactive effects are attenuated. Monitoring behavior, even inaccurately, may begin the self-regulatory process.

In a study conducted by Broden et al. (1971), students who self-monitored their own behavior showed reliable behavior change, even though the monitoring was grossly inaccurate and was not even carried out a large percentage of the time. Valins (1966) provided bogus heart-rate feedback to subjects so they could monitor their supposed responsiveness to pictures of seminude females. Even though monitoring was independent of the subjects' actual responses, preferences for pictures were altered with SM. As stated earlier, some studies suggest that accurate self-observation is not essential for behavior change. The feedback-loop model does not explain how a person can compare his behavior to a culturally desired standard if he does not record that behavior accurately. The self-regulation process, then, is not necessarily initiated by *accurate* self-observation. Perhaps, accurate feedback in self-regulation occupies the same place as KR does in motor learning. As Locke et al. (1968) concluded in a review of KR, differential goal setting can account for the effects of KR. In self-regulation and SM, perhaps the goal or standard for response performance contributes more importantly to behavior change than feedback does. Certainly research is needed to develop this hypothesis further by varying levels of standards or goals and types of SM in laboratory or therapy analogue studies, in which the goals can be readily manipulated.

The feedback model is useful in aligning SM with well-investigated areas of psychology, such as motor learning. In SM, the individual's present performance and his standards for performance require further study. An important feature of Kanfer's explanation is that standards of self-evaluation and self-reinforcement are developed vicariously and subsequently control behavior. Research evidence, much of it from Kanfer's own laboratory, suggests this is a plausible model for the self-regulatory processes.

Operant Consequences

An interpretation of SM related to the feedback explanation emphasizes the reinforcing and aversive consequences that are associated with SM. As Ferster et al. (1962) have noted, maladaptive approach behaviors (such as excessive eating, smoking, or alcohol consumption) often have immediate reinforcing consequences and delayed aversive consequences. One way to decrease these approach behaviors is to bring the ultimately aversive consequences closer to the response so that they immediately follow its performance. To control overeating, Ferster et al. required subjects to develop verbal repertoires of ultimate aversive consequences and to apply these immediately before eating high-caloric or otherwise undesirable foods.

Probably, individuals do not consider aversive consequences of maladaptive approach behaviors while they are performing these behaviors, despite the fact that they are aware of these consequences. Taking careful note of one's behavior, as in SM, may make the undesirable response and its consequences salient. SM and self-evaluation may become discriminative stimuli for either thoughts about the aversive consequences or the consequences themselves. Monitoring behavior can bridge the delay between the undesirable response and the ultimate aversive consequences. Thus, marking a point after smoking may be aversive, especially when high rates of marking and smoking occur, because higher rates are discriminative stimuli for the aversive consequences.

Conversely, when self-monitored behavior is a desirable behavior, SM may serve as a conditioned reinforcer that bridges the delay between the behavior and the long-term reinforcing consequences. Monitoring behavior can serve to reinforce the target response. For example, self-monitoring study behavior may bring the ultimate reinforcing consequences (such as good grades), which would otherwise be delayed, closer in the response sequence.

This interpretation of SM is not new. Homme (1965), in his excellent paper on coverant control, suggested that an individual monitor low-probability coverants with a hand counter prior to engaging in a high-probability behavior. Operation of the counter eventually becomes a reinforcer of the coverant. In SM, the reinforcer that directly follows recording may be a private event, such as "feeling better" as a result of self-control or self-reinforcement. Although the reinforcer that follows SM is a matter of conjecture, there is heuristic value in considering this paradigm. Events that immediately follow SM can be directly manipulated to determine their effect on behavior.

This brief outline of one operant interpretation of SM is closely related to the feedback model explicated by Kanfer (1970a). In both explanations, a standard of performance or goal on the part of the subject is implicit. Presumably, an individual has decided that his present performance is sufficiently aversive for him. This is tantamount to adherence to a consensually or personally validated norm of behavior, which Kanfer discusses.

Other interpretations of SM might be proffered readily. However, studies have focused entirely upon demonstrating rather than interpreting SM. Speculations about the events that mediate behavior change following SM may be premature. Kanfer's (1970a; Kanfer & Phillips, 1970) explanation of SM—its development and crucial ingredients—seems quite plausible in this author's opinion.

CONCLUSION

SM is often considered a therapeutic procedure in its own right, outside of its utility as an assessment technique in self-regulation investigations. In light of the present review, several tentative conclusions can be made.

1. Some studies have shown dramatic effects of SM on behavior (Broden et al., 1971; Gottman & McFall, 1972; Johnson & White, 1971; Mahoney, Moore, et al., 1973; McFall, 1970).
2. The effect of SM appears to attenuate with time (Broden et al., 1971; Fixsen et al., 1972; Mahoney, 1973; Stuart, 1971).
3. Numerous reports have shown that SM confounded with other procedures (such as contingent social reinforcement, punishment, nonspecific treatment effects, therapeutic instructions, and suggestion) effects change (Bayer, 1972; Herbert & Baer, 1972; Kolb, Winter, & Berlew, 1968; McFall & Hammen, 1971; Rehm & Marston, 1968; Rutner, 1967; Rutner & Bugle, 1969; Thomas et al., 1971).
4. SM alone has not altered the monitored response in a number of well-controlled and carefully executed studies (Berecz, 1972; Hall, 1972; McNamara, 1972; Mahoney et al., 1973; Stollak, 1967).
5. Change resulting from SM does not depend upon accurate or reliable recording on the part of the subject (Broden et al., 1971; Herbert & Baer, 1972). Conversely, highly reliable SM does not ensure behavior change in the absence of other contingencies (Powell & Azrin, 1968).

Several methodological issues remain to be resolved before definitive statements can be made about the effects of SM on behavior. First, when SM is used for assessment purposes, independent corroborative data are essential to validate the accuracy of assessment. If self-monitored responses cannot be easily monitored by an independent observer, independent corroboration may be made on a related response that is observable. For example, self-recording daily food intake cannot easily be verified by an omnipresent independent observer. However, corroborative data are readily available (for example, weight loss or gain). In the case of cigarette smoking, self-report data cannot be compared with objective measures of the amount of smoking, at least at the present time. Corroborative data from peers who also record instances of the subject's smoking are desirable. When SM is used to alter private events, it is desirable to make some behavioral prediction that will lend support that such events were indeed altered (for example, Mahoney et al., 1972).

Other methodological issues are the role of reactive versus nonreactive assessment and the role of self versus another individual as an observer. It is not clear what unique contribution *self*-observation makes to behavior change over and above the effects of reactive assessment carried out by an external observer. Often self-observation (which is reactive) is compared with observation by an external agent that is not reactive. There is an additional comparison that is important because it partials out reactivity—that is, the effect of assessment conducted by oneself and the effect of reactive assessment carried out by an observer.

An additional methodological issue concerns the role of SM in behavior change unconfounded by other behavior-change procedures. As McFall and Hammen (1971) point out, nonspecific factors in treatment require dismantling to illuminate the particular ingredients that lead to change. SM is often included in the nonspecific treatment package and therefore needs to be separated from instructions and suggestions to alter the target response, subject expectations, therapist contact, and experimental demand for behavior change. Few studies have minimized the effects of these other components so that they are eliminated as "plausible rival hypotheses" (Campbell & Stanley, 1966).

Research in SM is needed from several standpoints, including these methodological points. In addition, processes or events that mediate or account for the reactive effects of SM require elaboration. However, the major priority would seem to be additional investigations that demonstrate that SM can alter behavior and the conditions under which this occurs. The inconsistency of the effects of SM makes theoretical interpretations of the phenomenon somewhat secondary to unambiguous demonstrations of its efficacy.

RESEARCH ISSUES IN
SELF-MANAGEMENT

Michael J. Mahoney

Controlled research on self-control is an essential ingredient for both clinical and conceptual refinements of self-regulation methods. Mahoney presents a brief review of the existing research on clinical applications of self-control techniques. Self-management is divided into three main areas: (1) self-reinforcement, (2) self-punishment, and (3) auxiliary techniques (such as stimulus control). Self-reward and self-punishment are classified according to whether they involve the manipulation of a positive or negative stimulus (see Chapter Five).

The specific research issues addressed by Mahoney are (1) the relative effectiveness of different self-control strategies, (2) the use of current everyday events (such as coffee drinking) as consequences, (3) the relevance of Premack's hypotheses to self-control, (4) the importance of environmental stimuli in self-management, and (5) the conditions necessary to maintain individual self-control efforts. Several of the methodological problems associated with research in this area are discussed.

This article is a relatively technical survey that may present some difficulties for the beginning student. Since it discusses contemporary research issues and makes reference to actual clinical applications, however, the article merits inclusion in this book. Those who are interested in pursuing further read-

From *Behavior Therapy*, 1972, **3**, 45-63. Copyright © 1972 by Academic Press, Inc. Reprinted by permission.

ings and research in self-control are invited to use this article as a sourcework. The beginning student may simply want to briefly scan the breadth of self-control research surveyed and familiarize himself with the contemporary issues that are facing workers in this field.

Experimental studies and individual case histories have supported the contention that self-management is an area of considerable promise for the behavior modifier (Cautela, 1969; Kanfer, 1970a; Bandura, 1971). It is the intent of this paper to review some of the existing evidence on self-regulation and to point up several major issues which seem to face contemporary researchers in this area. Emphasis will be placed on variables within the self-management paradigm rather than on the acquisition of self-management behaviors (Bandura, 1971).

The terms "self-management," "self-regulation," and "self-control" have all been used with reference to the topic in question. Individual variation in the use of these terms has, however, caused some degree of confusion. For example, "self-control" has sometimes been used to denote all cases of self-imposed behavior modification (Cautela, 1969), while at other times it has been used only in instances of restraint or self-mediated response suppression (Kanfer, 1970a). For purposes of clarity, the term "self-management" (SM) will herein be employed as a summary label for all cases of self-regulated behavior change. Borrowing from Cautela (1969), SM is defined as any response made by an organism to modify the probability of another response. Note that the desired behavior change may involve either increases or decreases in some response pattern. An essential characteristic of SM is that the organism is itself the agent of change. Behavior change strategies (e.g., response consequation or stimulus control) are optionally implemented by the SM agent. This is not to deny that the initiation or maintenance of SM attempts may be influenced by external factors (Skinner, 1953). However, the controlling variables of a target behavior (discriminative stimuli, consequences, etc.) must lie in the hands of the SM agent.

SM may be divided into three main subclasses: (1) self-reinforcement, (2) self-punishment, and (3) auxiliary techniques. "Self-reinforcement" (SR) refers to any SM enterprise designed to increase the probability of some target behavior either by the self-presentation of positive consequences (SR+) or by the removal of negative consequences (SR−). Conversely, "self-punishment" (SP) refers to any SM enterprise designed to decrease the probability of a target behavior via the self-presentation of negative consequences (SP−) or by the removal of positive consequences (SP+). The emphasis in both SR and

SP is on consequences. Note that the categorization of a particular technique rests heavily on the definition and intended direction of rate change of a target behavior. For example, an attempt to self-manage smoking might fall under either subclass depending on whether one's procedural emphasis lay on the deceleration of smoking behavior or the acceleration of nonsmoking behavior. The "auxiliary techniques" subclass encompasses SM procedures which emphasize stimulus variables and incompatible responses. The above conceptualization does not, of course, deny the concurrent use of different SM subclasses and/or the significant overlap which often characterizes SM enterprises.

With these terminological clarifications in mind, we may turn our attention to a review of some of the major research issues in SM.

I. THE RELATIVE EFFICACY OF SELF-IMPOSED TECHNIQUES

A fairly substantial body of evidence exists indicating that—when compared to externally imposed behavior change strategies—self-imposed strategies are equally efficacious in the control of behavior (Lovitt & Curtiss, 1969; Glynn, 1970; Johnson, 1970; Johnson & Martin, 1972; Kanfer, 1970a; Bandura, 1971). However, very little research has been devoted to comparing the relative efficacy of different types of self-imposed techniques. For example, no comparisons have been made among the SM subclasses of SR, SP, and auxiliary techniques. Moreover, intraclass comparisons (e.g., SR+ versus SR−) have been totally lacking. Without such comparisons it is difficult to evaluate the appropriateness and prognosis of a SM technique in any particular situation. A brief summary of the existing evidence in each of the SM sub-classes follows. The sparsity of research in some areas—particularly interclass comparisons—will hopefully encourage future inquiries.

a. Positive Self-Reinforcement (SR+). When compared to other areas of SM, SR+ has received a substantial amount of research interest. A comprehensive review of the SR+ literature would consume more time and space than our current purpose would allow. The reviews by Kanfer (1970a) and Bandura (1971) provide valuable summaries of this area as well as some interesting speculations. It is worth noting that the SR+ strategy has become an increasingly popular one in academic and applied settings. Target behaviors ranging from heterosexual relations to studying have been modified (Rehm & Marston, 1968; Goodlet & Goodlet, 1969; Lovitt & Curtiss, 1969; Glynn, 1970; Mahoney, 1971).

The results of these and other studies have shown SR+ to be a very promising tool for behavior change and maintenance.

   b. *Negative Self-Reinforcement (SR−).*   No studies have yet been reported wherein an aversive state of affairs was first imposed and then self-removed contingent on some accelerative target behavior. This deficiency is somewhat surprising in light of the emphasis placed on avoidance and escape learning in infrahuman experimentation. The potential distastefulness of employing aversive stimuli cannot be invoked as an excuse since the area of SP− is densely researched. Cautela (1970b) has recently reported some research aimed at assessing the utility of experimenter-primed SR−. In his paradigm, an aversive scene is imagined and then replaced by an image of the desired target behavior. Unfortunately, this technique fails to parallel exactly the classical definition of negative reinforcement (which requires the target behavior to briefly precede—rather than follow—the termination of the aversive stimulus). Laboratory studies of SR− (e.g., Kanfer & Duerfeldt, 1968; Marston & Cohen, 1966) also suffer from possible analog deficiencies. Thus, the area of SR− has remained virtually unexplored and constitutes a worthwhile research direction for SM workers.
   Evaluative comparisons between SR+ and SR− have yet to be reported. It would seem reasonable, however, to predict that SR+ will prove more promising than SR− if and when such comparisons are made. This speculation draws on extrapolation from animal research with external consequation as well as on assumptions regarding the aversiveness of self-imposed negative consequences. Individual and situational variability, may, however, reveal that SR+ and SR− possess differential therapeutic effectiveness in specific instances. The need for empirical comparisons in this subarea is apparent.

   c. *Negative Self-Punishment (SP−).*   The self-presentation of aversive consequences has been fairly well researched in the applied therapeutic setting. To date, electric shock has been the most popular form of aversive stimulation in the SP− studies (cf. McGuire & Vallance, 1964; Wolpe, 1965; Mees, 1966; Ober, 1968; Bucher & Fabricatore, 1970). The behavioral problems in these studies have included smoking, drug addiction, hallucinations, and sexual disorders. Overall their results have ranged from partial success to out-and-out failures. Individual variations in methodology and targeted behavior, may, however, account for this dispersion. Likewise, the use of electrical aversion may itself be a variable. While there are several reasons which lobby in favor of its use (Rachman & Teasdale, 1969), it may often create undesirable by-products (cf. Bandura, 1969) and actually jeopardize fulfillment of the therapeutic contract (e.g., Powell & Azrin, 1968). Alternative modes of aversion have begun to be investigated with the hope that effective—but less aversive—techniques can be developed. Mees (1966) employed a breath-holding consequation as a form of self-imposed punishment for smoking. His results and those of others (cf. Keutzer, 1968; Tyler & Straughan, 1970) have failed to demonstrate any striking efficacy. More promising results have recently been obtained in some preliminary research employing a tactile aversion (Mahoney, 1971). Further research will be required for the delineation of aversion mode and treatment paradigm variables. At present the challenge in SP— would seem to involve finding a consequence negative enough to effect behavioral suppression without simultaneously jeopardizing follow-through in self-implementation. The potential applications and optimal parameters of SP— are certainly an area deserving further experimental interest.

It should be noted that nontherapeutic (and especially maladaptive) applications of SP— are in need of research. Bandura (1971) has noted some very interesting parallels between self-punitiveness and classical manifestations of behavior pathology. Recent studies by Sandler and Quagliano (1964) and Stone and Hokanson (1969) have shed light on the tenacious and dysfunctional maintenance of SP— behaviors in the absence of previously existent contingencies. An organism trained to self-impose punishment in order to avoid more painful consequences will continue to self-punish long after his punitiveness has ceased being functional. These findings might well be considered in future inquiries concerning the SP— technique.

d. Positive Self-Punishment (SP+).   SP+ includes those situations wherein an individual removes or avoids some positive consequence after the occurrence of an undesired target behavior. It is punitive in the sense that its goal is decelerative, and it is positive in the sense that it involves the removal of some positive stimulation. Conceptually, this subclass might be considered analogous to a self-imposed "time-out" from positive reinforcement (either by stimulus or self-removal). There is a surprising lack of evidence on the application of SP+. While some therapists have used time-out paradigms with clients, the contingency control in these instances has usually been in the hands of the therapist (cf. Fox, 1962; Tooley & Pratt, 1967; Rutner, 1967; Elliott & Tighe, 1968). The characteristic contingencies in these studies have involved threatened loss of money and/or therapist approval. The lack of controlled experimentation in this area is again disappointing.

As in SR, there have been no experimental comparisons between the positive and negative subdivisions of SP. Although the removal of positive consequences is generally considered the preferred punishment mode (Bandura, 1969), there is reason to doubt that a large efficiency difference exists between SP+ and SP−. As yet, the viability and effectiveness of SP strategies have been only marginally demonstrated. This research deficit is exacerbated by the fact that SP constitutes a major theme in nonprofessional conceptions and applications of SM. Well-controlled inquiries into this area are sorely needed.

e. Stimulus Control Techniques. The manipulation of stimulus variables was involved in some of the earliest SM conceptualizations and attempts (Skinner, 1953; Fox, 1962; Ferster, Nurnberger, & Levitt, 1962). Because of the significance of research findings in this area, an entire section will be devoted to their discussion.

f. Incompatible Response Approach. Several SM investigators have utilized techniques designed to establish responses which are incompatible with an undesired target behavior. Homme (1965), for example, relied heavily on this approach. In his paradigm for the SM of smoking behavior he emphasized the reinforcement of covert behaviors (especially thoughts) which are incompatible with (or at least antagonistic to) smoking behavior. One might also classify instances of self-induced relaxation in anxiety-arousing situations as examples of the incompatible response approach to SM (Goldfried, 1971). To date, research on self-managed anxiety reduction has predominated in this subarea. A research-worthy issue relates to the relative efficacy of SM strategies which address themselves to the target behavior itself rather than to responses incompatible with it. One might predict that SM approaches which combine techniques (e.g., SR+ of response X and SP− of response not-X) may prove superior to single-strategy approaches.

The foregoing summaries point up several specific research implications. Evaluative comparisons between SM strategies (e.g., SR versus SP) would seem of paramount importance. Likewise, data are needed on the relative effectiveness of different variations within strategies (e.g., SP+ versus SP−). Parametric explorations (e.g., type and magnitude of consequence) might also prove useful. Although scheduling variables have received some attention in laboratory research, no therapeutic applications have yet been reported. It may turn out that different consequation schedules are optimally suited to different stages in or applications of SM. Finally, the combination of various SM techniques requires systematic analysis.

II. CONSEQUENCES: CURRENT VERSUS POTENTIAL

Another research issue which has been pointed up by preliminary research in SM relates to whether or not the self-imposed consequation is one which is currently employed by the individual (perhaps infrequently or noncontingently) or whether it is one which could be potentially employed. A good illustration is in the area of SR+. An individual can choose to self-reward some target behavior either by making a current reinforcer (e.g., coffee drinking or cigarettes) contingent on that behavior or by introducing some new reinforcer (e.g., a long-awaited purchase). Homme (1965) utilizes the former in his coverant control paradigm. Other researchers have employed the introduction of a new reinforcer (e.g., Glynn, 1970). One research-worthy question has to do with the effect of self-deprivation on a current reinforcer (or "high probability behavior" (HPB)) when it is made contingent on some target behavior. If one views reinforcement from a probability framework (Premack, 1965, 1971), some interesting possibilities are generated by self-imposed modifications of response probability (e.g., extreme self-abnegation of a HPB may affect the probability of that behavior). Moreover, the act of self-deprivation may introduce aversive components to SR+ strategies. The act of depriving oneself of a current reinforcer (e.g., coffee) in order to use it as a self-reward may prove less effective than the self-presentation of new rewards. Neuringer (1969, 1970) has recently reported some studies dealing with a partial analog to self-imposed deprivation in pigeons and rats. He found that these animals would perform instrumental responses to obtain food even though they had a cup of free food available for ad libitum consumption. This was true even during shaping phases. The implications of Neuringer's research for SM studies have yet to be explored. However, the issues of self-imposed deprivation and current versus potential consequation offer fruitful areas for future SM inquiries.

III. THE PREMACK PRINCIPLE IN SELF-MANAGEMENT

An issue closely related to the "current versus potential consequences" question has to do with the application of the Premack principle to certain areas of SM. In essence, that principle states that—given ad libitum accessibility to various behavioral options—those behaviors engaged in most frequently (HPBs) can be employed contingently as reinforcers for those behaviors engaged in less frequently (LPBs) and vice versa (Premack, 1965, 1971). Along with the "probability hypothesis," Premack has stated several auxiliary hypotheses regarding the necessary and sufficient conditions for reinforcement. Among them have been a "contingency" and a partial reduction in the frequency of the HPB. Several research issues in SM are raised by these hypotheses.

   a. The Probability Paradox.   One intriguing implication of the probability hypothesis is that any HPB should reinforce any LPB, given that both response probabilities have been computed from observations of ad libitum consumption. Premack's probability hypothesis has frequently been interpreted as positing a strong correlation between free operant response probability and reinforcement value. Indeed, Premack's research (as well as that of several other investigators) has consistently supported such an interpretation. However, a paradoxical exception to this speculative equivalence lies in the area of obsessions and compulsions. These are HPBs which are reported as being subjectively aversive to the individual. One might wish to contend that these responses are not "free" operants in the sense that they may be maintained by their ability to reduce aversive states. Another possibility would be that—although these HPBs are reported as being subjectively aversive—they may be empirically reinforcing. The latter speculation could be tested by making obsessive-compulsive behaviors contingent on the performance of some target behavior. One could argue that, since Premack's definition of response probability incorporates a "transiency" clause, this experimental paradigm might not adequately probe the research question. However, the transiency clause could be likewise invoked to account for any disconfirmation of Premack's probability hypothesis (if so interpreted), rendering it empirically meaningless. At any rate, the seeming paradox between the probability hypothesis and the aversiveness of some HPBs remains unresolved. SM researchers would do well to investigate the relationship between response probability and reinforcement value rather than assume *a priori* that the Premackian extrapolation is warranted.
   It is noteworthy that several investigators employing Premackian approaches to SM have overlooked the crucial distinction between free operant response probability and actual response frequency. It is only in the case of the former that a reinforcement relationship can be presumed. A response which is frequently engaged in because of its contingent relationship to other motivational variables need not be moti-

vating in and of itself. For example, tax paying and domestic chores—although high in frequency—are not usually considered reinforcing. This distinction needs to be re-emphasized in Premackian SM strategies.

    b. Contingency and HPB Decrement.   Another Premackian issue in SM has to do with the hypothesized role of contingency relationships in reinforcement paradigms. His definition of "contingency" and "contiguity" rule out what had been previously considered demonstrations of contiguity relationships. According to Premack, in order for a response-consequence pairing to be contiguous, the probability of the consequence (HPB) can in no way be decreased from its ad libitum level. When a HPB decrement is present, a contingency is present. However, Premack goes on to show that a contingency is not sufficient for a reinforcement effect. When one targets a response whose operant level is extremely high and/or when one implements such a lenient contingency that no reinforcers are "lost" (i.e., there is no decrement from an ad lib rate), there is no reinforcement effect. This phenomenon—if applicable to the SM paradigm—could have important ramifications. It implicitly points up the necessity of self-imposed deprivation in SM. The latter, it will be recalled, constitutes a research issue in itself. Extrapolating Premack's hypothesis of HPB decrement to the SM situation, one might predict little or no change in a target behavior when the self-imposed contingency is such that no reduction in the now-contingent HPB occurs.

    Tangentially related to the contingency and HPB decrement requirements is the issue of the automaticity of reinforcement. The assumption of automaticity, which is usually left implicit, asserts that any response followed by a reinforcing event (or HPB) will be automatically strengthened. This conception of the reinforcement effect is implied in Homme's (1965) covariant control strategy. Homme proposes that an individual get maximum mileage out of daily reinforcers (coffee, cigarettes, etc.) by requiring accelerative target behaviors to precede them. Skinner (personal communication in Mahoney, 1970) has expressed doubts about the efficacy of throwing some to-be-accelerated target behavior in front of a preprogrammed reinforcer. The issue seems to be one of contingency versus simple contiguity. Does knowledge of the self-imposed nature of a contingency alter the effects of that contingency? Is a response modified despite the fact that the individual knows that its consequence was noncontingent (i.e., adventitious)? The question is that of perceived contingency or perceived reinforcement. Its ramifications for SM are as intriguing as they are research-deprived.

IV. STIMULUS VARIABLES IN SELF-MANAGEMENT

One of the more densely researched areas in SM has to do with the role of stimulus variables. Experimental studies on this issue have generally been of two types: (a) those which have investigated the role of stimuli in initiating and/or terminating response chains, and (b) those which have investigated the role of "attentional" variables in modifying target behaviors. While there has been some overlap between the two, we shall discuss them separately.

a. Stimulus Control.   When divided into the abovementioned dichotomy, the research issue of stimulus control emerges as a much more popular research topic. Several studies have been reported investigating the use of stimulus control techniques in interrupting and/or establishing competing response chains. These applications have been found to be successful in modifying maladaptive eating patterns (Ferster, Nurnberger, & Levitt, 1962; Stuart, 1967; Harris, 1969), inappropriate study habits (Fox, 1962), marital discord (Goldiamond, 1965a), and smoking (Nolan, 1968; Roberts, 1969; Upper & Meredith, 1970). Essentially, these stimulus control techniques involve the association of decelerative behaviors with progressively restrictive stimuli and the simultaneous association of competitive adaptive behaviors with progressively expansive stimuli. The rationale is directly borrowed from the laboratory research on discrimination learning. Note that there is often a concurrent emphasis on incompatible response and stimulus control techniques. The latter are apparently very effective and constitute one of the few subareas of SM which have received substantial investigation.

There are several subissues, however, which remain unexplored. For example, the differential effectiveness of stimulus control techniques with varying types of target behaviors requires further investigation. When the targeted behavior is decelerative, then the therapeutic strategy is one of interrupting a prepotent response chain and/or bringing it under restrictive stimulus control. The above-cited studies have addressed themselves for the most part to this strategy. However, there are instances wherein a response chain is so prepotent and/or resistant to change that the attainment of decelerative stimulus control is very difficult. Smoking, for example, has been one such target behavior (Keutzer, Lichtenstein, & Mees, 1968; Bernstein, 1969; Premack, 1970). Suggested techniques for facilitating the attainment of stimulus control under such conditions have been discussed elsewhere (cf. Mahoney, 1970).

In striking contrast to the problems encountered in attaining decelerative stimulus control, far fewer difficulties may be encountered when the target behavior is accelerative. This may be less true in instances in which the target behavior is context-bound. However, when the behavior of interest is both context-free (i.e., emittable in virtually any situation) and accelerative, attainment of stimulus control can be facilitated by artificial means. For example, if one wished to increase an individual's positive self-thoughts (which are accelerative and context-free) one could program an association between such thoughts and virtually any frequently encountered stimulus complex. This strategy has already been successfully employed with cigarette stimuli (Mahoney, 1971). Similar use of such stimuli as traffic lights or miniature timers (Upper & Meredith, 1970) also shows therapeutic promise.

b. Observation Versus Consequation.   A more recent issue in SM has centered on evaluating the relative contributions of self-observation and self-consequation to the behavior change process. Since most SM techniques involve some sort of self-monitoring, several investigators have begun to research the effects of such monitoring on target behaviors. The very fact that attention is directed toward a targeted response can have a significant effect on the probability of that response. This became especially apparent in early SM studies in which self-monitoring control groups demonstrated improvement. Kanfer, among others, has posited an evaluative component in the SM paradigm (Kanfer, 1970a, 1970b; Kanfer & Phillips, 1970). Essentially, this entails the subjective evaluation of the target behavior by the individual engaged in SM. If that behavior is negatively evaluated, then self-monitoring alone may have a decelerative effect on the behavior. Likewise, if the target behavior is positively evaluated, then self-monitoring may have an accelerative effect. Initial investigations of self-monitoring have lent support to this generalization (Fox, 1962; Rutner, 1967; Stollak, 1967; Kolb, Winter, & Berlew, 1968; Rutner & Bugle, 1969; McFall, 1970; Johnson & White, 1971). Methodological problems, however, pose a challenge to researchers interested in self-monitoring effects (cf. Orne, 1970; Simkins, 1971a). Reliability checks on self-monitoring data have shown the latter to be somewhat variable in their accuracy (Ober, 1968; Broden, Hall, & Mitts, 1971) although contingent consequation for accurate self-monitoring has shown some promise in reducing this variability (Fixsen, Phillips, & Wolf, 1972). When the target behavior is covert rather than overt, however, reliability may only be globally inferred from concomitant changes in overt behavior. As yet, no data have been reported which compare the effectiveness of self-monitoring to self-monitoring plus self-consequation. One may, of course, wish to interpret self-monitoring as integrally bound up with forms of covert self-consequation (Cautela, 1971) and/or self-instruction (Bem, 1967). Such an interpretation, however, does not alleviate the need for experimental research into the relative contributions of these processes to SM phenomena.

An interesting sidelight on this issue of observation versus consequation is that involving deliberate lack of observation on the part of the individual. The work of Mischel and his co-workers is again germane (Mischel & Ebbesen, 1970; Mischel, Ebbesen, & Zeiss, 1972). They found that attentional distractors aided children in prolonging waiting responses in a delay of gratification paradigm. Likewise, Kanfer & Goldfoot (1966) found that the availability of distraction allowed experimental subjects to prolong painful hand immersion in ice water. Bergin (1969) successfully employed distractional techniques as a means of interrupting deviant sexual patterns. The type of attentional distractor may play an important role in the success of such strategies. For example, Mahoney (1971) found that backward counting actually increased the frequency of obsessive ruminations in a client. Thus, it would appear that the therapeutic usefulness of attentional techniques must await clarification by further research.

V.   COVERT BEHAVIOR MODIFICATION

Another area which has recently gained prominence in SM has to do with the use of covert (and particularly cognitive) responses, either as target behaviors in themselves or as symbolic consequences. Behavior therapists have long been utilizing symbolic representations of behavior in treatment strategies. However, recent work by Cautela and others has further emphasized the potential role of cognitive responses in therapeutic behavior change.

Covert target behaviors have typically involved thought disorders (Rutner & Bugle, 1969; Bucher & Fabricatore, 1970), self-evaluative references (Mahoney, 1971), or cognitive antecedents of an overt response pattern (Lindsley, 1969; McFall, 1970). Homme's (1965) paper on "coverant control" laid much of the groundwork for empirically based attempts at the modification of cognitive responses. To date, only a handful of studies have addressed themselves to the assessment of coverant control techniques (Rutner, 1967; Keutzer, 1968; Tooley & Pratt, 1967; Lawson & May, 1970; Tyler & Straughan, 1970; Horan, 1971; Mahoney, 1971). Although definitive conclusions have been precluded by methodological problems, ambiguous findings, and a sparsity of research, the promising results obtained by some of the above researchers emphasizes the need for further experimentation in this area.

The use of covert responses as symbolic consequences was initially dominated by counter-conditioning paradigms. Affectively pleasant or unpleasant images were associated in systematized ways with hierarchies of responses (Lazarus & Abramovitz, 1962; Cautela, 1966, 1967). The "covert sensitization" procedures reported by Cautela have received particularly extensive application by other researchers (Kolvin, 1967; Anant, 1967; Davison, 1968b; Ashem & Donner, 1968; Barlow, Leitenberg, & Agras, 1969; Wisocki, 1970; Sachs, Bean, & Morrow, 1970; Wagner & Bragg, 1970; Lawson & May, 1970).

The use of cognitive responses as symbolic consequences in operant paradigms is corroborated by the work of Weiner (1965). Cautela (1970a, 1970b, 1971), in a series of experiments on covert conditioning, has examined the effects of imagined events on preceding behaviors. Although the evidence is still relatively sparse, preliminary results indicate that covert conditioning techniques may be very promising.

It should be noted that the area of covert behavior modification is inextricably bound up with many forms of SM. Since covert target behaviors require some form of self-reporting, a methodological attachment is necessary. Moreover, the role of the individual in producing symbolic consequences (even when therapist-prompted) requires some degree of SM conceptualization.

The most pressing research task in the area of covert SM is that of controlled replication and expansion. Although covert responses have recently become less controversial in behavior modification, researchers in this area would do well to remain very cautious in their inquiries. Weak data, premature conclusions, and/or inadequate designs could substantially reduce the import and expansion of covert behavior research. Particular attention to the control of demand characteristics and non-specific variables is advisable. The therapeutic promise of covert behavior modification has been explored elsewhere (Homme, 1965; Bandura, 1969; Cautela, 1971). However, until further evidence is available, this area must be viewed with cautious optimism.

VI.   CONSEQUATING THE SELF-IMPOSED CONSEQUENCE

Still another research issue in SM has to do with the maintenance of SM. Skinner (1953) makes an important distinction between the "controlled" and "controlling" responses. The controlled response would correspond to what we have heretofore termed the target behavior in SM. The controlling response consists of implementing those SM techniques prescribed for the modification of the target behavior. The maintenance of the latter has sometimes been termed the "contract problem" because it involves an obligation or commitment (cf. Marston & Feldman, 1970). The contract problem has been discussed elsewhere (Mahoney, 1970).

An interesting sidelight to the contract problem has to do with recent studies dealing with the possible reinforcement value of consequation control. Lefcourt (1966) points out that control over consequation is often preferred over random or externally controlled consequation. The recent laboratory work on instrumental responding in the presence of free reinforcers also bears on this issue (Neuringer, 1969, 1970). Recent investigations have shown that an experimental analog to SR+ can be demonstrated in pigeons (Mahoney & Bandura, 1972). Two pigeons were trained to self-reinforce (i.e., indulge in freely available grain only after having pecked a disc). Although external controls were employed in the development of this behavior, they were eventually removed so that the rate and duration of SR+ could be evaluated. The results indicated that SR+ is a relatively stable and enduring behavior under such conditions. These findings are suggestive of an experiment wherein organisms can choose between the self-imposition and external imposition of identical schedules. Information relevant to the contract problem and to various parameters of SM (e.g., schedule effects) may be obtained by such analogue investigations.

The SM strategy capitalizes on the fact that the individual is himself the best potential observer and modifier of his own behavior. However, this prestigious position is all but worthless if attempts at behavioral self-regulation are not maintained. Thus, the contract problem is one of the more challenging and far-reaching ones to be faced by SM researchers.

METHODOLOGICAL PROBLEMS IN SM

The processes and parameters of SM have remained relatively obscure partly because of research sparsity and partly due to the inadequacies of many SM inquiries. Some of these inadequacies stem from experimental naivete and/or carelessness on the part of SM workers. For example, the absence of experimental controls and treatment follow-ups has jeopardized the significance of some SM studies (e.g., Rutner, 1967). Likewise, the use of self-monitoring control groups to the exclusion of all others (e.g., Lawson & May, 1970) has probably led to inaccurate estimates of treatment effectiveness. The assumption that self-monitoring is nonreactive would seem questionable in light of recent data. Problems in causal interpretations are presented by the use of treatment combinations (e.g., Tooley & Pratt, 1967). Data reported from studies wherein the sole subject was the author's spouse (Nolan, 1968) or was the author himself (Roberts, 1969) are very suspect. Moreover, there is a need for more consistent efforts to avoid external controls if SM effects are to be isolated.

In addition to experimental deficiencies, there are several methodological problems which complicate SM research. The reliability of self-recorded behaviors is one such problem. Many SM studies have totally relied upon the accuracy and honesty of subjects' self-reports. Smoking research, for example, is typically plagued by this reliance. Studies wherein the end-product of SM is observable by an experimenter (e.g., obesity) must still rely on self-report data regarding the consistency and quality of self-imposed techniques. The ideal research situation in SM is one wherein a clearly defined target behavior and SM technique are unobtrusively observable by the experimenter. This allows for a reliability check on self-reported behavioral frequency and on actual SM technology. The SM of covert behaviors presents a more formidable problem to researchers seeking reliability. When such behaviors are presumptively linked to overt responses the latter may provide an indirect index of treatment effectiveness. Otherwise, a direct inference from self-report to the covert behavior must be employed. An initial investigation of the reliability and modifiability of covert behaviors has recently been reported (Mahoney, Thoresen, & Danaher, 1972). The data from that study have indicated that reliability checks can be made on some covert behaviors and that the latter appear to be a function of the same behavior principles as their overt counterparts. It should be noted that the current methodological problems posed by covert behavior SM should not deter continued experimental research on this topic. In addition to the dire need for clinical attempts at covert behavior modification, such efforts are at least partially justified by existing reports of successful applications.

A second methodological problem in SM deals with the aforementioned separation of self-monitoring and SM effects. It is virtually impossible to have an individual regulate his own behavior without his simultaneously attending to it. The latter, in turn, may have an effect in and of itself on the behavior of interest. There are no ready solutions to this dilemma. However, well-controlled experimentation on the effects of self-monitoring may provide a reliable means for partialling out its effects in SM inquiries.

One final research problem in SM has to do with experimental control. Almost all SM enterprises suffer from their susceptibility to demand characteristics and subject's expectations. To prescribe a particular SM technique for an individual is tantamount to asking for a given behavior change. The experimenter's confidence in a technique, the obvious implications of a self-imposed strategy, and similar uncontrolled variables complicate causal interpretation in self-managed behavior change. Many of the confounding effects associated with outright instruction (versus contingency manipulation) may be involved. The problem of experimental control looms especially large in SM studies employing a single subject design. The classical ABAB (or baseline, intervention, reversal, intervention) design is seldom used in such studies. This may be due to several factors (e.g., the unwillingness of a subject to "reverse" a successful SM project). One possible solution is that of multiple baselines—i.e., manipulating one behavior via SM while a second behavior is held constant (Sidman, 1960). The procedure is also appropriate when the behavior change is irreversible. The comparison of individual performances—while introducing intrasubject variability—may also provide some support for contentions regarding SM effects.

While the methodological problems posed by SM phenomena may exceed those encountered in other research areas, preliminary investigations have indicated that such problems are both surmountable and relatively nominal when measured against the practical ramifications of behavior control via SM (cf. Thoresen & Mahoney, 1974).

The foregoing has been a brief review of some of the evidence and issues in the area of SM. While a few subareas have received extensive research interest, there is an overall sparsity of empirical investigations into several SM topics. The relative efficacy of various techniques is especially devoid of research. Also lacking are the issues of current versus potential consequences, Premackian extrapolations to SM, and observation versus consequation. The contract problem remains virtually unexplored and covert SM issues have only recently begun to receive their experimental due. In addition to these research deficits, methodological problems complicate the interpretation of many SM investigations. In short, there is a great deal of work to be done in the experimental analysis of SM. While the foregoing review has discussed potential problems in the implementation and efficacious use of SM techniques, there should be little doubt that the area of SM is herein considered one of the most promising developments in behavior change research. It is hoped that some of the conceptualizations herein offered will facilitate expanding research inquiries into this fruitful area.

THE CLINICAL POTENTIAL OF MODIFYING WHAT CLIENTS SAY TO THEMSELVES

Donald Meichenbaum and Roy Cameron

One of the most exciting expansions of behavioral theory and research concerns "private events"—that is, what we think, imagine, and feel. In this text, we have consistently suggested that covert behaviors can be viewed as actions or responses susceptible to change in the same way that external actions are. Further, how a person perceives, anticipates, and evaluates events has been emphasized as mediating or influencing the effects of the external environment. Bandura, in Article Two and elsewhere, also highlights the prime role of covert actions in understanding all self-regulation processes. Meichenbaum and Cameron offer a broad array of case studies, field experiments, and laboratory investigations to emphasize the importance of what a person says to himself. These studies attempted to directly alter self-verbalizations. The studies also incorporated other actions, such as deep breathing and relaxation. Thus, extremely impulsive children have been trained to self-instruct themselves to attend more to academic tasks, hospitalized schizophrenics have learned to tell themselves to talk more coherently, and phobic subjects have learned to use "coping" self-instructions and physical relaxation to reduce their fears.

The promising results of these studies underscore several points. First, systematic training programs can be established to teach persons how to self-instruct themselves to act more effectively in problem situations by using modeling, rehearsal, and feedback. These procedures involve a fading strategy, from external instruction (that is, the person's observing others) to self-managed instruction. Second, a variety of covert and overt techniques, such as positive reinforcement, covert self-reward, self-punishment, modeling, and self-modeling combining imagery and words, can be used. What the optimal combination should be remains unexamined. Third, the use of "coping" treatments, in which the person observes a model who at first acts anxiously but gradually manages to reduce his anxiety, may enhance the effectiveness of current behavioral treatments. Fourth, combining physiological, cognitive, and overt techniques, as illustrated in Meichenbaum and Cameron's "stress-inoculation" procedure, seems very promising as a way of providing people with self-control skills that can *maintain* changes in a variety of everyday environments. Hopefully, more "treatment packages" that combine techniques rather than focus on single-treatment strategies will be developed during the next decade.

Our research efforts initially began in an attempt to systematically assess the validity of behavior-therapy procedures that have been described in a number of comparative studies and clinical case reports. The general research strategy has been to assess the efficacy of "standard" behavior-therapy procedures (such as operant and aversive conditioning, modeling, and desensitization) relative to the effectiveness of behavior-therapy procedures that have been modified to include a self-instructional component. In general, the results have indicated that, when the standard behavior-therapy procedures were augmented with a self-instructional package, greater treatment efficacy, more generalization, and greater persistence of treatment effects were obtained. Moreover, when the standard behavior-therapy procedures were put under the scrutiny of experimentation, their limitations were highlighted and, in some instances, the basis of their conceptualizations challenged. The by-product has been the development of new, and possibly more therapeutic, procedures.

One common theme has run through our research findings. It is that behavior therapies in their present form have overemphasized the importance of environmental consequences, thus underemphasizing (and often overlooking) how the subject perceives and evaluates those consequences. Our research on cognitive factors in behavior modification has highlighted the fact that it is not the environmental consequences per se that are of primary importance but what the subject says to himself about those consequences. However, what the subject says to himself—that is, how he evaluates and interprets these events —is explicitly modifiable by many of the behavior-therapy techniques that have been used to alter maladaptive behaviors. The following quasi-chronological summary of our research indicates how we have come to these conclusions.

The research program began with a rather serendipitous finding, which was observed in the senior author's Ph.D. dissertation (Meichenbaum, 1969). The study involved a laboratory operant-training program in which a group of hospitalized schizophrenic patients were trained to emit "healthy talk" in an interview setting. The effects of operant training generalized over time to a follow-up interview administered by the experimenter, to a post-test interview administered by a patient confederate, and to other verbal tasks (such as a proverbs test and a word-association test) administered under neutral conditions. Interestingly, a number of the schizophrenic patients who had been trained to emit "healthy talk" repeated aloud and spontaneously the experimental instruction "give healthy talk, be coherent and relevant" while being tested on the generalization measures.

This self-instruction seemed to mediate generalization and aid the subject in attending to the demands of the task by preventing any internally generated distracting stimuli from interfering with his language behavior. An intriguing question thus arose: can schizophrenics (and perhaps other clinical populations) be explicitly trained to talk to themselves in such a self-guiding fashion and to spontaneously produce such internally generated discriminative stimuli? A paradigm for training schizophrenics to self-instruct emerged from a series of studies with impulsive children.

A series of observational and experimental studies on impulsive children (Meichenbaum, 1971a; Meichenbaum & Goodman, 1969a) indicated that they exercise less verbal control over their motor behaviors and use private speech in a less instrumental fashion than reflective children do. Hence, it appeared that the impulsive children, like the schizophrenic patients, might benefit from learning to talk to themselves in a directive, self-regulatory fashion. Developmental literature from the Soviet psychologists Vygotsky (1962) and Luria (1961) inspired the training paradigm. On the basis of his work with children, Luria (1961, 1966) has proposed three stages by which the initiation and the inhibition of voluntary motor behaviors come under verbal control. During the first stage, the speech of others—usually adults—controls and directs a child's behavior. The child's own overt speech begins to effectively regulate his behavior during the second stage. Finally, the child's covert or inner speech comes to assume a self-governing role. From this hypothetical sequence, we developed a treatment paradigm that was successfully used to train impulsive children to talk to themselves as a means of developing self-control (Meichen-baum & Goodman, 1971). The children, who were given individual self-instructional training, had been placed in special-education classes because of their marked hyperactivity, impulsivity, and distractibility.

The cognitive self-guidance-training technique proceeded as follows: first, the experimenter performed a task while the subject observed (the experimenter acted as model); then the subject performed the same task while the experimenter instructed the subject aloud; then the subject was asked to perform the task again while instructing himself aloud; then the subject performed the task while whispering; and finally the subject performed the task while self-instructing covertly. The verbalizations that the experimenter modeled and the subject subsequently used included: (1) questions about the nature of the task; (2) answers to these questions in the form of cognitive rehearsal and planning; (3) self-instruction in the form of self-guidance; and (4) self-reinforcement. In this way, the impulsive child was trained to develop a new cognitive approach, or learning set, in which he could "size up" the demands of a task, cognitively rehearse, then guide his performance by means of self-instructions, and, finally, appropriately reinforce himself.

The following is an example of the experimenter's modeled verbalizations, which the subject subsequently used (initially overtly, then covertly):

> Okay, what is it I have to do? You want me to copy the picture with the different lines. I have to go slowly and carefully. Okay, draw the line down, down, good; then to the right; that's it; now down some more and to the left. Good, I'm doing fine so far. Remember, go slowly. Now back up again. No, I was supposed to go down. That's okay. Just erase the line carefully. . . . Good. Even if I make an error I can go on slowly and carefully. Okay, I have to go down now. Finished. I did it!

Note that in this example, an error in performance was included and the experimenter appropriately accommodated. This feature was included because prior research with "impulsive" children (Meichen-baum & Goodman, 1969a) indicated a marked deterioration in their performance following errors. The experimenter's verbalizations varied with the demands of each task, but the general treatment format remained the same throughout. The treatment sequence was also individually adapted to the capabilities of the subject and the difficulties of the task.

A variety of tasks was employed to train the child to use self-instructions to control his nonverbal behavior. The tasks varied along a dimension from simple sensorimotor abilities to more complex problem-solving abilities. The sensorimotor tasks, such as copying line patterns and coloring figures within certain boundaries, provided the subject with an opportunity to produce a narrative description of his behavior, both preceding and accompanying his performance. Over the course of a training session, the child's overt self-statements on a particular task were faded to the covert level. The difficulty level of the training tasks was increased over the training sessions, requiring more cognitively demanding activities. Hence, there was a progression from performing tasks such as reproducing designs and following sequential instructions taken from the Stanford-Binet Intelligence Test to completing pictorial series as on the Primary Mental Abilities Test to solving conceptual tasks such as the Ravens Matrices Test. The experimenter modeled appropriate self-verbalizations for each of these tasks and then had the child follow the fading procedure.

One can imagine a similar training sequence in the learning of a new motor skill such as driving a car with a stick shift. Initially, the driver actively goes through a mental checklist (sometimes aloud) that includes verbal rehearsal, self-guidance, and sometimes appropriate self-reinforcement. Only with repetition do the cognitions become short-circuited and does the sequence become automatic. If this observation has any merit, then a training procedure that makes these steps explicit should facilitate the development of self-control.

Subjects who participated in the self-instructional-training procedure showed significantly improved performance on the Porteus Maze Test, improved performance on the Wechsler Intelligence Scale for Children, and improved cognitive reflectivity on Kagan's (1966) Matching Familiar Figures Test (MFF), when compared with placebo and assessment control groups. The improved performance was evident in a one-month follow-up. A number of other investigators (Bem, 1967; Karnes, Teska, & Hodgins, 1970; Palkes, Stewart, & Freedman, 1972; Palkes, Stewart, & Kahana, 1968) have also demonstrated the therapeutic value of similar self-instructionally based treatment programs.

In a second study (Meichenbaum & Goodman, 1971), it became evident that the experimenter's cognitive modeling was a necessary, but not sufficient, condition for engendering self-control in impulsive children. The results indicated that the impulsive child's behavioral rehearsal in self-instructing was an indispensable part of the training procedures. It was necessary that the impulsive child not only be exposed to a self-instructing model but also "try out" the self-instructions himself. The treatment condition of cognitive modeling alone resulted in the impulsive child's slowing down his performance but did not result in a concomitant reduction in errors on the MFF test. However, cognitive modeling plus self-instructional rehearsal resulted in both a slower and a more accurate performance.

Our recent clinical work with impulsive, hyperactive children has raised a number of other treatment considerations. First, the self-instructional-training regimen can be supplemented with imagery manipulations, especially in treating young children. One can train the impulsive child to image and to subsequently self-instruct: "I will not go faster than a slow turtle." Secondly, it is often more productive to begin self-instructional training on tasks at which the child is somewhat proficient. The therapist can model the use of self-instructions in the midst of ongoing play activities and in turn have the child incorporate these self-statements into his repertoire. Thus, the therapist can, in a "playful" manner, teach the impulsive child the concept of talking to himself. Thirdly, we have found that it is helpful to evolve toward the complete package of self-statements through a series of successive approximations. Initially, the therapist can model and have the child rehearse simple self-statements, such as "Stop! I must think before I answer." Then, over the course of training sessions, the therapist can model (and have the child rehearse) a more complex set of self-statements.

Another observation is that children seem to readily accept the demand to "think aloud" as they perform a task, whereas the instruction to "talk aloud to oneself" seems to elicit negative connotations (for example, "that is something crazy people do").

The emphasis on playfulness needs to be underscored. In order to gain the impulsive child's attention, the therapist must actively participate in the child's play. For example, while playing with one impulsive boy, the therapist said "I have to land my airplane, slowly, carefully, into the hangar." The therapist then encouraged the child to have the control tower tell the pilot to go slowly, and so on. In this way, the therapist was able to have the child build up a repertoire of self-statements to be used on a variety of tasks.

We have employed two additional treatment procedures to train impulsive children to develop better verbal control of their behavior. The first involves the impulsive child's verbally directing another person to perform a task, such as the Porteus Maze Test, while the child sits on his hands. In this way, the child has to learn to use his language in an instrumental fashion in order to perform the task. Another technique designed to enhance self-control is to have an older impulsive child teach a younger child how to do a task. The older child, whose own behavior is actually the target of modification, is employed as a "teaching assistant" to model self-instructions for the younger child. In both of these instances, the goal is to have the impulsive child come to appreciate the ways in which language can be used to effect change.

Impulsive children vary markedly in how much training they need. Some require many trials of modeling and many trials of overt self-instructional rehearsal, whereas others may go covert quickly. The speed with which the therapist fades the self-instructional rehearsal depends on the child's performance. The importance of individually tailoring the self-instructional treatment package was illustrated by a study on the development of verbal control by Meichenbaum and Goodman (1969b). They found that forcing first-grade children to talk to themselves aloud while performing a motor-control task interfered with performance, whereas younger kindergarten children benefited from such overt self-instructions.

Finally, it should be made clear that the treatment-research results do not necessarily imply that reflective children actually talk to themselves in order to control their behavior. However, if one wishes to encourage an impulsive child to become reflective, then explicitly training him to talk to himself, initially overtly and eventually covertly, will enhance the change process.

The next step was to try the self-instructional-training paradigm with a group of schizophrenics. In an initial study, hospitalized schizophrenics were successfully trained to talk to themselves in order to improve their performance on attentional and cognitive tasks (Meichenbaum & Cameron, 1973). Using the same modeling and overt-to-covert cognitive-rehearsal paradigm that the impulsive children received, schizophrenics were trained to use such self-instructions as "pay attention, listen and repeat instructions, disregard distraction." The cognitive self-guidance training resulted in a significantly improved performance on such tasks as a digit-symbol task. On an individual case-study basis, several schizophrenic patients were given more extensive self-instructional training (for example, six hours), during which they were taught to monitor their own behavior and thinking as well as interpersonal cues. In this way, the schizophrenic patients were trained to become sensitive to the interpersonal cues (for example, to the facial and behavioral reactions of others) that indicated that they were emitting "schizophrenic behaviors" (such as bizarre, incoherent, or irrelevant behaviors and verbalizations). Both the interpersonal observations and the self-monitoring provided cues that were to be signals for the patient to emit the self-instructions "I will be relevant and coherent and make myself understood." An attempt was made to modify how the schizophrenic perceived, labeled, and interpreted such interpersonal and intrapersonal cues.

The sequence of the self-instructional-training regimen took into account Haley's (1963) hypothesis that schizophrenic symptoms function as covert messages aimed at grasping control of social interactions in a devious manner. This hypothesis was recently supported by Shimkunas (1972), who found that, as the demand for intense interpersonal relationships increased, the incidence of schizophrenic symptoms, such as bizarre verbalizations, also increased. Thus, the self-instructional training began with structured sensorimotor tasks in which the demands for social interactions and self-disclosure were minimal. On these initial straightforward tasks (such as digit-symbol tasks and the Porteus maze), the schizophrenics were trained to develop a set of self-controlling self-statements. When the schizophrenics had developed some degree of proficiency in the use of such self-statements, the task demands were slowly increased, requiring more cognitive effort and interpersonal interaction (for example, proverb interpretation and interviewing). In this way, an effort was made to have the schizophrenic initially develop, with high response strength, a set of self-instructional responses that he could apply in more anxiety-inducing interpersonal situations. Moreover, an attempt was made to have the schizophrenic become aware of instances in which he was using "symptomology" to control situations. This recognition was to be a cue to use the self-instructional controls that he had developed on the more simply structured sensorimotor and cognitive tasks. Thus, a continuum of training tasks was employed in which the degree of interpersonal closeness and the demand for self-disclosure were slowly increased.

The specific components of the self-instructional training included provision of general-"set" instructions; use of imagery, monitoring, and evaluation of inappropriate responses; and administration of self-reinforcement. These components were presented to the subject via a variety of procedures—namely, administration of instructions (by the experimenter and the subject, in overt and covert forms), modeling, provision of examples, behavioral rehearsal, operant chaining and shaping techniques, and discussion. Thus, all the clinical resources were used to develop attentional controls in schizophrenics.

The self-instructional-training group, compared with a yoked-practice control group, improved on a variety of measures, including the amount of "healthy talk" emitted in a structured interview, the level of proverb abstraction, the level of perceptual integration of responses in an inkblot test, and the amount of digit recall under distraction conditions. The consistent pattern of improvement for the schizophrenics who received self-instructional training was evident at a three-week follow-up assessment.

A word of caution is in order concerning the implementation of such self-instructional training with schizophrenics, as well as with other clinical populations. It is important to ensure that the subject does not repeat the self-statements in a relatively mechanical, rote, or automatic fashion without the accompanying meaning and inflection. This would approximate the everyday experience of reading aloud or silently when one's mind is elsewhere. One may read the paragraph aloud without recalling the content. What is needed instead is modeling and practice in synthesizing and internalizing the meaning of one's self-statements.

With the impulsive children and schizophrenic patients, appropriate self-instructional statements appeared to be absent from the subjects' repertoires before training. Self-instructional training was used to develop what Luria (1961) calls the "interiorization of language" in these populations. However, a large population of clients, who generally fall under the rubric of "neurotic," seem to emit a variety of maladaptive, anxiety-engendering self-statements.

Hence, the goal of intervention is not to remedy the absence of self-statements (as with the schizophrenics and impulsive children); rather it is to make the neurotic patients aware of the self-statements that mediate maladaptive behaviors and to train them to produce incompatible self-statements and behaviors.

This approach is not new. There is a long history of educational and semantic therapies that emphasize cognitive factors and that focus on maladaptive self-verbalizations (for example, Coue, 1922; Korzybski, 1933; Kelly, 1955; Phillips, 1957; Ellis, 1963; Blumenthal, 1969). A typical proponent of this view is Shaffer (1947), who defined therapy as a "learning process through which a person acquires an ability to speak to himself in appropriate ways so as to control his own conduct" (p. 463).

The second phase of our research explored the variety of ways in which "neurotic" clients can be trained to talk to themselves differently. In a series of studies using such varied populations as phobics, smokers, and speech-anxious, test-anxious, and uncreative college students, a variety of self-instructional-training techniques was examined. These treatment procedures included insight therapy, desensitization, modeling, anxiety relief, and aversive conditioning, all modified to be consistent with a self-instructional approach.

The therapeutic approach that has most explicitly emphasized the importance of a client's internal verbalizations is the rational-emotive therapy of Albert Ellis (1963). The Ellis approach attempts to make the client aware of his maladaptive self-statements and to change the client's behavior by means of persuasion, encouragement, and education in the form of rational analyses. The first experiment in treating speech-anxious clients (Meichenbaum, Gilmore, & Fedoravicius, 1971) was designed to assess the relative merits of a semantic insight-therapy approach similar to Ellis' versus systematic desensitization. In each case, treatment was conducted on a group basis. The desensitization treatment followed the general procedures described by Wolpe (1958) and Lazarus and Rachman (1960) and the detailed procedures of Paul and Shannon (1966). The procedure included progressive-relaxation training, group-hierarchy construction, imagery training, and group desensitization (Paul and Shannon, 1966). The group-insight-treatment approach emphasized the rationale that speech anxiety is the result of self-verbalizations and internalized sentences that are emitted while the individual is thinking about the speech situation. The clients were informed that the goals of therapy were for each subject to become aware of (or "gain insight into") the self-verbalizations and self-instructions that he emitted in anxiety-evoking interpersonal situations. The group members discussed the specific self-verbalizations that they emitted in speech situations and in interpersonal situations and the irrational, self-defeating, and self-fulfilling aspects of such statements. In addition, they learned to produce both incompatible self-instructions and incompatible behaviors.

The major results indicated that the insight approach was equally as effective as desensitization in reducing the behavioral and affective indicants of speech anxiety. However, a most interesting post hoc finding was that different types of clients received differential benefit from insight and desensitization treatment. Clients with high social distress who suffered anxiety in many varied situations benefited most from the insight procedure, which attends to and modifies the client's self-verbalizations. More recently, other investigators (Lazarus, 1971; Karst & Trexler, 1970) have also reported successful treatment outcome with a similar rational-emotive-based treatment approach. Desensitization treatment appeared to be significantly more effective with subjects whose speech anxiety was confined to formal speech situations. This latter finding is consistent with an increasing literature (Clarke, 1963; Gelder, Marks, Wolf, & Clarke, 1967; Lang & Lazovik, 1963; Lazarus, 1971; Marks & Gelder, 1965) which suggests that systematic desensitization works well with monosymptomatic phobias and poorly with so-called free-floating anxiety states.

Highly test-anxious clients represent another population whose self-statements or thinking processes evidently contribute to maladaptive behavior. Research by a variety of investigators (for example, Liebert & Morris, 1967; Mandler & Watson, 1966; Wine, 1971a,b) has indicated that highly test-anxious people, in situations in which their performance is being evaluated, spend much of their time (1) worrying about their performance and about how well others are doing; (2) ruminating over alternatives; and (3) being preoccupied with such things as feelings of inadequacy, anticipation of punishment, loss of status or esteem, and heightened somatic and autonomic reactions. In other words, a worry component diverts attention away from the task and results in performance decrement. Thus, a treatment procedure aimed at controlling the worry component and the attentional style of the highly test-anxious client should improve test performance.

Two studies have been conducted that use different training procedures to teach test-anxious college students to talk to themselves differently in order to control their attention. The first study (Meichenbaum, in press) compared subjects who received cognitive-modification treatment, subjects who underwent desensitization, and subjects in a waiting-list control group. The cognitive-modification-treatment group combined the insight-oriented approach of the previous treatment study of speech anxiety with a modified desensitization procedure. The first aspect of cognitive-modification therapy emphasized becoming aware of ("gaining insight into") the thoughts and self-verbalizations that are emitted both prior to and during test situations. The second phase of therapy was designed to train the test-anxious college students to emit task-relevant self-statements and to perform arousal-inhibiting behaviors, such as relaxation. Whereas the self-instructional-training procedures used thus far had involved explicit rehearsal and practice (for example, with schizophrenics and impulsive children), the therapeutic strategy tried with the test-anxious clients included self-instructional training as part of the imagery procedure of desensitization. In order to provide such self-instructional training, the therapists modified the desensitization component of the treatment to include coping imagery. The subjects were asked to visualize coping as well as mastery behaviors—that is, if they became anxious while imaging a scene, they were to visualize themselves coping with this anxiety by means of slow, deep breaths and self-instructions to relax and to be task relevant. The subjects were encouraged to use any personally generated self-statements that would facilitate their attending to the task and that would inhibit task-irrelevant thoughts. Only if the coping-imagery techniques did not reduce their anxiety were they to signal the therapist, terminate the image, and continue relaxing. Thus, the subjects in the cognitive-modification group rehearsed self-instructional ways of handling anxiety by means of imagery procedures. In this way, they provided themselves with a model for their own behavior—one that dealt with the anxiety they were likely to experience in reality.

This self-instructional coping imagery stands in marked contrast to the mastery-type imagery used in standard desensitization procedures. In the standard desensitization-treatment procedure, the subject is told to signal if the visualized image elicits anxiety and then to terminate that image and relax. This mastery-image procedure is consistent with the principle of counterconditioning, which pairs the subject's state of relaxation with the visualization of anxiety-eliciting scenes. There is no suggestion within the standard desensitization procedure that, following the completion of therapy, the subject will in fact realize or experience anxiety in the real-life situation. In contrast, the coping-imagery procedure required the subject to visualize the experience of anxiety and ways in which to cope with and reduce such anxiety. The coping-imagery technique was designed to have the test-anxious subject view the anxiety he might experience following treatment as an "ally," a signal for employing the previously trained coping techniques of relaxation and self-instructions. The cognitive-modification procedure required the client to explicitly rehearse by means of imagery (1) the ways in which he would appraise, label, and attribute the arousal he would experience, (2) the ways in which he would control his thoughts and cope with his anxiety, and, more specifically, (3) the self-statements he would make in evaluative situations.

The results of the study indicated that a cognitive-modification-treatment procedure, which attempts to make highly test-anxious subjects aware of the anxiety-engendering self-statements they *do* emit and of incompatible self-instructions and behaviors (such as relaxation) they *should* emit, was significantly more effective than standard desensitization in reducing test anxiety. The superiority of the cognitive-modification-treatment group was evident in an analogue test situation, on self-report measures, and on grade-point average. This improvement was maintained at a one-month follow-up assessment. It is noteworthy that, after treatment, the subjects in the cognitive-modification group did not significantly differ from low test-anxious subjects on the performance and self-report measures.

Most significantly, only the subjects in the cognitive-modification-treatment group reported a post-treatment increase in facilitative anxiety as assessed by the Alpert-Haber Anxiety Scale (1960). Following treatment, the cognitive-modification subjects labeled arousal as facilitative, as a cue to be task relevant, and as a signal to improve their performance. The self-report of reduced perceived anxiety *and* improved academic performance in the cognitive-modification subjects is most impressive in light of other investigators' reports (Lang & Lazovik, 1963; Paul, 1966) that desensitization results in modified behavior but in a minimal decrease in self-reports of fear and anxiety. Johnson and Sechrest (1968), who conducted a desensitization study of test-anxious subjects, failed to obtain changes in self-report on the Alpert-Haber scale, and they indicated that the verbal behavior of reporting oneself as an anxious student is not dealt with directly by the desensitization procedures. The cognitive-modification treatment demonstrated that the cognitions that accompany arousal are modifiable.

Further evidence for the effectiveness of training highly test-anxious college students to self-instruct was provided by Wine (1971a,b). Whereas Meichenbaum (in press) used a cognitive-rehearsal self-instructional *imagery* procedure, Wine (1971a,b) gave the subjects six hours of attentional training that involved the modeling and behavioral rehearsal of self-instructions (that is, a training procedure similar to that used with the schizophrenics and impulsive children). Subjects in Wine's self-instructional attention-training group improved significantly relative to the subjects in an insight group, which concentrated on the exploration of self-relevant verbalizations —namely, the thoughts that group members had in evaluative situations. Wine's results suggest that an insight procedure that concentrates only on making subjects aware of their anxiety-engendering self-statements *without* exploring and practicing the use of incompatible self-instructions and behaviors is ineffective in reducing test anxiety and is likely to reinforce a deteriorative process.

One additional note should be made concerning the treatment of speech- and test-anxious adults. In both of the Meichenbaum studies, a comparison was made between the group versus individual administration of the insight-treatment procedure. In both cases, group administration of the insight-treatment procedure was found to be as effective as individually administered insight treatment, and, thus, it represents a considerable saving in the therapist's time. In fact, the group administration of the insight-treatment approach appears easier and somewhat more effective than individual administration. In the group administration, the subjects can readily contribute to and benefit from a shared exploration of the personalized cognitive events that they emit and of the incompatible cognitions and behaviors that they must emit to reduce anxiety and improve performance. In addition, group pressure can be therapeutically employed to encourage and reinforce behavior change.

Interestingly, negative self-statements also seem to interfere with the functioning of college students who perform poorly on creativity tests. When such noncreative subjects were asked to describe the thoughts and feelings that they experienced while taking a battery of creativity tests, they reported task-irrelevant self-critical thoughts (such as "I'm not very original or creative; I'm better at organizing tasks than at being creative"), *or* they reported thoughts that disparaged the value of the creativity tests (such as "Is this what psychologists mean by creativity, telling all the uses of a brick? What a waste!")—*or*, if they did produce a creative response, they devalued their own performance by thinking that "anyone could have produced such an answer." Such cognitive activity is obviously counterproductive and likely interferes with the creative process.

Thus, the first aspect of self-instructional training of creativity was to make the subject aware of the variety of self-statements he emitted that inhibited creative performance. These negative self-statements fall into two general classes: (1) those by which the subject questions his own creative powers and (2) those by which he devaluates the task or situation.

The second aspect of training was to train subjects to produce incompatible, creativity-engendering self-statements. But what exactly do you train a subject to say to himself in order to become more creative? Some suggestions for the content of the self-statements come from the burgeoning literature on creativity training (see Parnes & Brunelle, 1967). Three conceptualizations of creativity seem to underlie the range of techniques that have been used to train creativity. The conceptualizations include a mental-abilities approach, which emphasizes deliberate training exercises (for example, Guilford, 1967; Torrance, 1965); an ego-analytic-levels analysis of thinking, which focuses on the role of the regression of the ego and on associational techniques (for example, Kris, 1953); and, finally, an approach that emphasizes the role of general attitudinal set, including factors that characterize creative individuals (for example, Barron, 1969). Each of these conceptualizations was translated into a set of self-statements that could be modeled and then practiced by subjects. Table 1 illustrates the variety of self-statements that characterize each conceptualization of creativity.

TABLE 1. *Examples of Self-Instructional Statements to En-hance Creativity.*

Conceptualizations of Creativity

Set-inducing attitudinal
self-statements

Two classes:
1.   What to do
2.   What not to do

Self-statements arising
from a mental-abilities
conceptualization

Two classes:
1.   Problem analysis—
what you say to
yourself before you
start a problem

2.   Task execution—what
you say to yourself
while doing a task

Self-statements arising from
an ego-analytic-levels
analysis of thinking

Self-Statements

1.   *Be creative, be unique.*
Break away from obvious, the
commonplace.
Think of something no one else will
think of.
Just be freewheeling.
If I push myself, I can be creative.
Quantity helps breed quality.

2.   *Get rid of internal blocks.*
Defer judgments.
No stop rule.
Don't worry about what others think.
Not a matter of right or wrong.
Don't give the first answer I think of.
No negative self-statements.

1.   *Size up problem. What is it I have to do?*
I have to put elements together
differently.
Use different analogies.

Do the task–as if I were Osborn
brainstorming or as if I were
Gordon of Synectics Training.
I'm going to elaborate on ideas.
Let's make the strange familiar or the
familiar strange.

2. *I'm in a rut, okay, try something new.*
How can I use this frustration to be more
creative?
Take a rest now; who knows when the
ideas will visit again?
Go slow, no hurry–no need to press.
Good, I'm getting it.
This is fun.
That was a pretty neat answer; wait until
I tell the others.
Release controls, let my mind wander.
Free-associate, let ideas flow.
Relax, just let it happen.
Let my ideas play.
Ideas will be a surprise.
Refer to my experience–just view it
differently.
Let my ego regress.
I feel like a bystander through whom
ideas are just flowing.
Let one answer lead to another.
Almost dreamlike, the ideas have a life
of their own.

The following is an example of the type of self-statements that the experimenter modeled and the subjects subsequently practiced. In this case, the task was product improvement, requiring a list of clever, interesting, and unusual ways of changing a toy monkey so that children would have more fun playing with it.

"I want to think of something no one else will think of—something unique. I'll be freewheeling, no hangups. I don't care what anyone thinks; I'll just suspend judgment. I'm not sure what I'll come up with; it will be a surprise. The ideas can just flow through me. Okay, what is it I have to do? Think of ways to improve a toy monkey. Toy monkey. Let me close my eyes and relax. I'll just picture a monkey. I see a monkey; now I'll let my mind wander; let one idea flow into another . . . let my ego regress."

After inducing this general set, the experimenter then thought aloud as he tried to come up with answers. For example:

"Now I'll do the task as if I were Gordon" [William Gordon of Synectics Training]. "I have to use analogies. Let me picture myself inside the monkey" (a fantasy analogy).

On another occasion the experimenter would model:

> "Now I'll do the task as if I were Osborn, who did that brainstorming research. How many different ways can I change the monkey? I must remember, the key word is *scram*. It stands for substitute, combine, rearrange, reverse, adapt, modify, magnify, minify."

Using such procedures, the experimenter would continue to provide both obvious and original answers to the task. Throughout the modeling, the experimenter often used self-reinforcement by manifesting spontaneous affect of pleasure, surprise, eagerness, and delight and by saying such things as "good" or "this is fun." The experimenter tried to capture a mood of self-mobilization, an attitude of determination to do the task, and a desire to translate into answers the excitement of creative thoughts. The modeling also included the experimenter's coping with getting into a rut, feeling frustrated, and then talking himself out of it. An example of a set of such coping self-statements follows:

> "I must stop giving the first answer that comes to my mind. I don't have to press. . . . I'll let the ideas just play; let things happen. The ideas seem to have a life of their own. If they don't come now, that's okay. Who knows when they will visit? Remember, no negative self-statements."

Following such modeling, the group practiced talking to themselves while performing on a variety of tasks. Gradually, at the subject's own pace, the explicit use of self-statements dropped out of the subject's repertoire. Most importantly, the subjects were not asked to merely parrot a set of self-statements; rather, they were encouraged to emit the accompanying affect and intention to comply with their self-statements. This involvement can be achieved by a variety of means, including (1) determining the subject's conceptualization of creativity and his expectations concerning training; (2) explaining the rationale for self-instructional training; (3) having the subject examine his personal experiences to find instances when he emitted similar negative and positive self-statements; and (4) having the subject rehearse or "try on" self-statements while performing personally selected meaningful activities (such as hobbies or homework).

In brief, the self-instructional creativity training began by calling attention to the largely counterproductive thinking patterns that were occurring. Then, through modeling and overt rehearsal, the subjects were trained to employ more productive thought patterns. Finally, the new patterns became covert. It is likely that, at this point, the new thought patterns themselves began to become automatic and occur without awareness.

In order to assess the beneficial effects of self-instructional training, two control groups were included in the study. The first group
afforded an index of improvement on creativity tests due to factors of
attention or placebo effects, exposure to creativity tests during training,
and any demand characteristics inherent in our measures of improvement. An attempt was made to include a group (1) that received a type
of training based on a conceptualization of creativity that did not
emphasize cognitive or self-instructional factors and (2) that had face
validity sufficient to elicit high expectations from the subjects. These
criteria were met by a procedure called "focusing," which Gendlin
(1969) and his colleagues suggest can be used to enhance creativity.
Focusing involves paying attention to one's present feelings and coming to a new formulation about them. In addition to the focusing group,
a waiting-list control group was included in the study.

The self-instructional-training group, compared with Gendlin's
focusing-training group and with the untreated waiting-list control
group, manifested a significant increase in originality and flexibility on
tests of divergent thinking, an increase in preference for complexity,
a significant increase in human-movement responses to an inkblot test,
and concomitant changes in self-concept. In contrast, subjects in the
focusing-training group showed no objective improvement on the
creativity tests, although they indicated by self-report that they felt more
creative.

Moreover, the self-instructional training engendered a generalized
set to view one's life style in a more creative fashion. The subjects
reported that they had spontaneously applied the creativity training to
a variety of personal and academic problems. This latter observation
suggests that psychotherapy clients may benefit from such a self-
instructional creativity or problem-solving regimen. Instead of the
clinician's dealing with the details of the client's maladaptive behaviors, he could provide the client with self-instructional creativity
training for solving personal problems. This suggestion is consistent
with D'Zurilla and Goldfried's (1971) view of a problem-solving approach to psychotherapy.

The research with the college students indicated that behavior-
modification techniques such as desensitization and modeling could
be improved by altering them in order to directly modify what clients
say to themselves. For example, the addition of an insight procedure
and of coping imagery to the desensitization treatment resulted in
greater improvement than did standard desensitization. Would other
behavior-modification procedures similarly benefit from changes designed to directly alter the client's cognitive processes? In separate

studies, the modification procedures of modeling, anxiety relief, and aversive conditioning were examined in order to compare the standard "traditional" manner in which the therapy procedure has been used with a procedure that would explicitly attempt to modify the client's self-statements as well as his maladaptive behavior.

The first study (Meichenbaum, 1971b) examined the use of modeling therapy to alter the self-statements of snake-phobic clients. The modeling study was designed to examine the efficacy of modeled self-verbalizations (that is, of the explicit modeling of self-statements the client could use) versus the efficacy of the absence of any modeled verbalizations. A second factor included in the study was the modeling style: coping models (that is, models who initially exhibited fearful behaviors, then coping behavior, and, finally, mastery behavior) versus mastery models (that is, models who demonstrated only fearless behavior throughout). The results clearly indicated that a coping model who self-verbalizes throughout facilitates the greatest behavioral change and the most self-reported affective changes. The effectiveness of a model who verbalizes self-instructions along with self-reassuring and self-rewarding statements was indicated by the fact that five of the nine clients in the coping-verbalization condition spontaneously and overtly self-verbalized in the post-test assessment.

It may be instructive to illustrate the coping verbalizations that were modeled. Initially, the models commented on their anxiety and fear and on the physiological accompaniments (sweaty palms, increased heart rate and breathing rate, tenseness, and so on). But, at the same time, the models attempted to cope with their fears by instructing themselves (1) to remain relaxed and calm by means of slow, deep breaths; (2) to take one step at a time; and (3) to maintain a determination to forge ahead and handle the snake. The models were preparing themselves to perform each task, and, upon completion of that task, they emitted self-rewarding statements and positive affective expressions. One model stated to the snake: "I'm going to make a deal with you. If you don't scare or hurt me, I won't scare or hurt you." After concluding the final step he added: "Wait until I tell my mom I was able to handle a snake barehanded for a full minute; she won't believe it. I'm so happy with myself: I was able to overcome my fear." It is interesting to note that two subjects who had observed this series of coping verbalizations stated aloud, on their return to the post-treatment-assessment room, stated aloud (in essence): "You [referring to the snake] made a deal with her [referring to the model]; I will make a similar deal. If you don't hurt me, I won't hurt you. I'm going to pick you up."

Bandura (1969) has emphasized that the information that observers gain from models is converted to covert perceptual-cognitive images and covert mediating-rehearsal responses that are retained by the client and later used by him as symbolic cues to overt behavior. The results of the modeling study suggest that the explicit modeling of self-verbalizations facilitates the learning process that Bandura has described. It is also interesting to note that treatments that provide clients with coping styles or imagery techniques (as in the previous study with test-anxious clients) facilitate greater behavioral change than do treatments that employ fearless mastery models or mastery images.

Another example of the efficacy of therapy designed to modify clients' self-verbalizations came from a series of studies (Meichenbaum & Cameron, 1972a) on Wolpe and Lazarus' (1966) anxiety-relief procedure. Wolpe and Lazarus have described their paradigm and its rationale as follows:

> If an unpleasant stimulus is endured for several seconds and is then made to cease almost immediately after a specified signal, that signal will become conditioned to the changes that follow cessation of the uncomfortable stimulus (p. 149).

Typically, the word "calm" is the signal that is paired with the offset of aversive stimulation (usually electric shock). Theoretically, the self-instruction "calm" takes on counterconditioning anxiety-relief qualities that generalize across situations. The notion is that the client will be able to reduce his anxiety level in virtually any situation by instructing himself to be "calm," thus evoking the conditioned relief response. A number of investigators (Solyom & Miller, 1967; Solyom, Kenny, & Ledwidge, 1969; Thorpe, Schmidt, Brown, & Castell, 1964) have presented data that demonstrate the therapeutic value of such anxiety-relief techniques in alleviating phobic and obsessive behaviors.

The first study in the series further assessed the therapeutic value of Wolpe and Lazarus' anxiety-relief procedure in reducing persistent avoidant fear behavior toward harmless snakes. The anxiety-relief group received five one-hour sessions of escape and avoidance training in which the self-instructions "relax" and "calm" terminated ongoing shock to the forefinger and eventually avoided the onset of shock. This shock-contingent group was compared to a self-instructional rehearsal group that did not receive shock and to a waiting-list control group. The anxiety-relief group showed significantly more behavioral and affective change than the rehearsal and control groups did.

A second study on the anxiety-relief procedure attempted to break new ground. An effort was made to modify the basic anxiety-relief paradigm so as to enhance its efficacy in reducing snake phobia. With this goal in mind, two alterations were made to the basic paradigm. First, we added a self-instructional component to the procedure. Phobic clients in an expanded anxiety-relief group now terminated shock by generating and emitting coping self-statements ("Relax—I can touch the snake; just one step at a time") rather than by verbalizing a single cue word (such as "relax" or "calm"). Our second revision of the paradigm involved employing the aversive stimulation as a punishing agent as well as using it as the basis for anxiety relief. The client was asked to verbalize the thoughts associated with his avoidant behavior. Shock onset was then made contingent upon these verbalizations.

In summary, the following Wolpe-Lazarus anxiety-relief procedure was used in Study I:

> The therapist says the cue word (for example, "shock"); then electric shock is administered to the client. When the client most desires relief from shock, he emits the self-instruction "relax," which terminates the shock. The client then relaxes.

In contrast, the expanded anxiety-relief group of Study II proceeded as follows:

> The therapist said the cue word "snake"; the client then verbalized the self-statements, thoughts, and descriptive images that he experienced when confronted by a snake (for example, "it's ugly," "it's slimy," "I won't look at it," and so on). The client was encouraged to emit the personal self-statements that he had experienced in the preassessment and in past encounters with the phobic object. Following the expression of these self-statements, shock was administered, thus punishing the anxiety-inducing, avoidant self-statements. The instrumental response that the client used to terminate shock (and in later sessions to avoid shock onset) was a set of positive self-instructions (for example, "Relax; you can touch it; one step at a time"). The clients were encouraged over the five treatment sessions to produce self-instructions indicating that they could look, touch, and handle the phobic object and that they were in control of how they felt. Throughout the training, all self-statements (both positive and negative) were to be said in a meaningful, personalized manner.

In addition to a waiting-list control group, two additional groups were included in Study II in order to assess (1) the rehearsal effects of such self-instructional training and (2) the importance of the contingency of shock onset and offset to the expanded anxiety-relief-treatment paradigm. The contingency variable was assessed by means of inverting the expanded anxiety-relief paradigm so that now the expression of avoidant thoughts was paired with relief, whereas positive, coping self-instructions were punished. The sequence for the *inverted* anxiety-relief group was as follows:

> The therapist said the cue word "snake"; the client then verbalized the self-instructions ("I'll relax; I can handle it," and so on). Following the expression of these self-instructions, shock was administered. The client terminated the shock by emitting the avoidant self-statements ("It's ugly"; "I can't touch the snake," and so on). In this way, anxiety relief was paired with the expression of the fear-avoidant self-statements, while the positive self-statements were punished.

In review, the groups included in Study II were (1) an expanded anxiety-relief group, (2) an inverted anxiety-relief group, (3) a self-instructional rehearsal group, and (4) a waiting-list control group.

The results proved most revealing. Findings were consistent across all behavioral and self-report measures, as indicated in the post-test and follow-up assessment. The two anxiety-relief groups (regular and inverted), which employed shock, were both equally effective in reducing fears. The cognitive-rehearsal group showed less substantial and less consistent behavioral change. Moreover, the two anxiety-relief shock groups in Study II yielded significantly more change than the anxiety-relief clients in Study I. The results of Studies I and II suggest that (1) self-instructional training in the form of anxiety relief is an effective treatment procedure in reducing persistent avoidant behavior; (2) the efficacy of Wolpe's anxiety-relief paradigm can be enhanced by having the client embellish his self-statements; (3) the addition of shock to the treatment paradigm has a therapeutic benefit in facilitating change; and (4) the importance of the contingency variable and the plausibility of a conditioning explanation for treatment efficacy are seriously called into question.

This last finding is especially noteworthy. Other investigators (Carlin & Armstrong, 1968; McConaghy, 1971) have recently reported similar instances of therapeutic benefit accruing from noncontingent and inverted aversive-conditioning paradigms. Carlin and Armstrong reported that smokers treated in a noncontingent-shock group showed greater reduction in smoking than smokers treated according to the traditional aversive-conditioning paradigm. McConaghy found that homosexuals who received a backward aversive-conditioning treatment improved as much as homosexuals who received a standard aversive-conditioning treatment. These studies, as well as our own research on anxiety relief, render suspect the basic "learning-theory" assumptions that have been offered to explain the treatment efficacy of aversive conditioning. A variety of alternative theories deriving from social psychology, such as dissonance theory, attribution theory, and self-perception theory, provide likely alternative explanations of the effects of aversive conditioning. In each case, these theories implicate the importance of the client's cognitions or self-statements in explaining treatment efficacy. More research is obviously required to assess the validity of each of these alternative interpretations.

Our research on the anxiety-relief procedure suggested that clients were developing a set of self-instructional coping skills, which they could employ to deal with the stress of shock, and that these skills were in turn employed by clients in overcoming their fear of snakes. This observation raised the possibility that one could further enhance the client's skills training by making the training more explicit and by giving the client application training in a more anxiety-inducing situation. A number of investigators (D'Zurilla, 1969; Goldfried, 1971; Suinn & Richardson, 1971; Zeisset, 1968) have provided data to indicate that a skills-training approach, followed by an opportunity for application practice or rehearsal, is effective in reducing anxiety.

Working within a skills-training framework, Meichenbaum and Cameron (1972b) developed a stress-inoculation-training procedure to treat multiphobic clients. The stress-inoculation training was designed to accomplish three goals. The first was to "educate" the client about the nature of stressful or fearful reactions; the second, to have the client rehearse various coping behaviors; and the third, to give the client an opportunity to practice his new coping skills in a stressful situation.

The educational phase conceptualized the client's anxiety in terms of a Schachterian model of emotion; that is, the therapist reflected that the client's fear reaction seemed to involve two major elements —namely, (1) his heightened arousal (for example, increased heart rate, sweaty palms, and bodily tension) and (2) his set of anxiety-engendering thoughts and self-statements. The therapist then suggested that treatment would be directed toward helping the client (1) control his physiological arousal by learning how to physically relax and (2) learn to modify his self-statements along more productive lines (see Table 2). Once having mastered such coping skills, the phobic client was given an opportunity to practice the coping mechanisms in a stress-inducing situation of unpredictable electric shock. Numerous investigators (Elliott, 1966; Pervin, 1963; Skaggs, 1926; Thornton & Jacobs, 1971) have demonstrated that unpredictable shock (in terms of intensity and timing) represents a very stressful, anxiety-inducing situation.

One can view this treatment approach as the client's receiving an inoculation to stress—one that builds "psychological antibodies" and

TABLE 2.   Examples of Coping Self-Statements Rehearsed by Stress-Inoculation Subjects.

Preparing for a Stressor

> What is it I have to do?
> I can develop a plan to deal with it.
> Just think about what I can do about it. That's better than getting anxious.
> No negative self-statements, just think rationally.
> Don't worry. Worry won't help anything.
> Maybe what I think is anxiety is eagerness to confront it.

Confronting and Handling a Stressor

> I can meet this challenge.
> One step at a time; I can handle the situation.
> Don't think about fear—just about what I have to do. Stay relevant.
> This anxiety is what the doctor said I would feel. It's a reminder to use my coping exercises.
> This tenseness can be an ally, a cue to cope.
> Relax; I'm in control. Take a slow, deep breath. Ah, good.

Coping with the Feeling of Being Overwhelmed

> When fear comes, just pause.
> Keep focus on the present; what is it I have to do?
> Let me label my fear from 0 to 10 and watch it change.
> I was supposed to expect my fear to rise.
> Don't try to eliminate fear totally; just keep it manageable.
> I can convince myself to do it. I can reason my fear away.
> It will be over shortly.
> It's not the worst thing that can happen.
> Just think about something else.
> Do something that will prevent me from thinking about fear.
> Just describe what is around me. That way I won't think about worrying.

Reinforcing Self-Statements

> It worked; I was able to do it.
> Wait until I tell my therapist about this.
> It wasn't as bad as I expected.
> I made more out of the fear than it was worth.
> My damn ideas—that's the problem. When I control them, I control my fear.
> It's getting better each time I use the procedures.
> I'm really pleased with the progress I'm making.
> I did it!

"psychological strategems and skills," which can be employed in a variety of settings that induce anxiety and fear. The skills-training-treatment approach was designed to translate the phobic client's sense of "learned helplessness" into a feeling of "learned resourcefulness" so that he could cope with any anxiety- or fear-inducing situation.

An interesting comparison would be to examine the efficacy of a treatment procedure based on self-instructions, such as stress inoculation, with the efficacy of a treatment procedure based on imagery, such as desensitization. In order to assess the relative effectiveness of the two procedures, the experimenters selected multiphobic clients (that is, phobic to both rats and snakes) for treatment. One group of such multiphobic subjects received desensitization treatment (half being desensitized to rats and the other half to snakes). The other groups received two self-instructionally based treatments—namely, stress-inoculation training and the expanded anxiety-relief procedure of Study II.

The results proved interesting. The most effective treatment approach was stress inoculation. The clients who received stress-inoculation training showed the most significant improvement in both behavioral approach and self-report measures with respect to both the snake and the rat. The expanded anxiety-relief groups did not differ behaviorally from the desensitization group with regard to the feared objects to which the desensitized group had received treatment. However, the desensitization group showed minimal generalization at post-test and only slight improvement at follow-up with regard to the nondesensitized phobic object. This latter result is consistent with the findings of Meyer and Gelder (1963) and Wolpe (1958, 1961), who indicate that desensitization seems to alleviate only those phobias that are being treated; it does not mitigate other coexisting phobias. These other phobias remain at a high level, and this indicates a specific treatment effect. On the other hand, the clients who were subjected to the elaborated anxiety-relief procedure showed marked reduction in avoidance behavior to both phobic objects. In summary, the rank ordering of the effectiveness of the treatments was: (1) stress inoculation, (2) expanded anxiety relief, and (3) desensitization. Each of these groups differed significantly from a waiting-list control group, which showed minimal change due to multiple exposures (from pretreatment assessment to post-test and follow-up assessment) to both phobic objects.

The stress-inoculation-training procedure is a complex, multi-faceted treatment package, and further research is required to assess the relative contribution of the different treatment components. However, one hypothesis that may explain the greater treatment generalization of the self-instructionally based treatment programs, as compared to the imagery-based programs, may involve the respective mediators. Verbal mediators, in the form of self-instructions, likely evoke a broader response hierarchy or a broader spectrum of responses than do imaginal mediators; thus, they contribute to greater treatment generalization. Paivio (1969, 1970) has suggested that visualizing an object or stimulus event is quite different from describing or talking about the same object and that dissimilar processes are involved. The visualization process, or the imagery that is involved in desensitization, is a more concrete representation of specific stimuli and therefore should lead to minimal treatment generalization across multiple phobias. In contrast, the stress-inoculation procedure emphasizes words and cognitive-coping processes that are more abstract representations of stimulus events and should result in greater treatment generalization across multiple phobias. Lang (1968) has indicated that "the absence of programs for shaping cognitive sets and attitudes may contribute to the not infrequent failure of transfer of treatment effects" (p. 94). This set of studies, which directly modified what phobic patients said to themselves, demonstrated the importance of such cognitive mediators in behavior modification.

With the increasing demand on individuals to deal with stress, the possibility of providing stress-inoculation training is most exciting. It was quite common for clients in the stress-inoculation group to spontaneously report that they had successfully used the training procedure in other stress situations, such as final exams and visits to the dentist. One client even taught the procedure to his pregnant wife. One could think of a variety of additional stressors that could be employed for inoculation purposes (for example, the cold pressor test, stress films, fatigue, deprivation conditions, speeches, and so on). The more varied and extensive the training to deal with a variety of stressors, the greater the likelihood that the client will develop a general learning set—a general way to talk to himself in order to cope. The research on stress by Janis (1958) and Lazarus (1966) provides further evidence for the importance of cognitive rehearsal and stress inoculation in learning to cope.

The last behavior-modification procedure that was examined in order to determine how a client's self-statements and behavior can be modified was aversive conditioning. The aversive-conditioning paradigm typically involves showing the client a taboo stimulus or its representation (for example, a slide). When the client responds (as indicated by galvanic skin response, penile erection, and so forth), he is shocked. Shock is terminated by the reduction of the autonomic arousal or by an instrumental response such as choosing another slide. In some paradigms, the onset and offset of shock are made contingent upon the initiation and termination of an instrumental act such as drinking alcohol or smoking. A study was conducted in which the aversive-conditioning paradigm was elaborated on in order to modify what clients say to themselves. Steffy, Meichenbaum, and Best (1970) treated a group of smokers by making the shock contingent upon the self-statements, thoughts, and images that accompany the smoking act. Termination of the shock was contingent upon the expression of self-instructions to put out the cigarette or self-statements such as "I don't want a cancer weed." In this way, an explicit attempt was made to influence the chain of covert behaviors that control the smoking behavior. The clients were very inventive and serious in generating self-persuasive and self-rewarding self-statements that they could use to combat their urges to smoke.

This treatment approach is consistent with Premack's (1970) analysis of the self-control mechanisms that contribute to the termination of smoking behavior. Premack proposed that the decision to stop smoking results in a self-instruction that interrupts the automatic quality of the smoking chain. An increase in self-monitoring of one's smoking behavior sets the stage for such self-instructions. Thus, a treatment procedure that focuses on the development of such self-instructions should prove efficacious.

Postassessment and a six-month follow-up indicated substantial and significant improvement for the treatment group that attended to covert verbalizations as compared with a standard aversive-conditioning group. Having the clients self-verbalize an image while performing the maladaptive overt motor act (smoking) and then making the onset and offset of shock contingent upon the verbalized covert processes was highly effective in modifying self-verbalizations and in reducing smoking behavior.

Our self-instructional-treatment approach might also be applied to aversive conditioning of other clinical populations. For example, if a therapist were treating a pedophile by means of such an aversive-conditioning procedure, and, if the conditioned stimuli were slides of young children, he could make the onset of shock contingent upon the meaningful expression of the set of self-statements and descriptive images, feelings, and fantasies that the pedophile experiences when confronted by a real child. Shock offset could then be made contingent upon incompatible self-statements, which may involve self-instructions that he is mislabeling his arousal as sexual, that he should remove himself from the playground, or that he is not that kind of person. The possibility of making consequences, either positive or negative, contingent upon the self-statements that clients emit seems to hold much promise for future treatment development.

It should be apparent by now that, as Farber (1963) has indicated, "the one thing psychologists can count on is that their subjects will talk, if only to themselves; and not infrequently, whether relevant or irrelevant, the things people say to themselves determine the rest of the things they do" (p. 336). The present set of studies indicates that the recently developed group of behavior-modification techniques can be successfully used to modify what the client says to himself.

Finally, evidence (Krasner, 1968; Traux, 1966) has convincingly indicated that the therapist can and does significantly influence what the client says to him. Now it is time for the therapist to *directly* make use of this influence to change what clients say to themselves.

BEHAVIOR MODIFICATION IN THE TREATMENT OF OBESITY

Sydnor B. Penick, Ross Filion,
Sonja Fox, Albert Stunkard

Obesity has been a frequent subject for research in self-control. Following the pioneering efforts of Stuart (1967), investigators have explored the influence of both environmental-planning and behavioral-programming strategies in the treatment of weight problems. This article represents a blending of these two strategies in a well-controlled obesity study.

Of particular interest is the extent to which diverse self-control techniques were combined to offer a powerful treatment package. In addition to self-monitoring their eating habits, obese persons used several environmental-planning (stimulus-control) strategies as well as positive and negative self-reinforcement. They rewarded themselves with points for improvements in eating habits (positive self-reward). An ingenious form of negative self-reward was also employed: they stored bags of suet (pork fat) in their refrigerators as reminders of their own body fat and systematically removed portions of this aversive stimulus as they lost weight. Extensive social reinforcement (environmental feedback) was also provided.

The superiority of behavioral techniques over traditional group-therapy methods is noted. Although individuals varied widely in their responsiveness to treatment, the overall performance of the persons who received self-control training was quite impressive.

"Most obese persons will not stay in treatment for obesity. Of those who stay in treatment most will not lose weight and of those who do lose weight, most will regain it" (Stunkard, 1958). Until recently, this summary of the results of outpatient treatment for obesity has been unchallenged. Reports in the medical literature agree that no more than 25% of obese persons entering treatment will lose as much as 20 pounds and only 5% will lose as much as 40 pounds.

The current interest in behavior modification and the evidence of its effectiveness in the control of several conditions rendered inevitable its application to the problems of overeating and obesity. Yet the results of the first such application, by Ferster, Nurnberger, & Levitt (1962) were disappointing. The modal weight loss of the 10 patients in his program was only 10 pounds, with a range from 5 to 20 (Ferster, personal communication). A second study reported significantly greater weight losses among a group treated behaviorally than among a no-treatment control group; few of these patients were really obese, however, and only 21% of those remaining in treatment lost as much as 20 pounds (Harris, 1969).

Against this background, Stuart's recent report on *Behavioral Control of Overeating* stands out (Stuart, 1967). Eighty per cent of patients who began treatment (and all who continued) lost more than 20 pounds and 30% lost more than 40 pounds—the best results of outpatient treatment for obesity yet reported. These results persuaded us to assess the effectiveness of behavior modification in the treatment of obesity.

METHODS AND MATERIALS

The assessment of behavior modification was carried out in a day-care program for the treatment of obesity which is described more fully elsewhere (Penick, Filion, & Fox, 1971). Duration of treatment was 3 months, carried out once a week from 10:30 AM to approximately 3 PM. Activities consisted of an exercise period, preparation and eating of a low calorie lunch, and group therapy.

Thirty-two patients, all at least 20% overweight (Metropolitan Life Insurance Company, 1960), composed the study group. Median per cent overweight of patients treated by behavior therapy was 78%; that of the control patients was 80%. Median age of the behavior therapy patients was 39 (range 22–61); that of the control group was 44 (range 15–61). Most of the subjects were middle-class private patients referred for weight reduction, while 6 were lower-class persons referred by a state rehabilitation agency. Twenty-four were women and 8 were men.

Two cohorts were studied, the first composed entirely of private patients, the second containing also the rehabilitation patients. Patients from each source were randomly assigned to either a behavior therapy or a control group. Private patients paid in advance for the entire program and the fees were not refundable; welfare patients' fees were paid by the state.

Therapy of both groups lasted about 2 hours and was carried out by a man-and-woman team. The control group received supportive psychotherapy, instruction about dieting and nutrition and, upon demand, which was infrequent, appetite suppressants. The male therapist (SP) was an internist with long experience in the treatment of obesity. He is currently undertaking residency training in psychiatry, which has given him considerable additional training in group therapy. The female therapist was a research nurse with long association with her co-therapist, but no previous experience in group therapy.

The behavior modification therapists had had experience with group therapy only once before, in a 2-month pilot study of a group of obese women. The male therapist (RF), an experimental psychologist, had a strong background in learning theory but little clinical experience. The female therapist (SF), a research technician, had had extensive experience in clinical research, particularly in obesity. No appetite suppressants were used with these groups. The behavioral program is described below.

RESULTS

The Behavioral Program

The behavioral program was similar to that described by earlier writers and involved four general principles.

1. Description of the Behavior To Be Controlled. The patients were asked to keep daily records of the amount, time and circumstances of their eating. The immediate results of this time-consuming and inconvenient procedure were grumbling and complaints. Eventually, however, each patient reluctantly acknowledged that keeping these records had proved very helpful, particularly in increasing his awareness of how much he ate, the speed with which he ate, and the large variety of environmental and psychologic situations associated with eating. For example, after 2 weeks of record-keeping, a 30-year-old housewife reported that for the first time in her life, she recognized that anger stimulated her eating. Accordingly, whenever she began to get angry, she left the kitchen and wrote down how she felt, thereby decreasing her anger and aborting her eating.

2. Modification and Control of the Discriminatory Stimuli Governing Eating. Most of the patients reported that their eating occurred in a wide variety of places and at many different times during the day. They were accordingly encouraged to confine their eating, including snacking, to one place. In order not to disrupt domestic routines, this place was usually the dining room. Further efforts to control the discriminatory stimuli included the use of a distinctive table setting, including an unusually colored place mat and napkin. Patients were encouraged to make eating a pure experience, unaccompanied by any other activity, particularly reading, watching television or arguing with their families.

3. Development of Technics Which Control the Act of Eating. Specific technics were utilized to help patients decrease the speed of their eating, to become aware of the various components of the eating process, and to gain control over these components. Exercises included counting each mouthful of food eaten during a meal, and placing utensils on the plate after every third mouthful until that mouthful was chewed and swallowed.

4. Prompt Reinforcement of Behaviors Which Delay or Control Eating. A reinforcement schedule, utilizing a point system, was devised for control of eating behavior. Exercise of the suggested control procedures during a meal earned a certain number of points; devising an alternative to eating in the face of strong temptation earned double this number of points. Points were converted into money which was brought to the next meeting and donated to the group. At the beginning of the program, the group decided how the money should be used, and, to our surprise, highly altruistic courses were chosen. Each week, the first group donated its savings to the Salvation Army; the second, to a needy friend of one of the members, a widow with 14 children.

In addition to positive reinforcement, negative reinforcement was utilized. For example, control over snacking was facilitated by "doctoring" favorite snack foods with castor oil or other aversive taste. Furthermore, failure to exercise control resulted in the loss of points.

Our program differed from previous behavioral methods in at least two ways: (a) infrequent weighings and (b) separate reinforcement schedules for exercise of self-control and for weight loss.

(a) Previous workers, ourselves included, had weighed patients more frequently, and had attached contingencies to weighings as frequent as four times a day. Such short-term weight fluctuations, however, may result from physiologic factors such as fluid shifts, and are therefore probably imperfectly related to the exercise of behavioral control of eating. Their reinforcement could thus be counter-productive at times.

(b) The primary objective of this program was the development of self-control of eating, and weight loss was considered a consequence of the adaptive behaviors resulting from self-control. Separate reinforcement systems were therefore established for self-control and for weight loss. Reinforcements for self-control have been described. Various reinforcements for weight loss were devised by individual patients and therapists. An example of a popular and effective method utilized by all group members was purchase of a pound of suet which was cut into 16 pieces and placed in a plastic bag in a prominent place in the refrigerator. The patient attempted to visualize this fat on his body. For each pound lost, he removed 1 ounce of fat from the bag and tried to imagine its disappearance from his body. If he gained weight, he took home an ounce of fat for each pound gained and added it to his fat bag. When a patient had lost the entire fat bag, a prize such as a book or cosmetics was presented to him by the group, along with lavish praise.

Weight Loss

The results of treatment of the two cohorts are summarized in Table 1. The weight losses in the control group are comparable to those reported for a variety of treatments in the medical literature; none lost

TABLE 1. *Results of Treatment: Percent of Groups Losing Specified Amounts of Weight.*

Weight	Behavior modification groups (%) (N = 15)	Control therapy groups (%) (N = 17)	Average medical literature (%)
More than 40 pounds	13	0	5
More than 30 pounds	33	0	—
More than 20 pounds	53	24	25

40 pounds and 24% lost more than 20 pounds. By contrast, 13% of the behavioral modification group lost more than 40 pounds and 53% lost more than 20 pounds. Although neither of the differences between behavior modification and control groups for weight losses of over 20 and 40 pounds is statistically significant, that for weight losses of over 30 pounds is ($p = 0.015$ by Fisher exact probability test).

The weight losses for each subject are plotted in Figs. 1 and 2. Two findings should be noted. First, in each cohort the median weight loss for the behavior modification group was greater than that of the control group—24 versus 18 pounds for the first cohort and 13 versus 11 pounds for the second. The second finding is the far greater variability of the results of the behavior modification groups ($f = 4.38$, $p < 0.005$). The 5 best performers belonged to these groups as did the single least effective one, the only patient who actually gained weight during treatment. Because of this great variability, the overall differences in weight loss between the behavior modification and the control groups did not reach statistical significance.

Follow-up of the two cohorts at 6 and 3 months, respectively, provided evidence of the continuing influence of treatment, in contrast to the usual experience of rapid regaining of weight after treatment. Table 2 reveals that the number of persons in the behavior modification group

TABLE 2.   Follow-Up at 3-6 Months: Percent of Groups Losing Specified Amounts of Weight.

Weight	Behavior modification groups (%) (N = 15)	Control therapy groups (%) (N = 17)
More than 40 pounds	27	12
More than 30 pounds	40	18
More than 20 pounds	53	29

who lost more than 40 pounds doubled after termination of treatment (from 2 to 4), and 3 have actually lost more than 50 pounds. The control group similarly showed an increase in the number of persons losing large amounts of weight, a finding which attests to the effectiveness of this treatment. The median weight losses of the groups again showed differences favoring behavior modification: 18.5 versus 13.5 pounds for the first cohort and 22 versus 15 pounds for the second cohort.

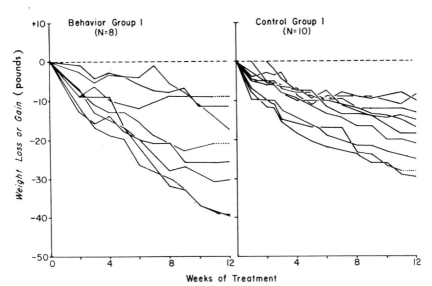

FIGURE 1. *Weight Changes of Patients in First Cohort.* Dotted lines represent interpolated data based upon weights obtained during follow-up. Note greater weight loss of behavior modification group and greater variability of this weight loss as compared with that of control group.

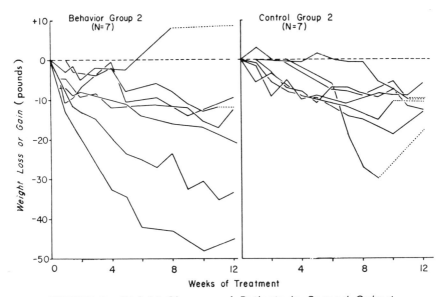

FIGURE 2. *Weight Changes of Patients in Second Cohort.* Dotted lines again represent interpolated data. Variability of weight loss of behavior modification group is even larger than that of first cohort, while variability of weight loss in control group is even smaller.

DISCUSSION

This study showed that behavior modification, devised by a team with little experience in this modality, was more effective in the treatment of obesity than was the best alternate program that could be devised by an internist with long experience in the treatment of this disorder. These results, and those of Stuart (1967) and of Harris (1969) cited earlier, strongly suggest that behavior modification represents a significant advance in the treatment of obesity.

Two factors increase our confidence in the significance of these results. First, the weight losses in the control group are representative of the majority of reports in the medical literature. The difference between behavior modification and control groups is thus not due to decreased effectiveness of treatment in the control group. Second, although the weight losses of the behavior modification group are not as great as those reported by Stuart in his pecedent-making report cited earlier, they are a result of only 3 months of treatment, compared with the year's duration of treatment in Stuart's series. Indeed, they are greater than the weight losses after 3 months among Stuart's patients, none of whom had lost as much as 20 pounds at that time. This significant difference ($p = 0.013$ by Fisher exact probability test) suggests that a group setting may increase the effectiveness of behavior modification when compared with individual treatment as utilized by Stuart.

The major limitation of this study must be considered—the use of different therapists *as well as* different therapies. Ideally, each therapist should utilize each modality of therapy in an unbiased manner. Since this ideal cannot be realized, the next best procedure is to control the bias by utilizing frankly biased therapists, some whose bias is for behavior modification and some whose bias is against it. We are now beginning such a study, which is both laborious and time-consuming. Short of such an investment, the design utilized in the present study is the most efficient. Until almost the end of the study, each therapist team believed that the treatment it used was the better, and it was biased in favor of it. Furthermore, SP's experience in the treatment of obesity and as a group therapist was far greater than that of the leaders of the behavior modification groups.

A possible limitation of the study is that the day hospital setting may have had differential effects upon the behavior modification and supportive psychotherapy groups. If the former group responded more favorably to this setting, such an interaction, rather than behavior modification alone, could account for the apparently greater effectiveness of behavior modification.

The great variability in the performance of the patients in the behavior modification groups raises intriguing questions for further research, as both the best and the worst results were obtained in these groups. It appears that behavior modification can be remarkably effective for certain patients and quite ineffective for others. None of the criteria we utilized, primarily our clinical impressions and MMPI data, predicted which patients would respond. A major goal of our further research will be to develop such predictors, as even limited success in this endeavor, coupled with the replication of the current findings, would mean a significant advance in the treatment of obesity. For selected persons, an effective treatment for their obesity would be at hand.

SUMMARY

The effectiveness of behavior modification in the treatment of obesity was assessed in a group of 32 patients divided into two cohorts. Half of each cohort was treated as a group with a behavior modification program, and half received more conventional group psychotherapy. Treatment modalities were compared with each other and with the results of treatment for obesity as reported in the medical literature.

All four treatment groups performed well by accepted standards. In each cohort, however, the weight loss of the behavioral modification group exceeded that of the traditional therapy group, and even in this small sample, this difference reached statistical significance by one criterion. Furthermore, 13% of this group lost more than 40 pounds and 53% lost more than 20 pounds, results which rank with the best reports in the medical literature.

The results of the behavior modification groups were far more variable than those of traditional group therapy programs, with individual patients performing both more and less effectively than those of the traditional therapy groups. Available data were insufficient to distinguish responders to behavior modification from nonresponders. The development of predictors of response to behavior modification, in combination with replication of the current findings, could mean a significant advance in the treatment of obesity.

SMOKING ON CUE: A BEHAVIORAL APPROACH TO SMOKING REDUCTION

David Shapiro, Bernard Tursky,
Gary E. Schwartz, Susan R. Shnidman

A popular focus for self-control is smoking. Shapiro, Tursky, Schwartz, and Shnidman present an innovative technique for the self-regulation of smoking. Applying stimulus-control principles, they trained smokers to use small portable timers to change the many social and physical cues that influenced their smoking behavior.

This strategy had an impressive effect on individual smoking rates. Although total abstention was rare, significant reductions were reported. In light of the fact that smoking has been one of the most difficult behaviors to change, these findings show substantial promise for clinical applications.

In recent years, behavioral scientists have been called on to offer practical solutions to problems of social relevance. In matters of public health, cigarette smoking is now recognized as a major hazard, and significant efforts are being directed toward examining the reasons why

From *Journal of Health and Social Behavior*, 1971, **12**(2), 108-113. Copyright 1971 by the American Sociological Association. Reprinted by permission.

people develop, maintain, and modify their smoking habits (U.S. Department of Health, Education and Welfare, 1964; Keutzer et al., 1968). A great deal of attention is being paid to the elimination of smoking through mass education and antismoking advertising, particularly to discourage young people from taking on the habit. A major problem in which there has been little progress to date, however, is the availability of alternatives for a large segment of the population who have been smoking cigarettes for many years. Many habitual smokers report that they want to give up smoking but find it extremely difficult to reduce their rate of smoking to safer levels or to quit entirely.

There is general agreement that smoking is primarily a psychological habituation, and not a physiological addiction (U.S. Department of Health, Education and Welfare, 1964; Keutzer et al., 1968). Although the pleasure associated with smoking may in part be connected with its physiological effects, these appear to vary widely from individual to individual and are probably not as critical as the environmental contingencies connected with and serving to maintain the habit.

This article describes a behavioral conception of smoking as a habit formed and maintained by a complex process of conditioning. This process results in a strong association between the response of smoking and a number of specific stimulus events occurring in the individual's daily life. These events become conditional stimuli that are linked with the urge to smoke and act as cues for the smoking response.

A method of smoking reduction and control was derived from this conception of the smoking habit. It is based on the transfer of the smoking response to a controllable neutral stimulus that has no meaning in the natural environment. The method permits the tailoring of smoking reduction to each individual's smoking rate and allows the gradual extinction of the responses associated with one's usual smoking cues. Unlike laboratory-based procedures, moreover, this behavioral method has the advantage of being readily self-administered.

Initial smoking experiences usually occur at an early age and are in most cases aversive. The persistence of smoking behavior despite its unpleasant beginnings is an indication of the strength of the early social reinforcement for smoking, such as approval by one's peers or a sense of rebellion against parents or authority. With continued smoking, individuals develop various degrees of tolerance for the smoke, and the behavior of smoking becomes more and more unconscious and automatic as the habit is successively reinforced.

Smoking soon becomes linked with specific events in the environment. The young smoker starts the process by seeking the company of his peers when he smokes and establishing a smoking routine that will enable him to smoke in secret. The process of conditioning continues, and eventually smoking tends to become linked with a number of different specific events in the environment that effectively cue the smoking response. In a questionnaire on smoking habits administered to 750 subjects, this linking of smoking to environmental events was corroborated. It appears to be typical for people to smoke on specific occasions, unique but consistent for each person, rather than at equal intervals throughout the day. Even very heavy smokers reported that they are more likely to smoke at certain times than at others. Signal situations frequently noted were after meals, on awakening, answering the telephone, on retiring, drinking coffee, watching TV, driving a car, and periods of stress, mental concentration, or relaxation. These stimulus situations function as cues for the smoking response. This response is overtly initiated by lighting the cigarette, but must be preceded by a chain of events that occur with each cue and are associated with the urge to smoke. It follows that every time the individual smokes in response to the cuing stimuli, further conditioning takes place and the habit comes more and more under their control.

One of the major difficulties in smoking reduction is the persistence of the urge to smoke when the cues occur. Other smoking reduction programs recommend the elimination of so-called unnecessary cigarettes associated with less urgent cues (American Cancer Society, No. 2666; Guttman and Marston, 1967). Our analysis of the smoking habit suggests that this procedure would serve to strengthen the dominant cues for which smoking occurs characteristically and therefore further condition the smoking habit.

Inasmuch as the ordinary cues themselves cannot be eliminated from the environment, our approach to smoking reduction is to substitute an entirely new cue for the individual to follow. A signaling device is used to produce an auditory signal at random times, and the response of smoking is now conditioned to this new signal. This serves the dual purpose of providing a smoking cue that will not have any environmental meaning to the individual and permitting the extinction of the events associated with the smoking response. The new controlled signal is programmed initially at the individual's current smoking rate and is then gradually phased out. As the new cue competes with the old cues in controlling the urge to smoke, the latter lose their cuing function because only the new signal is reinforced. Furthermore, since the new cue itself is gradually phased out, any possible physical or psychological disturbances brought on by suddenly stopping smoking and withdrawing from the use of tobacco can be lessened or avoided.

In the feasibility study reported here, two different signaling devices were used: (1) the Bellboy-paging device operated by standard telephone equipment and initiated at random by a tape programmer and relays and (2) a hand-operated watch timer set by the subject himself for times up to two hours, with dual settings required for longer times. The Bellboy device has several limitations: high costs of operation, restriction of transmission range, and frequent transmission difficulties. The hand device is a small, relatively inexpensive pocket timer. In the study, most subjects followed lists of controlled random times predetermined by the experimenters in setting their hand devices. A few subjects were required to use fixed time intervals. In the total sample of 40 subjects, 8 used the Bellboy, 23 the randomized-time hand device, and 9 the fixed-time device. The slight differences in results for the different procedures are not discussed in this article. In current work, the hand signaling device has been modified so that relatively random times can be programmed easily by the individual without the inconvenience of following lists of numbers.

The timing procedure is a means of regulating cigarette consumption in a manner similar to other types of prescribed regimes that limit the amount of intake, and may be thought of as a cigarette diet. In this diet, however, the occasions as well as the amount of intake are prescribed in such a way as to randomize the relationship between the individual's smoking and other activities. Moreover, to the extent that other pleasurable events typically associated with smoking (for example, eating, drinking, or social interaction) also serve to reinforce smoking (Premack, 1970), further extinction of the habit is made possible by smoking at random times.

On the basis of a newspaper story (Boston Globe, 1969) describing the concept of smoking cues and the need for volunteers in a smoking reduction study, about 1,000 letters and phone calls were received. Those inquiring were sent a questionnaire, and potential subjects were selected who stated that they were in good health and did not regularly use drugs or medication. From this group, subjects were randomly selected and asked by telephone if they wished to participate. A feasibility study was carried out on a sample consisting of seven Very Heavy (50-70 cigarettes daily), twenty-two Heavy (30-50), and eleven Moderate (20-30) smokers for whom six-week follow-up data are also available. The sample consisted of 18 men and 22 women, ranging in age from 21 to 54, with a median of 35. Years of habitual smoking varied from 6.5 to 35, with a median of 17.5 years. The subjects reported that they tried to quit smoking from never to ten times, with a median of two times.

The feasibility test was designed to determine (1) the degree to which smokers would follow such a program in the absence of other prescribed forms of therapy (individual counseling, group meetings, drugs), and (2) the relationship between the extent of the program completed and the final smoking reduction obtained.

The procedure was structured so that in the first week of the program subjects smoked at approximately their normal rate. In succeeding weeks, the daily rate was reduced by four cigarettes at the beginning of the program and by two cigarettes at the end. The weekly rates were 54, 48, 44, 40, 36, 32, 28, 24, 20, 16, 12, 10, 8, 6, 4 cigarettes per day. The very heavy group started at 54, the heavy at 40, and the moderate at 24 cigarettes daily. The entire procedure was explained to subjects in an initial orientation meeting. Subjects were asked to smoke *only* when their signaling device provided the cue, not to refuse to smoke on this cue unless they were in a situation where it is illegal to smoke (in a theatre) or impossible to smoke (taking a shower), and not to make up missed cigarettes. Not smoking on impulse was stressed.

In questionnaire and interview data obtained at the completion of the program, subjects reported varying degrees of difficulty in complying with the instructions to smoke only on the cue provided by the signaling device. Instances of cheating declined as many subjects became accustomed to the procedure. Other subjects at various points in time discontinued the procedure, reporting difficulty in following the schedule or maintaining successive weekly reductions in smoking rate.

The median number of weeks subjects continued following the program was nine, eight, and seven for the Very Heavy, Heavy, and Moderate smokers, respectively, and eight for all subjects pooled. The median smoking reduction obtained during the program was 67 per cent for Very Heavy, 75.5 per cent for Heavy, 80 per cent for Moderate smokers, and 75 per cent for all subjects combined. Out of the 40 volunteers, all of whom showed some reduction during the program, 27 decreased their smoking rate to twelve or fewer cigarettes and 19 to eight or fewer cigarettes daily.

The subjects were asked about their smoking rate six weeks following the program's termination. Comparing this rate with their rate prior to the program, the median reductions were 27 per cent, 43 per cent and 50 per cent for Very Heavy, Heavy, and Moderate smokers, respectively, and 43 per cent for all subjects pooled. These data are for the entire sample, including those subjects who followed little of the program.

The relationship between extent of the program completed and smoking reduction on follow-up is shown in Figure 1. The data indicate

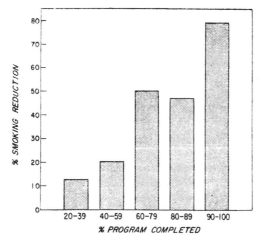

FIGURE 1. Per Cent Program Completed (abscissa) is based on the ratio of number of weeks the individual followed the program to the total number of weeks required to reduce to four cigarettes daily. From left to right, the number of subjects represented in each bar are four, seven, eleven, six, and twelve. The 80-to-100 per cent group was split into two bars to show the greater effectiveness of the method for the twelve subjects completing more than 90 per cent of the program. Per Cent Smoking Reduction (ordinate) is based on the ratio of follow-up smoking rate to pretreatment smoking rate subtracted from 100 per cent. The follow-up data were obtained six weeks after termination of the program.

that time on the program has its predicted relationship with smoking outcome. The more a person smokes on the new cues, and the more the new cues are reduced, the greater the reduction in his smoking behavior after the cues have been removed. The most important finding is that the procedure proves effective in reducing final smoking if subjects complete most or all of the program. This observation is seen with other types of successful treatments, such as those involving medicinal drugs or food diets, where it is reasonable to expect that effectiveness is directly related to the extent the treatment is followed.

Subjects who were able to complete the program may of course differ in terms of motivation or other pretreatment variables from those who dropped out prior to the final week. This issue may be put into perspective by examining data obtained from a waiting control group of nineteen smokers randomly selected from the total original volunteer group. These nineteen subjects were told they would be taken into the program in a future study. They received a smoking schedule each week similar to that received by the experimental subjects and were asked to return an enclosed postcard listing their daily smoking rate. Thirteen out of the nineteen subjects continued to provide this information for at least eight weeks, and their reports indicated a 2 per cent median reduction in smoking. This small, nonsignificant amount of reduction in equally motivated control subjects may be compared with a 75 per cent median reduction in smoking achieved in the 24 experimental subjects remaining in the program for an eight-week period.

In personal interviews, subjects were almost uniformly enthusiastic about the procedure and its potential as a means of reducing smoking. Many reported increasing difficulty as the program approached rates of about twelve cigarettes daily and less. Several stated they gave up the program when certain stressful events in their lives seemed to trigger the urge to smoke more often. Typical events were sickness in the family, a sudden change such as returning to work from summer vacation, and unusual stress.

There was no communication between the experimenters and the subjects by which these complications could be handled. In subsequent experience with individual cases, we found that such complete relapses may be avoided by advising the person to (1) maintain a particular rate for as many weeks as necessary until he is comfortably able to continue further reduction or (2) return to higher smoking rates temporarily when unusual stress occurs, so long as he continues to follow the signal, and then to proceed along the schedule normally. By the same token, subjects who have completed the program and are at low levels of cigarette consumption or have stopped smoking can go back on the signaling device if they begin to feel compelled to smoke at higher levels again.

No attempt was made in this feasibility study to move subjects from low rates of smoking to nonsmoking. This step was made optional, and a number of subjects quit voluntarily when they completed the last week of scheduled smoking. We now believe this final move to nonsmoking can be built into the smoking regime. Then, if the pressure to smoke becomes too urgent, the individual can return to smoking at a low rate using the signaling device. As with other problems requiring continuing self-control, such as excessive food or alcohol, there is reason to anticipate the need for using the cigarette diet as needed to bring the problem back under control until new habits of nonsmoking are firmly established. On theoretical grounds, it is to be expected that a long-term habit like smoking can quickly be re-established; hence a means of returning to a method of control, such as this procedure, is needed.

On the clinical level, with suitable modification each individual may be able to utilize the smoking reduction procedure according to his own needs and progress in controlling the habit. As in other dietary and self-control procedures (Skinner, 1953; Premack, 1970) other kinds of support may be desirable for individuals unable to continue to comply with the procedure. The method described in this article can readily be used in conjunction with other techniques of social or motivational support, such as group discussions. Now that large numbers of smokers in our society have been motivated to quit because of the health hazard, the availability of a method that is psychologically sound and easily administered may help make this possible.

In conclusion, we would like to reiterate that this study was primarily conducted to prove the feasibility of the effectiveness of gradual smoking reduction by substituting a controlled neutral stimulus for normal smoking cues. Further research must be conducted to prove its superiority to other methods of controlling the smoking habit. While a variety of antismoking procedures have been attempted (Bernstein, 1970), no comparative data on systematic gradual reduction are available. We plan to continue this work by comparing the described gradual reduction method with gradual tapering off in which the subject is permitted to smoke whenever he wishes, and with immediate cessation. We will attempt to determine how best to enhance the effectiveness of our technique by evaluating the degree of therapist contact and social intervention (group support) that is necessary to achieve the final goal of sustained cessation of smoking. Finally, we will solicit long-term follow-up information from all participants to evaluate the effectiveness of the various experimental techniques.

BEHAVIORAL MEANS AND HUMANISTIC ENDS

Carl E. Thoresen

The behaviorist's position in psychology is typically presented as antagonistic to that of the humanist. The humanist is often portrayed as someone concerned with the "inside" dimensions of human experience, whereas the behaviorist is portrayed as a strict environmentalist with an "outside" perspective. Further, the humanist is seen as the staunch ally of "natural" man against the "rat-like," mechanistic determinism of the behaviorist.

Thoresen challenges these oversimplified and dichotomous perspectives that pit humanist against behaviorist. Neither caricature is accurate. The terms *humanist* and *behaviorist* are extremely broad ones, each encompassing a variety of viewpoints. Some humanists reject the relevance of empirical science as a means of solving human problems, while others believe that science represents the ultimate humanistic endeavor. Similarly, some conventional behaviorists reject anything that cannot be readily observed and measured by others—that is, they see cognitive or covert events as a return to "mentalism." On the other hand, social-learning theorists and practitioners view covert or internal processes as crucial elements in understanding human behavior (for example, Bandura, Article Two; Meichenbaum & Cameron, Article Eleven).

Thoresen suggests that the major goals of humanists—such as heightening awareness, fostering compassion, developing a sense of unity (mind and

An expanded version of this paper appears in the *72nd Yearbook of the National Society for the Study of Education* (1973). This adaptation is used by permission of the National Society for the Study of Education.

body), and transcending the immediate environment—may be achieved by using behavioral techniques. He argues that humanistic concerns can be translated into human-action terms—that is, into what persons would *do*. Behavioral techniques can then be used to encourage these humanistic actions. Attempting such a translation raises several questions. Can, for example, the highly literary and abstract conceptions of many humanists be conceived as specific human actions without somehow altering their meaning?

A host of techniques purporting to enhance and expand human growth have gained popular attention—for example, biofeedback, yoga, meditation, self-hypnosis, sensory awareness, and encounter groups methods. Can the empirical and scientific orientation of contemporary behaviorism adequately encompass a broadening range of techniques to foster behavioral freedom? The synthesis referred to by Thoresen as *behavioral humanism* will require changes by all concerned. The ongoing changes already noted within humanistic and behavioral perspectives point to the real possibility of a synthesis in the coming decade.

Educators and behavioral scientists can act to help the individual act in positive, meaningful ways with himself and with others. There are many ways to take such actions. One way offers considerable promise: the synthesizing of social-learning principles and techniques with the goals and concerns of "humanistic" psychologists and educators. This effort to synthesize is referred to as *behavioral humanism*. We can benefit from the work of both behaviorists and humanists if we reduce the confusion, ambiguity, and misunderstanding about contemporary behaviorism and humanism and if we develop and use new scientific methods tailored to the study of human phenomena.

The term *humanistic* of course means many things to many people. A variety of humanisms have existed since the time of Hellenic civilization. Today there are classical, ethical, scientific, religious, Christian, and rational humanists. Many people are essentially humanists *even though they do not label themselves as such*. Those who identify with humanistic psychology can be seen as advocating a blending of psychology as a discipline with ethical forms of humanism (Wilson, 1970).

Humanism was and remains primarily a philosophical and literary movement. Concern is more with ideas and concepts—with "matters of the mind"—and less with methods and techniques—with specific human behavior. The humanistic-psychology/growth/encounter-group movement, however, is a modern-day exception to this. Here, mind and body, idea and technique have been blended.

Humanism emerged (or re-emerged, if the classical Greeks are taken as the original humanists) in the early Renaissance as a reaction against the revealed truth of the Church and the dominance of Aristotelian thinking (Abbagnano, 1967). The early humanists argued that man, through his own intellect, had the power (and the responsibility) to determine his own destiny. It was the Renaissance humanists who made the definitive break that opened the way for the rise of Western science. Interestingly, some contemporary humanists now oppose the scientific view introduced by earlier humanists.

Kurtz (1969) suggests that two basic principles characterize humanism: (1) a rejection of any supernatural world view as established fact and (2) a rejection of any metaphysical divinity as the source of human values. Some people may believe in supernatural powers, but, since there is no known empirical means to prove or refute these views, the existence of such powers is a matter of personal belief, not of fact. For the humanist, man must be responsible for himself, especially in deciding what is good, desirable, and worthwhile. Man is the maker of values, and man's actions represent, in effect, his values.

Not all humanists, however, accept two other basic principles offered by Kurtz: (1) that ethical principles and value judgments should be open to empirical, rational scrutiny and (2) that the methods of science can be applied in solving man's problems. The humanist is generally concerned with what people do in this life—that is, with human actions in life's present circumstances. Many humanists further believe that the use of reason and scientific methods provides the best single means of solving human problems and improving the quality of human life. For example, Eysenck (1971a, p. 25) states that "the use of reason in human affairs applied in the service of compassion" reflects the basic spirit of many humanists.

Definitions of what constitutes humanism are as diverse as the individuals offering the definitions. Interestingly, many contemporary "behaviorists"—that is, behavior therapists, behavioral counselors, and operant- or social-learning psychologists—consider themselves humanists (for example, Day, 1971; Hosford & Zimmer, 1972; Kanfer & Phillips, 1970; Lazarus, 1971; MacCorquodale, 1971; Skinner, 1971; Staats, 1971; Ullmann & Krasner, 1969). There are several reasons why behavior-oriented professionals see themselves this way. First, they focus on what the individual person *does* in the present life and not on who the person *is* in terms of vague social labels or obscure descriptions. Second, they emphasize human problems primarily as learning situations in which the person is capable of changing. Third, they examine how environments can be altered to reduce and prevent human problems. Finally, they use scientific procedures to improve techniques for helping individuals.

Differences or distinctions between contemporary behaviorists and humanists do exist. For example, many contemporary humanists have rejected methods of science as means of problem solving, where-as behaviorists are strongly committed to rigorous empirical inquiry. As many differences exist, however, *within* heterogeneous groupings of those called *behaviorists* or of those called *humanists*, as exist between them. The issue is not behaviorism versus humanism—that is a pseudo-issue that has been promoted by caricatures of these positions. Instead, the issue is how best to utilize the concepts and methodologies of both behavioral and humanistic psychology.

HUMANISTIC PSYCHOLOGY AND EDUCATION

Many people have written about the concerns of humanistic psychology and education (for example, Allport, 1963; Brown, 1970; Bühler, 1971; Edwards, 1969; Fairfield, 1971; Heath, 1969; Huxley, 1966; Jourard, 1968, 1971; Landsman, 1968; Maslow, 1969; Matson, 1964, 1971; Murphy, 1969; Platt, 1966; Rogers, 1969; Weinstein & Fantini, 1970). Humanistic psychology and education have been influenced by a host of Eastern and Western schools of philosophy, psychology, and religious thought. Abraham Maslow, Carl Rogers, Rollo May, and Viktor Frankl in particular have extended this influence. The tolerance for diversity and pluralism that characterizes humanistic psychology brings about a confluence of theoretical orientations, such as neopsychoanalytic, phenomenological, Gestalt, existential, and Rogerian. As a result, the field at present lacks a coherent and integrated theoretical rationale. This theoretical looseness, though cherished by some, has discouraged empirical research. Bühler (1971), in presenting the basic theoretical concepts of humanistic psychology, has distinguished it from the philosophy of humanism by its use of different concepts, methods, and goals. For Bühler, humanistic psychology must use scientific methods to discover ways of helping the person "experience his existence as real." The humanistic psychologist is seen as more action-oriented than the traditional literary humanist, who engages in philosophical disputes and antireligious quarrels.

Jourard (1968) has emphasized *transcendent* behaviors—that is, he argues that the individual learns by committing himself fully in thinking, perceiving, and achieving; by going beyond the typical; by acting divergently; by taking risks; and by using fantasy. Transcendent behavior is made possible by an openness to experience, an ability to focus selectively, skill in using symbols and metaphors, and self-confidence. For Landsman (1968), the key unit of behavior is "positive experiencing." He suggests that effort should be directed toward the "experimental creation of positive experiences." According to Maslow (1966, 1969), the major task of humanistic psychology is to collaborate with the behavioral sciences in finding out how to create physical and social environments that will nurture self-actualization. In discussing humanistic education, Brown (1970) has stressed the need for a confluence of the cognitive and the affective aspects of learning. With this integration, the curriculum could provide planned educational experiences for all kinds of human learning.

Maslow (1969, p. 732) offered what can be viewed as the basic theme of humanistic psychology and education: "The first and overarching Big Problem is to make the Good Person." The concept of creating the good person permeates the writings of humanistic psychology. The task of psychology is to develop methods that will help the individual act in more positive, meaningful ways with himself and with others. An examination of the literature of humanistic psychologists and educators reveals the following concerns:

1. The person as the unit of focus—that is, emphasis on the individual rather than on the average performance of large groups and populations.
2. The search for unity and harmony in human experience—that is, the goal of putting the "mind" and the "body" together.
3. Awareness and awakening—that is, attempts to increase the conscious range of the person's behavior, especially in his own internal behavior (such as thoughts, images, and physiological responses).
4. The need for compassionate persons—that is, the need for individuals who can communicate personally and intimately with others in a variety of ways and who can also help others experience life more positively.
5. Transcendence—that is, the ability to move beyond the immediate external environment and create new environments internally as well as externally.
6. Self-determination and responsibility—that is, the ability to identify alternatives, clarify values, make decisions, and accept the responsibility for one's actions.
7. Diversity and pluralism—that is, a reverence for the idiosyncratic and the unique in individuals.

The focus of action-oriented humanists is on what the individual person does, internally and externally. The concerns listed here highlight the *interdependence* of human activity, stressing the need for unity and harmony in experience. The self-actualizing person is aware of a variety of responses taking place both within himself and between himself and his environment. Further, such a person has the skills to "make things happen," to reduce the influence of the immediate environment, and to act in ways that create new environments.

CONTEMPORARY BEHAVIORISM

The term *behaviorist* represents a variety of theoretical positions and technical practices. There are diversity and disagreement among those who consider themselves to be behaviorists (Day, 1969; Rachlin, 1970). While all aspects of what constitutes behaviorism cannot be discussed here, it may be possible to eliminate some stereotypes.

Clearly, some of its critics (Koch, 1964; Koestler, 1967; Matson, 1964) offer a dated and inaccurate representation of behaviorism. Behaviorism is not, for example, the simple(minded) application of reinforcement schedules to persons as if they were no different from rats or pigeons. Neither is all behaviorism a physicalistic, empty(headed) black-box psychology. Behaviorism (or behavior therapy) does not deny thoughts and complex emotions; neither does it treat individuals as "simple mechanical entities" (Portes, 1971). At present, there is no one type of behaviorism. Behaviorists today range from experimental psychologists who meticulously study animal responses in highly controlled laboratories to counselors and therapists who work with the immediate complex problems of individuals. Contemporary behaviorism is, in fact, a rich conglomeration of principles, assumptions, and techniques.

Perhaps what characterizes all behaviorists is (1) their use of experimental methods, (2) their reliance on empirical ,data based on careful observation, (3) their concern for objectivity and the replication of results, (4) their focus on the environment and what the organism is currently doing, and (5) their rejection of inner causes or entities as either the sole or the most important determinants of human action. To the behaviorist, the "here-and-now," contemporary environment is important because much of what a person does is a function of environmental events.

Popular conceptions of behaviorism often fail to acknowledge differences between behaviorists. Some conventional behaviorists have used internal processes, such as drive reduction or habit strength, to explain behavior (Hull, 1943; Miller & Dollard, 1941). Others have suggested that curiosity and exploratory drives that are elicited by external stimuli account for human actions (Berlyne, 1960; Harlow, 1953). And still others have conceptualized internal sensory-feedback processes to explain behavior (Mowrer, 1960). In addition, conventional behaviorism has emphasized operational definitions and direct observation of physical responses. Some conventional behaviorists are also dualistic in the Cartesian mind-body sense; to them, the events of the mind are not to be understood in the same fashion as is physical behavior—that is, sensorimotor behavior (Rachlin, 1970). Conventional behaviorists have also relied heavily on extensive deductive theories and have typically employed experimental group designs in their research (for example, Hull, 1943).

By contrast, *radical* behaviorists reject mind-body dualism, reliance on operational definitions, and mentalistic explanations such as drive states and drive reduction (Skinner, 1945). They view private events—that is, what goes on within the person—as subject to the same learning principles as external behavior. The radical behaviorist also rejects elaborate experimental group designs and reliance on inferential statistics based on the average performance of groups of subjects. Instead, he argues that the individual organism should serve as the focus of research and that observations should be made *continuously* before, during, and after planned interventions. There is a strong emphasis on careful description and recording of actions.

A distinction is sometimes made between the early radical behaviorism of John Watson (1919) and the contemporary radical behaviorism of B. F. Skinner (Day, 1969; Terrace, 1971). Both are labeled radical for rejecting mentalistic explanations. However, Watson's highly physicalistic stimulus-response rationale, coupled with a dualistic perspective, differs markedly from Skinner's operant theory (Skinner, 1969). Interestingly, the "radical" position of Skinner is shared considerably by the radical phenomenology of Sartre and Merleau-Ponty (1965), who reject what they regard as the introspective, dualistic, and idealistic views of American phenomenologists (such as Rogers and May). These French phenomenologists argue that human behavior is understood by examining the person's behavior and its interaction with his environment (see Kvale & Grenners, 1967).

Besides conventional and radical behaviorists, there are social-learning or cognitive behaviorists (for example, Bandura, 1969), who emphasize internal processes such as thoughts and imagery in explaining how learning occurs. At present, the term *behaviorist* may therefore refer to conventional, radical, or cognitive-oriented behaviorism.

Social Learning

The most recent development in contemporary behaviorism can be called the *social-behavior* or *social-learning approach* (Bandura, 1969; Mischel, 1971). This type of behaviorism does not conceptualize behavior exclusively in operant-response terms—that is, in terms of discriminative stimuli, responses, and reinforcing stimuli. Further, it does not utilize the traits, motives, and drive explanations of conventional behaviorism (Dollard & Miller, 1950; Eysenck, 1960); neither does it reject the relevance of internal processes and events. Indeed, to social-learning behaviorists, the often-cited empty "black box" is considered very much full.

In the social-behavior view, individual actions are regulated by three basic processes: stimulus control, internal symbolic control, and outcome control (Bandura, 1969). A major focus of social-behavior theory is on the person's covert symbolic responses. Mediation—that is, what goes on within the person—is important, as is the "meaning" or significance of a particular situation to the person. Staats (1972), for example, discusses how words, as conditional cues and as consequences, convey a great deal of personal meaning. Words subvocalized as well as spoken can arouse a broad range of emotional behavior, mediating positive and negative experiences. Bandura (1969) has emphasized the importance of vicarious or observational learning, which takes place by means of symbolic processes within the individual. Observational learning is not explained in an external-stimulus-cue-and-reinforcement paradigm. Rather, observational learning is presented as a sequence of complex processes involving attentional, retentional, reproductive, and motivational factors.

In the social-learning perspective, a distinction is made between the acquisition of behavior (learning) and its performance. Internal symbolic and sensory processes play the major role in *learning* new behavior; the external contingencies of reinforcement (outcomes) determine whether the behavior is then *performed*. Reinforcement is seen as chiefly of informational and incentive value. The person can learn without overtly performing the behavior and without any direct reinforcement. Social behaviorists view the individual person as a dynamically changing organism rather than as a passive receptacle of enduring responses. The internal and external actions of each person are primarily influenced by specific here-and-now experiences.

Both social behaviorism and Skinner's radical behaviorism emphasize that current environmental situations are prime determinants of human action. Although Skinner's theoretical work has clearly acknowledged the importance of private events and the individual's internal environment, the research and practice of radical behaviorists have generally avoided this area. Social behaviorists have pursued the more complex area of symbolic behavior, seeking to understand how covert events-as-responses interact with external responses to influence what the person does.

Behaviorism today is far more than either the psychology of Watson, with its physicalistic concerns, or the drive-reduction-oriented animal experiments of the conventionalists. *Behaviorism* as a term denotes an emphasis on the comprehensive and systematic study of the individual and on the use of empirical methods to examine how current environments may be influencing the individual's action. What goes on within the individual—that is, covert responses—represents important data.

Some basic characteristics of contemporary radical-behaviorism and social-learning approaches are as follows:

1. a monistic view of the individual and a rejection of a dualistic mind-body theory;
2. a belief that public or observable events are functionally similar to private or covert events and that both kinds of events are influenced by the same learning processes and principles;
3. a rejection of exclusive, inner, "mentalistic" explanations of behavior;
4. a belief that behavior is determined primarily by the immediate environment, including the person's own internal environment;
5. a use of scientific methods that stress careful, systematic observation and control of behavior, including self-observation and self-control; and
6. a rejection of the use of trait-state labels (such as *introvert*) to describe the person, based on the belief that the individual is best described and understood by examining what he does in particular situations.

FREEDOM AND SELF-CONTROL

A growing area of behavioral research is concerned with self-control. What actions can a person take to influence his own internal and external behavior? Behavioral researchers have recently developed techniques to teach individuals how to manage their own actions. Some humanistic writers (Blanshard, 1970; Matson, 1971) have criticized behaviorists for their failure to consider freedom and self-direction. Believing that the person is and should be free to decide what he should do in a given situation and that human action is neither predetermined nor predictable, they see the behaviorist as someone who would deprive the person of this freedom to determine his own actions. They equate the prediction and control of human behavior by others with the demise of freedom and dignity. However, they view the individual's ability to predict and control his *own* actions as freedom.

The problem with this view of the individual's freedom is that past and present experiences with other persons do subtly influence what an individual may decide to do in the present.[1] Common sense would seem to suggest that the person can decide to do something independently of anything else; a venerable literary tradition also supports the view that self-direction operates entirely within the person as a consequence of some inside entity or agent. The person who thus charts his own course and makes his own choices is seen as a free and dignified individual (Lamont, 1967).

Freedom and dignity, however, are measured in individual actions. The free person has the power to take certain actions. The power, and therefore the freedom, depends on being aware—that is, on the conscious processing of all kinds of information. Recall the premium placed on awareness by humanistic psychologists. Awareness is crucial, since the information (stimuli, to use a technical term) influences the individual's behavior. The person who has information and who can control it is free. Terrace (1971) points out that awareness is actually a learned behavior. The person learns to distinguish certain internal responses that he then labels *angry, happy, upset,* and so on. Awareness therefore consists of discriminating information and describing it in some way. How a person labels information about his own behavior has been studied recently in self-perception and attribution research (for example, Ross, Rodin, & Zimbardo, 1969; Bem, 1972). Inaccurate labeling and faulty stimulus discrimination may be one type of maladaptive behavior pattern. For example, the person who is unable to explain adequately to himself the high arousal that he is experiencing may conclude that he is irrational and mentally disturbed and thus label himself as *crazy* (Zimbardo, Maslach, & Marshall, 1972). Faulty awareness leads to errors in attributing the causes of one's behavior; often, the person concludes that he has no control when in fact he does (see Nisbett & Valins, 1971).

In many ways, the difference between individual freedom and control by others lies in "who is manipulating what stimuli" (London, 1969, p. 214) or in who is using and controlling information that influences human action. Awareness is the basis of freedom and self-control, because it provides the individual with the information he needs to change his own sources of stimulation, both internal and external. Freedom versus determinism therefore is not a real issue. The freedom to

[1]A related issue is the prediction and control of behavior. To many humanists, freedom and choice are antithetical to any kind of prediction and control. Most behaviorists, however, argue that prediction is involved when a person makes a choice between alternatives. Indeed, to be really free, the person must be able to predict the consequences of certain alternatives.

act depends on the person's being aware of, or knowing, what kinds of information (stimuli) influence his own behavior. This knowledge must include internal or covert stimuli as well as external data on both internal and external behavior.

Staats (1971, 1972) has suggested that the very young child learns self-control by observing others. The young child talks aloud to himself at first and then gradually replaces these overt verbalizations with covert talk, or self-verbalization, in the form of self-instructions. After the first few years of life, the person engages in a great deal of covert speech (Luria, 1961; Vygotsky, 1962). However, his awareness of this internal behavior quickly diminishes. Thus, over time, it *seems* to the person as if what he does is spontaneous and totally determined from within. Once behavior such as covert speech is learned from environmental experiences, however, that behavior can determine, in part, what the person will do. In this way, it may be said that the person causes his own current and future behavior through what he has learned in the past. He learns covert responses, such as self-verbalization, from others in his verbal community. The availability of these learned covert responses to the person determines whether that person is "free to act" (see Meichenbaum and Cameron, Article Eleven).

Viktor Frankl's modern classic *Man's Search for Meaning* (1959) exemplifies how the verbal community in most Western cultures teaches the person to conceptualize self-control as a vague inner force. Throughout Frankl's moving description of life in a concentration camp, he describes circumstances in which he used self-verbalization or vivid imagery. For long periods of time, Frankl managed his inner environment by carrying on imaginary conversations with his wife or with friends, coupling them with "mental pictures" of persons and situations. In this way, aversive external stimuli—the sight of dead bodies and the verbal and physical abuse of guards—and physiological cues such as hunger, over which he had no control, were managed—that is, made more tolerable. Frankl, however, did not conceptualize his covert actions as influencing other behaviors. Instead, he explained them in terms of inner life and freedom. Frankl states that he survived because he possessed an inner strength, a sense of meaning, and personal dignity. Yet it might be said that he survived because he had learned to use vivid images and to carry on covert dialogues with himself in very aversive situations. In effect, Frankl transcended the environment by creating a new internal environment.

Techniques for self-control have had a long, though somewhat obscure, history. Varieties of yoga and Zen procedures for self-managing thoughts and physiological responses have existed for more than 2000 years. There is evidence that certain individuals have achieved astonishing levels of self-control. Green (1971), for example, has reported laboratory studies with a yoga master who radically altered his heart rate, body temperature, and brain-wave patterns repeatedly on demand. The yogi was engaging in a complex pattern of coverants that altered these responses. The unanswered questions are: "What are the controlling behaviors?" and "How did they function to effect such changes?"

Research by behaviorally oriented investigators has been expanding recently into physiological feedback (biofeedback) training, cognitive focusing, and the instrumental (operant) conditioning of glandular and visceral responses (DuPraw, 1972; Green, Green, & Walters, 1970; Wegner, Bagchi, & Anand, 1963). These developments merit acknowledgment for their relevance in understanding self-control. Comprehensive discussions of these developments are available elsewhere (see Barber, DiCara, Kamiya, Miller, Shapiro, & Stoyva, 1970; Kamiya, Barber, DiCara, Miller, Shapiro, & Stoyva, 1971). Thoresen and Mahoney (1974), in reviewing covert methods of self-control (such as thought stopping), cite the importance of distinguishing between controlling actions and behavior to be controlled. Covert behavior in the form of self-verbalizations or images can be used to change other behavior (covert or overt), as cues to some action and as consequences. Freedom as a continuum emerges when the person increases his ability to manage the many environments (including the one inside) that influence control.

HUMANISTIC BEHAVIORS

Earlier, a summary of humanistic concerns was presented. These concerns were stated in rather abstract terms. It seems possible, however, to reconceptualize these important ideas and translate them into statements of human action. Such a translation should encourage empirical research that examines how the frequency and magnitude of these human actions can be changed. In addition, it is reasonable to consider these humanistic concepts in terms of internal (covert) and external (overt) behavior. Because the human organism is a complex system that responds within and without *simultaneously*, the use of an internal-external classification is arbitrary. Such a classification may be helpful at this point, however, in facilitating understanding and in fostering controlled research.

Some humanists may argue that translating these concerns into human-response terms is oversimplistic and reductionistic (for example, Matson, 1971). Admittedly, the approach is simple and may fail to capture *all* aspects of the phenomena involved. However, proceeding from the simple to the more complex has been one of the most successful strategies of modern science (Maslow, 1966). In an area in which relatively little empirical data is available, moving from the simple to the complex on the basis of empirically derived data is crucial. The major question concerns the *development of methods to help persons act in more humanistic ways.* If a translation is indeed too simple, the methods will not work. The answer therefore will be found empirically, not solely in logical argument.

Internal Responses

An examination of the humanistic literature suggests a variety of statements that can be translated into response terms. First, let us consider internal actions. The following are a sample of internal-response categories in which the importance of the increase-decrease factor is evident. The humanistic phrases typically found in the literature are in parentheses.

1. Increase the frequency, variety, and accuracy of self-observation of internal responses such as thoughts, images, and physiological responses. ("Increase self-knowledge; know what is going on within; be really aware of self.")
2. Increase the frequency of perceptually accurate responses. ("See things for what they really are; know what others are experiencing.")
3. Increase the frequency and variety of low-probability responses. ("Have new and unusual thoughts, physical sensations, and images.")
4. Decrease the frequency of stress and tension responses within the body. ("Experience tranquility and calmness in everyday life.")
5. Increase the frequency of highly consistent psychophysiological responses. ("Experience a sense of unity within; put the body in agreement with the head.")
6. Increase the frequency and variety of imagery responses. ("Engage in rich fantasy; develop your imagination.")
7. Increase the frequency of using psychophysiological responses in specific situations as criteria. ("Trust your own experiences; 'read' yourself and use personal reactions to decide.")
8. Decrease the frequency and variety of self-critical, negative responses. ("Accept yourself as worthy; experience yourself as positive; think positively about self and others.")

Let us explore a few of these translations. The first item, self-observation, can be described as the systematic recording of a particular internal response, such as positive self-thoughts. Here the person makes discriminations about whether certain covert verbalizations constitute positive self-thoughts and records these thoughts by tallying each occurrence on a card or by using a wrist counter. At the end of a particular time period, such as a day, the person notes the total number of positive self-thoughts. By this means, knowledge of one's internal events can be obtained. Item 4, concerning stress and tension responses, might be dealt with by teaching the person how to use deep muscle-relaxation techniques or how to stop stressful thoughts when they occur. Once instructed, the person may come to experience more tranquility and calmness in his everyday life.

Self-critical, negative responses (Item 8) are a major factor in self-esteem and self-acceptance. Thus, helping a person reduce the frequency and variety of self-critical thoughts is one way of encouraging self-esteem. Of course, the person should also be engaging in external actions that encourage positive thoughts about himself. Since some persons manifest high frequencies of negative self-thoughts that lack any external basis, reducing these negative internal responses may be prerequisite to promoting more positive responses about oneself (Hannum, Thoresen & Hubbard, Article Five).

Admittedly, speaking of responses and frequencies fails to convey the warmth and positive connotation of the "humanistic phrases." Yet the changes listed will do a great deal in "turning on" persons and helping them experience their "inner space" more positively (Gustaitis, 1969).

External Responses

Here are a few tentative translations of other humanistic phrases into external-response categories—that is, actions that can be directly observed by others.

1. Increase the frequency, variety, and accuracy of external observation responses, both of the self and of others. ("Know what is happening with others around you; know what is happening with yourself.")
2. Increase the frequency and variety of positive verbal responses. ("Self-disclose; be assertive when necessary; empathize with others.")
3. Increase the frequency and variety of positive nonverbal responses. ("Relate to others in many ways; really care and be concerned.")
4. Increase the frequency of using environmental stimulus cues by altering physical environments. ("Make things happen for yourself and for others.")
5. Decrease the frequency and variety of socially aversive, negative verbal and nonverbal responses. ("Be a positive, accepting person; deal with disagreement and disapproval in constructive ways.")
6. Increase the frequency and variety of positive verbal and nonverbal responses to animate and inanimate natural situations. ("Have good relationships with nature; feel close to nature.")

"Positive verbal responses" (Item 2) is obviously a very broad response category. The notion of what constitutes a positive verbal response is relative to the consequences of such behavior in particular situations. However, specific verbal responses, such as self-disclosing behavior, can be defined, and planned learning situations can be used to increase such behaviors. Stuhr, Thoresen, and Anton (1973), for instance, designed a treatment to increase "personal-feeling questions" for persons who lacked self-disclosing experiences (and friends). Similarly, aversive talk and gestures (Item 5) can be identified and then altered through structured learning situations. One way of "making things happen" (Item 4) is to change certain features of the physical environment. For example, the person can rearrange room furnishings to prompt certain behaviors and discourage others.

Well-controlled empirical studies of how individuals change will reveal whether or not these suggested translations have missed the humanistic mark.

IN SUMMARY

Complex contemporary environments have reduced the individual person's power to manage his own life. Modern humanists and contemporary behaviorists are both concerned with helping the person experience life more positively. The translation of humanistic concerns into human-response terms is one way of encouraging meaningful scientific inquiry. Literary, nonempirical, and antiscientific orientations cannot provide the data needed to develop techniques for giving power to the individual. Polemics and stereotyping by humanists have accomplished little, except to retard scientific progress. Furthermore, the myopic perspective of conventional behaviorists and other scientists preoccupied with "hard" data has also impeded research.

We need a synthesizing perspective that draws from a variety of sources and avoids invidious dichotomies—such as humanist versus behaviorist. The beginnings of such a perspective have been suggested. Humanistic psychologists and educators share much with contemporary behaviorists. All are concerned with increasing our understanding of the overt and covert processes that influence the actions of individuals. The intensive, empirical study of the individual offers a methodology well suited to the concerns of both groups.

Misunderstanding and misinformation among behavioral scientists, educators, and humanistic scholars have prevented much-needed scientific inquiry. Well-controlled empirical research can provide valuable data. With such data, we can learn how to help the individual engage in self-actualizing behavior. It's time to start putting it together.

REFERENCES

Abbagnano, N. Humanism. In P. Edwards (Ed.), *The encyclopedia of philosophy*. Vol. 4. New York: Macmillan, Free Press, 1967.

Adams, J. A closed-loop theory of motor learning. *Journal of Motor Behavior*, 1971, **3**, 111-149.

Allen, K. E., Hart, B., Buell, J. S., Harris, R. T., & Wolf, M. M. Effects of social reinforcement on isolate behavior of a nursery school child. *Child Development*, 1964, **35**, 511-518.

Allport, G. W. *Pattern and growth in personality*. New York: Holt, Rinehart & Winston, 1963.

Alpert, R., & Haber, R. N. Anxiety in academic achievement situations. *Journal of Abnormal and Social Psychology*, 1960, **61**, 205-207.

American Cancer Society. *If you want to give up cigarettes*. Publication No. 2666.

Anant, S. S. A note on the treatment of alcoholics by a verbal aversion technique. *Canadian Psychologist*, 1967, **8**, 19-22.

Aronfreed, J. The effects of experimental socialization paradigms upon two moral responses to transgression. *Journal of Abnormal and Social Psychology*, 1963, **66**, 437-448.

Aronfreed, J. The origin of self-criticism. *Psychological Review*, 1964, **71**, 193-218.

Aronfreed, J., & Reber, A. Internalized behavioral suppression and the timing of social punishment. *Journal of Personality and Social Psychology*, 1965, **1**, 3-16.

Aronson, E., & Carlsmith, J. M. Experimentation in social psychology. In G. Lindzey & E. Aronson (Eds.), *Handbook of social psychology*. Reading, Mass.: Addison-Wesley, 1968.

Arthur, A. Z. Diagnostic testing and the new alternatives. *Psychological Bulletin*, 1969, **72**, 183-192.

Ashem, B., & Donner, L. Covert sensitization with alcoholics: A controlled replication. *Behaviour Research and Therapy*, 1968, **6**, 7-12.

Axelrod, S., Hall, R. V., Weis, L., & Rohrer, S. Use of self-imposed contingencies to reduce the frequency of smoking behavior. Paper presented at the Fifth Annual Meeting of the Association for the Advancement of Behavior Therapy, Washington, D.C., September 1971.

Ayllon, T., & Azrin, N. H. Reinforcement and instructions with mental patients. *Journal of the Experimental Analysis of Behavior*, 1964, **7**, 327-331.

Ayllon, T., & Azrin, N. H. *The token economy.* New York: Appleton-Century-Crofts, 1968.

Azrin, N. H., & Holz, W. C. Punishment. In W. K. Honig (Ed.), *Operant behavior.* New York: Appleton-Century-Crofts, 1966.

Azrin, N. H., & Powell, J. Behavioral engineering: The reduction of smoking behavior by a conditioning apparatus and procedure. *Journal of Applied Behavior Analysis*, 1968, **1**, 193-200.

Azrin, N. H., & Powell, J. Behavioral engineering: The use of response priming to improve prescribed self-medication. *Journal of Applied Behavior Analysis*, 1969, **2**, 39-42.

Azrin, N. H., Rubin, H., O'Brien, F., Ayllon, T., & Roll, D. Behavioral engineering: Postural control by a portable operant apparatus. *Journal of Applied Behavior Analysis*, 1968, **1**, 99-108.

Bachrach, A. J. *Psychological research: An introduction.* New York: Random House, 1965.

Baer, D. M. Behavior modification: You shouldn't. In E. A. Ramp & B. I. Hopkins (Eds.), *A new direction for education: Behavior analysis 1971.* Vol. 1. Lawrence: The University of Kansas, 1971. Pp. 358-369.

Baer, D. M., Wolf, M. M., & Risley, T. R. Some current dimensions of applied behavior analysis. *Journal of Applied Behavior Analysis*, 1968, **1**, 91-97.

Bandura, A. *Principles of behavior modification.* New York: Holt, Rinehart & Winston, 1969.

Bandura, A. Vicarious and self-reinforcement processes. In R. Glaser (Ed.), *The nature of reinforcement.* New York: Academic Press, 1971. Pp. 228-278.

Bandura, A., Grusec, J. E., & Menlove, F. L. Some social determinants of self-monitoring reinforcement systems. *Journal of Personality and Social Psychology*, 1967, **5**, 449-455.

Bandura, A., & Kupers, C. J. The transmission of patterns of self-reinforcement through modeling. *Journal of Abnormal and Social Psychology*, 1964, **69**, 1-9.

Bandura, A., & Perloff, B. Relative efficacy of self-monitored and externally imposed reinforcement systems. *Journal of Personality and Social Psychology*, 1967, **7**, 111-116.

Bandura, A., & Walters, R. H. *Social learning and personality development*. New York: Holt, Rinehart & Winston, 1963.

Bandura, A., & Whalen, C. K. The influence of antecedent reinforcement and divergent modeling cues on patterns of self-reward. *Journal of Personality and Social Psychology*, 1966, **3**, 373-382.

Barber, T., DiCara, L. V., Kamiya, J., Miller, N. E., Shapiro, D., & Stoyva, J., (Eds.) *Biofeedback and self-control*. Chicago: Aldine, 1970.

Barber, T. X., & Hahn, K. W. Jr. Experimental studies in "hypnotic" behavior: Physiological and subjective effects of imagined pain. *Journal of Nervous and Mental Disease*, 1964, **139**, 416-425.

Barlow, D. H., Leitenberg, H., & Agras, W. S. Experimental control of sexual deviation through manipulation of the noxious scene in covert sensitization. *Journal of Abnormal Psychology*, 1969, **74**, 597-601.

Barrish, H., Saunders, M., & Wolf, M. M. Good behavior game: Effects of individual contingencies for group consequences on disruptive behavior in a regular classroom. *Journal of Applied Behavior Analysis*, 1969, **2**, 119-124.

Barron, F. *Creative person and creative process*. New York: Holt, Rinehart & Winston, 1969.

Bates, H., & Katz, M. Development of the verbal regulation of behavior. *Proceedings, 78th Annual Convention, American Psychological Association*, 1970, **5** (Pt. 1), 299-300.

Bayer, C. A. Self-monitoring and mild aversion treatment of trichotillomania. *Journal of Behavior Therapy and Experimental Psychiatry*, 1972, **3**, 139-141.

Bechtoldt, H. P. Construct validity: A critique. *American Psychologist*, 1959, **14**, 619-629.

Bem, D. Self-perception theory. In L. Berkowitz (Ed.), *Advances in experimental social psychology*. Vol. 6. New York: Academic Press, 1972. Pp. 1-62.

Bem, S. L. Verbal self-control: The establishment of effective self-instruction. *Journal of Experimental Psychology*, 1967, **74**, 485-491.

Bennis, W. G. The temporary society. In W. G. Bennis & P. E. Slater (Eds.), *The temporary society*. New York: Harper & Row, 1968, 124-128.

Berecz, J. Modification of smoking behavior through self-administered punishment of imagined behavior: A new approach to aversive therapy. *Journal of Consulting and Clinical Psychology*, 1972, **38**, 244-250.

Bergin, A. E. Self-regulation technique for impulse control disorders. *Psychotherapy: Theory, Research and Practice*, 1969, **6**, 113-118.

Bergin, A. E. The evaluation of therapeutic outcomes. In A. E. Bergin & S. L. Garfield (Eds.), *Handbook of psychotherapy and behavior change: An empirical analysis*. New York: Wiley, 1971. Pp. 217-270.

Bergin, A. E., & Garfield, S. L. (Eds.), *Handbook of psychotherapy and behavior change: An empirical analysis*. New York: Wiley, 1971.

Bergmann, G. *Philosophy of science*. Madison: University of Wisconsin Press, 1957.

Berlyne, D. E. *Conflict, arousal, and curiosity*. New York: McGraw-Hill, 1960.

Berne, E. *Transactional analysis in psychotherapy*. New York: Grove Press, 1961.

Berne, E. *Games people play*. New York: Grove Press, 1964.

Bernstein, D. A. Modification of smoking behavior: An evaluative review. *Psychological Bulletin*, 1969, **71**, 418-440.

Bernstein, D. A. The modification of smoking behavior: An evaluative review. In W. A. Hunt (Ed.), *Learning mechanism in smoking*. Chicago: Aldine, 1970. Pp. 3-41.

Bijou, S. W., Peterson, R. F., & Ault, M. H. A method to integrate descriptive and experimental field studies at the level of data and empirical concepts. *Journal of Applied Behavior Analysis*, 1968, **1**, 175-191.

Blanshard, B. The limits of naturalism. In *Contemporary philosophic thought: The international philosophy year conferences at Brockport. Vol. 2. Mind, science, and history*. Albany: State University of New York Press, 1970.

Bledsoe, J. C. Self-concepts of children and their intelligence, achievement, interests, and anxiety. *Journal of Individual Psychology*, 1964, **20**, 55-58.

Bledsoe, J. C., & Garrison, K. C. The self-concepts of elementary school children in relation to their academic achievement, intelligence, interests, and manifest anxiety. (Cooperative Research Project No. 1008.) Washington, D.C.: Department of Health, Education, and Welfare, 1962.

Blumenthal, A. The base of objectivist psychotherapy. *The Objectivist*, 1969.

Bolstad, O. D., & Johnson, S. M. Self-regulation in the modification of disruptive behavior. *Journal of Applied Behavior Analysis*, 1972, **5**, 443-454.

Boston Globe. Want to give up cigarettes? Harvard needs 60 volunteers. April 6, 1969.

Boudin, H. M. Contingency contracting as a therapeutic tool in the deceleration of amphetamine use. *Behavior Therapy*, 1972, **3**, 604-608.

Boulding, K. General systems theory—the skeleton of science. *Management Science*, 1956, **2**, 197-208.

Boyd, H. S., & Sisney, V. V. Immediate self-image confrontation and changes in self-concept. *Journal of Consulting Psychology*, 1967, **31**, 291-294.

Boyd, L. M. Most disappointed men in the world. *San Francisco Chronicle*, March 15, 1969.

Breger, L. The ideology of behaviorism. In L. Breger (Ed.), *Clinical-cognitive psychology: Models and integrations*. Englewood Cliffs, N.J.: Prentice-Hall, 1969. Pp. 25-55.

Bridger, W. H., & Mandel, I. J. A comparison of GSR fear responses produced by threat and electric shock. *Journal of Psychiatric Research*, 1964, **2**, 31-40.

Broden, M., & Hall, R. V. Effects of teacher attention on the verbal behavior of two junior high school pupils. Paper presented at Council for Exceptional Children convention, New York, 1968.

Broden, M., Hall, R. V., Dunlap, A., & Clark, R. Effects of teacher attention and a token reinforcement system in a junior high school special education class. *Exceptional Children*, 1970, **36**, 341-349.

Broden, M., Hall, R. V., & Mitts, B. The effect of self-recording on the classroom behavior of two eighth-grade students. *Journal of Applied Behavior Analysis*, 1971, **4**(3), 191-199.

Brown, G. *Human teaching for human learning*. New York: Viking, 1970.

Brown, J. M. Intervention packages: An approach to self-management. *Personnel and Guidance Journal*, 1972, **50**, 809-815.

Browning, R. M., & Stover, D. D. *Behavior modification in child treatment*. Chicago: Aldine, 1971.

Bucher, B., & Fabricatore, J. Use of patient-administered shock to suppress hallucinations. *Behavior Therapy*, 1970, **1**, 382-385.

Buckley, W. (Ed.), *Modern systems research for the behavioral scientist*. Chicago: Aldine, 1968.

Bühler, C. Basic theoretical concepts of humanistic psychology. *American Psychologist*, 1971, **26**, 378-386.

Campbell, D. T., & Fiske, D. W. Convergent and discriminant validation by the multitrait-multimethod matrix. *Psychological Bulletin*, 1959, **56**, 81-105.

Campbell, D. T., & Stanley, J. C. *Experimental and quasi-experimental designs for research*. Chicago: Rand McNally, 1963.

Cannon, W. B. Self-regulation of the body. In W. Buckley (Ed.), *Modern systems research for the behavioral scientist*. Chicago: Aldine, 1968. Pp. 256-258.

Carlin, A. S., & Armstrong, H. E. Aversive conditioning: Learning or dissonance reduction. *Journal of Consulting and Clinical Psychology*, 1968, **32**, 674-678.

Carson, R. C. *Interaction concepts of personality*. Chicago: Aldine, 1969.

Cautela, J. R. Treatment of compulsive behavior by covert sensitization. *Psychological Record*, 1966, **16**, 33-41.

Cautela, J. R. Covert sensitization. *Psychological Record*, 1967, **20**, 459-468.

Cautela, J. R. Behavior therapy and self-control: Techniques and implications. In C. M. Franks (Ed.), *Behavior therapy: Appraisal and status*. New York: McGraw-Hill, 1969. Pp. 323-340.

Cautela, J. R. Covert reinforcement. *Behavior Therapy*, 1970, **1**, 33-50. (a)

Cautela, J. R. Covert negative reinforcement. *Journal of Behavior Therapy and Experimental Psychiatry*, 1970, **1**, 273-278. (b)

Cautela, J. R. Covert conditioning. In A. Jacobs & L. B. Sachs (Eds.), *The psychology of private events: Perspectives on covert response systems*. New York: Academic Press, 1971. Pp. 109-130.

Cautela, J. R., & Kastenbaum, R. A reinforcement survey for use in therapy, training, and research. *Psychological Reports*, 1967, **20**, 1115-1130.

Chaplin, J. P., & Krawiec, T. S. *Systems and theories of psychology*. New York: Holt, Rinehart & Winston, 1960.

Chapman, J., & McGhie, A. A comparative study of disordered attention of schizophrenia. *Journal of Mental Science*, 1962, **108**, 187-500.

Chapman, R. F., Smith, J. W., & Layden, T. A. Elimination of cigarette smoking by punishment and self-management training. *Behaviour Research and Therapy*, 1971, **9**, 255-264.

Chassan, J. B. *Research design in clinical psychology and psychiatry*. New York: Appleton-Century-Crofts, 1967.

Clarke, D. The treatment of monosymptomatic phobia by systematic desensitization. *Behaviour Research and Therapy*, 1963, **1**, 63-68.

Colle, H. A., & Bee, H. L. The effects of competence and social class on degree of modeling of self-reward patterns. *Psychonomic Science*, 1968, **10**, 231-232.

Coopersmith, S. *The antecedents of self-esteem.* San Francisco: Freeman, 1967.

Coue, E. *The practice of autosuggestion.* New York: Doubleday, 1922.

Cox, L. E. The effects of social contract conditions on the tolerance of noxious stimulation. Unpublished master's thesis, University of Cincinnati, 1972.

Creer, T. L., & Miklich, D. R. The application of a self-modeling procedure to modify inappropriate behavior: A preliminary report. *Behaviour Research and Therapy,* 1970, **8**, 91-92.

Cronbach, L. J. *Essentials of psychological testing.* New York: Harper & Row, 1960.

Crowne, D. P., Stephens, M. W., & Kelly, R. The validity and equivalence of tests of self-acceptance. *Journal of Psychology,* 1961, **51**, 101-112.

Danto, A., & Morgenbesser, S., (Eds.) *Philosophy of science.* New York: Meridian Books/World Publishing, 1960.

Davison, G. C. Systematic desensitization as a counter-conditioning process. *Journal of Abnormal Psychology,* 1968, **73**, 91-99. (a)

Davison, G. C. Elimination of a sadistic fantasy by a client-controlled counter-conditioning technique: A case study. *Journal of Abnormal Psychology,* 1968, **73**, 84-90. (b)

Davison, G. C. Self-control through "imaginal aversive contingency" and "one-downmanship": Enabling the powerless to accommodate unreasonableness. In J. D. Krumboltz & C. E. Thoresen (Eds.), *Behavioral counseling: Cases and techniques.* New York: Holt, Rinehart & Winston, 1969. Pp. 319-327.

Dawson, M. E. Comparison of classical conditioning and relational learning. Unpublished master's thesis, University of Southern California, 1966.

Dawson, M. E., & Grings, W. W. Comparison of classical conditioning and relational learning. *Journal of Experimental Psychology,* 1968, **76**, 227-231.

Day, W. F. Radical behaviorism in reconciliation with phenomenology. *Journal of the Experimental Analysis of Behavior,* 1969, **12**, 315-328.

Day, W. F. Humanistic psychology and contemporary humanism. *The Humanist,* 1971, **31**, 13-16.

Delgado, J. M. R. *Physical control of the mind.* New York: Harper & Row, 1969.

Dollard, J., & Miller, N. *Personality and psychotherapy: An analysis in terms of learning, thinking, and culture.* New York: McGraw-Hill, 1950.

Dukes, W. F. N=1. *Psychological Bulletin,* 1965, **64**, 74-79.

DuPraw, V. Self-management of internal responses: Heart rate control. Unpublished doctoral dissertation, Stanford University, 1972.

D'Zurilla, T. Reducing heterosexual anxiety. In J. Krumboltz & C. E. Thoresen (Eds.), *Behavioral counseling: Cases and techniques.* New York: Holt, Rinehart & Winston, 1969.

D'Zurilla, T., & Goldfried, M. Problem solving and behavior modification. *Journal of Abnormal Psychology*, 1971, **78**, 107-126.

Eaton, J. W., & Weil, R. J. *Culture and mental disorders.* New York: Free Press, 1955.

Edgington, E. S. Statistical inference and nonrandom samples. *Psychological Bulletin*, 1966, **66**, 485-487.

Edwards, A. L. *The social desirability variability in personality assessment and research.* New York: Dryden, 1957.

Edwards, A. L. *Experimental design in psychological research.* New York: Holt, Rinehart & Winston, 1964.

Edwards, A. L., & Cronbach, L. J. Experimental design for research in psychotherapy. *Journal of Clinical Psychology*, 1952, **8**, 51-59.

Edwards, I. *A humanistic view.* Sydney, Australia: Angus & Robertson, 1969.

Edwards, W. The theory of decision making. *Psychological Bulletin*, 1954, **51**, 380-417.

Egan, G. *Encounter: Group processes for interpersonal growth.* Monterey, Calif.: Brooks/Cole, 1970.

Ehrlich, P. R. *The population bomb.* New York: Ballantine, 1968.

Elliott, R. Effects of uncertainty about the nature and advent of a noxious stimuli (shock) upon heart rate. *Journal of Personality and Social Psychology*, 1966, **3**, 353-356.

Elliott, R., & Tighe, T. Breaking the cigarette habit: Effects of a technique involving threatened loss of money. *Psychological Record*, 1968, **18**, 503-513.

Ellis, A. *Reason and emotion in psychotherapy.* New York: Lyle Stuart, 1963.

Etzioni, A., & Remp, R. Technological "shortcuts" to social change. *Science*, 1972, **175**, 31-38.

Evans, G., & Oswalt, G. Acceleration of academic progress through the manipulation of peer influence. *Behaviour Research and Therapy*, 1967, **5**, 1-7.

Eysenck, H. J. *Behavior therapy and the neuroses.* London: Pergamon, 1960.

Eysenck, H. J. Reason with compassion. *The Humanist*, 1971, **31**, 24-25. (a)

Eysenck, H. J. Behavior therapy as a scientific discipline. *Journal of Consulting and Clinical Psychology*, 1971, **36**, 314-319. (b)

Fairfield, R. P., (Ed.) *Humanistic frontiers in American education.* Englewood Cliffs, N.J.: Prentice-Hall, 1971.

Farber, N. E. The things people say to themselves. *American Psychologist*, 1963, **6**, 185-197.

Ferkiss, V. C. *Technological man.* New York: Mentor, 1969.

Ferster, C. B. Classification of behavior pathology. In L. Krasner & L. P. Ullman (Eds.), *Research in behavior modification.* New York: Holt, Rinehart & Winston, 1965. Pp. 6-26.

Ferster, C. B., Nurnberger, J. I., & Levitt, E. B. The control of eating. *Journal of Mathetics*, 1962, **1**, 87-109.

Ferster, C. B., & Perrott, M. C. *Behavior principles.* New York: Appleton-Century-Crofts, 1968.

Festinger, L. A theory of social comparison processes. *Human Relations*, 1954, **7**, 117-140.

Fiske, D. W., Hunt, H. F., Luborsky, L., Orne, M. T., Parloff, M. B., Reiser, M. F., & Tuma, A. H. Planning of research on effectiveness of psychotherapy. *Archives of General Psychiatry*, 1970, **22**, 22-32.

Fixsen, D. L., Phillips, E. L., & Wolf, M. M. Achievement place: The reliability of self-reporting and peer-reporting and their effects on behavior. *Journal of Applied Behavior Analysis*, 1972, **5**, 19-30.

Flannery, R. B. Use of covert conditioning in the behavioral treatment of a drug-dependent college dropout. *Journal of Counseling Psychology*, 1972, **19**, 547-550.

Fox, L. Effecting the use of efficient study habits. *Journal of Mathetics*, 1962, **1**, 75-86.

Frankl, V. E. *Man's search for meaning: An introduction to logotherapy.* New York: Washington Square Press, 1959.

Franks, C. M., Fried, R., & Ashem, B. An improved apparatus for the aversive conditioning of cigarette smokers. *Behaviour Research and Therapy*, 1966, **4**, 301-308.

Freud, S. Further recommendations on the technique of psychoanalysis (1913). Reprinted in P. Rieff (Ed.), *Freud: Therapy and technique.* New York: Collier, 1963. Pp. 135-156.

Fromm, E. *Escape from freedom.* New York: Holt, Rinehart & Winston, 1941.

Geer, J., & Turtletaub, A. Fear reduction following observation of a model. *Journal of Personality and Social Psychology*, 1967, **6**, 321-327.

Gelder, M., Marks, I., Wolff, H., & Clarke, M. Desensitization and psychotherapy in the treatment of phobic states: A controlled inquiry. *British Journal of Psychiatry*, 1967, **113**, 33-73.

Gelfand, D. M. The influence of self-esteem on rate of verbal conditioning and social matching behavior. *Journal of Abnormal and Social Psychology*, 1962, **65**, 259-265.

Gelfand, D. M., & Hartmann, D. P. Behavior therapy with children: A review and evaluation of research methodology. *Psychological Bulletin*, 1968, **69**, 204-215.

Gelfand, D. M., & Hartmann, D. P. Manual of child behavior modification exercises. Unpublished manuscript, University of Utah, 1972.

Gendlin, E. Focusing. *Psychotherapy: Theory, Research and Practice*, 1969, **6**, 4-15.

Gergen, K. Self-theory and the process of self-observation. *Journal of Nervous and Mental Disease*, 1969, **148**, 437-448.

Gewirtz, J. L. The roles of covert responding and extrinsic reinforcement in "self-" and "vicarious-reinforcement" phenomena and in "observational learning" and limitation. In R. Glaser (Ed.), *The nature of reinforcement*. Columbus, Ohio: Merrill, 1971. Pp. 279-309.

Gewirtz, J. L., & Stingle, K. G. Learning of generalized imitation as the basis for identification. *Psychological Review*, 1968, **75**, 374-397.

Glynn, E. L. Classroom applications of self-determined reinforcement. *Journal of Applied Behavior Analysis*, 1970, **3**, 123-132.

Goldfried, M. R. Systematic desensitization as training in self-control. *Journal of Consulting and Clinical Psychology*, 1971, **37**(2), 228-234.

Goldfried, M. R. Reduction of generalized anxiety through a variant of systematic desensitization. In M. R. Goldfried & M. Merbaum (Eds.), *Behavior change through self-control*. New York: Holt, Rinehart & Winston, 1973. Pp. 297-304.

Goldfried, M. R., & Merbaum, M., (Eds.) *Behavior change through self-control*. New York: Holt, Rinehart & Winston, 1973.

Goldiamond, I. Self-control procedures in personal behavior problems. *Psychological Reports*, 1965, **17**, 851-868. (a)

Goldiamond, I. Fluent and nonfluent speech (stuttering): Analysis and operant techniques for control. In L. Krasner & L. P. Ullmann (Eds.), *Research in behavior modification*. New York: Holt, Rinehart & Winston, 1965. Pp. 106-156. (b)

Goldstein, A. P., Heller, K., & Sechrest, L. B. *Psychotherapy and the psychology of behavior change*. New York: Wiley, 1966.

Goldstein, K. M. Note: A comparison of self-reports and peer-reports of smoking and drinking behavior. *Psychological Reports*, 1966, **18**, 702.

Goodlet, G. R., & Goodlet, M. M. Efficiency of self-monitored and externally imposed schedules of reinforcement in controlling disruptive behavior. Unpublished manuscript, University of Guelph, 1969.

Gordon, S. B., & Sachs, L. B. Self-control with a covert aversive stimulus: Modification of smoking. Unpublished manuscript, West Virginia University, 1971.

Gottman, J. M., & McFall, R. M. Self-monitoring effects in a program for potential high school dropouts: A time-series analysis. *Journal of Consulting and Clinical Psychology*, 1972, **39**, 273-281.

Gough, G. G., & Heilbrun, A. B. *Adjective checklist manual*. Palo Alto, Calif.: Consulting Psychologists Press, 1965.

Green, E. Varieties of healing experiences. Address given at DeAnza College, October 30, 1971.

Green, E., Green, A., & Walters, E. Self-regulation of internal states. In J. Rose (Ed.), *Progress of Cybernetics. Proceedings of the International Congress of Cybernetics, London, 1970*. London: Gordon & Breach, 1971.

Greene, R. J. Modification of smoking behavior by free operant conditioning methods. *Psychological Record*, 1964, **14**, 171-178.

Grings, W. W. Verbal-perceptual factors in the conditioning of autonomic responses. In W. F. Prokasy (Ed.), *Classical conditioning: A symposium*. New York: Appleton-Century-Crofts, 1965. Pp. 71-89.

Grose, R. F. A comparison of vocal and subvocal conditioning of the galvanic skin response. Unpublished doctoral dissertation, Yale University, 1952.

Grossberg, J. M. Behavior therapy in review. *Psychological Bulletin*, 1964, **62**, 73-88.

Grusec, J. Some antecedents of self-criticism. *Journal of Personality and Social Psychology*, 1966, **4**, 244-252.

Guerney, B. G., (Ed.) *Psychotherapeutic agents: New roles for nonprofessionals, parents, and teachers*. New York: Holt, Rinehart & Winston, 1969.

Guilford, J. P. *Psychometric methods*. New York: McGraw-Hill, 1936.

Guilford, J. P. Some theoretical views of creativity. In H. Helson & W. Bevan (Eds.), *Contemporary approaches to psychology*. New York: Van Nostrand, 1967.

Gustaitis, R. *Turning on*. New York: Macmillan, 1969.

Guttman, M., & Marston, A. Problems of Ss motivation in a behavioral program for reduction of cigarette smoking. *Psychological Reports*, 1967, **20**, 1107-1114.

Gygi, C., & Saslow, G. An interactional approach to weight reduction. Paper presented at the meeting of the Western Psychological Association, San Francisco, April, 1971.

Haley, J. *Strategies of psychotherapy*. New York: Grune & Stratton, 1963.

Hall, R. V., & Broden, M. Behavior changes in brain-injured children through social reinforcement. *Journal of Experimental Child Psychology*, 1967, **5**, 463-479.

Hall, R. V., Cristler, C., Cranston, S., & Tucker, B. Teachers and parents as researchers using multiple baseline designs. *Journal of Applied Behavior Analysis*, 1970, **3**, 247-255.

Hall, R. V., Fox, R., Weis, L., & Quinn, A. Three studies using changing criterion research designs. Submitted for publication.

Hall, R. V., Fox, R., Willard, D., Goldsmith, L., Emerson, M., Owen, M., Davis, F., & Porcia, E. The teacher as observer and experimenter in the modification of disputing and talking-out behaviors. *Journal of Applied Behavior Analysis*, 1971, **4**, 141-149.

Hall, R. V., Lund, D., & Jackson, D. Effects of teacher attention on study behavior. *Journal of Applied Behavior Analysis*, 1968, **1**, 1-12.

Hall, R. V., Panyan, M., Rabon, D., & Broden, M. Teacher applied contingencies and appropriate classroom behavior. *Journal of Applied Behavior Analysis*, 1968, **1**, 315-322.

Hall, S. M. Self-control and therapist control in the behavioral treatment of overweight women. *Behaviour Research and Therapy*, 1972, **10**, 59-68.

Hannum, J. W. The modification of evaluative self-thoughts and their effect on overt behavior. Unpublished doctoral dissertation, School of Education, Stanford University, 1972.

Harlow, H. F. Motivation as a factor in the acquisition of new responses. In *Current theory and research in motivation: A symposium*. Lincoln: University of Nebraska Press, 1953, Pp. 24-49.

Harris, M. B. Self-directed program for weight control: A pilot study. *Journal of Abnormal Psychology*, 1969, **74**, 263-270.

Harris, M. B., & Bruner, C. G. A comparison of self-control and a contract procedure for weight control. *Behaviour Research and Therapy*, 1971, **9**, 347-354.

Hartig, M., & Kanfer, F. H. The role of verbal self-instruction in children's resistance to temptation. *Journal of Personality and Social Psychology*, 1973, **25**, 259-267.

Hartmann, D. P. Current developments in behavior modification with children. In L. D. Clark (Ed.), *Proceedings of the Sixteenth Annual Institute of Professors of Psychiatry West of the Mississippi*. Salt Lake City: University of Utah Medical School, 1970. Pp. 10-24.

Hartmann, D. P. Notes on methodology: 1. On choosing an interobserver reliability estimate. Unpublished manuscript, University of Utah, 1972. (a)

Hartmann, D. P. Some neglected issues in behavior modification with children. Paper presented at the meeting of the Association for the Advancement of Behavior Therapy, New York, October 1972. (b)

Hayakawa, S. I. *Language in thought and action*. (Rev. ed.) New York: Harcourt Brace Jovanovich, 1964.

Heath, R. S. *The reasonable adventurer*. Pittsburgh: University of Pittsburgh Press, 1969.

Heider, F. *The psychology of interpersonal relations*. New York: Wiley, 1958.

Heimstra, N. W., & Ellingstad, V. S. *Human behavior: A systems approach*. Monterey, Calif.: Brooks/Cole, 1972.

Heisenberg, W. *Physics and philosophy*. New York: Harper Torch, 1958.

Hempel, C. G. *Philosophy of natural science*. Englewood Cliffs, N.J.: Prentice-Hall, 1966.

Herbert, E. W., & Baer, D. M. Training parents as behavior modifiers: Self-recording of contingent attention. *Journal of Applied Behavior Analysis*, 1972, **5**, 139-149.

Herbert, E. W., Gelfand, D. M., & Hartmann, D. P. Imitation and self-esteem as determinants of self-critical behavior. *Child Development*, 1969, **40**, 421-430.

Hess, E. H., & Polt, J. M. Pupil size as related to interest value of visual stimuli. *Science*, 1960, **132**, 349-350.

Hill, W. F. Learning theory and the acquisition of values. *Psychological Bulletin*, 1960, **67**, 317-331.

Hobbs, N. Sources of gain in psychotherapy. *American Psychologist*, 1962, **17**, 741-747.

Homme, L. E. Perspectives in psychology: XXIV. Control of coverants, the operants of the mind. *Psychological Record*, 1965, **15**, 501-511.

Homme, L. E., C'deBaca, P., Cottingham, L., & Homme, A. What behavioral engineering is. *Psychological Record*, 1968, **18**, 425-434.

Homme, L. E., C'deBaca, P. C., Devine, J. V., Steinhorst, R., & Rickert,

E. J. Use of Premack principle in controlling the behavior of nursery school children. *Journal of the Experimental Analysis of Behavior*, 1963, **6**, 544.

Homme, L. E., & Tosti, D. *Behavior technology: Motivation and contingency management*. San Rafael, Calif.: Individual Learning Systems, 1971.

Honig, W. K., (Ed.) *Operant behavior: Areas of research and application*. New York: Appleton-Century-Crofts, 1966.

Horan, J. J. The effect of coverant conditioning on weight reduction. Paper presented at the meeting of the American Educational Research Association, New York, February 1971.

Hosford, R. E., & Zimmer, J. Humanism through behaviorism. *Counseling and Values*, 1972, **16**, 1-7.

Hovland, C. I., Janis, I. L., & Kelly, H. H. *Communication and persuasion*. New Haven, Conn.: Yale University Press, 1953.

Hughes, C. C., Tremblay, M., Rapoport, R. N., & Leighton, A. H. *People of cove and woodlot: Communities from the viewpoint of social psychiatry*. New York: Basic Books, 1960.

Hull, C. L. *Principles of behavior*. New York: Appleton-Century-Crofts, 1943.

Hunt, W. A., (Ed.) *Learning mechanisms in smoking*. Chicago: Aldine, 1970.

Huxley, A. Education on the nonverbal level. In R. M. Jones (Ed.), *Contemporary educational psychology*. New York: Harper Torch, 1966. Pp. 44-60.

Jackson, B. Treatment of depression by self-reinforcement. *Behavior Therapy*, 1972, **3**, 298-307.

Jacobson, E. *You must relax*. New York: Whittlesey House, 1934.

Janis, I. L. Personality correlates of susceptibility to persuasion. *Journal of Personality*, 1954, **22**, 504-518.

Janis, I. L. *Psychological stress: Psychoanalytic and behavioral studies of surgical patients*. New York: Wiley, 1958.

Janis, I. L., & Field, P. B. Sex differences and personality factors related to persuasibility. In C. I. Hovland & I. L. Janis (Eds.), *Personality and persuasibility*. New Haven, Conn.: Yale University Press, 1959. Pp. 55-68.

Jeffrey, D. B. Relationships between internal-external control of reinforcements, study reinforcements and school performance. Paper presented at the meeting of the Western Psychological Association, Los Angeles, April 1970.

Jeffrey, D. B. The effects of external-control versus self-control procedures on the modification and maintenance of weight. Unpublished doctoral dissertation, University of Utah, 1973.

Jeffrey, D. B., & Christensen, E. R. The relative efficacy of behavior therapy, willpower, and no treatment control procedures on the modification of obesity. In A. Stunkard (Chm.), Behavior modification approaches to the treatment of obesity: Recent trends and developments. Symposium presented at the meeting of the Association for the Advancement of Behavior Therapy, New York, October 1972.

Jeffrey, D. B., Christensen, E. R., & Pappas, J. P. Developing a behavioral program and therapist manual for the treatment of obesity. *The Journal of the American College Health Association*, 1973, in press.

Johnson, S. M. Self-reinforcement versus external reinforcement in behavior modification with children. *Developmental Psychology*, 1970, **3**, 147-148.

Johnson, S. M., & Bolstad, O. D. Methodological issues in naturalistic observation: Some problems and solutions for field research. Paper presented at the Fourth Banff International Conference on Behavior, Calgary, Alberta, March 1972.

Johnson, S. M., & Martin, S. Developing self-evaluation as a conditioned reinforcer. In B. Ashem & E. G. Poser (Eds.), *Behavior modification with children*. New York: Pergamon, 1972.

Johnson, S. M., & Sechrest, C. Comparison of desensitization and progressive relaxation in treating test anxiety. *Journal of Consulting and Clinical Psychology*, 1968, **32**, 280-286.

Johnson, S. M., & White, G. Self-observation as an agent of behavioral change. *Behavior Therapy*, 1971, **2**, 488-497.

Johnson, W. *People in quandries*. New York: Harper, 1966.

Johnson, W. G. Some applications of Homme's coverant control therapy: Two case reports. *Behavior Therapy*, 1971, **2**, 240-248.

Johnston, J. M. Punishment of human behavior. *American Psychologist*, 1972, **27**, 1033-1054.

Jourard, S. M. *Disclosing man to himself*. Princeton, N.J.: Van Nostrand, 1968.

Jourard, S. M. *The transparent self*. (Rev. ed.) New York: Van Nostrand-Reinhold, 1971.

Kagan, J. Reflection-impulsivity: The generality and dynamics of conceptual tempo. *Journal of Abnormal Psychology*, 1966, **71**, 17-24.

Kamiya, J., Barber, T., DiCara, L. V., Miller, N. E., Shapiro, D., & Stoyva, J., (Eds.) *Biofeedback and self-control*. Chicago: Aldine, 1971.

Kanfer, F. H. Influence of age and incentive conditions on children's self-rewards. *Psychological Reports*, 1966, **19**, 263-274.

Kanfer, F. H. Verbal conditioning: A review of its current status. In T. R. Dixon & D. L. Horton (Eds.), *Verbal behavior and general behavior theory*. Englewood Cliffs, N.J.: Prentice-Hall, 1968. Pp. 254-290.

Kanfer, F. H. Self-regulation: Research, issues, and speculations. In C. Neuringer & J. L. Michael (Eds.), *Behavior modification in clinical psychology*. New York: Appleton-Century-Crofts, 1970. Pp. 178-220. (a)

Kanfer, F. H. Self-monitoring: Methodological limitations and clinical applications. *Journal of Consulting and Clinical Psychology*, 1970, **35**, 148-152. (b)

Kanfer, F. H. The maintenance of behavior by self-generated stimuli and reinforcement. In A. Jacobs & L. B. Sachs (Eds.), *The psychology of private events*. New York: Academic Press, 1971, 39-59.

Kanfer, F. H., & Duerfeldt, P. H. Effects of pretraining on self-evaluation and self-reinforcement. *Journal of Personality and Social Psychology*, 1967, **7**, 164-168.

Kanfer, F. H., & Duerfeldt, P. H. Comparison of self-reward and self-criticism as a function of prior external reinforcement. *Journal of Personality and Social Psychology,* 1968, **8**, 261-268.

Kanfer, F. H., & Goldfoot, D. A. Self-control and tolerance of noxious stimulation. *Psychological Reports,* 1966, **18**, 79-85.

Kanfer, F. H., & Karoly, P. Self-control: A behavioristic excursion into the lion's den. *Behavior Therapy*, 1972, **3**, 398-416. (a)

Kanfer, F. H., & Karoly, P. Self-regulation and its clinical applications: Some additional considerations. In R. C. Johnson, P. R. Dokecki, & O. H. Mowrer (Eds.), *Conscience, contract, and social reality*. New York: Holt, Rinehart & Winston, 1972. Pp. 428-437. (b)

Kanfer, F. H., & Marston, A. R. Conditioning of self-reinforcing responses: An analogue to self-confidence training. *Psychological Reports*, 1963, **13**, 63-70. (a)

Kanfer, F. H., & Marston, A. R. Human reinforcement: Vicarious and direct. *Journal of Experimental Psychology*, 1963, **65**, 292-296. (b)

Kanfer, F. H., & Phillips, J. S. Behavior therapy: A panacea for all ills or a passing fancy? *Archives of General Psychiatry*, 1966, **15**, 114-128.

Kanfer, F. H., & Phillips, J. S. *Learning foundations of behavior therapy*. New York: Wiley, 1970.

Kanfer, F. H., & Seidner, M. Self-control: Factors enhancing tolerance of noxious stimulation. *Journal of Personality and Social Psychology*, 1973, **25**, 381-389.

Kantor, J. R. *Principles of psychology*. Bloomington, Ind.: Principia Press, 1924.

Karnes, M., Teska, J., & Hodgins, A. The effects of four programs of classroom intervention on the intellectual and language development of 4-year-old disadvantaged children. *American Journal of Orthopsychiatry*, 1970, **40**, 58-76.

Karst, T., & Trexler, L. Initial study using fixed-role and rational-emotive therapy in treating public-speaking anxiety. *Journal of Consulting and Clinical Psychology*, 1970, **34**, 360-366.

Katz, R. C. A procedure for concurrently measuring elapsed time and response frequency. *Journal of Applied Behavior Analysis*, in press.

Kazdin, A. E. Covert self-modeling and the reduction of avoidance behavior. *Journal of Abnormal Psychology*, 1973, **81**, 87-95.

Kazdin, A. E., & Bootzin, R. R. The token economy: An evaluative review. *Journal of Applied Behavior Analysis*, 1972, **5**, 343-372.

Kelly, G. *The psychology of personal constructs*. Vol. 2. New York: Norton, 1955.

Keutzer, C. S. Behavior modification of smoking: The experimental investigation of diverse techniques. *Behaviour Research and Therapy*, 1968, **6**, 137-157.

Keutzer, C. S., Lichtenstein, E., & Mees, H. L. Modification of smoking behavior: A review. *Psychological Bulletin*, 1968, **70**, 520-533.

Kidder, L. H., & Campbell, D. T. The indirect testing of social attitudes. In G. I. Summers (Ed.), *Attitude Measurement*. Chicago: Rand McNally, 1970. Pp. 333-385.

Kiesler, D. J. Experimental designs in psychotherapy research. In A. E. Bergin & S. L. Garfield (Eds.), *Handbook of psychotherapy and behavior change: An empirical analysis*. New York: Wiley, 1971. Pp. 36-74.

Koch, S. Psychology and emerging conceptions of knowledge as unitary. In T. W. Wann (Ed.), *Behaviorism and phenomenology–contrasting bases for modern psychology*. Chicago: The University of Chicago Press, 1964.

Koestler, A. *The ghost in the machine*. New York: Macmillan, 1967.

Kohlberg, L., Yaeger, J., & Hjertholm, E. Private speech: Four studies and a review of theories. *Child Development*, 1968, **39**, 691-736.

Kolb, D. A., Winter, S. K., & Berlew, D. E. Self-directed behavior change: Two studies. *Journal of Applied Behavioral Science*, 1968, **4**, 453-471.

Kolvin, L. Aversive imagery treatment in adolescents. *Behaviour Research and Therapy*, 1967, **5**, 245-249.

Korzybski, A. *Science and sanity*. Lancaster, Pa.: Lancaster Press, 1933.

Krasner, L. The therapist as a social reinforcement machine. In H. Strupp & L. Luborsky (Eds.), *Research in psychotherapy*. Vol. 3. Washington, D.C.: American Psychological Association, 1968.

Krasner, L. Behavior therapy. In P. H. Musser & M. A. Rosenzweig (Eds.), *Annual review of psychology*. Palo Alto, Calif.: Annual Reviews, 1971. Pp. 483-532.

Kris, E. *Psychoanalytic explorations in art*. London: Allen & Unwin, 1953.

Krumboltz, J. D., & Thoresen, C. E. (Eds.) *Behavioral counseling: Cases and techniques*. New York: Holt, Rinehart & Winston, 1969.

Kurtz, P. What is humanism? In R. Kurtz (Ed.), *Moral problems in contemporary society*. New York: Prentice-Hall, 1969.

Kvale, S., & Grenners, C. E. Skinner and Sartre: Towards a radical phenomenology of behavior? *Review of Existential Psychology and Psychiatry*, 1967, **7**, 128-148.

Lackenmeyer, C. W. Experimentation—a misunderstood methodology in psychological and social-psychological research. *American Psychologist*, 1970, **25**, 617-624.

Lamont, C. *Freedom of choice affirmed*. New York: Horizon Press, 1967.

Lana, R. E. Pretest sensitization. In A. Rosenthal & R. L. Rosnow (Eds.), *Artifact in behavioral research*. New York: Academic, 1969. Pp. 119-141.

Landsman, T. Positive experience and the beautiful person. Presidential address at the meeting of the Southeastern Psychological Association, Miami, Fla., April 1968.

Lang, P. Fear reduction and fear behavior: Problems in treating a construct. In J. M. Shlien (Ed.), *Research in Psychotherapy*, Vol. 3. Washington, D.C.: American Psychological Association, 1968.

Lang, P. The mechanics of desensitization and the laboratory study of human fear. In C. Franks (Ed.), *Assessment and status of the behavior therapies*. New York: McGraw-Hill, 1969.

Lang, P., & Lazovik, A. Experimental desensitization of a phobia. *Journal of Abnormal and Social Psychology*, 1963, **66**, 519-525.

Lawson, D. M., & May, R. B. Three procedures for the extinction of smoking behavior. *Psychological Record*, 1970, **20**, 151-157.

Lazarus, A. A. *Behavior therapy and beyond*. New York: McGraw-Hill, 1971.

Lazarus, A. A., & Abramovitz, A. The use of "emotive imagery" in the treatment of children's phobias. *Journal of Mental Science*, 1962, **108**, 191-195.

Lazarus, A. A., & Davison, G. C. Clinical innovation in research and practice. In A. E. Bergin & S. L. Garfield (Eds.), *Handbook of psychotherapy and behavior change: An empirical analysis.* New York: Wiley, 1971. Pp. 196-213.

Lazarus, A. A., & Rachman, S. The use of systematic desensitization in psychotherapy. In H. Eysenck (Ed.), *Behavior therapy and the neurosis.* London: Pergamon, 1960.

Lazarus, R. *Psychological stress and the coping process.* New York: McGraw-Hill, 1966.

Leak, G. K., & Fraser, S. C. The effects of self-monitoring and reinforcement on weight reduction and its maintenance in obese females. Paper presented at the meeting of the Western Psychological Association, Portland, Ore., April 1972.

Lefcourt, H. M. Internal versus external control of reinforcement: A review. *Psychological Bulletin,* 1966, **65**, 206-220.

Lefcourt, H. M. Effects on cue explication upon persons maintaining external control expectancies. *Journal of Personality and Social Psychology,* 1967, **5**, 372-378.

Lesser, G. S., & Abelson, R. P. Personality correlates of persuasibility in children. In C. I. Hovland & I. L. Janis (Eds.), *Personality and persuasibility.* New Haven, Conn.: Yale University Press, 1959. Pp. 187-206.

Levine, F. M., & Greenspoon, L. Telemetered heart rate and skin potential of a chronic schizophrenic patient especially during periods of hallucinations and periods of talking. *Journal of Consulting and Clinical Psychology,* 1971, **37**, 345-350.

Levy, L. *Conceptions of personality.* New York: Random House, 1970.

Lewinsohn, P. M., Weinstein, M. S., & Shaw, D. A. Depression: A clinical research approach. In R. Rubin & C. M. Franks (Eds.), *Advances in behavior therapy.* New York: Academic Press, 1969. Pp. 231-240.

Liebert, R. M., & Allen, M. K. Effects of rule structure and reward magnitude on the acquisition and adoption of self-reward criteria. *Psychological Reports,* 1967, **21**, 445-452.

Liebert, R. M., Hanratty, M., & Hill, J. H. Effects of rule structure and training method on the adoption of a self-imposed standard. *Child Development,* 1969, **40**, 93-101.

Liebert, R. M., & Morris, L. Cognitive and emotional components of test anxiety: A distinction and some initial data. *Psychological Reports,* 1967, **20**, 975-978.

Liebert, R. M., & Ora, J. P. Jr. Children's adoption of self-reward patterns: Incentive level and method of transmission. *Child Development,* 1968, **39**, 537-544.

Lindsley, O. R. A reliable wrist counter for recording behavior rates. *Journal of Applied Behavior Analysis*, 1968, **1**, 77-78.

Lindsley, O. R. Should we decelerate urges or actions? Thou shalt not covet. Paper presented at the meeting of the American Psychological Association, Washington, D.C., 1969.

Locke, E. A., Cartledge, N., & Koeppel, J. Motivational effects of knowledge of results. *Psychological Bulletin*, 1968, **70**, 474-485.

Loeb, A., Beck, A. T., Diggory, J. C., & Tuthill, R. Expectancy, level of aspiration, performance, and self-evaluation in depression. *Proceedings of the 75th Annual Convention of the American Psychological Association*, 1967, **2**, 193-194.

London, P. *Behavior control*. New York: Harper & Row, 1969.

Lord, F. M. Elementary models for measuring change. In C. W. Harris (Ed.), *Problems in measuring change*. Madison: The University of Wisconsin Press, 1967. Pp. 21-38.

Lovitt, T. C., & Curtiss, K. Academic response rate as a function of teacher and self-imposed contingencies. *Journal of Applied Behavior Analysis*, 1969, **2**, 49-53.

Lundin, R. W. *Personality: A behavioral analysis*. New York: Macmillan, 1969.

Luria, A. R. *The role of speech in the regulation of normal and abnormal behavior*. New York: Liveright, 1961.

Luria, A. R. *Higher cortical functions in man*. New York: Basic Books, 1966.

Lykken, D. Statistical significance in psychological research. *Psychological Bulletin*, 1968, **70**, 151-159.

Maccoby, E. E. Role-taking in childhood and its consequences for social learning. *Child Development*, 1959, **30**, 239-252.

MacCorquodale, K. Behaviorism is a humanism. *The Humanist*, 1971, **31**, 12-13.

Maddi, S. *Personality theories: A comparative analysis*. Homewood, Ill.: Dorsey Press, 1968.

Madsen, C. Jr., Becker, W., & Thomas, D. Rules, praise, and ignoring: Elements of elementary classroom control. *Journal of Applied Behavior Analysis*, 1968, **1**, 139-150.

Mahoney, M. J. Toward an experimental analysis of coverant control. *Behavior Therapy*, 1970, **1**, 510-521.

Mahoney, M. J. The self-management of covert behavior: A case study. *Behavior Therapy*, 1971, **2**, 575-578.

Mahoney, M. J. Research issues in self-management. *Behavior Therapy*, 1972, **3**, 45-63. (a)

Mahoney, M. J. Self-reward and self-monitoring techniques for weight control. Unpublished doctoral dissertation, Stanford University, 1972. (b)

Mahoney, M. J. Self-control strategies in weight loss. Paper presented at the Sixth Annual Meeting of the Association for the Advancement of Behavior Therapy, New York, 1972. (c)

Mahoney, M. J. Self-reward and self-monitoring techniques for weight control. *Behavior Therapy*, in press.

Mahoney, M. J., & Bandura, A. Self-reinforcement in pigeons. *Learning and Motivation*, 1972, **3**, 293-303.

Mahoney, M. J., Moore, B. S., Wade, T. C., & Moura, N. G. M. The effects of continuous and intermittent self-monitoring on academic behavior. *Journal of Consulting and Clinical Psychology*, 1973, **41**, 65-69.

Mahoney, M. J., Moura, N. G. M., & Wade, T. C. The relative efficacy of self-reward, self-punishment, and self-monitoring techniques for weight loss. *Journal of Consulting and Clinical Psychology*, 1973, **40**, 404-407.

Mahoney, M. J., Thoresen, C. E., & Danaher, B. G. Covert behavior modification: An experimental analogue. *Journal of Behavior Therapy and Experimental Psychiatry*, 1972, **3**, 7-14.

Mandler, G., & Watson, D. Anxiety and the interruption of behavior. In C. Speilberger (Ed.), *Anxiety and behavior*. New York: Academic Press, 1966.

Mann, R. A. The use of contingency contracting to control obesity in adult subjects. Paper presented at the Meeting of the Western Psychological Association, San Francisco, April 1971.

Marcus, J. N., & Morgan, W. G. *A guidebook for systematic densensitization*. Palo Alto, Calif.: Veterans Workshop, 1968.

Marks, I., Boulougouris, J., & Marset, P. Flooding versus desensitization in the treatment of phobic patients. *British Journal of Psychiatry*, 1971, **119**, 353-375.

Marks, I., & Gelder, M. A controlled retrospective study of behavior therapy in phobic patients. *British Journal of Psychiatry*, 1965, **111**, 561-573.

Marlatt, G. A., & Kaplan, B. E. Self-initiated attempts to change behavior: A study of New Year's resolutions. *Psychological Reports*, 1972, **30**, 123-131.

Marquis, J. N., & Morgan, W. G. *A guidebook for systematic desensitization*. Palo Alto, Calif.: Veterans Workshop, Veterans Administration Hospital, 1968.

Marston, A. R. Response strength and self-reinforcement. *Journal of Experimental Psychology*, 1964, **68**, 537-540. (a)

Marston, A. R. Variables affecting incidence of self-reinforcement. *Psychological Reports*, 1964, **14**, 879-884. (b)

Marston, A. R. Imitation, self-reinforcement, and reinforcement of another person. *Journal of Personality and Social Psychology*, 1965, **2**, 255-261. (a)

Marston, A. R. Self-reinforcement: The relevance of a concept in analogue research in psychotherapy. *Psychotherapy: Theory, Research and Practice*, 1965, **2**, 1-5. (b)

Marston, A. R. Self-reinforcement and external reinforcement in visual-motor learning. *Journal of Experimental Psychology*, 1967, **74**, 93-98.

Marston, A. R. The effect of external feedback upon the rate of positive self-reinforcement. *Journal of Experimental Psychology*, 1969, **80**, 175-179.

Marston, A. R., & Cohen, N. J. The relationship of negative self-reinforcement to frustration and intropunitiveness. *Journal of General Psychology*, 1966, **74**, 237-243.

Marston, A. R., & Feldman, S. F. Toward the use of self-control in behavior modification. Paper presented at the meeting of the American Psychological Association, Miami, 1970.

Marston, A. R., & Kanfer, F. H. Human reinforcement: Experimenter and subject controlled. *Journal of Experimental Psychology*, 1963, **66**, 91-94.

Marx, M. H., (Ed.) *Psychological theory: Contemporary readings*. New York: Macmillan, 1951.

Maslow, A. H. *The psychology of science*. New York: Harper & Row, 1966.

Maslow, A. H. Towards a humanistic biology. *American Psychologist*, 1969, **24**, 724-735.

Matson, F. *The broken image*. New York: Braziller, 1964.

Matson, F. W. Counterrebuttal. *The Humanist*, 1971, **31**, 18-19.

McConaghy, N. Aversive therapy of homosexuality: Measures of efficacy. *American Journal of Psychiatry*, 1971, **127**, 1221-1223.

McFall, R. M. The effects of self-monitoring on normal smoking behavior. *Journal of Consulting and Clinical Psychology*, 1970, **35**, 135-142.

McFall, R. M., & Hammen, C. L. Motivation, structure, and self-monitoring: The role of nonspecific factors in smoking reduction. *Journal of Consulting and Clinical Psychology*, 1971, **37**, 80-86.

McGinnies, E. *Social behavior: A functional analysis*. Boston: Houghton Mifflin, 1970.

McGuire, R. J., & Vallance, M. Aversion therapy by electric shock, a simple technique. *British Medical Journal*, 1964, **1**, 151-153.

McKenzie, H., Clark, M., Wolf, M., Kothera, R., & Benson, C. Behavior modification of children with learning disabilities using grades as tokens and allowances as backup reinforcers. *Exceptional Children*, 1968, **34**, 745-753.

McMains, M. J., & Liebert, R. M. Influence of discrepancies between successively modeled self-reward criteria on the adoption of a self-imposed standard. *Journal of Personality and Social Psychology*, 1968, **8**, 166-171.

McNamara, J. R. The use of self-monitoring techniques to treat nail biting. *Behaviour Research and Therapy*, 1972, **10**, 193-194.

McNamara, J. R., & MacDonough, T. S. Some methodological considerations in the design and implementation of behavior therapy research. *Behavior Therapy*, 1972, **3**, 361-378.

Mees, H. L. Placebo effects in aversive control: A preliminary report. Paper read at the joint meeting of the Oregon-Washington State Psychological Association, Ocean Shores, Wash., 1966.

Meichenbaum, D. The effects of instructions and reinforcement on thinking and language behaviors of schizophrenics. *Behaviour Research and Therapy*, 1969, **7**, 101-114.

Meichenbaum, D. The nature and modification of impulsive children. Paper presented at the meeting of the Society for Research in Child Development, Minneapolis, 1971. (a)

Meichenbaum, D. Cognitive factors in behavior modification: Modifying what people say to themselves. Paper presented at the Fifth Annual Meeting of the Association for the Advancement of Behavior Therapy, Washington, D.C., 1971. (b)

Meichenbaum, D. Examination of model characteristics in reducing avoidance behavior. *Journal of Personality and Social Psychology*, 1971, **17**, 298-307. (c)

Meichenbaum, D. Enhancing creativity by modifying what Ss say to themselves. Unpublished manuscript, University of Waterloo, 1972. (a)

Meichenbaum, D. Cognitive modification of test anxious college students. *Journal of Consulting and Clinical Psychology*, 1972, **39**, 370-380. (b)

Meichenbaum, D., & Cameron, E. An examination of cognitive and contingency variables in anxiety relief procedures. Unpublished manuscript, University of Waterloo, 1972. (a)

Meichenbaum, D., & Cameron, E. Reducing fears by modifying what

clients say to themselves: A means of developing stress innocula-
tion. Unpublished manuscript, University of Waterloo, 1972. (b)

Meichenbaum, D., & Cameron, E. Training schizophrenics to talk to
themselves: A means of developing attentional controls. *Behavior
Therapy*, 1973, **4**, 515-534.

Meichenbaum, D., Gilmore, J., Fedoravicius, A. Group insight vs. group
desensitization in treating speech anxiety. *Journal of Consulting
and Clinical Psychology*, 1971, **36**, 410-421.

Meichenbaum, D., & Goodman, J. The developmental control of operant
motor responding by verbal operants. *Journal of Experimental
Child Psychology*, 1969, **7**, 553-565. (a)

Meichenbaum, D., & Goodman, J. Reflection-impulsivity and verbal
control of motor behavior. *Child Development*, 1969, **40**, 785-797.
(b)

Meichenbaum, D., & Goodman, J. Training impulsive children to talk
to themselves: A means for developing self-control. *Journal of
Abnormal Psychology*, 1971, **77**, 115-126.

Menninger, K. *Theory of psychoanalytic technique*. New York: Harper
& Row, 1958.

Merleau-Ponty, M. *The structure of behavior*. London: Methuen, 1965.

Metropolitan Life Insurance Company. New weight standards for men
and women. *Statistical Bulletin*, 1969, **40**, 3.

Meyer, V., & Gelder, M. Behavior therapy and phobic disorders. *British
Journal of Psychiatry*, 1963, **109**, 19-28.

Miller, G. A., Galanter, E., & Pribram, K. H. *Plans and the structure
of behavior*. New York: Holt, Rinehart, & Winston, 1960.

Miller, M. M. Treatment of chronic alcoholism by hypnotic aversion.
Journal of the American Medical Association, 1959, **171**, 1492-
1495.

Miller, M. M. Hypnotic-aversion treatment of homosexuality. *Journal of
the National Medical Association*, 1963, **55**, 411-415.

Miller, N. E. Experimental studies of conflict. In J. McV. Hunt (Ed.), *Personality and the behavior disorders*. Vol. 1. New York: Ronald
Press, 1944. Pp. 431-465.

Miller, N. E. Learnable drives and rewards. In S. S. Stevens (Ed.), *Handbook of experimental psychology*. New York: Wiley, 1951. Pp. 435-
472.

Miller, N. E. Liberalization of basic S-R concepts: Extensions to conflict
behavior, motivation, and social learning. In S. Koch (Ed.),
Psychology: A study of a science. Vol. 2. New York: McGraw-Hill,
1959. Pp. 196-292.

Miller, N. E. Learning of visceral and glandular responses. *Science*, 1969, **163**, 434-453.

Miller, N. E., & Dollard, J. *Social learning and imitation*. New Haven, Conn.: Yale University Press, 1941.

Mischel, W. *Personality and assessment*. New York: Wiley, 1968.

Mischel, W. *Introduction to personality*. New York: Holt, Rinehart & Winston, 1971.

Mischel, W., & Ebbesen, E. B. Attention in delay of gratification. *Journal of Personality and Social Psychology*, 1970, **16**, 329-337.

Mischel, W., Ebbesen, E. B., & Zeiss, A. R. Cognitive and attentional dynamics in delay of gratification. *Journal of Personality and Social Psychology*, 1972, **21**, 204-218.

Mischel, W., & Liebert, R. M. Effects of discrepancies between observed and imposed reward criteria on their acquisition and transmission. *Journal of Personality and Social Psychology*, 1966, **3**, 45-53.

Moos, R. H. Behavioral effects of being observed: Reactions to a wireless radio transmitter. *Journal of Consulting and Clinical Psychology*, 1968, **32**, 383-388.

Mowrer, O. H. *Learning theory and behavior*. New York: Wiley, 1960.

Murphy, G. Psychology in the year 2000. *American Psychiatrist*, 1969, **24**, 523-530.

Nadel, S. F. Social control and self-regulation. *Social Forces*, 1953, **31**, 265-273.

Neisworth, J. T. Elimination of cigarette smoking through gradual phase-out of stimulus controls. *Behaviorally Speaking*, October 1972, 1-3.

Nelson, C. M., & McReynolds, W. T. Self-recording and control of behavior: A reply to Simkins. *Behavior Therapy*, 1971, **2**, 594-597.

Neuringer, A. J. Animals respond for food in the presence of free food. *Science*, 1969, **166**, 399-401.

Neuringer, A. J. Many responses per food reward with free food present. *Science*, 1970, **169**, 503-504.

Nisbett, R. E., & Gordon, A. Self-esteem and susceptibility to social influence. *Journal of Personality and Social Psychology*, 1967, **5**, 268-276.

Nisbett, R. E., & Valins, S. *Perceiving the cause of one's own behavior*. New York: General Learning Press, 1971.

Nolan, J. D. Self-control procedures in the modification of smoking behavior. *Journal of Consulting and Clinical Psychology*, 1968, **32**, 92-93.

Notterman, J. M., & Trumbull, R. Note on self-regulatory systems and stress. *Behavioral Science*, 1950, **4**, 324-327.

Nowlis, D., & Kamiya, J. The control of electroencephalographic alpha rhythms through auditory feedback and the associated mental activity. *Psychophysiology*, in press.

Nunnally, J. C. *Psychometric theory*. New York: McGraw-Hill, 1967.

Ober, D. C. The modification of smoking behavior. *Journal of Consulting and Clinical Psychology*, 1968, **32**, 543-549.

Ofstad, N. S. The transmission of self-reinforcement patterns through imitation of sex-role appropriate behavior. Unpublished doctoral dissertation, University of Utah, 1967.

O'Leary, D. K., Becker, W. C., Evans, W. C., & Saudargas, R. A. A token reinforcement program in a public school: A replication and systematic analysis. *Journal of Applied Behavior Analysis*, 1969, **2**, 171-179.

O'Leary, D. K., & Drabman, R. Token reinforcement programs in the classroom: A review. *Psychological Bulletin*, 1971, **4**, 324-327.

Orne, M. T. Demand characteristics and the concept of quasi-controls. In R. Rosenthal & R. L. Rosnow (Eds.), *Artifact in behavioral research*. New York: Academic Press, 1969. Pp. 147-179.

Orne, M. T. From the subject's point of view, when is behavior private and when is it public? Problems of inference. *Journal of Consulting and Clinical Psychology*, 1970, **35**, 143-147.

Paivio, A. Mental imagery in associative learning and memory. *Psychological Review*, 1969, **76**, 241-263.

Paivio, A. On the functional significance of imagery. *Psychological Bulletin*, 1970, **73**, 385-392.

Palkes, H., Stewart, M., & Freedman, J. Improvement in maze performance of hyperactive boys as a function of verbal-training procedures. *Journal of Special Education*, 1972, **5**, 337-342.

Palkes, H., Stewart, W., & Kahana, B. Porteus maze performance of hyperactive boys after training in self-directed verbal commands. *Child Development*, 1968, **39**, 817-826.

Parnes, S., & Brunelle, E. The literature of creativity. Part 1. *Journal of Creative Behavior*, 1967, **1**, 52-109.

Patterson, G. R. An application of conditioning techniques to the control of a hyperactive child. In L. P. Ullman & L. Krasner (Eds.), *Case studies in behavior modification*. New York: Holt, Rinehart & Winston, 1965. Pp. 370-375.

Patterson, G. R. A community mental health program for children. In L. A. Hamerlynck, P. O. Davidson, & L. E. Acker (Eds.), *Behavior modification and ideal mental health services*. Calgary, Alberta: University of Calgary, 1969. Pp. 131-179.

Patterson, G. R. Behavior modification with families. Colloquium presented to the Department of Psychology, University of Utah, 1970.

Patterson, G. R., & Harris, A. Some methodological considerations for observation procedures. Paper presented at the meeting of the American Psychological Association, San Francisco, September 1968.

Patterson, G. R., Ray, R. S., & Shaw, D. R. Direct intervention in families of deviant children. *Oregon Research Institute Bulletin*, 1968, **8**, No. 9.

Paul, G. L. *Insight vs. desensitization in psychotherapy: An experiment in anxiety reduction*. Palo Alto, Calif.: Stanford University Press, 1966.

Paul, G. L. Behavior modification research: Design and tactics. In C. M. Franks (Ed.), *Behavior, therapy: Appraisal and status*. New York: McGraw-Hill, 1969. Pp. 29-62.

Paul, G. L., & Shannon, D. Treatment of anxiety through systematic desensitization in therapy groups. *Journal of Abnormal Psychology*, 1966, **71**, 124-135.

Penick, S. B., Filion, R. D. L., & Fox, S. A day hospital approach to human obesity. Unpublished manuscript, University of Pennsylvania, 1971.

Penick, S. B., Ross, F., Fox, S., & Stunkard, A. J. Behavior modification in the treatment of obesity. *Psychosomatic Medicine*, 1971, **33**, 49-55.

Pervin, L. The need to predict and control under conditions of threat. *Journal of Personality*, 1963, **31**, 570-585.

Phillip, R. E., Johnson, G. D., & Geyer, A. Self-administered systematic desensitization. *Behaviour Research and Therapy*, 1972, **10**, 93-96.

Phillips, E. L. *Psychotherapy: A modern theory and practice*. Englewood Cliffs, N.J.: Prentice-Hall, 1957.

Phillips, E. L., & Wiener, D. N. *Short-term psychotherapy and structured behavior change*. New York: McGraw-Hill, 1966.

Piaget, J. *The language and thought of the child*. London: Routledge & Kegan Paul, 1926.

Platt, J. R. *The step to man*. New York: Wiley, 1966.

Portes, A. On the emergence of behavior therapy in modern society. *Journal of Consulting and Clinical Psychology*, 1971, **36**, 303-313.

Powell, J., & Azrin, N. The effects of shock as a punisher for cigarette smoking. *Journal of Applied Behavior Analysis*, 1968, **1**, 63-71.

Pratt, S., & Tooley, J. Contract psychology: Some methodological considerations and the research contract. Unpublished paper, Wichita State University, 1964.

Premack, D. Reinforcement theory. In D. Levine (Ed.), *Nebraska symposium on motivation: 1965*. Lincoln: University of Nebraska Press, 1965. Pp. 123-180.

Premack, D. Mechanisms of self control. In W. Hunt (Ed.), *Learning and mechanisms of control in smoking*. Chicago: Aldine, 1970. Pp. 107-123.

Premack, D. Catching up with common sense or two sides of a generalization: Reinforcement and punishment. In R. Glaser (Ed.), *The nature of reinforcement*. New York: Academic Press, 1971. Pp. 121-150.

Proctor, S., & Malloy, T. E. Cognitive control of conditioned emotional responses: An extension of behavior therapy to include the experimental psychology of cognition. *Behavior Therapy*, 1971, **2**(3), 294-306.

Pyle, W. New accounting system measures human assets. *Newsletter*, Institute for Social Research, University of Michigan, Spring 1970.

Rachlin, H. *Introduction to modern behaviorism*. San Francisco: Freeman, 1970.

Rachman, S., & Teasdale, J. *Aversion therapy and behavior disorders: An analysis*. Coral Gables, Fla.: University of Miami Press, 1969.

Rao, C. R. Least squares theory using an estimated dispersion matrix and its application to measurement of signals. *Proceedings of the Fifth Berkeley Symposium on Mathematical Statistics and Probability*, 1967, **1**, 355-372.

Rehm, L. P., & Marston, A. R. Reduction of social anxiety through modification of self-reinforcement: An instigation therapy technique. *Journal of Consulting and Clinical Psychology*, 1968, **32**, 565-574.

Reid, J. B. Reliability assessment of observation data: A possible methodological problem. *Child Development*, 1970, **41**, 1143-1150.

Resnick, J. H. Effects of stimulus satiation on the over-learned maladaptive response of cigarette smoking. *Journal of Consulting and Clinical Psychology*, 1968, **1**, 267-281.

Risley, T. R. Behavior modification: An experimental-therapeutic endeavor. In L. A. Hamerlynch, R. O. Davidson, & L. E. Acker (Eds.), *Behavior modification and ideal mental services*. Calgary, Alberta: University of Calgary Press, 1969. Pp. 103-127.

Risley, T. R., & Hart, B. Developing correspondence between the nonverbal and verbal behavior of preschool children. *Journal of Applied Behavior Analysis*, 1968, **1**, 267-281.

Roberts, A. H. Self-control procedures in modification of smoking behavior: Replication. *Psychological Reports*, 1969, **24**, 675-676.

Rogers, C. *On becoming a person*. Boston: Houghton Mifflin, 1961.

Rogers, C. *Freedom to learn.* Columbus, Ohio: Merrill, 1969.

Rosenberg, M. J. *Society and the adolescent self-image.* Princeton, N. J.: Princeton University Press, 1965.

Rosenberg, M. J. The conditions and consequences of evaluation apprehension. In R. Rosenthal & R. Rosnow (Eds.), *Artifact in behavioral research.* New York: Academic Press, 1969. Pp. 280-349.

Rosenhan, D., Frederick, F., & Burrowes, A. Preaching and practicing: Effects of channel discrepancy on norm internalization. *Child Development*, 1968, **39**, 291-301.

Rosenthal, R. Interpersonal expectations: Effects of the experimenter's hypothesis. In R. Rosenthal & R. L. Rosnow (Eds.), *Artifact in behavioral research.* New York: Academic Press, 1969. Pp. 181-277.

Rosenthal, R., & Rosnow, R. L., (Eds.) *Artifact in behavioral research.* New York: Academic Press, 1969.

Ross, L., Rodin, J., & Zimbardo, P. Toward an attribution therapy: The reduction of fear through induced cognitive misattribution. *Journal of Personality and Social Psychology*, 1969, **12**, 279-288.

Roszak, T. *The making of a counter culture: Reflections on the technocratic society and its youthful opposition.* Garden City, N.Y.: Doubleday, 1969.

Rotter, J. B. *Social learning and clinical psychology.* Englewood Cliffs, N.J.: Prentice-Hall, 1954.

Rotter, J. B. Generalized expectancies for internal versus external control of reinforcement. *Psychological Monographs*, 1966, **80** (I, Whole No. 609).

Rotter, J. B., Seeman, M., & Liverant, S. Internal versus external control of reinforcements: A major variable in behavior theory. In N. F. Washburne (Ed.), *Decisions, values, and groups.* Vol. 2. London: Pergamon, 1962. Pp. 473-516.

Rutner, I. T. The modification of smoking behavior through techniques of self-control. Unpublished master's thesis, Wichita State University, 1967.

Rutner, I. T., & Bugle, C. An experimental procedure for the modification of psychotic behavior. *Journal of Consulting and Clinical Psychology*, 1969, **33**, 651-653.

Sachs, L. B., Bean, H., & Morrow, J. E. Comparison of smoking treatments. *Behavior Therapy*, 1970, **1**, 465-472.

Sandler, J., & Quagliano, J. Punishment in a signal avoidance situation. Paper presented at the meeting of the Southeastern Psychological Association, Gatlinburg, Tenn., 1964.

Schmidt, G. W., & Ulrich, R. E. Effects of group-contingent events upon classroom noise. *Journal of Applied Behavior Analysis*, 1969, **2**, 3-13.

Schwartz, M. L., & Hawkins, R. P. Application of delayed reinforcement procedures to the behavior of an elementary school child. *Journal of Applied Behavior Analysis*, 1970, **3**, 85-96.

Schwitzgebel, R. Survey of electromechanical devices for behavior modification. *Psychological Bulletin*, 1968, **70**, 444-459.

Sears, P. S. The pursuit of self-esteem, the middle childhood years. Paper presented at the meeting of the American Psychological Association, Chicago, September 1960.

Sears, R. R. Identification as a form of behavioral development. In D. B. Harris (Ed.), *The concept of development*. Minneapolis: University of Minnesota Press, 1957. Pp. 149-161.

Seligman, M. E. P. Chronic fear produced by unpredictable electric shock. *Journal of Comparative and Physiological Psychology*, 1968, **66**, 402-411.

Shaffer, L. The problem of psychotherapy. *American Psychologist*, 1947, **2**, 459-467.

Shimkunas, A. Demand for intimate self-disclosure and pathological verbalizations in schizophrenia. *Journal of Abnormal Psychology*, 1972, **80**, 197-205.

Sidman, M. *Tactics of scientific research: Evaluating experimental data in psychology*. New York: Basic Books. 1960.

Siegel, S. *Nonparametric statistics for the behavioral sciences*. New York: McGraw-Hill, 1956.

Simkins, L. The reliability of self-recorded behaviors. *Behavior Therapy*, 1971, **2**, 83-87. (a)

Simkins, L. A rejoinder to Nelson and McReynolds on the self-recording of behavior. *Behavior Therapy*, 1971, **2**, 598-601. (b)

Skaggs, E. Changes in pulse, breathing, and steadiness under conditions of startledness and excited expectancy. *Journal of Comparative and Psychological Psychology*, 1926, **6**, 303-318.

Skinner, B. F. The operational analysis of psychological terms. *Psychological Review*, 1945, **52**, 270-278.

Skinner, B. F. *Science and human behavior*. New York: Macmillan, 1953.

Skinner, B. F. *Contingencies of reinforcement*. New York: Appleton-Century-Crofts, 1969.

Skinner, B. F. *Beyond freedom and dignity*. New York: Knopf, 1971.

Solyom, L., Kenny, T., & Ledwidge, B. Evaluation of a new treatment paradigm for phobias. *Behaviour Research and Therapy*, 1967, **5**, 313-324.

Solyom, L., & Miller, S. Reciprocal inhibition by aversion relief in the treatment of phobias. *Behaviour Research and Therapy,* 1969, **14**, 3-9.

Spaulding, R. L. Achievement, creativity, and self-concept correlates of teacher-pupil transactions in elementary schools. In C. B. Stendler (Ed.), *Readings in child behavior and development.* (2nd. ed.) New York: Harcourt Brace Jovanovich, 1964. Pp. 313-318.

Staats, A. W. *Child learning, intelligence, and personality.* New York: Harper & Row, 1971.

Staats, A. W. Language behavior therapy: A derivative of social behaviorism. *Behavior Therapy,* 1972, **3**, 165-192.

Steffy, R., Meichenbaum, D., & Best, A. Aversive and cognitive factors in the modification of smoking behavior. *Behaviour Research and Therapy,* 1970, **8**, 115-125.

Stollak, G. E. Weight loss obtained under different experimental procedures. *Psychotherapy: Theory, Research and Practice,* 1967, **4**, 61-64.

Stollak, G. E., Guerney, B. G., & Rothberg, M. *Psychotherapy research: Selected readings.* Chicago: Rand McNally, 1966.

Stone, L. J., & Hokanson, J. E. Arousal reduction via self-punitive behavior. *Journal of Personality and Social Psychology,* 1969, **12**, 72-79.

Stotland, E., & Zander, A. Effects of public and private failure on self-evaluation. *Journal of Abnormal and Social Psychology,* 1958, **56**, 223-229.

Strupp, H. H., & Bergin, A. W. Some empirical and conceptual bases for coordinated research in psychotherapy: A critical review of issues, trends, and evidence. *International Journal of Psychiatry,* 1969, **72**, 1-90.

Stuart, R. B. Behavioral control over eating. *Behaviour Research and Therapy,* 1967, **5**, 357-365.

Stuart, R. B. A three-dimensional program for the treatment of obesity. *Behaviour Research and Therapy,* 1971, **9**, 177-196.

Stuart, R. B. Situational versus self-control. In R. D. Rubin, H. Fensterheim, J. D. Henderson, & L. P. Ullmann (Eds.), *Advances in behavior therapy.* New York: Academic Press, 1972. Pp. 129-146.

Stuart, R. B., & Davis, B. *Slim chance in a fat world: Behavioral control of obesity.* Champaign, Ill.: Research Press, 1972.

Stuhr, D. E. The effects of social model characteristics in eliciting personal feeling questions. Unpublished doctoral dissertation, School of Education, Stanford University, 1972.

Stuhr, D. E., Thoresen, C. E., & Anton, J. L. The effects of social model characteristics in producing changes in conversational behavior. Stanford University, unpublished manuscript, 1973.

Stunkard, A. J. The management of obesity. *New York State Journal of Medicine*, 1958, **58**, 79-87.

Suinn, R., & Richardson, R. Anxiety management training: A non-specific behavior therapy program for anxiety control. *Behavior Therapy*, 1971, **2**, 498-510.

Sullivan, H. S. *The interpersonal theory of psychiatry*. New York: Norton, 1953.

Sulzer, E. S. Reinforcement and therapeutic contract. *Journal of Consulting Psychology*, 1962, **9**, 271-276.

Surratt, P. R., Ulrich, R. E., & Hawkins, R. P. An elementary student as a behavioral engineer. *Journal of Applied Behavior Analysis*, 1969, **2**, 85-92.

Suzuki, D. T. *An introduction to Zen Buddhism*. London: Rider, 1949.

Tabachnick, B. R. Some correlates of prejudice toward Negroes in elementary age children. *The Journal of Genetic Psychology*, 1962, **100**, 193-203.

Tart, C. T. States of consciousness and state-specific sciences. *Science*, 1972, **176**, 1203-1210.

Tasto, D. L., & Suinn, R. M. Fear survey schedule changes on total and factor scores due to nontreatment effects. *Behavior Therapy*, 1972, **3**, 275-278.

Taylor, G. R. *The biological time bomb*. New York: Signet Books, 1968.

Terrace, H. S. Awareness as viewed by conventional and radical behaviorism. Paper presented at the annual meeting of the American Psychological Association, Washington, D.C., September, 1971.

Tharp, R. G., & Wetzel, R. J. *Behavior modification in the natural environment*. New York: Academic Press, 1969.

Thibaut, J., & Kelley, H. H. *The social psychology of groups*. New York: Wiley, 1959.

Thomas, D., Becker, W., & Armstrong, M. Production and elimination of disruptive classroom behavior by systematically varying teacher's behavior. *Journal of Applied Behavior Analysis*, 1968, **1**, 35-45.

Thomas, E. J., Abrams, K. S., & Johnson, J. B. Self-monitoring and reciprocal inhibition in the modification of multiple tics of Gilles de la Tourette's syndrome. *Journal of Behavior Therapy and Experimental Psychiatry*, 1971, **2**, 159-171.

Thoresen, C. E. Relevance and research in counseling. *Review of Educational Research*, 1969, **39**, 263-281.

Thoresen, C. E. The intensive design: An intimate approach to counseling research. Paper presented at the American Educational
Research Association, Chicago, 1972. (a)

Thoresen, C. E. Training behavioral counselors. In F. W. Clark, D. R.
Evans, & L. A. Hamerlynch (Eds.), *Implementing behavioral programs for schools and clinics*. Champaign, Ill.: Research Press,
1972. Pp. 41-62. (b)

Thoresen, C. E. Behavioral humanism. In C. E. Thoresen (Ed.), *Behavior
modification in education*, 72nd Yearbook of the National Society
for the Study of Education. Chicago: University of Chicago Press,
1973. (a)

Thoresen, C. E. Behavioral self-observation in reducing drinking
behavior: A case study. Unpublished manuscript, Stanford University, 1973. (b)

Thoresen, C. E. The healthy personality as a sick trait. *The Counseling
Psychologist*, in press.

Thoresen, C. E., Hubbard, D. R. Jr., Hannum, J. W., Hendricks, C. G.,
& Shapiro, D. Self-observation training with a nursery school
teacher. Research and Development Report No. 110, Palo Alto,
Calif.: Stanford Center for Research and Development in Teaching,
June 1973.

Thoresen, C. E., & Mahoney, M. J. *Behavioral self-control*. New York:
Holt, Rinehart & Winston, 1974.

Thornton, J., & Jacobs, P. Learned helplessness in human subjects.
Journal of Experimental Psychology, 1971, **87**, 367-372.

Thorpe, J., Schmidt, E., Brown, P., & Castell, D. Aversion-relief therapy:
A new method for general application. *Behaviour Research and
Therapy*, 1964, **2**, 71-82.

Tighe, T. J., & Elliott, R. A technique for controlling behavior in natural
life settings. *Journal of Applied Behavior Analysis,* 1968, **1**, 263-
266.

Todd, F. J. Coverant control of self-evaluative responses in the treatment of depression: A new use for an old principle. *Behavior
Therapy*, 1972, **3**, 91-94.

Toffler, A. *Future shock*. New York: Random House, 1970.

Tooley, J. T., & Pratt, S. An experimental procedure for the extinction
of smoking behavior. *Psychological Record*, 1967, **17**, 209-218.

Torrance, E. *Rewarding creative behavior*. Englewood Cliffs, N.J.:
Prentice-Hall, 1965.

Truax, C. Reinforcement and nonreinforcement in Rogerian psychotherapy. *Journal of Abnormal Psychology*, 1966, **71**, 1-9.

Tyler, V. O., & Straughan, J. H. Coverant control and breath holding as techniques for the treatment of obesity. *Psychological Record*, 1970, **20**, 473-478.

Ullmann, L. P., & Krasner, L. *A psychological approach to abnormal behavior.* Englewood Cliffs, N.J.: Prentice-Hall, 1969.

Underwood, B. J. *Psychological research.* New York: Appleton-Century-Crofts, 1957.

Upper, D., & Meredith, L. A stimulus control approach to the modification of smoking behavior. Paper presented at the American Psychological Association, Miami, 1970.

Upper, D., & Meredith, L. A timed interval procedure for modifying cigarette smoking behavior. Submitted for publication, 1971.

U.S. Department of Health, Education, and Welfare. Report on the Advisory Committee to the Surgeon General of the Public Health Service, 1964. Public Health Service Publication No. 1103.

Valins, S. Cognitive effects of false heart-rate feedback. *Journal of Personality and Social Psychology*, 1966, **4**, 400-408.

Valins, S., & Ray, A. Effects of cognitive desensitization on avoidance behavior. *Journal of Personality and Social Psychology*, 1967, **7**, 345-350.

Vygotsky, L. S. *Thought and language.* New York: Wiley, 1962.

Wagner, M. K., & Bragg, R. A. Comparing behavior modification approaches to habit decrement-smoking. *Journal of Consulting and Clinical Psychology*, 1970, **34**, 258-263.

Walters, R. H., Parke, R. D., & Cane, V. A. Timing of punishment and the observation of consequences to others as determinants of response inhibition. *Journal of Experimental Child Psychology*, 1965, **2**, 10-30.

Wasik, B. H., Senn, K., Welch, R. H., & Cooper, B. R. Behavior modification with culturally deprived school children: Two case studies. *Journal of Applied Behavior Analysis*, 1969, **2**, 181-194.

Watson, D. L., & Tharp, R. G. *Self-directed behavior: Self-modification for personal adjustment.* Monterey, Calif.: Brooks/Cole, 1972.

Watson, J. B. *Psychology from the standpoint of a behaviorist.* Philadelphia: Lippincott, 1919.

Webb, E. J., Campbell, D. T., Schwartz, R. D., & Sechrest, L. *Unobtrusive measures: Nonreactive research in social sciences.* Chicago: Rand McNally, 1966.

Webb, E. J., & Salancik, J. R. Supplementing the self-report in attitude research. In G. F. Summers (Ed.), *Attitude measurement.* Chicago, Rand McNally, 1970. Pp. 317-327.

Weber, S. J., & Cook, T. D. Subjects effects in laboratory research: An examination of subject roles, demand characteristics, and valid inference. *Psychological Bulletin*, 1972, **77**, 273-295.

Wegner, M. A., Bagchi, B. U., & Anand, G. Voluntary heart and pulse control by Yoga methods. *International Journal of Parapsychology*, 1963, **5**, 25-40.

Weick, K. E. Systematic observation methods. In G. Lindzey & E. Aronson (Eds.), *The handbook of social psychology.* (2nd ed.) London: Addison-Wesley, 1968. Pp. 357-451.

Weiner, H. Some effects of response cost upon human operant behavior. *Journal of the Experimental Analysis of Behavior*, 1962, **5**, 201-208.

Weiner, H. Real and imagined cost effects upon human fixed-interval responding. *Psychological Reports*, 1965, **17**, 659-662.

Weinstein, G., & Fantini, M. (Eds.), *Toward humanistic education: A curriculum of affect.* New York: Praeger, 1970.

Weis, L., & Hall, R. V. Modification of cigarette smoking through avoidance of punishment. In R. V. Hall (Ed.), *Managing behavior: Part III.* Merriam, Kan.: H & H Enterprises, 1970. Pp. 54-55.

Weisberg, P. Operant procedures with the retardate: An overview of laboratory research. In N. R. Ellis (Ed.), *International review of research in mental retardation.* New York: Academic Press, 1971. Pp. 113-145.

Wilson, E. H. Humanism's many dimensions. *The Humanist*, 1970, **30**, 35-36.

Wine, J. Investigations of attentional interpretation of test anxiety. Unpublished doctoral dissertation, University of Waterloo, Waterloo, Ontario, 1971. (a)

Wine, J. Test anxiety and direction of attention. *Psychological Bulletin*, 1971, **76**, 92-104. (b)

Wisocki, P. Treatment of obsessive-compulsive behavior by covert sensitization and covert reinforcement: A case report. *Journal of Behavior Therapy and Experimental Psychiatry*, 1970, **1**, 233-239.

Wolf, M., & Risley, T. Reinforcement: Applied research. In R. Glaser (Ed.), *The nature of reinforcement.* New York: Academic Press, 1971. Pp. 310-325.

Wolpe, J. *Psychotherapy by reciprocal inhibition.* Palo Alto, Calif.: Stanford University Press, 1958.

Wolpe, J. The systematic desensitization treatment of neuroses. *Journal of Mental Disease*, 1961, **132**, 189-203.

Wolpe, J. Conditioned inhibition of craving in drug addiction: A pilot experiment. *Behaviour Research and Therapy*, 1965, **2**, 285-288.

Wolpe, J. *The practice of behavior therapy.* New York: Pergamon Press, 1969.

Wolpe, J., & Lazarus, A. *Behavior therapy techniques.* New York: Pergamon, 1966.

Wright, H. F. Observational child study. In P. Mussen (Ed.), *Handbook of research methods in child development*, New York: Wiley, 1960. Pp. 71-139.

Yamagami, T. The treatment of an obsession by thought stopping. *Journal of Behavior Therapy and Experimental Psychiatry*, 1971, **2**, 133-136.

Yates, A. *Behavior therapy*. New York: Wiley, 1970.

Zeissit, R. Desensitization and relaxation in the modification of patients' interview behavior. *Journal of Abnormal Psychology*, 1968, **73**, 18-24.

Zifferblatt, S. Behavioral systems. In C. E. Thoresen (Ed.), *Behavior modification in education*, 72nd Yearbook of the National Society for the Study of Education. Chicago: University of Chicago Press, 1973.

Zimbardo, P., Maslach, C., & Marshall, G. Hypnosis and the psychology of cognitive behavioral control. In E. Fromm & R. Shor (Eds.), *Current trends in hypnosis research*. Chicago: Aldine, 1972. Pp. 539-574.

Zimmerman, E., & Zimmerman, J. The alteration of behavior in a special classroom situation. *Journal of the Experimental Analysis of Behavior*, 1962, **5**, 59-60.

AUTHOR INDEX